New Perspectives in Early Childhood
Teacher Education: Bringing Practitioners
into the Debate
  STACIE G. GOFFIN & DAVID DAY, Eds.

Assessment Methods for Infants and
Toddlers: Transdisciplinary Team
Approaches
  DORIS BERGEN

The Emotional Development of Young
Children: Building an Emotion-Centered
Curriculum
  MARION C. HYSON

Young Children Continue to Reinvent
Arithmetic—3rd Grade: Implications of
Piaget's Theory
  CONSTANCE KAMII with
  SALLY JONES LIVINGSTON

Moral Classrooms, Moral Children:
Creating a Constructivist Atmosphere in
Early Education
  RHETA DeVRIES & BETTY ZAN

Leadership in Early Childhood:
The Pathway to Professionalism
  JILLIAN RODD

Understanding Assessment and Evaluation
in Early Childhood Education
  DOMINIC F. GULLO

Diversity and Developmentally
Appropriate Practices:
Challenges for Early Childhood Education
  BRUCE L. MALLORY &
  REBECCA S. NEW, Eds.

Changing Teaching, Changing Schools:
Bringing Early Childhood Practice
into Public Education—
Case Studies from the Kindergarten
  FRANCES O'CONNELL RUST

Physical Knowledge in Preschool
Education: Implications of Piaget's Theory
  CONSTANCE KAMII & RHETA DeVRIES

Caring for Other People's Children:
A Complete Guide to Family Day Care
  FRANCES KEMPER ALSTON

Family Day Care: Current Research for
Informed Public Policy
  DONALD L. PETERS &
  ALAN R. PENCE, Eds.

The Early Childhood Curriculum:
A Review of Current Research, 2nd Ed.
  CAROL SEEFELDT, Ed.

Reconceptualizing the Early Childhood
Curriculum: Beginning the Dialogue
  SHIRLEY A. KESSLER &
  BETH BLUE SWADENER, Eds.

Ways of Assessing Children and
Curriculum: Stories of Early Childhood
Practice
  CELIA GENISHI, Ed.

The Play's the Thing:
Teachers' Roles in Children's Play
  ELIZABETH JONES &
  GRETCHEN REYNOLDS

Scenes from Day Care:
How Teachers Teach and
What Children Learn
  ELIZABETH BALLIETT PLATT

Raised in East Urban:
Child Care Changes in a
Working Class Community
  CAROLINE ZINSSER

United We Stand:
Collaboration for Child Care
and Early Education Services
  SHARON L. KAGAN

Making Friends in School:
Promoting Peer Relationships
in Early Childhood
  PATRICIA G. RAMSEY   (Continued)

Assessment Methods for Infants and Toddlers

Transdisciplinary Team Approaches

Doris Bergen

Foreword by Stephen J. Bagnato

TEACHERS COLLEGE, COLUMBIA UNIVERSITY
NEW YORK AND LONDON

Published by Teachers College Press, 1234 Amsterdam Avenue, New York, N.Y. 10027

Grateful acknowledgment is offered to the following for permission to reprint the figures indicated:

Fig. 1.2: Sequence of Prenatal Development. From Rosenblith (1992), *In the Beginning—Development from Conception to Age Two*, p. 22. Reprinted by permission of Sage Publications, Inc.

Fig. 1.3: Developmental Vulnerabilities in Infants and Toddlers. From Kalmanson (1989), "Assessment Considerations—Developmental Vulnerabilities." Early Childhood Update, 5(4), Fall 1989, p. 7.

Figure 2.1: Immediate Evaluation of the Newborn: The Apgar Score. From Apgar (1953), "A Proposal for a New Method of Evaluation of a Newborn Infant." Anesthesia and Analgesia, 32:260–7. Reprinted by permission of the International Anesthesia Research Society.

Figure 2.4: Contents of the Physician Psychosocial Assessment Form. From Horwitz, Leaf, Leventhal, Forsyth, & Speechley (1992), "Identification and Management of Psychosocial and Developmental Problems in Community-Based Primary Care Pediatric Practices." Pediatrics, Vol. 89, p. 480, 1992. Reprinted by permission of Pediatrics.

Figure 4.1: Model of Arena Assessment. From Benner (1992), Assessing Young Children with Special Needs: An Ecological Perspective, p. 56. Adapted from Project KAI (Brighton, MA). Reprinted by permission of Adrienne Frank MS OTR, Child Development Resources, Lightfoot, VA.

Figure 5.1: Movement Terminology. Reprinted with the permission of Macmillan College Publishing Company from *Assessing Infants and Toddlers with Handicaps* by Donald Bailey, Jr. and Mark Wolery, p. 304. Copyright 1989 by Macmillan College Publishing Company, Inc.

Library of Congress Cataloging-in-Publication Data
Bergen, Doris.
    Assessment methods for infants and toddlers: transdisciplinary
  team approaches/Doris Bergen
        p.   cm.—(Early childhood education series)
    Includes bibliographical references (p.   ) and index.
    ISBN 0-8077-3380-6 (alk. paper). —ISBN 0-8077-3379-2 (alk. paper
  pbk.)
      1. Child development—Testing.   2. Infants—Development—Testing.
  3. Child development deviations—Diagnosis   I. Title.   II. Series.
  RJ51.D48547   1994
  618.92'0075—dc20   94-12519

ISBN 0-8077-3380-6
ISBN 0-8077-3379-2 (pbk.)

Printed on acid-free paper
Manufactured in the United States of America
99 98 97 96 95 94 93   8 7 6 5 4 3 2 1

Assessment Methods for Infants and Toddlers

Transdisciplinary Team Approaches

Doris Bergen

Foreword by Stephen J. Bagnato

TEACHERS COLLEGE, COLUMBIA UNIVERSITY
NEW YORK AND LONDON

Published by Teachers College Press, 1234 Amsterdam Avenue, New York, N.Y. 10027

Grateful acknowledgment is offered to the following for permission to reprint the figures indicated:

Fig. 1.2: Sequence of Prenatal Development. From Rosenblith (1992), *In the Beginning—Development from Conception to Age Two*, p. 22. Reprinted by permission of Sage Publications, Inc.

Fig. 1.3: Developmental Vulnerabilities in Infants and Toddlers. From Kalmanson (1989), "Assessment Considerations—Developmental Vulnerabilities." Early Childhood Update, 5(4), Fall 1989, p. 7.

Figure 2.1: Immediate Evaluation of the Newborn: The Apgar Score. From Apgar (1953), "A Proposal for a New Method of Evaluation of a Newborn Infant." Anesthesia and Analgesia, 32:260–7. Reprinted by permission of the International Anesthesia Research Society.

Figure 2.4: Contents of the Physician Psychosocial Assessment Form. From Horwitz, Leaf, Leventhal, Forsyth, & Speechley (1992), "Identification and Management of Psychosocial and Developmental Problems in Community-Based Primary Care Pediatric Practices." Pediatrics, Vol. 89, p. 480, 1992. Reprinted by permission of Pediatrics.

Figure 4.1: Model of Arena Assessment. From Benner (1992), Assessing Young Children with Special Needs: An Ecological Perspective, p. 56. Adapted from Project KAI (Brighton, MA). Reprinted by permission of Adrienne Frank MS OTR, Child Development Resources, Lightfoot, VA.

Figure 5.1: Movement Terminology. Reprinted with the permission of Macmillan College Publishing Company from *Assessing Infants and Toddlers with Handicaps* by Donald Bailey, Jr. and Mark Wolery, p. 304. Copyright 1989 by Macmillan College Publishing Company, Inc.

Library of Congress Cataloging-in-Publication Data
Bergen, Doris.
    Assessment methods for infants and toddlers: transdisciplinary
  team approaches/Doris Bergen
        p.   cm.—(Early childhood education series)
      Includes bibliographical references (p.   ) and index.
      ISBN 0-8077-3380-6 (alk. paper). —ISBN 0-8077-3379-2 (alk. paper
  pbk.)
        1. Child development—Testing.   2. Infants—Development—Testing.
    3. Child development deviations—Diagnosis   I. Title.   II. Series.
    RJ51.D48547   1994
    618.92'0075—dc20   94-12519

ISBN 0-8077-3380-6
ISBN 0-8077-3379-2 (pbk.)

Printed on acid-free paper
Manufactured in the United States of America
99 98 97 96 95 94 93   8 7 6 5 4 3 2 1

Contents

FOREWORD

Teamwork is synonymous with and critical to the effectiveness of family-centered early intervention for young children at developmental risk. Unfortunately, most professionals are ill-prepared to collaborate with families and other professionals in a cohesive fashion. Needs assessment surveys of practicing professionals and students in training rank systematic experience in team assessment and family collaboration as one of the top five needs in early intervention. Few resources have been available to fulfill this field-identified need. Dr. Bergen's text on transdisciplinary team assessment is a much needed, well-conceived, and important contribution to the early intervention field. This book provides professionals in training from various disciplines with a clear understanding of both the dynamics (interpersonal strategies) and the mechanics (team assessment strategies) of teamwork—a blend that has been absent in similar texts.

For infants, toddlers, and preschoolers with special needs, the "teamwork" concept is the organic structure that defines, synchronizes, and links various diverse and crucial processes: establishing a family-centered context; defining the appropriate mode of teaming; conducting developmental assessments; explicating distortions in neurodevelopment; facilitating team decision-making and consensus; setting integrated child and family goals; delivering integrated services; and monitoring child/family progress and program outcome and efficacy.

Too often administrators and professionals concentrate on the mechanics rather than the dynamics of teamwork. Therefore, many programs establish inflexible rules and procedures that make few accommodations for the idiosyncratic needs of infants and families and that are by their very nature *developmentally inappropriate*. In the assessment process, a few of the common and damaging errors include: the exclusive use of standardized norm-referenced measures and discipline-specific scales; failure to assess in natural settings; failure to accommodate different response modes and adaptations for various functional impairments; failure to include parents as partners in assessment activities; reliance on standardized scores rather than team consensus data to determine developmental characteristics and intervention needs; failure to use toys, chairs, tables, mats, and other materials that stage, motivate, and optimize the assessment of individual infants; and failure to use transdisciplinary strategies during assessment activities to reduce redundancy and refine the sampling of child/family strengths and needs.

At its foundation, early intervention assessment requires teamwork, and teamwork requires family–professional collaboration. Yet, teamwork must be viewed as much larger than what is the most appropriate test to use, for assessment in early intervention is not a test-based process:

> Early childhood assessment is a flexible, collaborative decision-making process in which teams of parents and professionals repeatedly revise their judgments, reach consensus, and make collective decisions about the changing developmental educational, mental health, and medical needs of young children and their families and the services that they require. . . . The mission of assessment for early intervention is the planning and delivery of family-centered developmental support (Bagnato & Neisworth, 1991, xi).

In other resources, we have advocated for fundamental changes in team assessment and team decision-making practices in the early intervention field. Most notably, we have emphasized linking team assessment and early intervention (Bagnato, Neisworth, & Munson, 1989); best practices in assessment for early intervention (Bagnato & Neisworth, 1991); and the use of convergent assessment data for collaborative parent–professional team decision-making (Bagnato & Neisworth, 1990). Dr. Bergen's book is exemplary in building upon these and other foundations in the early intervention field to underscore the need for systematic training in teamwork for professionals.

Stephen J. Bagnato, Ed. D., NCSP
Associate Professor of Pediatrics & Psychology
University of Pittsburgh School of Medicine
Coordinator, Early Childhood Diagnostic Services and
Developmental Neuropsychology Services
Children's Hospital of Pittsburgh

REFERENCES

Bagnato, S. J. & Neisworth, J. T. (1990). *System to Plan Early Childhood Services (SPECS)*. Circle Pines, MN: American Guidance Service, Inc.

Bagnato, S. J. & Neisworth, J. T. (1991). *Assessment for early intervention: Best practices for professionals.* New York: Guilford.

Bagnato, S. J., Neisworth, J. T., & Munson, S. M. (1989). *Linking developmental assessment and early intervention: Curriculum-based prescriptions.* 2nd edition. Rockville, MD: Aspen Publishers.

ACKNOWLEDGMENTS

Because I used a transdisciplinary team approach in the writing of the text, there were many persons who provided valuable contributions to its content. I wish to thank them for their interactive assistance.

Many faculty associates at the Miami University Center for Human Development, Learning, and Teaching served as my co-authors on some of the chapters and as reviewers of many of the dialogue sections. Although they are listed as contributors at the back of the book, I would like to thank them here: Caroline Everington, Kathleen Hutchinson, Elizabeth Johnston, Susan Mosley-Howard, Julie Rubin, Alex Thomas, and Margaret Wright. Another colleague also served as a co-author of one chapter: Sharon Raver-Lampman.

A number of professional colleagues who assisted in the preparation of other chapters, by providing insights from their disciplines through in-depth interviews, and who reviewed those chapters and some of the dialogue sections: Amy Badanes, Licensed Speech Pathologist (L.S.P.), Early Intervention Service Coordinator, Butler County MRDD, Hamilton, OH; Judith Cooper, Supervisor of Early Childhood Education, Hamilton County MRDD, Cincinnati, OH; Corrine Welt Garland, Executive Director of Child Development Resources, Lightfoot, VA; Kate Gordon, Licensed Social Worker (L.S.W.), Donna Lilley, Licensed Physical Therapist (L.P.T.), Cincinnati, OH; Christine Piepmeier, Director of Fairacres Center, Butler County MRDD, Hamilton, OH; and B. Kristine Holt, Early Intervention Services Coordinator, Hamilton County MRDD, Cincinnati, OH.

Three of my former graduate students served as collectors of case and dialogue data, wrote a number of the case drafts, and provided other special material: Joan Dolgin, Early Childhood Special Educator, Toronto, Canada; Tanya Katterheinrich, School Psychologist, Fairfield, OH; and Margery Pitzer, Early Intervention Specialist, Hamilton County MRDD, Cincinnati, OH.

My former graduate assistant—Shireen Pavri, School Psychologist Intern, Oxford, OH—reviewed and checked references, coordinated the development of the assessment appendices, served as a chapter and case reader, and provided other technical preparation support.

Other academic and professional colleagues provided material incorporated in the text and/or served as reviewers of chapters and of dialogue sections: Connie Betts, Special Education Teacher, Cincinnati, OH; Ellen Buerk, M.D., Oxford, OH; Scotty Cooper, L.S.W., Early CARE Tracking Coordinator, Middletown Regional Hospital, Middletown, OH; James Davis, M.D., Oxford, OH; Bette Downs, L.P.T., Mosinee, WI; Mary Ann Dykstra, L.P.T., Hamilton, OH; Mary Gormally-Franzoso, Visiting Assistant Professor, Department of Educational Psychology, Miami University, Oxford, OH; Child Advocacy Center, Cincinnati, OH; Kathy McMahon-Klosterman, Associate Professor, Department of Educational Psychology, Miami University, Oxford, OH; Garry Mesibov, Director, Division TEACCH, The School of Medicine, The University of North Carolina at Chapel Hill, NC; Mary Porter, R.N., L.S.W., Middletown Regional Hospital, Middletown, OH; Nikki Rosen, O.T.R/L, W. Bloomfield, MI; Gloria Segal, O.T.R/L, Hamilton, OH; Carrie Ann Shook, Early Intervention Specialist, Hamilton Country MRDD, Cincinnati, OH; Sue Skinner-Kidd, Early Intervention Specialist, Lima, OH; Kammy Wise, L.P.N., Tampa, FL; and Francis Wright, M.D., Oxford, OH.

I especially want to thank the group of parents who permitted the case information about their children to be revised and adapted for the dialogues. I also wish to express my appreciation for both these parents and the many professionals from early intervention teams who permitted their comments to be revised and adapted for the dialogue sections. A special thanks to parents Scott and Sonie Halcomb for the unique insights they provided to me.

Finally I wish to thank my husband, Joel Fink, whose patience and support contributed to my ability to meet (almost!) all of my deadlines.

Doris Bergen

Defining Developmental Risk and Transdisciplinary Assessment

There are advantages and disadvantages to teaching a course in a field that is emerging. A disadvantage is that there may be no text available that is completely appropriate; an advantage is that one can conceptualize such a text and try out versions of it while teaching the course. My course in infant and toddler assessment and early intervention is such a course, and this text has been crafted from the experiences I have had in teaching it.

I use a team teaching approach because I believe that university teachers should provide models of the behaviors that students are to learn. The course is intended to meet the needs not only of early childhood special educators but also of the wide range of professionals who must now work together as members of early intervention teams to carry out the mandates initiated by Public Law 99-457. This law requires states to plan for a coordinated approach to the provision of assessment and intervention services for young children, and to use a multifactored, multi-disciplinary, family-centered approach to assessment.

The university preparation programs for the professionals who must now collaborate in providing such services have typically been single-discipline-based, and thus have rarely engaged students in understanding or practicing team approaches of any kind. In my view, helping professionals understand the perspectives of members of the various disciplines that form early intervention teams is an essential step in preparing them to work together. This text has been designed to make these varied perspectives explicit and to encourage dialogue among the professionals and professionals-to-be who are expected to be early intervention team members.

FORMAT AND CONTENT OF THE BOOK

This book focuses on assessment of young children at developmental risk. It takes the perspective of professionals expected to be members of the transdisciplinary teams who work with these children and their families. It addresses the assessment of children who are in the chronological *and* the developmental age range from birth to 3 years. It is particularly focused on identifying ways team assessments can be effectively used to gather the information needed for design of intervention activities and delivery of appropriate services.

Because assessment of developmental delay or differences must be interpreted within the context of normative human development, Chapter 1 reviews major developmental principles and processes, and describes the characteristics of young children who are developing typically, along with those who are at risk for developmental problems. It includes a brief discussion of some characteristics of adolescent and adult developmental change that may affect caregiver–child interactions.

Chapters 2 through 7 present the assessment perspectives of a wide variety of professionals, including medical personnel in hospital and primary care settings; clinical, developmental, and school psychologists; early childhood special educators; occupational and physical therapists; speech pathologists and audiologists; and personnel having case management responsibilities, such as social workers and family educators or service coordinators. The perspectives of parents whose children may receive these assessment and intervention services are also discussed in each of the chapters. All of these perspectives are integrated with my own views, drawn from over 20 years of experience as a university early childhood educator and early childhood special educator.

The brief explications in the chapters are meant only to expose readers to general knowledge of the assessment processes common to each professional discipline and to give guidelines for understanding how that discipline may contribute to team assessment approaches. Advanced professional training in the discipline is essential for a full a picture of the assessment methods, and even that training cannot prepare these professionals to be aware of every problem manifested by young children with developmental disabilities.

Assessment issues related to special populations of infants and toddlers (e.g., culturally diverse, severely or multiply disabled, neglected or abused) are explored in Chapters 8 and 9, and influential ecological factors in family and community contexts are related to the issues. The strengths of transdisciplinary team assessment models and the problems encountered in using these models are made explicit throughout the chapters, as are the policy issues that must be addressed when there is a com-

mitment to such an approach. In the final chapter (Chapter 10), the ideal transdisciplinary model is again discussed, evaluations of the model are reported, and guidelines for effective use of the model are given. The epilogue provides a look into the future of transdisciplinary assessment.

ASSESSMENT METHODS

The content of the book includes descriptions of assessment methods derived from psychometric, developmental, educational, therapeutic, and medical practice. The typical contexts for their use are briefly discussed in the chapters and more fully described in Appendices A and B. No attempt was made to include all relevant or useful instruments now available for early assessment. Rather, those that were selected serve as representations of the types of instruments that are being used in this field. They include standardized norm- and criterion-referenced instruments, nonstandardized research-based measures and scales, and formal and informal observational techniques. The criteria used in selecting those to be included were fourfold:

1. Frequency or "typicality" of use by professionals in a particular discipline or in a number of disciplines
2. Potential as effective innovative assessment approaches
3. Representativeness as a method used in assessing difficult-to-assess developmental domains
4. Potential for being a valid measure for children from diverse cultural and ethnic groups

The descriptions are designed to make the reader aware of general characteristics, technical features, and measurement purposes of the assessment methods and to provide a basis for evaluating and selecting these or other instruments presently in use or being developed.

TEAM DIALOGUES

Integration of diverse professional and family perspectives is provided in the "dialogue" sections interspersed between chapters. The team dialogues are based on a series of actual early intervention team meetings, which were audio taped, edited, and revised to disguise identifiable details (e.g., names, family history, location, cultural group), highlight or expand issues, or increase the diversity of perspectives. As a whole, they show how information gained from assessment is being used (or could be used) in practice to develop Individualized Family Service Plans (IFSP), to monitor and reevaluate the plans, and to provide transitions to other services. The placement of particular dialogues is designed to reflect aspects of the perspectives that were discussed in the chapter immediately preceding, although all of the dialogues include a variety of discipline perspectives. They also include family perspectives, although I found a wide variation in level of parent participation in actual team cases.

The dialogues illustrate the variety of approaches currently being used by teams. Although some of them have similarities to the ideal transdisciplinary model advocated in the literature, some are adaptations of this model designed to meet particular assessment situations, and others are reflections of the realities in the field at the present time, which may include meetings at which not all relevant team members are present or in which the interactions are not always as productive as expected.

The dialogues are planned to help students understand the thinking of various team members as the problem-solving process is played out in these specific child and family cases. By being able to simulate participation in the team problem-solving process, students can gain an understanding of the roles of the various team members and of how the interactions of these roles affect the outcomes for children and families. Students may be assigned roles and actually simulate the team meetings, or they may study them as cases to be analyzed and reported to the class. In either of these approaches, the dialogues may serve as discussion starters and integrative experiences.

The writing of this text itself has been a team effort. The chapter perspectives were constructed with the help of a number of university colleagues, who served as co-authors of certain chapters, and colleagues in practice, who provided extensive interview information about their disciplines. Dialogues were developed with the assistance of a team of my graduate students and those practitioners and family members who consented to the taping of their team meetings. Graduate and undergraduate students in early intervention courses assisted in review and evaluation of assessment instruments. Many of these colleagues and students also provided assistance by reading various chapters and dialogues and evaluating the validity of the information presented.

DEFINING DEVELOPMENTAL RISK

A number of excellent sources have given extensive descriptions of conditions that may impede or distort young children's developmental progress (e.g., Raver, 1991); this information is not repeated in detail here. Three types of developmental risk category, described below, have been described by Tjossem (1976) and further detailed by Bergen and Raver (1991):

Established risk conditions include neurological, genetic, orthopedic, cognitive, or sensory impairments or other physical or medical syndromes that have been strongly linked to developmental problems. These problems may be evident at or shortly after birth, especially in children with severe physical, sensory, or cognitive impairments. Some well defined conditions, even when diagnosed early, do not retard or distort development until later in the child's life. However, in children with most established risk conditions, developmental problems usually begin to be evident by the time the child is 6 months to 1 year of age. Established risks are often called disabilities. They include diagnoses such as Down's syndrome, spina bifida, cerebral palsy, blindness, limb loss or deformity, and other such genetic, motor, sensory, and cognitive impairments.

Biological risk conditions are physical or medical trauma experiences that occur in the prenatal period, during the birth process, or in the neonatal period that have a high probability of resulting in developmental delay but that do not always cause delay. Many of these biological risks are acute during the hours, days, or weeks immediately following the child's birth; thus, intensive medical care is usually required. If the child comes through that period successfully, there may or may not be long-term detrimental results. For example, extremely low birth weight is often related to developmental delay; however, some children who are of low birth weight are able to overcome this condition and do not experience permanent delays in development.

Environmental risk conditions are those factors in the physical setting (e.g., substandard housing, exposure to lead paint) or in the family or other social institutions (e.g., parent caregiving capabilities, low socioeconomic level, cultural values that preclude medical care) that have the potential to influence negatively young children's developmental progress. Negative environmental conditions internal to the family (e.g., family violence, parental drug abuse) and external to the family (e.g., unemployment, lack of access to health care) have an impact both on the development of all family members and on the capacity of these families to provide appropriate environments for their young at-risk children.

The vast array of environmental factors that can influence development have been conceptualized by Bronfenbrenner (1979, 1993). They include the persons in the immediate and broad family system, neighborhood, community, state, and nation. Often, a number of these conditions exist together and the prognosis for delay is greater when there is a combination of negative factors. For example, if the physical environment is poor (e.g., substandard housing in a deteriorating neighborhood), the caregiving interaction is of low quality (e.g., a depressed parent), and the family members exhibit tendencies associated with a history of school failure (e.g., are unlikely to read story books to the child), the potential delay for the child may be greater than if only one of these conditions is present. Also, when environmental risk is combined with either biological or established risk, the interactions of these factors increases the potential for developmental delay.

It is always difficult to determine the proportion of risk from biological or medical conditions and from environmental factors that may exist during the child's first few years of life. For example, research about the effects of early cocaine exposure on children's long-term development is inconclusive. Prenatal cocaine exposure, which is a major biological risk at birth and results in documented problems for neonates, does not seem to predict major developmental problems during the latter part of the first or second year of life (Chasnoff, Griffith, Freier, & Murray, 1992). Because this condition also has environmental risks associated with it (e.g., the capacity of the parent to care effectively for the child), it is very difficult to determine whether the major factor in learning problems identified in drug-exposed children at later ages are from the early biological risk of drug exposure or from the environmental risk of experiencing a drug-addicted caretaker.

DEFINING A TRANSDISCIPLINARY PERSPECTIVE

The term *transdisciplinary assessment* has been gaining increasing prominence as early interventionists attempt to fulfill the mandates of Public Law 99-457. One of the requirements of that law is that collaborative teamwork be evident in meeting the needs of young children who are at risk for developmental delay. This requires efforts to involve the family in determining appropriate early intervention, to ensure that public and private agencies collaborate in facilitating smooth transitions to other services, and to use team approaches and multifactored methods in assessment and intervention.

For those professionals who have been working in assessment and intervention services for some time, the term *transdisciplinary* is difficult to differentiate from the various types of interactive teaming in which they may have already been engaged. Foley (1990) explains that it is an approach that was devised to remedy the deficits in other models of assessment that had been used primarily with older children and adults. The differences between multi-, inter-, and transdisciplinary team approaches have been discussed at length in numerous other publications (e.g., Foley, 1990; Morsink, Thomas, & Correa, 1991; Raver, 1991; Woodruff & McGonigel, 1988) and do not need to be discussed at length here. However, a few essential differences need to be highlighted and the rationale for an integrative (i.e., transdisciplinary) rather than multi- or interdisciplinary approaches explained.

The *multidisciplinary assessment* approach involves having each professional conduct a separate evaluation, using the major instruments or procedures common in that discipline. The results are then reported in writing to an individual who is central to the process (e.g., a director of a medical or clinical team). In this model, the professionals who do the assessment are often not involved in developing the intervention plan; the plan is usually made by one or two centrally involved individuals or by a different set of professionals who use the written assessment result reports in making their decisions. Parents are involved primarily in making sure their children get to the various professional offices where the assessments will be made and in hearing the results of the assessment from each professional's individual perspective.

In the *interdisciplinary assessment* model, the assessments are still conducted independently by the professionals, using their discipline-specific instruments. However, there are usually communication and results-sharing among the assessors, often through a meeting with the parent and at least some of the team members. Typically, at the group meeting each professional takes a turn in telling the parent the results and giving recommendations for intervention. Rarely does one professional question or even comment on another's report, and although the parent is asked to question or comment, the assessment profile and the decisions regarding appropriate intervention are usually made by each professional prior to the meeting and are not often changed as a result of the team meeting.

The *transdisciplinary assessment* approach differs both in the procedures for assessment and in the determination of actions based on the assessment. At least in its ideal form, parents are involved even before the actual assessment procedures begin; they are asked to give their own assessment of the child and to identify areas of concern that the parents feel are particularly important to assess and remediate. The parents also have the opportunity to identify needs of the family that relate to their child, and to affirm the strengths they can bring to that child's care and education. Then the team as a whole decides on the appropriate methods for assessing each child and conducts an integrated assessment, using the methods from all disciplines that appear to be appropriate. Often, the assessment is done in an arena in which one or two of the professionals interact with the child while the others observe, noting the specific developmental areas on which their expertise is focused.

At other times the team may determine that not all team members need to be present because they have already shared enough of their own expertise with one or two other team members who are then able to conduct the complete assessment. If a deeper level of diagnosis is judged to be needed, then there may be an individual assessment in the problematic areas. In planning the intervention, one team member serves as primary coordinator of the plan but the team as a whole discusses the results and integrates the findings from various disciplines before the intervention plan is put in place. The parent is present throughout the assessment and intervention planning and is a fully contributing member of the team.

THEORETICAL RATIONALE FOR A
TRANSDISCIPLINARY APPROACH

There are four transactional principles that provide the theoretical rationale for this approach. They are described by Foley (1990), as follows:

1. Multiple factors converge to produce any given symptom complex (e.g., systemic analysis is needed to understand developmental problems).
2. The child must be understood as a whole person in an environmental context (e.g., the interaction of familial and social factors with individual child factors determine the depth and range of risk).
3. There are developmental "domino" or "cross-over" effects (e.g., all zones of development are affected because of the unity of development in infancy).
4. There are cumulative adversity effects (e.g., a developmental problem is a result of the accumulation of events, not one single event).

According to Foley, the transdisciplinary approach was designed to take into account the principles of this theoretical perspective.

PRACTICE RATIONALE FOR A
TRANSDISCIPLINARY APPROACH

The framers of Public Law 99-457 believed that there were several major drawbacks to current practice that could be addressed through collaborative teamwork, such as duplication of services, lack of communication between disciplinary groups serving the same or similar populations, and cost-effectiveness problems, that could be addressed through collaborative teamwork. Anyone who has worked in a social service, health, or education oriented profession can give examples of such dysfunctional conditions. They probably agree that better communication and collaborative efforts would be more cost- and time-efficient, and more effective in bringing needed services to young children and their families. Most of those same professionals, however, can point to resource and personnel needs, to family problems, and to health, education, and social services gaps that cannot be overcome simply by a commitment to teamwork.

Thus, transdisciplinary assessment and intervention will not solve all of the problems evident in our systems of service to young children and their families. However, the approach may serve to improve present assessment methods, to demonstrate the truth of the Gestalt principle that the "whole is greater than the sum of its parts," and to give young children their best chance of getting the range of prevention and intervention services that they need. Specifically, transdisciplinary assessment is useful for the following reasons.

First, it takes into account the ecological factors that impinge on and interact with the developmental problems of infants and toddlers. Typically, professionals from different disciplines attend to different ecological factors; as a team they can get a complex picture of the ecology surrounding children's developmental progress and thus be better prepared to have an effect on that progress.

Second, it directly addresses many of the validity and reliability problems that are evident when only one or two assessment instruments are used with infants and toddlers. Even the best of instruments has relatively poor predictive validity (i.e., a child whose early assessment results show delay or lack of delay often does not show that same pattern at a later age). Many also have poor concurrent validity (i.e., results from two measures that purport to assess a similar developmental construct are not in agreement) and poor reliability (i.e., a child's performance on the same or a similar test will differ if taken again, especially if in a different context). Few tests supply normative data representative of performance of children with disabilities or delays; thus, determining delay is difficult. Having a number of team members concurrently using different measures and giving perspectives on the same domains of development can serve not only as a practical confirmation or disconfirmation of validity and reliability questions but also as an indicator of the context variables that may have influenced assessment performance.

Third, it provides for families an integrated and comprehensive picture of their children's strengths and areas of developmental delay. In the typical multi- and interdisciplinary models of assessment, families are often confused about the meaning of the jargon from various disciplinary fields. They cannot understand or resolve the differences in disparate or conflicting reports. Often, they must provide the same set of background information numerous times because this information is not shared among discipline groups; they must interact separately with a range of professionals, who often have no knowledge of or interest in the reports of other professionals; and the team has no plan for integrating the various assessment reports into a coherent picture that leads to a useful plan of intervention. Transdisciplinary assessment has the potential for making the process more meaningful to and empowering of parents and thus more useful to their children.

Fourth, it gives professionals from many disciplines new insights into their own and others' perspectives on assessment and intervention. While being required to share expertise and viewpoints with other professionals is often threatening and time consuming, it is rewarding in at least two ways. First, by making explicit the understandings and principles of their own discipline, they can gain a deeper level of knowledge about that discipline. As the old saying goes, "the teacher learns the most." Second, by giving up a part of their role and responsibility and taking on parts of the roles of other professionals in order to achieve a shared goal, they can experience a broadening and deepening of their own knowledge base. This process can result in professional development in its truest sense.

PROMOTING CHILD AND TEAM READINESS

In the past few years, there has been great interest in the first goal of the *Commission 2000 Report* (Task Force on Education, 1990), which has again called attention to the need for early experiences that will make all children "ready to learn." While I have some quarrel with the way this goal has been stated, because I believe young children are *always* ready to learn, I do agree that a collaborative approach that helps all children reach their full developmental potential is an important societal goal.

Unfortunately, domestic policy and practice have not provided the resources needed to enable all young children to learn at their highest capacity. In fact, societal "benign neglect" or active restriction of access to health and other basic resources has forced many children to grow up in environments that are not conducive to their optimal development. The challenge we now face is that of ensuring that the policies and practices we advocate and implement result in improving the chances for life success of all young children, but especially those who are judged to be at risk.

Child readiness, however, cannot be accomplished out of the context of team readiness. The present readiness level of early intervention teams to meet the challenges of collaborative, comprehensive, and family-centered assessment and intervention merits immediate attention. Transdisciplinary team assessment is only beginning to be implemented throughout the nation. Many hybrid team versions exist, especially ones that combine aspects of the interdisciplinary and transdisciplinary models. While there are problems in getting transdisciplinary teams to function successfully, evidence is accumulating that supports the effectiveness of such models (Morsink et al., 1991). My hope is that this book will help professionals from a wide range of disciplines become ready to work in an integrated, effective way that promotes young children's developmental achievement and supports the empowerment of their families.

chapter 1

Doris Bergen

Interactive Perspectives on Infant and Toddler Development

The months before birth and the first 3 years after birth are times of great developmental change. Some changes are gradual and others seem to occur with astounding suddenness, although the precursors for the changes usually have been building for some time. In the first year of life the rate of change is often so rapid that physical and behavioral differences can be noted almost on a daily basis. By the age of 3, children who are developing typically have amassed a broad foundation of knowledge, skills, and attitudes on which their subsequent developmental changes will be based.

The processes and stages of infant and toddler development have fascinated a number of our most noted scientists, including Darwin (1877), who recorded observations of his own son's development in one of the first "baby biographies"; Skinner (1945, 1972) who designed a special infant learning environment in which to observe his child; and Piaget (1954, 1962), whose observations of his infants' play influenced his theory of sensorimotor cognition.

The early development knowledge-base has been greatly enriched by a physician, Arnold Gesell (1925, 1928, 1949), who systematically observed children, charted the typical developmental milestones occurring in their first years of life, designed one of the first methods of assessing normative development, and recommended procedures for diagnosing developmental problems and delays. Although inappropriate uses of his developmental schedules and interpretations of his work that have stressed its maturational focus have been effectively criticized (e.g., Kelley & Surbeck, 1991; Meisels, 1987), Gesell's fundamental perspective—that diagnosis of developmental problems must be done within the context of knowledge of typical developmental processes—is still relevant.

Many of the standardized assessment measures currently in use draw on information collected by Gesell and other researchers who studied young children during the middle decades of the century. In the past 20 years, however, another group of researchers and theorists has been at work, using technologically sophisticated methods to observe early developmental processes more precisely. For example, they have studied prenatal and infant brain development (Epstein, 1978); the effects of nutritional and health factors on early neurological processes (Lozoff, 1989); infant perception, attention, and memory processes (Bornstein, 1988; Rovee-Collier, 1993); and infant sensorimotor intelligence (Uzgiris, 1976). They have also looked at social, emotional, and communicative issues such as infant temperament (Thomas & Chess, 1977); attachment to caregivers (Lamb, 1977); language and symbolic play (McCune-Nicolich, 1981); and parent-child reciprocal interaction processes (Field, 1979).

Other researchers have investigated how culturally diverse family values and behaviors affect development (Laosa, 1982), and what the effects of various disabilities may be in influencing developmental patterns (Casby & Ruder, 1983). The insights into child development gained from this research are only beginning to be used in formal assessment, although some assessment measures have been designed that draw specifically on this information. For example, there are measurements of temperament (Carey & McDevitt, 1978); attention (Fagan & Shepherd, 1987); social–emotional interactions (Greenspan Leiberman, & Poisson, 1990); and play (Linder, 1993). Revisions of psychometric instruments are also beginning to incorporate recent developmental information in test items (e.g., Bayley, 1993).

An understanding of basic developmental principles and "typical" developmental milestones and the awareness of biological and environmental interactions that affect development is essential in order to choose and use developmentally appropriate assessment methods, make decisions based on these measures, and plan relevant interventions. The overview provided here does not take the place of an in-depth study of life span development, which should be an important requirement in the educational program of all professionals who work in educational, psychological, medical, communication, or social disciplines related to early intervention. All professionals on early intervention teams must have a well-grounded human development knowledge-base in order to make valid judgments about developmental delays in young children and to initiate appropriate interventions to promote their development.

DEVELOPMENTAL CHANGE AS ACHIEVEMENT

Although theorists have defined human development in various ways (e.g., Ausubel, Sullivan, & Ives, 1980; Baltes, 1989; Bronfenbrenner, 1993;

Scarr, 1991), most of them would agree that it includes the following characteristics:

1. *Changes* in the structure, function, or behavior of the human organism
2. that occur *over some time period* (which may be of long or brief duration)
3. and are *due to an interactive combination* of maturation and learning (heredity/environment interaction)

According to Feinman (1991), American cultural values that emphasize accomplishment, hard work, upward striving, and individual effort have resulted in a societal view of "development as achievement." Thus, American parents and teachers see young children's developmental changes as the attainment of milestones or stages that mark progress. Feinman states, "In industrial society, development is the realm in which the infant is encouraged to achieve" (p. 290). Moreover, it is an individual achievement rather than a group achievement. He notes American emphasis on the accomplishment of developmental tasks in early childhood and questions our view that development is progress rather than just change, recalling Bruner's (1983) comment that "Human beings, whatever their age, are completed forms of what they are" (p. 138).

Although this argument is provocative and certainly in need of further consideration, especially in regard to people who have been diagnosed with disabilities, it is also clear that early intervention is now strongly in the philosophical camp that defines "development as achievement." If it were not, then there would be no such concept as "developmental delay," which implies that, for some young children, developmental achievements have not occurred in a timely, sequential fashion.

The sequences, milestones, and stages outlined by numerous researchers and theorists describe normative developmental features, usually called *universals* of development. However, these professionals, like most parents, have also found that wide *individual variations* occur within the universal developmental patterns. These individual variations form a range within typical development that has been called the "range of normality." Extreme variations that go beyond the borders of these ranges have traditionally been categorized as atypical developmental patterns or disabilities.

Individual variations are partly due to genetically based characteristics, but are also the result of experiences that children have prenatally, at birth, and throughout their early years as they interact with the physical objects and sensory stimuli in the environment and with the social world of parents, siblings, extended family members, and nonrelated caregivers. The exact nature of the complex interactions between young children's biologically based characteristics and the factors in their pre- and postnatal environments is not yet clear. However, the importance of early environments on the developmental changes that occur between birth and age 3 has been well established, and current studies continue to support that conclusion (e.g., Brooks-Gunn, Klebanov, Liaw, & Spiker, 1993).

In infancy, developmental change has a high biological and maturational component; that is, many changes occur universally as a part of the growth process. Children carry within them a genetic potential, sometimes called a "genetic reaction range" or a "genotype," and it provides the parameters within which all development occurs. For example, physical characteristics, such as height potential, are influential in determining developmental terminals (i.e., how tall a child will eventually be). The exact influence of genetic characteristics is only beginning to be explored; however, there appear to be temperament, as well as physical characteristics that are biologically based (Chess & Thomas, 1989).

Environmental factors may interact with biologically based dispositions in positive or negative ways. The human organism is a system and, as such, has interactive components within itself (e.g., an illness affects a child's demonstration of walking ability). However, aspects of the social and physical environment (e.g., the care received during the illness, a safe or unsafe place in which to walk, an encouraging parent) also determines whether and how the child's genetic potential will be manifested. The manifestations of developmental potential that result from these interactions is called the "phenotype." The phenotype is observed during assessments. From observations and comparisons of phenotypic behaviors, predictions are made about the developmental potential of children.

Given their acceptance of the achievement definition of development and their commitment to maximizing that achievement, early intervention team members need to know basic developmental *principles* and *processes*, have a base of developmental *knowledge*, and understand the potential effects of biological and environmental *interactions* on developmental change.

BASIC DEVELOPMENTAL PRINCIPLES AND PROCESSES

Theorists and researchers often disagree on developmental issues such as whether there are discrete stages or how important a role heredity plays. However, they do agree that there are a number of principles that characterize human development throughout the life span. Figure 1.1 describes these principles and gives examples illustrating how they are manifested in typical development.

In regard to these developmental principles, young children with disabilities or delays are more similar to than different from typically developing human beings. Thus, the same developmental principles apply to children who are at risk for delay, although there may be some differences in how the principles are manifested. It is especially important for early intervention team members to keep these principles in mind as they plan ways to help these children reach their developmental potential. Figure 1.1 also shows the relationship of these principles to the development of young children who are at risk for delay.

DEVELOPMENT DURING THE PRENATAL PERIOD

The developmental stages of the prenatal period unfold in a relatively predictable fashion, although they are influenced by genetic and environmental factors. Figure 1.2 shows the timetable for initial development for typically developing children.

Rosenblith (1992) identifies the following genetic factors that can affect prenatal development: chromosomal disorders (e.g., Down's syndrome), gene defects (e.g., cystic fibrosis), the Rh factor, and problems in the balance of negative and positive genetic characteristics (e.g., sickle-cell anemia). She indicates that environmental factors that may affect prenatal development include maternal diseases (e.g., rubella, HIV), maternal chronic illness (e.g., diabetes), maternal malnutrition, prenatal oxygen deprivation, nonpsychotropic drugs (e.g., thalidomide, steroids), and psychotropic drugs (e.g., alcohol, nicotine, heroin, cocaine). Other possible environmental influences include radiation and physical or psychological stress. The type and severity of effects that environmental factors have depend on the time and intensity of exposure and on interactions with the genetic characteristics of the fetus.

During the birth process there are changes in the circulatory and the respiratory systems that enable the neonate to survive without the placenta. For example, impulses from the sensory receptors of the skin and chemical receptors in blood gases stimulate the respiratory center of the brain at birth so that breathing movements begin (Rosenblith, 1992). If such processes do not occur, death or disability for the neonate may result.

DEVELOPMENTAL ACHIEVEMENTS
FROM BIRTH TO AGE THREE

The period from birth to age 3 is one of extremely rapid development. The major developmental achievements that occur form the basis for all assessments of developmental delay. For some children these achievements occur over a longer chronological period than the first 3 years, and for others some of these achievements are never attained or have unique char-

FIGURE 1.1
DEVELOPMENTAL PRINCIPLES, TYPICAL EXAMPLES, AND RELATION TO RISK CONDITIONS

Principles	Typical Examples	Risk Conditions
1. Human beings are active in the process of their own development.	Infants actively seek stimulation by visual search and by grasping or moving toward novel phenomena.	Children who are at risk actively select and attend to environmental stimuli and attempt to act on these stimuli; if disabilities hamper self-efficacy, adaptive devices and social stimulation must be enablers of action.
2. Developmental change can occur at any point in the life span.	Adolescent parents and middle adult parents experience developmental change when they have a child.	Those at risk may not reach some developmental milestones until they are older, but they will continue to make progress; education continues to make a difference throughout the life span.
3. The process is not a smooth, additive one; it involves transitions and cycles, which include chaotic and disorganized as well as integrated and coordinated periods.	In the "terrible twos" the child strives for autonomy while still being dependent and so behavior fluctuates between seeking nurturing and gaining control of self and others.	Those at risk also experience setbacks, plateaux, disorganized periods, and new beginnings; these cycles may not be evidence of pathology but of developmental transition periods similar to those of typical children.
4. Biological maturation and hereditary factors provide the parameters within which development occurs.	A child's physique (e.g., wiry or solidly built) may affect timing of walking.	Biological and hereditary factors affect the levels of progress and the end points of development in areas of risk.
5. Environments can limit or expand developmental possibilities.	A child with poor nutrition or who is confined to a crib may walk later than is typical.	Certain types of delay (e.g., language, social) are very much influenced by home, school, and community environments.

6. There are both continuity and discontinuity (i.e., gradual, stable growth, and abrupt changes) in development.	The temperament of a child (e.g., slow-to-warm-up) may be evident throughout life; thinking patterns will differ qualitatively from infancy to adolescence.	Continuity of development may be less easily recognized and discontinuities may be more noticeable or attributed to nondevelopmental causes in those at risk.
7. Many developmental patterns and processes are universal (i.e., they follow similar time intervals, durations, and sequences of change in most individuals, no matter what their cultural group).	Children in all cultures use a type of "baby" grammar when they first learn to talk.	Children at risk will also show these patterns, although they may be distorted or delayed due to disabilities.
8. There are unique individual biological characteristics as well as culturally and environmentally contingent qualities that influence timing, duration, sequence, and specificity of developmental change.	Most girls talk earlier than boys, but in cultures where mothers talk more to boys, they talk early; girls in some cultures are permitted to be active and in those cultures they show higher activity levels.	Children at risk are more likely to have unique characteristics and experiences that influence how universals of development are manifested.
9. Developmental changes may be positive or negative, as they are affected by health and other factors.	A chronic illness may affect a child's progress and cause some regression to "baby" behavior.	Children with severe or progressive syndromes may show deteriorating development; a balance between maintenance of positive developmental signs and control of negative indicators may be required.
10. Developmental change intervals tend to be of shorter time spans for younger than older individuals.	Infants' motor skills are very different at 6 months and at 1 year, but there is not much change in motor skills between ages 15 and 17.	Time intervals of change are often long with children with disabilities, but developmental progress will usually occur more quickly at younger rather than older ages, making early intervention important.

FIGURE 1.2
SEQUENCE OF PRENATAL DEVELOPMENT

Name of Stage	Time After Fertilization	Events
Initial development		
Zygote	0–40 hours	Cleavage divisions.
Morula	40 hours to 4 days	Reaches uterus; embryonic cell masses develop.
Blastocyst	4–8 days	Development of 2-layered (bilaminar) disk; implantation begins; embryonic membranes start to develop.
Embryo—Early	12–13 days	Implantation complete.
	14 days	Mature placenta begins to develop.
	15–20 days	Development of 3-layered (trilaminar) disk; neural tube begins to form; disk becomes attached to uterine wall by short, thick umbilical cord; placenta develops rapidly.
	21–28 days	Eyes begin to form; heart starts beating; crown–rump length 5 mm (less than .25 in); growth rate about 1 mm per day; neural tube closes (otherwise spina bifida); vascular system develops (blood vessels); placental maternal–embryonic circulation begins to function.
Embryo—Late	5 weeks	Arm and leg buds form.
	7 weeks	Facial structures fuse (otherwise facial defects, e.g., cleft palate).
	8 weeks	Crown–rump length 3 cm (slightly over 1 in); weight 1 gm (about .03 oz); major development of organs completed; most external features recognizable at birth are present.

Fetal development

Fetus		
	8–12 weeks	Movements of arms and legs; startle and sucking reflexes, facial expressions, and external sex organs appear; fingerprints develop; respiratory and excretory systems develop, but are not functional; lanugo develops.
	end of first trimester	Length 7.6 cm (about 3 in); weight 14 g (about .5 oz); simple abortion by curettage no longer possible.
	13–16 weeks	Skin and true hair develop; skeleton becomes bony.
	17–24 weeks	Length 20 cm (about 8 in); weight 450 g (less than 1 lb); movements become obvious to mother ("quickening"); heartbeat can be heard through stethoscope; old cells discarded and replaced by new (hence cells in amniotic fluid).
	25–28 weeks	Begins to acquire subcutaneous fat; terminals of lung and associated blood vessels develop.
	end second trimester	Good chance of survival if born prematurely.
	by 38 weeks	Fetus becomes plump; lanugo usually shed; testes of male usually descend.

Source Note: Reprinted with permission from Rosenblith, JF (1992).

19

acteristics. Although human development is holistic, proceeding in an integrated fashion across all domains, the convention of the field is that developmental changes are observed and evaluated in discrete domain categories. The domains of development typically described are physical–motor, sensory–perceptual, cognitive, language, social–emotional, and play. Developmental disabilities or risk conditions may affect the attainment of developmental goals in each of these domains.

Physical–Motor Development

Changes in physical growth and motor coordination during the first 3 years of life can be readily observed. Perhaps because of this ease of observation, assessment instruments for young children use many items from this domain. However, the predictive validity of these assessment instruments for cognitive delay has not been high (Columbo, 1993). This may be because early physical–motor development is strongly maturationally based and thus less influenced by cultural or experiential factors than other developmental domains. Super (1976), however, found that in some cultures these skills were achieved early and were related to the amount of teaching of motor skills in which the mothers engaged.

Infants' heads are proportionally large in relation to the rest of their body at birth, and movement is dominated by primitive reflexes. The average infant weighs about 7 pounds and is approximately 20 inches long at full-term birth (Rosenblith, 1992). Their heart and breathing rates are twice as fast as those of adults. The skeletal maturity of girls is typically about four weeks ahead of that of boys (Fischer & Lazerson, 1984). During the first year of life weight typically triples, and length increases by about 10 inches.

Premature infants who are considered at *high* risk are those who weigh less than 3 1/2 pounds; those who weigh between 3 1/2 and 5 1/2 pounds are also considered at risk. Small-for-gestational-age (SGA) infants are also considered at high risk. Premature birth is associated with high risk primarily because the development of organs necessary for survival (e.g., the lungs) may not be sufficiently complete to enable the infant to be viable (Rosenblith, 1992). Much of the activity in neonatal nurseries is devoted to helping premature or low-birth-weight infants to survive until their systems can function without assistance.

The pattern of "states of consciousness" also seems to be important in the neonatal period. Infants typically go through a cycle of sleep and arousal states, ranging from deep sleep to active crying. Seven behavioral states have been categorized by Brazelton (1984), who built on the knowledge of infant states in his assessment scale in order to observe movement from state to state and to elicit best performance during the assessment. The active alert state seems to be the one in which most infant learning occurs. Although typical young infants average about 15 to 16 hours of sleep per day, there is great variation in sleep patterns, with some infants sleeping as little as 10 hours per day. The number of sleep periods also varies: infants of 13 weeks range from 2 to 17 sleep periods (Rosenblith, 1992).

At full-term birth, infants' brains have almost all the neurons (i.e., nerve cells) they will ever have; however, the receptor connections (i.e., dendrites) between the neurons are not yet complete, and the cortical portion of the brain has not been fully developed (Rosenblith, 1992). During the first 2 years of life the dendritic connections multiply extensively and the development of the insulating material that speeds message transmission (i.e., myelinization) occurs.

The brain grows in spurts during this early period (Epstein, 1978). By age 2, children's brains are already about 75% of adult size, but there is a spurt of growth beginning at age 2 that results in the brain being almost full size by age 6 (Tanner, 1978). There is some evidence that nutritional deficits during these first years can affect cognitive and physical development (Pollitt, Gorman, Engle, Martorel, & Rivera, 1993; Super, Herrera, & Mora, 1990, 1991). However, nutritional rehabilitation by itself is often not enough to remediate cognitive delays (Lozoff, 1989).

The presence in neonates of motor reflexes, such as sucking, rooting, and grasping, aid infant survival. Most reflexes (e.g., sucking, grasping) become incorporated in voluntary movements later. Others typically disappear during the first year. For example, the Moro (startle) reflex disappears in about 4 months. Infants' failure to lose such reflexive behaviors as their voluntary motor coordination is established serves as a strong indicator of a serious developmental disability (Gallagher & Cech, 1988).

The general sequence of changes in mobility and gross motor coordination (e.g., sitting, standing, walking) and in fine motor coordination (e.g., picking up small objects and transferring them from one hand to the other) has been outlined since the 1930s (Gesell, 1925; Shirley, 1931). For example, rolling over and sitting usually occur by about 6 months, standing by 8 months, and walking by about 11 months. Infants reach for objects by about 2 months, are successful at grasping them by about 5 months, and have a thumb-finger grasp that enables them to pick up small objects by about 10 months. Although the exact time these milestones are achieved is not crucial, the occurrence of motor skills within the range of the typical sequence is an important assessment standard. Young children who have conditions such as cerebral palsy or spina bifida, who are missing limbs, or who have visual impairments almost always have delays or distortions in their motor coordination achievements.

The process of motor coordination follows cephalocaudal (top-to-bottom) and proximodistal (inner-to-outer) change principles. An example of the cephalocaudal principle is that infants gain head control before trunk control, which occurs before leg control. The proximodistal principle is shown in children's ability to coordinate their whole body in space before they can use precise fine motor skills, such as picking up a small object. Young children must master two aspects of motor coordination: (1) coordination with self (e.g., moving one's own body to sit or stand) and (2) coordination of self with objects and other people (e.g., locating objects in space and moving to reach, touch, grasp, catch, and manipulate them). These types of coordination are essential for achieving more complex coordinated movement (Keogh, 1978). Of course, these coordination achievements also require the ability to integrate movement patterns with information from sensory stimuli. Sensorimotor integration problems are often identified in children who have delayed motor coordination.

Sensory–Perceptual Development

Although early researchers saw infants as primarily passive and reactive in regard to the sensory stimuli with which they were bombarded, more recent research on the development of sensory and perceptual processes and their relation to cognition have indicated that, from birth, infants selectively attend to, attempt to control, and perceptually organize their sensory environment (Bornstein, 1988). Infants can see and discriminate among patterns presented at close range even during the newborn period (Fantz, 1963), but they can not see well at distances. During their first 3 years distance vision improves greatly. Infants are particularly interested in the human face and by 6 months can recognize familiar and unfamiliar faces (Gibson, 1969). Hearing is already well developed at birth, although sounds must be relatively loud to be heard. Newborns react to sounds, and their ability to locate the direction of sound improves greatly by 5 months (Morrongiello & Clifton, 1984). By 4 months they are beginning to discriminate among and organize speech sounds (Eimas & Miller, 1992).

Even very young infants are responsive to odor, taste, touch, and probably pain (Steiner, 1979; Gunnar, Malone, & Fisch, 1987). Intermodal perception, which is the ability to integrate information simultaneously from several sensory modalities, is evident within the first year of life (Meltzoff, 1990). For example, 6-month-old infants can recognize moving objects (Ruff, 1982) and by 1 year they coordinate vision and touch (Acredolo & Hake, 1982). An important achievement is gaining the ability to reach for and grasp an object, which usually occurs by about 4 months of age. Some infants begin with large and vigorous movements and refine them, others start quietly and gradually generate more energetic movements (Thelen, Corbetta, Kamm, Spencer, Schneider, & Zernicke, 1993).

Infants show by their defensive motor responses to approaching objects that they have a basic understanding of speed and trajectory of movement of objects in space before they are 6 months old (Ball & Tronick, 1971). They demonstrate depth perception by hesitating when expected to crawl across surfaces that appear to be far below them during the latter part of the first year (Gibson & Walk, 1960).

Infants also demonstrate the ability to synchronize the rhythm of their movements with those of their caregivers; monitor and control their arousal level through motoric withdrawal and gaze aversion when interaction is too intense; and use their facial expressions and body movements to elicit responses from caregivers when the caregivers are nonresponsive (Brazelton, Koslowski, & Main, 1974; Stern, 1974). Because of the importance of visual, auditory, and other sensory stimuli in motor coordination, reciprocal interactions, and exploratory movement, the visually or otherwise sensorily impaired young child will be likely to have delays or distortions in these behaviors, which may then have implications for development in cognitive, language, and social-emotional domains.

The sensorimotor actions of infants demonstrate the close tie between these action schemes and their increasing knowledge of objects (Piaget, 1954). At first, infants use the same action schemes (e.g., mouthing or shaking) on all objects they encounter, but by the end of the first year they use differentiated action schemes that are appropriate for the objects. For example, they will mouth a cookie, shake bells, and rub cotton on their cheek. The appearance of differentiated action schemes, described in detail by Uzgiris and Hunt (1975), show the infant is beginning to recognize and use objects appropriately.

Cognitive Development

The link of infant cognition to sensory and motor development was made explicit by Piaget (1954), who described stages of infant *sensorimotor* thought and the transition to representational thinking during the toddler years. He characterized sensorimotor cognition as having 6 stages. The stage sequence progresses from simple reflexes (first month) to attempts to reproduce chance events (1 to 4 months) to focused action on the objects in the environment (4 to 8 months) to intentional coordination of schemes (8 to 12 months) to exploration of new scheme possibilities (12 to 18 months) to ability to represent objects and use primitive symbols (18 to 24 months). If voluntary coordination of reflexive behaviors is the source of cognition, as Piaget asserts, then problems in timing of onset and disappearance of reflexes are strong indicators of potential cognitive problems.

Piaget theorized that the ability to use representational thinking, which occurs between 18 and 24 months, is evidenced when infants demonstrate object permanence (i.e., being able to hold the idea of an object in mind even when it cannot be seen); pretend play (i.e., transforming objects and actions to be other than they actually are); and language (i.e., understanding and using verbal symbolic labels for objects and actions). The demonstration of these capabilities marks the end of the sensorimotor period, which occurs at about age 2. Symbolic representation also enables infants to understand that pictures, television images, and replica models can represent persons, animals, objects, actions on objects, and social interactions. The transition from sensorimotor to representational thought is crucial for the development of higher level thinking abilities. According to Piaget, from age 3 to 7, children's representational thinking is still highly based on perceptual information (i.e., appearance), focuses on one dimension, and is characterized by egocentric speech, in which the child uses vocal sounds or narratives to accompany actions but not for communicative intent. He terms this age period *preoperational* because children are not yet capable of performing logical mental operations.

Most children who have developmental delays eventually reach this transition period from sensorimotor to preoperational thinking. However, the timing depends on the type and severity of delay. For example, visually impaired children are usually delayed in developing object permanence and symbolic play (Rogers & Puchalski, 1984) and children with autism may be delayed in or may never attain the ability to understand or produce language and to play in pretend modes (Clune, Paolella, & Foley, 1979). Using Piaget's concepts, Uzgiris & Hunt (1975) designed a method of assessment that gives insights into sensorimotor thought and the transition to representational thought. Dunst (1980) has adapted this instrument for use with children who have disabilities.

Vygotsky (1962), who studied young children's categorization and language abilities, indicated that young children demonstrate categorical thinking first by grouping objects using unorganized trial and error or spatial nearness criteria. By age 3 they are able to associate objects and organize complexes of objects using criteria based on perceptual or semantic associations. Vygotsky differs with Piaget in his view of the role of egocentric speech, which Piaget asserted was a nonsocial behavior that paralleled thinking. Vygotsky sees egocentric speech of the type that accompanies action as arising from social awareness and as playing an important role in influencing young children's development of conceptual thought.

A number of current theorists have revised aspects of Piagets' stage descriptions. For example, Case (1986) has indicated that the *preoperational* period, which begins about age 2 or 3, might be better termed *relational* because children are learning the relationships among the phenomena in their world. Fischer (1980; Fischer, Bullock, Rotenberg, & Raya, 1993) rejects the idea of stages, preferring instead to describe "tiers" of behavior that take into account the fact that the same level of thinking is not used across all domains. He characterizes early sensorimotor thought as "single set representations" (i.e., reaching), which then proceeds to "mapping" (i.e., connecting the single sets of seeing, reaching, and grasping). Ability to coordinate conceptual "systems" of representations does not begin until after the toddler age; however, toddlers do begin to show they can coordinate their actions among sensorimotor systems (e.g., taking note of object distance and speed in their reaching and grasping acts). Baldwin, Markman, & Melartin (1993) report that by 9 months infants can draw simple inferences about object properties after only brief experiences with the objects. They presented infants with similar looking novel toys, one of which had a hidden but salient property (such as making noise). Infants attempted to reproduce that property in the similar toy, but did not attempt to do so when given a dissimilar toy.

Some cognitive skills may occur earlier than Piaget proposed. For example, newborns are able to form prototypes and recognize familiar schemes (Walton & Bower, 1993); infants of 3 and 6 months can demonstrate long-term memory of events in which they have actively participated (Rovee-Collier, 1993); and those of 7 months can remember where objects had been placed at an earlier time (Fox, Kagan, & Weiskopf, 1979). Also, newborns can imitate adult emotional expressions (Field, 1982) and infants of 9 months can imitate actions 24 hours after they have seen them performed, a phenomenon Piaget said did not occur until 18 months (Meltzoff, 1988). During infancy, children begin to acquire a sense of intentionality, recognizing that people are responsive to their requests and attempts to communicate (Flavell, 1993).

Many recent research findings about infant cognitive competence have not yet found their way into standard assessment measures, but they have potential for being especially useful in assessing young children who have severe motor or sensory problems that prevent them from demonstrating their understanding through sensorimotor actions. An example is a measure derived from perception of visual stimuli, which is now being used to make inferences about infant cognitive development (e.g., Fagan, 1987). In this assessment technique, the length of time infants pay attention to pictures of novel and familiar faces is used as an indicator of cognitive competence. Typical infants habituate to familiar stimuli and look longer at novel stimuli. Research indicates this method has predictive validity for later cognitive competence (Fagan & Singer, 1983; Fagan, Singer, Monte, & Shepherd, 1986). It is not a measure that can be used with the visually impaired infant; however, it does provide an assessment alternative that requires no language and minimal movement. It is described further in Appendix B. Because the close interface of language with cognition is evident after the first year of life, most assessment methods used with 2- and 3-year-olds require children to demonstrate comprehension and production of language when cognition is being assessed.

Language Development

The processes of language acquisition and the sequence of language development milestones have been well charted over the past 25 years (e.g., Brown, 1973; Nelson, 1973). Even very young infants rapidly learn to use their vocal apparatus to attract attention to their needs and engage in social interactions through crying and "cooing" vocalizations. Beginning at about three or four months and continuing throughout the first year is a babbling stage, during which infants gain the ability to articulate the sounds of all languages and gradually learn to approximate the phonetic elements and intonations used in their native language. Babbling seems to be a maturationally based behavior because its initial phases occur even in deaf infants, who have had no opportunity to hear language (Lenneberg, 1967).

Hearing-impaired infants do not continue to progress to later stages unless they have hearing augmentation, confirming that exposure to a language environment is necessary for language acquisition. The learning of sign language is apparently slightly easier than the learning of spoken language; however, the cognitive capabilities of memory, categorization, and symbolization must be present for either to occur (Goodwyn & Acredolo, 1993). For example, children who exhibit pervasive communication disorders, such as those resulting from autism, usually have delays or distortions in their cognitive and play capabilities and in their language (Riguet, Taylor, Benaroya, & Klein, 1981). Prematurity alone does not seem to preclude the typical development of language, however. For example, in a longitudinal study of 30 premature low-birth-weight children, only 4 showed language problems at age 3 (Craig, Evans, Meisels, & Plunkett, 1991).

Understanding of language (also called "reception" or "comprehension") begins at about 9 to 10 months with the comprehension of single words, and increases exponentially, with more than 50 words being understood by 13 to 14 months (Bates, Bretherton, & Snyder, 1981). During the second year of life, children begin to follow simple directions, point to pictures or objects when given a label, and participate in repetitive familiar games or stories. By age 3 they respond to word-order cues and can understand sentences using active voice, although understanding of passive voice sentences takes longer (Savage-Rumbaugh, Murphy,

Sevcik, Brakke, Williams, & Rumbaugh, 1993). Savage-Rumbaugh et al. assert that "when similar requirements are used for both skills, comprehension is found to precede production without exception" (p. 22).

Nelson (1973) found that comprehension at 13 to 15 months predicted children's level of language production at 2 and 2½ years. Comprehension was a better predictor of late production than the number of words spoken at this same age. Language comprehension is often difficult to assess because much language occurs in meaningful contexts and is accompanied by gestures, facial expressions, or tones that also convey meaning. However, by 18 to 24 months, if comprehension of well formed sentences voiced by familiar adults is not beginning to occur, concern for the child's hearing or cognitive capabilities is warranted. The "range of normality" for demonstrating the basics of receptive language is relatively narrow (about 9 to 24 months).

Infants' ability to use spoken language (also called "expression" or "production") typically begins during the last few months of their first year, although there is a much wider "range of normality" in regard to onset, quantity, and quality of speech. For example, although parents are often concerned about articulation of sounds, age of mastery of particular sounds ranges from age 3 (b, m, n, f, w, h) to over age 6 (th, ing) (Goldman & Fristoe, 1986) and achieving speech that is understandable by familiar adults can occur anywhere from age 2 to age 4 (Frankenburg & Dodds, 1990). Echolalic vocalization (i.e., long streams of sounds that mimic speech) is a form of egocentric speech that is characteristic of some children with language, cognitive, and social–emotional disabilities. It is not true speech and does not have a communicative intent. Persistent echolalic speech without development of one- and two-word sentences of intentional speech is a sign of developmental problems.

According to Nelson (1973), the first words spoken are personal and mostly action-related, having salient properties of change. That is, they express the child's desires to affect the environment and reflect "the child's mode of structuring the world" (p. 33). The use of holophrastic speech (i.e., using one word to express the meaning of a sentence) occurs by about 12 to 15 months. For example, "Cookie" could mean "I want a cookie," "Here is a cookie for you," or "The cookie jar is empty." Holophrastic speech is usually accompanied by gestures in context that enable parents to guess the meaning. (Greenfield & Smith, 1976).

Toddler speech is usually telegraphic (i.e., a sentence without modifiers), such as "Go store" or "Daddy work." These sentences are also accompanied by gestures and tones that convey meaning within the context. Slobin (1972) has identified twelve types of meaning that toddlers convey, including identifying, locating, repeating, negation, possession, attribution, questioning, and various agent–action–object combinations.

Toddlers from countries throughout the world convey these meanings in their early speech. Toddlers may show a preference for words that are object referenced ("car" or "book") or that are expressive or interpersonal ("Hi" or "baby") (Nelson, 1973). Whether this is due to temperament or personality differences or to environmental influences is not clear.

In addition to the phonetic (sound), syntactic (structure), and semantic (meaning) aspects of language, pragmatics, the ability to use language appropriately in social interactions, is a very important aspect of language knowledge. Young children must learn that language communicates messages and how to show communicative intent. They must also know how to access the knowledge that they share with the listener in order to make it meaningful (presupposition) and how to maintain a dialogue with others over conversational turns (discourse) (Roth, 1990).

Adults demonstrate communicative intent, presupposition, and discourse rules when they engage in early social games or caregiving activities with infants. Vocalization responsiveness in a "turn taking" pattern of communication with adults can be observed as early as 3 or 4 months (Brazelton, Koslowski, & Main, 1974), and infants' active communication participation with family members during social game routines, such as peek-a-boo, is highly evident by the latter part of the first year (Bruner & Sherwood, 1976). Adults and older children interact with typically developing infants asymmetrically, adjusting their language and interaction patterns to compensate for the young child's lack of expertise in communication (e.g., Stern, 1977). They tend to use a simplified and highly expressive speech style, which has been referred to as "motherese" (Snow, 1983; Dunn & Kendrick, 1981). Recent research indicates that there are similarities in these patterns across cultures but that parents from different cultural and socioeconomic groups also have differences in the amount of speech directed at the child and in the specific content of their language during communicative interactions (Fernald & Morikawa, 1993; Heath, 1989). Because language is culturally transmitted and socially interactive, its development is greatly affected by the social and emotional world that young children are provided.

Social–Emotional Development

Knowledge of the social and emotional development of infants and toddlers has greatly increased in recent years as these domains have become subjects of research interest. Emotional expression seems to arise from an innate base because of its survival value in gaining caregiver attention and responsive care (Izard, 1980). However, there are cultural influences that determine what primary emotions the infant will express in the eliciting context (Kagan, 1984).

Izard indicates that infants show a neonatal smile (not a true smile), startle responses, distress, and disgust. By 4 to 6 weeks the social smile appears, and by 3 to 4 months infants show anger, surprise, and sadness. Fear and shame or shyness are evident in the second half of the first year and contempt and guilt appear during the second year. Damon (1988) indicates that these early emotions form part of the basis of moral development. For example, infants show empathy by reacting with an emotional response that is similar to the one being expressed by the parent or peer. Toddlers show shame or embarrassment when they fail to live up to parental standards and show guilt by taking personal blame for the distress of others.

Building upon the work of Freud (1923–24), who theorized about the emotional, social, and personality consequences of early relationships between young children and their parents, a number of theorists have posited stages of social–emotional development. According to Greenspan and Greenspan (1985), there are 6 stages of emotional development during the first 3 years, beginning with self-regulation, falling in love (e.g., forming an emotional attachment), developing interactional communication, gaining an organized sense of self, creating emotional ideas, and using emotional thinking (fantasy). These stages may be observed in children with disabilities also, but they have some differences. For example, emotional expression is both delayed and less intense among children with cognitive disabilities (Cicchetti & Sroufe, 1976) and children with autism display emotional expressions that are incongruent with contextual events (e.g., sad during pleasant events, happy during unpleasant events) (McGee, Feldman, & Chernin, 1991). Some studies of prenatally drug-exposed infants show effects on temperament. Exposed neonates are more irritable and arrhythmic than nonexposed neonates. Prenatally drug-exposed toddlers may also exhibit disorganized play and insecure attachment, although their cognitive test scores are usually in the normal range (Hawley & Disney, 1992).

Erikson (1963) identified psychosocial crises that occur in the infant and toddler years and made caregivers aware of the social interaction base from which emotional and social competence arises. He called the infant crisis that of *trust versus mistrust* and the toddler crisis *autonomy versus shame and doubt*. According to Erikson, infants who are in relatively predictable, caring environments develop the ability to trust themselves, other people, and the environment, thus enabling them to give and receive love and to reach out confidently to other people. It is fostered by the "affective reciprocity" (Emde, 1980) established between the infant and caregiver. Typically, infants demonstrate their trust of the caregivers both by engaging in positive interactions with those persons and by becoming suspicious of unfamiliar adults. In the second half of the first year (7 to 10 months) stranger anxiety and separation anxiety occur. Bowlby (1989) explains these anxieties as having an innate base and being related to the attachment process.

By 12 months, when mobility has been achieved, infants show a strong desire to explore and control their environment, but they usually stay in range of the "secure base" of the caregiver. If this trusting base has been established and if the environment is safe and responsive, toddlers are then ready to gain control of their own body functions, seek autonomy, and explore a widening social and physical environment. One of the hindering factors in the lives of children with severe motoric disabilities is that, even if they are capable of becoming cognitively and socially autonomous, they have few opportunities to engage in behaviors that promote autonomy.

By 18 months, children demonstrate a sense of self as different from others (Lewis & Feinman, 1991). Mahler, Pine, & Bergman (1975) identify 4 stages in the process of self development, which begins with separation and moves to individuation by age 3. The sense of self is very evident between $2\frac{1}{2}$ and 3 years, when toileting and feeding behaviors are coming under the child's control. The phrase, the "terrible twos" is an indicator of the interpersonal adjustments that must be made when children are in the process of self-development. Parents and teachers do not always see this behavior as an indicator of developmental achievement and so may resist the child's attempts at self-direction. This reluctance to permit independent behaviors is often especially strong in parents who have had premature or medically fragile infants because their mind set may still be geared toward protection (or overprotection) long after that is necessary.

The young child's ability to have a secure attachment, which is the strong affectional relationship to parents or other caregivers, is based on both the trusting and the autonomous behaviors. For example, the securely attached child is more likely to be socially competent with peers during the toddler age (Pastor, 1981). According to Bowlby (1989), attachment behaviors are partly innate because forming an emotional linkage with a caregiver is essential for infant survival. However, they also have a strong cognitive component because person awareness, stranger wariness, and separation protests all are required in order for the child to differentiate among familiar and unfamiliar persons and to have object permanence (Teti & Nakagawa, 1990). Status of attachment can therefore be of interest in assessing the development of children with disabilities or suspected cognitive delays. Numerous studies of the attachment of maltreated infants have indicated that these children are much more likely to have insecure attachments, when assessed by the Ainsworth Strange Situation procedure (Ainsworth, 1979; Teti & Nakagawa, 1990). Studies of children with cognitive disabilities indicate that they do not exhibit typical attachment patterns, although they do show attachment-like behaviors (Blacher, 1987). This assessment procedure is explained in Appendix B.

Through interactions with parents, other caregivers, and peers, young children also gain understanding of the social rules that should be followed and attempt to influence the social behaviors of others. The process of socialization is reciprocal because parents and children are socialized during these interactions. As Rogoff (1991) states, "infants are active participants in their own development" (p. 258). For example, infants become upset and withdraw or cry if parents respond inappropriately or fail to respond to their interaction attempts (Trevarthen, 1977), and the temperament of the infant affects the interaction style of the parents (Chess & Thomas, 1989). Infants with regular responses and reactions of moderate intensity are easier for most parents than those with erratic behaviors and intense reactions. Also, certain disabilities, such as visual or hearing impairment, cognitive delay, or severe motor problems, may distort the reciprocal interaction process. For example, Fraiberg (1974) found that mothers of blind infants thought the children were not responsive because of the lack of visual regard and differentiated facial expressions, and this feeling then negatively affected the mother's interactive style. Also, the temperaments of infants who have been exposed to drugs may make them less easily soothed and less consistently responsive (Edmondson & Smith, 1992).

Young children typically display prosocial behavior such as cooperating in play with parents by 6 months (Hay, Ross, & Goldman, 1979) and spontaneously "helping" with tasks by age 2 (Rheingold, 1979). Infants also show awareness of peers (Hay, Nash, & Pedersen, 1983). Toddlers exhibit preferences for play with particular children (Vandell & Mueller, 1978); show empathy for siblings' problems (Dunn & Kendrick, 1981); and share objects with peers (Mueller & Lucas, 1975). Many assessment instruments used with young children examine social-emotional development under the rubric of "adaptive behavior" or "personal-social behavior." These categories typically focus on self-help skills and compliance with prosocial rules. Some of these instruments are described in Appendix B.

Damon (1988) indicates that social cognition, which is understanding the social world, can be observed in children's concern for distributive justice (e.g., sharing); respect for rules (e.g., learning to obey "no"); and reciprocity (e.g., turn-taking). They also exhibit social referencing, which is perceiving the other person's feelings and interpretations of events and using them as cues for their own feelings and interpretations (Feinman, 1991). They are particularly likely to use familiar persons as social referents when they are in ambiguous situations (i.e., unsure how to act or feel).

Because play is the primary mode of interaction in young children, much of their social-emotional development is fostered in their play.

Play Development

Young children's play is highly related to other developmental domains. As infants initially explore the physical environment, using their sensori-motor abilities (e.g., looking, tasting, touching), they also begin to play with the objects in the environment by repeating actions over and over and gradually elaborating on these actions. This object play has been called practice play by Piaget (1962) because the repetition with variations assists infants in consolidating and reorganizing their behavior.

By 9 months infants typically select slightly novel rather than famil-iar objects and enjoy playing with responsive objects (e.g., those that make noise or move when touched) (McCall, 1979). They are interested in cause–effect relationships around 1 year and like to try to make toys work and to order unstructured play materials by arranging them or grouping them. During the second year they begin to understand the social mean-ing of objects and their play reflects the functions, categories, and verbal criteria they have learned. Toddlers' practice play typically includes activ-ities such as stacking and knocking down, filling and dumping, and putting objects in and taking them out of containers. They also use objects to enhance their interactions with adults and peers by showing, giving, and receiving objects and by observing object play of others (Mueller & Bren-ner, 1977).

Adults facilitate social play development by involving infants in social games or routines such as peek-a-boo. These routines occur within a "play frame" created by adults, who give signals that tell infants the interaction is play. Signals such as close facial contact, open eyes and mouth, exag-gerated features, high-pitched voices, and exaggerated speech sounds all show the infant that "this is play" (Sutton-Smith, 1979). Fathers and mothers interact differently in play; fathers are more active and mothers more initiating and responsive.

Adults also play differently with male and female children (Lamb, 1977; Power & Parke, 1983). They react differently in play interactions even with 1-year-old children when they know the gender of the child (Goldberg & Lewis, 1969). Although play content and activity level in play are very similar in boys and girls of age 2, by age 3 gender differences in play choices begin to be observed (Fagot, 1988). There appear to be sub-tle differences in teacher responsiveness to "gender appropriate" play that may account for the growing differences in play materials and content shown by boys and girls by age 2 1/2 (Fagot, Hagen, Leinbach, & Krons-berg, 1985). Adults also interact differently in play with children who have disabilities. For example, mothers of cognitively delayed infants take a more directive and managerial role in the play; that is, the reciprocity balance is more toward mother-initiated action rather than infant-initiated (Bailey & Slee, 1984).

There are also some differences in the way children with disabilities play with objects in their sensorimotor practice play. When nonfamiliar toys are presented, children with cognitive delays explore for a longer time before beginning to engage in practice play (Switzky, Ludwig, & Haywood, 1979). However, the type of disability and the severity of the condition determine whether there will be a problem in practice-play abilities (Rogers, 1988).

At the end of the first year, pretend play begins. This involves the ability to transform objects and act as if they had other qualities. The first transformations are with realistic objects and self-focused actions (Fenson, 1984). For example, the infant may "drink" from an empty cup. Slightly later, the pretend actions can be focused on someone other than self, such as "feeding" a doll from an empty bottle. Most early pretend play replicates details of ordinary life events and roles and follows a predictable sequence, although it is also affected by context variables (Bretherton, O'Connell, Shore, & Bates, 1984).

By about 24 months coordinated pretend sequences are seen, with more than one action (e.g., doll is fed, rocked, put to bed) or more than one object (e.g., many dolls are put to bed). By age 3, the pretend play will have a planned sequence and be accompanied by language. Toddlers give labels to objects (e.g., calling a block a "cake") and also name actions (e.g., riding in a wagon is called "going shopping"). Adults facilitate pretend play during the toddler years by creating a context for pretend, providing props, initiating a role for themselves, responding by taking a role, and accepting the appropriateness of the child's pretend actions (e.g., Miller & Garvey, 1984).

Play with the sounds of language is also common during the period from about 12 to 24 months (Cazden, 1976). Toddlers use nonsense rhyming sounds or repeat sounds in definite patterns, with evident enjoyment. Although older toddlers' pretend play often revolves around the use of objects and performance of actions that represent social acts of immediate family members (e.g., giving a bottle to a doll; setting the table), they may also act out simple scripts based on television characters (e.g., cartoon characters); make a game of pointing out and labeling family members portrayed in videos or photographs and animals shown in books; and respond to requests for giving the names of familiar people or animal sounds by deliberately giving the wrong ones (and laughing about their teasing!).

This topsy-turvy play with concepts indicates that they have mastered the right labels and find it funny if they give an incongruous answer

(Chukovsky, 1963). The appearance of humor is also a sign of cognitive development because much humor is based on visual incongruity (e.g., seeing a hat on a dog) or verbal incongruity (e.g., deliberately calling a dog an incorrect name). Parents often observe the development of humor with these characteristics in their children when they are as young as 2 years (Bergen, 1989). These behaviors are all evidences of the influence of the ways symbolic portrayals in the social environment influence play, cognitive, language, and social–emotional development. Children in all cultural groups demonstrate symbolic awareness in play, but because the symbols provided by adults and the media differ among cultures, the themes and roles of play also differ.

Children with cognitive delays also engage in pretend play; however, it does not begin until they have reached the developmental equivalent of the 18– to 24-month period, when representational thought, holophrastic speech, and understanding of the word *no* are achieved (Casby & Ruder, 1983; Rogers & Puchalski, 1984). Pretend play in cognitively delayed children is usually more repetitive and contains fewer symbolic substitutions, but it has many similarities to that of typically developing children (Hill & McCune-Nicolich, 1981). Pretend play in autistic children is also impoverished in content, with few object transformations and little symbolic fluency (Riguet, Taylor, Benaroya, & Klein, 1981) and it is closely linked to receptive language development (Ungerer & Sigman, 1981). When with peers, children who have disabilities spend more time looking and listening than playing with other children (Brophy & Stone-Zukowski, 1984).

INTERACTIONS OF ADULT DEVELOPMENT WITH CHILD DEVELOPMENT

One developmental process posited by Gesell and colleagues (Ilg & Ames, 1955) was that of "cycles of behavior." Their data showed that children's developmental change is manifested in alternating periods of equilibrium and disequilibrium. Disequilibrium periods include first a "breaking up" state, movement through states of "inwardness" and "expansiveness," and reintegration into another state of equilibrium. The first cycle occurs between birth and age 5, but throughout childhood the cycle seems to repeat about every 5 years. Although the exact descriptions and age levels may not always apply, many parents can attest to being surprised when their smoothly functioning child suddenly began to exhibit disorganized or clumsy behavior, their confident child became inward and anxious, or their cooperative child became an expansive risk-taker.

One of the most interesting discoveries of life span developmental researchers and theorists is that cycles of equilibrium and disequilibrium also occur throughout the adult years (e.g., Gould, 1980; Levinson, 1978; Vaillant, 1977). The length of time between the equilibrium periods may be much longer than 5 years, and the changes may involve much less dramatic or visible states of breaking up, inwardness, expansiveness, and new consolidation. However, such common terms as "mid-life crisis" attest to the presence of this process; it may be evident in external behaviors (e.g., quitting a job) or in internal states only (e.g., adult self-report data showing breaking down of old ways of thinking, increased preoccupation with self, or imagining risk-taking new behaviors).

The timing and nature of developmental change in adults is more dependent on environmental influences than is the case with children, most of whom tend to have relatively similar life experiences during their childhood years. Adults' range of life experiences is much greater and the triggering factors that precipitate developmental change may be different and may occur at early or later age periods. Although the majority of developmental themes are similar for men and women (Neugarten, 1964), the pattern of experiences for men traditionally has been different from that for women (Levenson, 1978; Rosenfeld & Stark, 1987).

For example, the experience of parenthood produces developmental change in both parents, but that change is usually more extreme for women, who typically bear the primary psychological and care responsibility for children. The influence of parenting experiences on developmental change is also affected by whether it is a *normative* event (i.e., one encountered by most adults) or a *nonnormative* event (i.e., one experienced by only a small subset of adults) (Santrock, 1992). For example, getting married at age 20 to 25, and becoming a parent at age 22 to 30 are normative events, while becoming a single unmarried parent at age 14, becoming a first-time parent at 40, being divorced at 30, and then becoming a single parent, or, at any age, becoming a parent of a child with disabilities are all nonnormative events.

Parents at any life stage, whether their life circumstances are excellent or less than ideal, face developmental crises when they have a child who is disabled or at risk for delay. Because developmental changes are influenced by both biological and environmental factors, it is difficult to predict the extent of parental and family developmental change that will occur when they have a child who needs early intervention. D'Amato and Yoshida (1991) found that 75% of parents of young children with disabilities reported childrearing concerns, with the most difficult aspect being coming to terms with their child's development in comparison to typical peers. Although most research shows that families exhibit a great deal of stress when they have a child with disabilities, there is also evidence that the range of adaptive reactions is wide and that some families have remarkable coping powers (Simeonsson, 1988). Because adult developmental changes are major influences on child–caregiver interactions, professionals who work with families must view the child's development in the context of the developmental state of the adults who care for the child. Thus, the interactive perspective must include consideration of adult, as well as child development.

INTERACTIONS OF RISK CONDITIONS ON DEVELOPMENTAL ACHIEVEMENT

As this brief overview of developmental achievements in the first 3 years of life makes clear, there are many important developmental changes that young children achieve in that time span. There is much variation in how and when typical developmental stages or milestones are exhibited in children who are categorized as at risk, because the nature and severity of the disability or risk condition influence what developmental domains are affected and what limits will be set on the child's response capabilities. Children with severe or multiple disabilities will be affected in many domains; other children may experience problems of delay or distortion in only one domain. However, this primary delay may then have an effect on development in other domains.

For children without clearly identified disabilities, recognition of problematic behaviors that are outside the range of normality is not so easily accomplished. According to Kalmanson (1989), patterns of behavior are more important to identify because they may be likely to indicate intervention is needed, while "singular behaviors are likely to indicate individual differences within the normal range of development" (p. 6). Determining the duration of the problem behavior, its pervasiveness, and its intensity are also crucial in the assessment process. Infant specialists have attempted to differentiate between developmental vulnerabilities that are likely to point to the need for intervention as compared to typical states of developmental transition or stress. Kalmanson (1989) suggests that it is useful to assess the pervasiveness of vulnerabilities over five domains: self-organization, social–emotional, motor, sensory integration and perception, and language. Her indicators are in Figure 1.3. Although her example does not include all domains discussed in this chapter, it does give an indication of the levels of duration, pervasiveness, and intensity of problematic behavior that should be considered in determining whether intervention is needed.

FIGURE 1.3
DEVELOPMENTAL VULNERABILITIES IN INFANTS AND TODDLERS

	Infancy	Toddlerhood
Self-Organization	Difficulty with regulation of states, irritability, crying, trouble falling asleep Attention seems random, not focused or responsive to adult interaction	Little organized attention to people or objects Difficulty falling asleep, wakes up irritable Irregular food intake
Social–Emotional	Unresponsive Lack of reciprocal gaze Absence of anticipatory response to being held Seems to prefer being alone Fails to form strong personal attachments	Little or no reciprocal interaction/play Little attachment to primary caregivers Indifference or extreme prolonged distress at comings or goings of primary caregivers Absence of imitative play
Motor	Lack of motor response to voice Arches back when held Doesn't mold to parent's body, limp	Disorganized, random movement Impulsive racing and falling Apathetic, little interest in movement
Sensory Integration	Easily upset by extraneous sounds/sights, startles easily Trouble coordinating input from parents (can't look at mother while being held and talked to)	Easily startled Doesn't localize sound Overwhelmed by moderate stimulation and withdraws Engages in self-stimulation
Language	Absence of cooing in response to parents' vocalizations Lack of attention to parent's voice	Absence of communication/gestures Little imitation of words No words for important people/objects Lack of intentionality in communication

SUMMARY

The foundation for early intervention rests on the concept of development as achievement and its corollary, that assessment of developmental delay is needed in order to intervene and promote child achievement. In order to be effective, the assessment and intervention team must have a thorough knowledge of human developmental processes and principles; the ability to consider both universal and individual aspects of developmental stages and milestones; and an understanding of how these processes, principles, stages, and milestones vary as a function of established, biological, or environmental risk conditions interacting with adult developmental issues. Effective assessment and intervention must be built on this developmental knowledge-base.

QUESTIONS FOR DISCUSSION

1. What physical–motor, sensory–perceptual, cognitive, language, social–emotional, and play development indicators would be most important to observe if there were concerns about developmental delay in a child of 6 months, 12 months, 18 months, and 24 months?
2. How can the developmental principles outlined in Figure 1.1 influence childrearing and early intervention practice?

PROBLEMS OF PRACTICE

Observe an infant (3 to 12 months) and a toddler (13 to 20 months) who have not been identified as having any type of disability or developmental delay, and note their behaviors for at least one hour, respectively. Then make a summary of their developmental achievement levels in physical–motor, sensory–perceptual, cognitive, language, social–emotional, and play domains. Ask each child's parent or caregiver whether the behavior you observed was typical. Note any discrepancies. Using this "typical" achievement list, observe for 1 hour a child aged about 2 years who has been identified as having delay in at least one domain and summarize that behavior. Check with the child's parent to determine whether your observation is representative of the child's achievements. Compare that child's achievements with those of the two "typical" children, and indicate whether this observation confirms the diagnosis of delay that was identified in the early intervention referral.

SUGGESTED READINGS

Gonzalez-Mena, J., & Eyer, D. W. (1993). *Infants, toddlers, and caregivers* (2nd ed.). Mountain View, CA: Mayfield.

Rosenblith, J. F. (1992). *In the beginning: Development from conception to age two.* Newbury Park, CA: Sage.

chapter 2

Doris Bergen
Margaret Wright

MEDICAL ASSESSMENT PERSPECTIVES

The number of infants born at risk has grown exponentially over the past several decades. Many of these infants have long-term, medically complex problems that require multifaceted and costly care. Infants assessed by medical personnel can be placed into one of three categories: (1) those born with known genetic disorders (e.g., Down's syndrome) or physical disabilities (e.g., cerebral palsy, deafness, blindness) who need immediate intervention at birth and long-term comprehensive care to achieve their potential; (2) those born prematurely or at very low birth weight who are at risk for disability because of prematurity or medical procedures performed to prevent their death (iatropic causes); and (3) those whose future development could be severely compromised by psychosocial risk factors such as poverty, poor nutrition, in utero drug exposure, or family environments that include persons with severe mental illness, substance abuse problems, or neglectful or abusive behaviors (Anastasiow & Harel, 1993; Chasnoff, Griffith, Freier, & Murray, 1992; Green, 1991; Kopp & Kaler, 1989; Shonkoff, Hauser-Cram, Krauss, & Upshur, 1992; Werner & Smith, 1982, 1992; Wright & Masten, in press).

Several epidemiological studies of the use of health services by families with children indicate that a small sub-group use a disproportionate amount of these services (Boyce, Sobolewski, & Schaefer, 1989; Forsarelli, DeAngelis, & Mellits, 1987; Starfield et al., 1979, 1985). Boyce (1992) suggests that only 15% to 20% of all children use over 50% of available physician services. These children cluster in four groups: (1) those with parents who are excessively anxious; (2) those with illnesses or problems caused by parental action (e.g., child abuse, Munchausen syndrome); (3) those with chronic illness, such as asthma, seizure disorders, cystic fibrosis; and (4) those predisposed to illness because of psychosocial risk factors, environmental toxins, such as lead, susceptibility to viral or infectious illnesses, and constitutionally or genetically based vulnerability to stress (Green, 1986; Starfield et al., 1984).

A number of recent studies have documented that many young children now being seen by primary care physicians are at risk because of psychological and social problems (Boyce, 1992; Green, 1991; Horwitz, Leaf, Leventhal, Forsyth, & Speechley, 1992). Haggerty, Roghmann, & Pless (1975) refer to this as the "new morbidity" in pediatric practice. In response to the need for physicians to assess, treat, or refer more children with psychosocial problems, the Task Force on Pediatric Education has recommended that, in addition to rotations in child psychiatry, further rotation in developmental pediatric areas (behavioral, family, social, and educational) be incorporated into pediatric curriculum.

UNDERLYING ASSUMPTIONS

The multiplicity of problems and the complexity of required medical services make assessment and provision of coordinated care in the hospital and following discharge quite a challenge. An important assumption of this perspective is that comprehensive assessment and care relies on the cooperation and energy of many individuals from a variety of professions, all of whom must work effectively together in the medical setting. In the hospital setting a case management approach has often been selected as the most effective way to manage health assessment needs, plan and coordinate services, and monitor the services for quality control. Providing for these multiple service needs is particularly important for the medically fragile infant. The quality of the interactions among physicians, nurses, allied health professionals, parents, health care providers, and the infant determines the effectiveness of case management.

A second assumption underlies the medical perspective on assessment: cost effectiveness. Because the cost of health care today is a crucial issue facing health care providers and administrators, third-party payers, employers, and families of high-risk infants, conducting comprehensive diagnoses, planning and coordinating services, and directing patient care activities require a balance between concern for quality of patient care and cost containment (Hamric & Spross, 1989; Nine, Bayes, Christian, & Dillon, 1992; Norris & Hill, 1991).

A third assumption that directs early medical assessments is that the family's role is very important. In the past, hospital personnel were not so aware of the need for involving the family in all aspects of early assessment and intervention; however, the present approach is highly cognizant of the contribution the family makes to the well-being and progress of the child.

The importance of the family has always been recognized by physicians and nurses in pediatric and public health practice. Early tracking programs, which identify and monitor infants judged to be at risk, are also based on the importance of linking the practices of medical personnel with family concerns and issues (Anastasiow & Harel, 1993; Shonkoff et al., 1992).

METHODS OF ASSESSMENT

Assessment of infant well-being by medical personnel begins during the pre-natal period and continues during the birth process and early hours of the infant's life. Systematic assessment of a neonate's physical health and behav-ioral state is routinely conducted. Clinical judgment is the primary means of assessment, although some standardized measures are used. For typically developing infants, a primary care physician usually takes over the assess-ment role after the infant's first few days of life. For infants with risk condi-tions that may result in severe developmental problems, extensive and long-term assessment and intervention may be required in the hospital setting.

HOSPITAL SETTINGS

Hospitals usually use a case management approach in dealing with assess-ment issues. In the assessment phase of case management, a comprehen-sive evaluation of the infant's physical health status and functional capa-bility is combined with assessment of the family's and community's support systems, financial resources, and environmental conditions that may promote or adversely affect health outcome.

    Standardized assessment instruments are often used to obtain assess-ment of the infant's neuro-behavioral state. These include the Apgar Score, which is an evaluation measure used at 1 minute and 5 minutes after birth, and Brazelton's Neonatal Behavioral Assessment Scale, which measures behavioral and neural organization. It can identify neuro-behavioral deficits, describe the level and quality of the infant's behavior, assess the impact of treatment interventions, detect changes in the infant's behavior, and predict future development and function. It is a better predictor of later developmental outcome than the Apgar Score. In the Apgar Score, five physical signs are evaluated 1 minute and 5 minutes after the complete birth of the infant (not regarding the cord and placenta). Each sign is given a score of 0, 1, or 2. A total score of 10 indicates that the infant is in the best possible condition. The score taken at 1 minute is a good index of asphyxia and the need for assisted ventilation; at 5 minutes, the score is a more accurate index of the likelihood of death or later neurologic deficits (Apgar, 1953). These tests are described further in Figures 2.1 and 2.2. If warranted by the infant's condition, a variety of other diagnostic tests and procedures are used, such as ultrasound, electrocardiogram, spinal tap, and magnetic resonance imaging (MRI). Descriptions of the most frequently used medical diagnostic tests are in Figure 2.3.

FIGURE 2.1
IMMEDIATE EVALUATION OF THE NEWBORN: THE APGAR SCORE

	Sign	0	1	2
1.	Heart rate	Absent	Below 100	Over 100
2.	Respiratory effort	Absent	Slow, irregular	Good, crying
3.	Muscle tone	Limp	Some flexion of extremities	Active, motion
4.	Response to catheter in nostril (tested after oro-pharynx is clear)	No response	Grimace	Cough or sneeze
5.	Color	Blue, pale	Body pink, extremities blue	Completely pink

Source Note: Reprinted with permission from Apgar (1953).

FIGURE 2.2
INFANT NEURODEVELOPMENTAL ASSESSMENT: BRAZELTON NEONATAL BEHAVIORAL ASSESSMENT SCALE (BNBAS)

A 7 cluster scoring scheme summarizes the Brazelton Scale Scores:

1. Habituation:
   Habituation to a bright light, a rattle, a bell, a pinprick

2. Orientation:
   Attention to visual and auditory stimuli

3. Motor processes:
   Quality of movement and tone

4. Range of state:
   Peak of excitement
   Rapidity of buildup
   Irritability
   Lability of state

5. Regulation of state:
   Cuddliness
   Consolability
   Self-quieting
   Hand-to-mouth activity

6. Autonomic stability:
   Tremors
   Startles
   Reactive skin color changes

7. Reflexes:
   Number of abnormal reflexes

Source Note: Information from Brazelton, Nugent, & Lester, 1987.

FIGURE 2.3
Common Diagnostic Tests and Procedures

Ultrasound scan	Uses sound waves to look inside different parts of the body. The image on the screen is transferred to a regular X-ray film for the doctor to interpret.
Electrocardiogram (EKG)	A recording of the child's heartbeats. The EKG detects changes or alterations in heart rate and rhythm, in heart ventricular size and heart strain (e.g., coronary artery occlusion).
Computed tomography (CT)	A type of X-ray that takes pictures of the child's brain and abdomen. At certain times medication is given intravenously. This medicine circulates in the blood and causes parts of the brain or abdomen to show up more clearly on the pictures.
Spinal tap	Measures the amount of pressure in the spinal canal; removes a small amount of fluid for examination. After the lower part of the spine has been anesthetized, a needle is inserted in the spinal canal and fluid is withdrawn.
Electroencephalogram (EEG)	A recording of the electrical activity generated by the brain that represents the summed results of excitatory and inhibitory postsynaptic potentials.
Magnetic resonance (MRI)	A noninvasive imaging method of examining the brain and other internal organs of the body. This test uses magnetic fields instead of X-ray to produce images on film by computer analysis. The MRI provides excellent detail of anatomic structures.
Event related potential (ERP)	Assesses a transient electrical signal following stimulation of a peripheral sensory modality (e.g., ear-brainstem evoked response; eye-visual evoked response; peripheral nerve-somatosensory evoked response). The signal is recorded over the appropriate area of the scalp with EEG electrodes. The small signal needs to be averaged to be detectable and differentiated from ongoing EEG activity.
Extracorporeal membrane oxygenation (ECMO)	Machine acts as an artificial heart and lung membrane adding oxygen for a baby whose own heart or lungs cannot get enough oxygen into the blood to circulate through the body. The goal of ECMO is to let the heart and lungs recover while the baby is supported by the ECMO.

Ventricular shunt	A small tube that has been placed in the child's head to reduce hydrocephalus. The shunt carries extra fluid from the head to the blood stream (ventriculo-jugular [VJ] shunt) or to the abdomen (ventriculo-peritoneal [VP] shunt) where it is absorbed.
Shunt-o-gram	Used to determine why a child's ventricular shunt is not working properly. A small needle is put into the valve of the shunt. Fluid is drawn out of the valve and sent to the laboratory for testing. A dye that shows up on X-rays is put into the valve and X-rays are taken. After pumping the shunt, X-rays are again taken to watch the dye pass through the shunt tube.

Source Note: Adapted from "Helping Hand," Children's Hospital Homegoing Education and Literature Program, Columbus, OH, with permission.

Comprehensive functional assessment of the infant is frequently performed by an inter- or multidisciplinary team consisting of a nurse, social worker, and other allied health professionals. A variety of methods are used, such as informal direct observation of the infant, observation of parent responses to information, use of an infant observation checklist, maintenance of anecdotal chart notes of critical incidents, and ongoing monitoring of physiological measures of infant health status. A developmental assessment instrument such as the Bayley may also be included if the infant is in long-term care. Parental ability to cope with the medical needs of the infant following hospital discharge is monitored also.

A clinical example of the process used for an infant in a neonatal intensive care unit (NICU) follows: An infant born 2 months prematurely (birth weight approximately 2 lbs; less than 1000 g) who tested positively for cocaine (and whose mother was a cocaine and alcohol user) would be placed in the neonatal unit. The life-threatening condition of the neonate and the high risk for mortality or morbidity presents a number of challenges that need to be addressed by the NICU team. They are concerned with the infant's survival and quality of life because 27% of infants born at very low birth weight die (Claflin & Meisels, 1993). Infants exposed to drugs in utero are at high risk for compromised neuro-developmental outcome, infection, congenital abnormalities, and neonatal drug withdrawal, which leads to symptoms of irritability and hypersensitivity to touch, sound, and light (Bingol, Fuchs, Diaz, Stone, & Gromisch, 1987; Chasnoff et al. 1992; Singer, Farkas, & Kliegman, 1992).

While the infant is in the NICU, safety and security issues are crucial, and careful documentation and monitoring of all medications, intravenous therapy, and diagnostic procedures is essential. The margin of error is extremely small when dealing with medically fragile and premature infants, who are particularly susceptible to infection.

There may be extensive diagnostic testing, numerous procedures, and much transferring of the infant to and from various facilities. Monitoring of apnea, respiratory distress, intraventricular hemorrhage, and hydrocephalus is often needed. In addition, the metabolic and physiological needs of very low-birth-weight infants necessitate extensive monitoring of all physiological parameters, such as heart rate, body temperature, blood pressure, and oxygen saturation.

Clinical judgment regarding the infant's diagnosis and treatment involves a complex intellectual process of decision making among a number of different individuals. Most in-patient units comprise inter- or multidisciplinary teams that meet weekly to discuss case management plans. At these meetings decisions regarding which target behaviors or symptoms need to be observed for a particular infant are discussed, and assignments of individuals responsible for performing such observations are made. Inferential decisions about diagnosis and treatment are then derived from the observational data, diagnostic test findings, laboratory data, and clinical examination. This complex process results in a medical diagnosis, at times accompanied by the delineation of additional psychosocial problems within the family. Decisions regarding medical and psychosocial treatment are usually made during team meetings and documented extensively in the hospital medical record (Hamric & Spross, 1989).

To develop a plan that meets the needs of the family and the infant, the NICU must implement a monitoring and evaluation program that meets the requirements of the Joint Commission on Accreditation of Health Care Organizations (JCAHO). The hospital must also comply with quality assurance (QA) guidelines. The physician–director of the NICU has overall responsibility for quality assurance, although this responsibility is shared by the staff. The head nurse assists the medical director in evaluating the neonate's initial needs and stabilizing the infant's condition.

Following diagnostic assessment and formulation of a medical treatment plan, infants categorized as having identified disabilities are usually referred to early intervention programs at the time they are ready to leave the hospital. Those whose risk conditions have not yet resulted in demonstrated developmental delay are included in hospital tracking programs, when they are available. These programs rely on public health nurses, social workers, and physicians in the community to monitor the developmental progress of infants at risk of delay during their first few years.

If the infant's medical problem is extremely complex (e.g., needing organ transplantation, dependent on monitoring devices at home, or severely medically compromised), a case management approach is developed to facilitate access to home support services and to prevent avoidable episodes of illness (American Nurses Association [ANA], 1988). Public health nurses can assist directly in the home, advocate for services on behalf of the child and family, and help the family identify appropriate institutional or community resources. A social worker may be involved to facilitate coordination of services needed, such as home care or therapeutic visits, and to work with the family to find sources of financial assistance, such as third-party payments, or of reductions in cost of care.

Home health education of the parents in the care of their medically fragile infant is often vitally important to help them develop the expertise needed to handle an acute exacerbation of the child's medical problem. For many high-risk infants, an effective treatment plan following hospital discharge involves parent education, community resource assessment, coordination of needed services, possible home health care assistance, respite care, and patient advocacy (ANA, 1988; Hamric & Spross, 1989). Collaboration with primary care providers in developing and implementing health care management prior to, during, and following hospitalization is essential. With such intervention, the potential for maximizing the self-care potential of the family can be enhanced.

PRIMARY CARE PEDIATRIC SETTINGS

The primary care physician is usually the monitor of developmental delay for young children. Infants judged to be at risk at birth may be under the care of their primary care physician while still in the hospital. However, if the early weeks of the infant's life have been spent in a hospital specializing in neonatology, the community physician to whom the infant is referred on leaving the hospital may have had only minimal contact with the assessment team from the hospital setting. Some infants continue to be seen by hospital well-baby clinics, others will not have contact with a primary care physician unless an acute illness requires care. Tracking programs monitor whether the parent does maintain medical care for immunizations and other illness prevention services.

Routine health assessments are completed by the primary care physician and nurse clinician. These include a general physical and neurological examination, measurement of height, weight, blood pressure, and head circumference, and vision and hearing screening tests. In addition, primary care physicians or nurses can assess the overall developmental level of infants with a measure such as the Denver Developmental Screening Test (DDST), which was initially designed for pediatricians' use. This recently revised test, Denver II (Frankenburg & Dodds, 1990), is designed to provide a clinical impression of a child's overall development, in particular, to identify children who may need further comprehensive assessment because of developmental delay. It assesses social–emotional, fine motor, gross motor, and language development and is considered one of the most reliable and valid measures for screening purposes. Appendix B describes it further.

Parents are a primary source of information for physicians, especially in relation to psychosocial problems that may influence the child's development. Physicians routinely ask parents questions about their children's health, nutrition, developmental progress, and family conditions. Although many physicians have medical associates in the same office, few use a team assessment approach. Rather, they and their nurses collect the diagnostic information and the physician refers children directly to other specialists, if intervention or further diagnosis is needed.

A study of the rates of identification and predictors of psychological problems in children under the care of physicians in a group of pediatric practices in New England reported that 27% of the children were identified as having at least one problem (Horwitz et al., 1992). Data were collected using the checklist of psychosocial and developmental problems (based on the World Health Organization's primary care child classification system) shown in Figure 2.4.

The physicians in the study were found to be more likely to identify problems under the following circumstances: during a well-child rather than a sick-child visit; when the clinician knew the child well; when the child was male; and when the child's parents were not married. The most commonly identified problems were family difficulties, child behavior problems, and child language problems. When a problem was identified, 31% received no active treatment although the problem was noted in the child's record (these were usually problems in motor development). In the cases that received further attention, 40% were treated by the pediatrician, 16% were referred to an appropriate specialist, and further evaluation indicated that no treatment was necessary for 13% of the children. The more severe the problem, the more likely the referral. The study conclusions point to the need for medical personnel to receive training in identifying and intervening when developmental, behavioral, family, and school-related concerns emerge.

INFORMATION EXCHANGE WITH FAMILIES AND REFERRAL AGENCIES

Because parents can experience psychosocial stressors when their infants are born with immediate medical problems, many families benefit from consultation with the psychology staff and, if needed, joint planning with child welfare and social services agencies, in addition to close involvement

FIGURE 2.4
CONTENTS OF THE PHYSICIAN PSYCHOSOCIAL ASSESSMENT FORM

Category	Specific Problems
Physical growth	Slow weight gain, non-organic failure and development to thrive, obesity
Sleep	Trouble sleeping, sleepwalking, night terrors
Motor	Hyperactivity, overactivity; gross motor delay, fine motor delay
Cognitive–language	Mental retardation, learning disabilities, language delay, attention problems, speech problems
School	School failure, school refusal, absenteeism or truancy
Behavior	Enuresis, temper tantrums, fire setting, stealing, tics, encopresis, excessive masturbation
Psycho-physiological	Recurring stomach pain, headaches, recurring knee or leg pain
Feelings	Anxiety or nervousness, feelings of depression, low self-esteem, excessive anger or irritability
Thought	Delusions, hallucinations, incoherence
Peer activity	No confidence, social isolation, fighting and bullying
Parent-child	Problems separating, physical abuse, psychological abuse, sexual abuse, physical neglect
Social	Lack of housing, frequent moves, financial problems, sexual abuse (other than parent)
Family	Divorce or separation, physical or mental illness of parent, drug or alcohol abusing parent, parental discord, spouse abuse, few social ties, problems with siblings, death of parent

Source Note: Reprinted with permission from Horwitz, McLeaf, Leventhal, Forsyth, & Speechly (1992).

with the medical staff. Therefore, while attending to the physiological needs of the infant, members of the NICU team are also responsible for attending to the psychological and psychosocial needs of the family.

For parents, the neonatal intensive care unit is a very strange and unpleasant environment in which to become acquainted with a new baby. Parents are surrounded by "high-tech" equipment (e.g., ventilators, apnea monitors, temperature control devices, and intravenous lines) and are often bombarded by high noise levels. In addition, they encounter a series of experts who communicate in extremely technical medical language that may be confusing and frightening. The parents face great uncertainty about the infant's likelihood of survival or disability and they often have limited physical contact with their infant (Claflin & Meisels, 1993; Field, 1993; O'Dougherty & Brown, 1990). Thus, parent education and support become integral parts of the NICU's team functioning. To facilitate this information exchange, many units have developed family-centered nursing and provide psychological supportive care on the units.

Staff education is also essential to ensure competence in meeting infants' medical needs and in providing assistance to parents coping with fear, confusion, and anxiety. Effective communication of professionals, across disciplines and with the parents to establish trust, is crucial.

A number of clinical interventions have been shown to reduce family stress, and a variety of questionnaires have been used to assess the family's ability to cope with the demands of the medically fragile infant. Several intervention studies have examined the usefulness of parent observation of the nurse or physician administration of the Brazelton Scale (Field, 1993; Widmayer & Field, 1980; Worobey & Belsky, 1982). Demonstration of the test with the parent watching has been shown to have long-term implications for maternal sensitivity to behavior of the infant. One study (Widmayer & Field, 1981), which compared mothers' scores on the Mother's Assessment of Behavior of the Infant (MABI) with the Brazelton Scale results showed that mothers who observed the test administration performed better on developmental assessments and during face-to-face interactions with their infants. The infants also performed better on the Brazelton interactive process items. Other investigators explored the effects of observation of the Brazelton with other samples and detected similar gains (Anderson, 1981; Worobey & Belsky, 1982). This improved performance is attributed to facilitation of parental sensitivity and responsiveness to their newborn infants. By observing the Brazelton and subsequently performing the rating, parents may learn about the infant's capabilities and respond more sensitively to their infant's signals and be more effective at interpreting their infant's cues.

It is also imperative that the health care providers know about the community resources available to children and families so that they can make appropriate referrals. The referral process has often been fragmented: parents are given separate information about isolated resources in their communities or, if the problem requires a specialist, they are referred to a person whose location may not be convenient. The initiative for contacting these resources has usually been the responsibility of parents, who vary greatly in their motivation to seek and ability to obtain other community health and education services. To diminish these difficulties, many hospital-based tracking programs not only provide referrals but also initiate contacts with public health nurses, early intervention programs, physicians, and other community resources needed by the child and family.

Because primary care physicians are particularly concerned about motor and language development during the first years of life, they often make referrals to physical therapists, occupational therapists, and speech pathologists, and to early intervention programs. Although some physicians are very knowledgable about community resources, others are aware of only a few of the services in their communities. Thus, referrals by primary care physicians may vary greatly in terms of comprehensiveness, cost, and usefulness. With the recent state and national mandates requiring interagency cooperation, the information about available community resources and the accessibility of these resources to parents has been much improved, and more coordination of referral sources is becoming evident. There are as yet few transdisciplinary models of assessment that incorporate medical, educational, psychological, and social work personnel, however, so referral networks are not as comprehensive as they could be.

USEFULNESS OF A TRANSDISCIPLINARY MODEL

There are a number of assessment and intervention team models that consist of or incorporate medical personnel. Their composition depends somewhat on the setting in which the team is working. University hospitals provide a high degree of specialization across many areas of health care, and include students in training and faculty doing research on the teams. Private hospitals and ambulatory care facilities may provide a range of comprehensive services that involve those professionals on the teams or they may be composed of specialty clinics that individually assess the child. Short-term stay hospitals provide surgical and non-surgical acute treatment, diagnostic procedures, and prescription and monitoring of medications, primarily employing medical personnel.

There are a number of chronic care programs that incorporate psychological and educational personnel in their teams. Clinics typically have a team that includes one or two representatives from psychosocial disciplines. Rural clinics provide a range of primary care for all income levels, while family health centers and community care centers provide care for low-income families. Primary care settings focus on the integration of physiological, psychological, social, and cultural factors that are likely to have an impact on the child's health status and developmental prognosis. However, they usually do not have a full range of team disciplines.

The models of inter-, multi-, or transdisciplinary teamwork vary in these different settings. For early intervention personnel to operate effectively in these settings, they must be knowledgeable about the specific ways health assessment planning and delivery of services occur and about the types of available community resources. The typical medical model has been one of inter- or multidisciplinary interaction, with experts from each discipline sharing information, either without integration into the broader assessment picture (a multidisciplinary approach) or with an integrative discussion of the separately gathered assessment information (an interdisciplinary approach), which takes place before the intervention plan is complete. The transdisciplinary approach, in which experts from a range of disciplines permit information from their area of expertise to be collected by other team members or engage in a global discussion of the child's needs across discipline areas, is not a common model.

The commitment to team approaches is certainly high in hospital settings, especially in neonatal and child care. However, the team is usually not broadly representative of a range of disciplines, consisting primarily of medical personnel and perhaps a psychologist or social worker. Primary care physicians often provide information to educationally and developmentally oriented transdisciplinary teams, but they rarely participate in the team discussions or intervention plans.

There are a number of constraints that work against incorporating medical personnel in transdisciplinary models of assessment and intervention once the child is out of the hospital or clinic. First, medical personnel are often located in areas that are not close to the early intervention site. Second, the time commitment required for this model is high, and most medical personnel do not feel they have this time to devote to assessment and intervention planning. Finally, the cost of on-site medical professionals is often prohibitive.

One example of a transdisciplinary model is when an early intervention team meeting is held at a hospital, with the early interventionist, parent, and social worker present. Even then, the meeting may result in being more of an information sharing session by the medical personnel than a collaborative effort to observe, discuss, and plan together for the child's developmental progress.

Other efforts to incorporate medical personnel in teams have had varied success. Public health or school nurses are often included as central team members; physicians have been most difficult to integrate. Interpretation of the physician's views has often been left to other team members or to parents and, in some cases, this information is not even available to the teams who are making decisions about children's educational and developmental needs.

Because many of the infants and toddlers who need early intervention have chronic or crisis-based medical needs, it is imperative that collaborative approaches are implemented when possible. Currently, transdisciplinary teamwork that incorporates personnel from medical, educational, and psychosocial disciplines is not used extensively out of neonatal hospital settings.

POLICY ISSUES

All health services organizations are presently facing important policy challenges related to resource organization and management (McLaughlin & Kaluzny, 1990). These challenges are coming from health care professionals, state and national governments, and the population. There has been recent interest in "total quality management" (TQM), a framework for organizational change initially implemented by businesses. Since the JCAHCO has made revision of health care provision a primary agenda item, TQM concepts are being studied. This represents a paradigmatic shift in health care management, with potential conflict with past practices (Arikian, 1991; Flower, 1991; McLaughlin & Kaluzny, 1990). TQM's philosophy of operation requires basic revisions in health care organizations, including visible management, informal communication across disciplines, timely decision making, support of experimental approaches and risk taking, time for innovative projects and research, and concern about patient care quality and employee job satisfaction. TQM principles have been applied in a number of magnet hospitals (Kramer & Schalenberg, 1988).

The TQM approach may be instrumental in fostering transdisciplinary assessment and intervention in hospital and primary care settings, because many of its principles are congruent with the goals of a transdisciplinary team in early intervention. In a TQM approach, improvement of health care delivery is the responsibility of all personnel, not just those designated as quality assurance personnel; this requires teamwork that builds on the creativity and worth of each team member. The typical professional model now in use has been particularly effective in handling technical information from medical research and specialization issues, but it fosters individual professional autonomy, which is not the focus of TQM.

Although the magnet hospitals report improved quality of care, greater team-related autonomy in practice, and facilitation of best performance in each team member, there are many potential conflicts with present practice, especially in relation to cost containment issues. Many issues of individual versus collective responsibility, clinical versus managerial leadership, administrative authority versus participation, goal-directed versus process and performance expectations, and rigid versus flexible planning need to be addressed, if policy changes that promote TQM are to be initiated.

Federal policy on health care also affects primary care physicians, health maintenance organizations, and professionals of other disciplines that collaborate with medical personnel. Policies may be conducive to transdisciplinary approaches in early assessment and intervention or have a negative impact on these approaches. As the health care system continues to be examined and revised, managerial style, cost containment mandates, and team–individual interface will affect the functioning of early intervention teams.

Another issue that may eventually affect policy is arising from initial research on how effective the commonly used risk factors are in predicting poor developmental outcomes. For example, a recent study of 985 low-birth-weight, preterm infants showed that few of the individual risk factors listed in federally mandated state definitions of risk predicted poor developmental outcomes (Kirby, Swanson, Kelleher, Bradley, & Casey, 1993). In this study, most specific factors had positive predictive values of only 12% to 40%, and even composite factors yielded only 25% to 35% predictive values. Those factors, such as hypothyroidism, that had values greater than 50% occurred in less than 6% of the sample. As this study and other longitudinal studies have indicated, the determinants of individual outcome are extremely complex and difficult to predict. Risk and continued vulnerability need to be evaluated in multiple domains, including assessment of specific biological, psychological, and social stresses as well as changes in these areas over time and at different stages of the disease and the child's development (Wright & Masten, in press.)

One of the best known and most illustrative projects in this regard is the 30-year longitudinal study of 698 infants born on the Hawaiian island of Kauai in 1955 (Werner & Smith, 1982, 1992). While moderate-to-severe perinatal stress did emerge as a risk factor, key factors identified in this study that predicted later developmental problems included chronic poverty, low maternal education, and family conflict or instability. Thus, multiple levels of analysis (biological, cognitive, social, emotional, and environmental) are needed to understand individual vulnerability and resilience. While severe biological insult can permanently affect the development of some children, the longitudinal studies to date have provided clear documentation that children have a remarkable capacity for recovery and adaptive growth. Further research exploring the processes underlying recovery and resilience is needed.

These studies also raise questions about the policy implications of medical risk evaluation on the design and funding of early intervention programs. Further longitudinal study is needed to determine the effectiveness of both identification criteria and early intervention practice. Whether the present intensive service models being advocated and used are necessary, successful in identifying the appropriate target populations, providing sufficient developmentally and socially appropriate services, and cost effective are questions that should lead to policy debate in the future.

SUMMARY

Medical personnel are often engaged in providing assessment and intervention services to young children with complex and multifaceted developmental problems. In hospital settings, they rely on a model of professional teamwork that seeks to involve the family as well. Primary caregivers outside of the hospital setting usually work independently with families, using other early intervention services as referral possibilities. Medical approaches usually work well, especially when the child's initial survival and long-term health depend on the expertise of these professionals. However, medical personnel are concerned with how family involvement can be promoted, cost effectiveness improved, and communication among professional groups enhanced. These issues, which are important aspects of transdisciplinary team approaches, have begun to be addressed, but are not yet resolved.

QUESTIONS FOR DISCUSSION

1. What are the strengths of the professional team model used in hospital settings and what aspects of that approach have been identified as problematic?
2. How do primary care physicians typically evaluate young children, what intervention decisions are they most likely to make, and what sources of referral do they use most often?

PROBLEMS OF PRACTICE

Visit a neonatal nursery and observe the types of assessment and intervention being practiced. Ask at least three team members who have worked together in providing early intervention services for a child and family to point out the practices that worked well and the areas that could be improved. Investigate the referrals that families are likely to receive as follow-up to their child's hospital experiences. Evaluate ways to improve or expand referral linkages.

SUGGESTED READINGS

Claflin, C. J., & Meisels, S. J. (1993). Assessment of the impact of very low birth weight infants on families. In N. J. Anastasiow & S. Harel (Eds.), *At-risk infants: Interventions, families, and research* (pp. 57–79). Baltimore: Paul H. Brookes.

Widmayer, S. M., & Field, T. M. (1980). Effects of Brazelton demonstrations on early interactions of preterm infants and their teenage mothers. *Infant Behavior and Development, 3,* 79–89.

DIALOGUE

IFSP Review of Arlo

GENDER, AGE, ETHNIC ORIGIN OF CHILD: Male, 16 months, Euro-American.

OCCASION OR PURPOSE OF DIALOGUE: Second review of Arlo, 6 months after initial assessment, to assess developmental progress and further define the nature of the child's disabilities. The child is presently enrolled in an early intervention program that provides once-a-week visits in his home.

TEAM MEMBERS: Two pediatricians (staff physician, pediatric fellow), a physical therapist, a clinical nurse, a social worker, an early intervention specialist, a psychologist, and Arlo's mother and grandfather. (This is the same team who conducted the initial assessment.)

SETTING: A hospital-affiliated clinical center for developmental disabilities.

OVERVIEW OF THE CASE

RISK CONDITIONS

Arlo was a full-term baby, born by cesarean section, reported to be blue at time of delivery. He was sent to the intensive care nursery, diagnosed as having aspiration pneumonia (from aspiration of meconium), and placed on a ventilator for 3 weeks. Since birth he had a deep cough that worsened whenever he was active. Two months ago, during routine adenoid surgery, the surgeon discovered an artery was growing around Arlo's trachea. Its further growth would have resulted in an obstructed windpipe and death The problem was corrected surgically and his cough is now gone. His recovery from surgery has been good and his color is better since the operation.

REASON FOR REFERRAL

At 10 months, Arlo was referred to the hospital clinical center by his private pediatrician, who had concerns about his slow rate of developmental progress in motor areas. Although Arlo's developmental delay in gross and fine motor domains was observed by the team at the initial assessment, no specific diagnosis giving the etiology of the delays was confirmed. Three objectives were identified at that time, two of which have been achieved:

1. Enrollment in a home-based early intervention program. (Achieved.)
2. Provision of a sling-type sitting device to give Arlo more stability. (After consultation with the physical therapist.)
3. Clarification for the family of the sequence of events that occurred at Arlo's birth, which might have led to his delays. (A family-initiated objective, not yet achieved.)

BACKGROUND INFORMATION

Arlo's mother is a 19-year-old single parent in a close extended family from a low socioeconomic rural Appalachian background. Although the mother lives with her son in an apartment by herself, her three sisters assist in the child's day-to-day care. The mother does not work outside the home. The child's father (a member of the extended family) has limited ongoing contact with the family.

FAMILY STRENGTHS AND NEEDS

Family strengths include the support provided by the extended family, in particular by the child's three aunts. The early interventionist has observed that Arlo's mother seems to enjoy the child, often smiling at, hugging, and kissing him. She talks about Arlo in a caring way that conveys her enjoyment of motherhood.

Arlo's mother has identified some family needs, which include finding a more affordable apartment that has better heating and access to public transportation. She believes that the poor heating is responsible for the frequent illnesses of Arlo and of herself. She has incurred high electric bills by using space heaters to try to warm the apartment. There may also be exposure to toxins in the apartment atmosphere (not yet tested). The apartment is outside of the metropolitan public transit limits. The family does not believe the mother can learn to drive because she has physical and learning disabilities, and therefore family members transport her to appointments.

SOURCES OF ASSESSMENT INFORMATION

In addition to physical examination of Arlo, the pediatricians reviewed the birth records and the results of a range of tests, requested after the initial assessment. These included MRI, blood tests, and chromosome studies to rule out a variety of syndromes. Other assessment instruments used by the team included the Bayley Scales of Infant Development, the Battelle Developmental Inventory, physical manipulation tests and clinical observations of Arlo's natural movements, family interview, and home observation data. Although the private pediatrician administered a routine hearing check, no other assessment of hearing has been made. Based on the results from the assessment sources used, Arlo's developmental status is as follows:

Social–Emotional Development

Arlo is a sociable baby who seems to enjoy being with people. He smiles reciprocally and seeks attention by performing in ways that gain positive social interaction. When he is upset, he shows displeasure and protest by crying and arching his back. He exhibits shyness with strangers and prefers to sit on his mother's lap during new situations. Although these behaviors are not uncommon for a child in his age range, the pattern of scores on the Battelle show his social–emotional and self-help skills to be inconsistent, with Arlo's performance in the personal–social domain ranging from 9 to 14 months and his adaptive behavior being demonstrated at 10 months.

Physical–Motor and Sensory–Perceptual Development

Arlo appears to have low muscle tone in the trunk. He has just begun to sit alone: get himself into a sitting position unassisted, sit for 10 to 30 seconds, and brace himself when he begins to lose balance. He is beginning to crawl short distances, but must rest his stomach on the floor every 10 to 20 seconds while in the crawling position. Arlo typically uses a raking motion to pick up small food objects. He can bang objects at midline and take objects in and out of containers. Although he uses both hands to play with toys at midline, he must frequently stop manipulating the toys in order to steady himself. He has difficulty releasing objects in midline with a purposeful release and often misses his midline target. Battelle scores in gross motor areas show him to be functioning in the 7- to 10-month range and in fine motor areas in the 8- to 10-month range. On the Bayley Motor Scales, Arlo received a Psychomotor Development Index Score of 54, and his raw score is 58, which is equivalent to approximately 10 months in developmental age.

Cognitive–Language Development

Arlo demonstrates knowledge of the functions of objects (e.g., balls, cars, blocks) in his play with toys. He responds to one-step directions but does not yet point to pictures of objects or to body parts on request. He is beginning to use a few holophrastic sound approximations to communicate his desires (e.g., "dink" for "I want a drink") and to imitate words and label objects. His expressive language is in the 11- to 14-month range, his receptive language at the 14- to 17-month level, and his cognitive functioning in the 16- to 18-month range, according to the Battelle scores. His Bayley Mental Development Index Score is 103, and his raw score is 104, which indicates a developmental age of approximately 16 months. There is a significant discrepancy between his motor index score (54) and his mental index score (103).

THE TEAM DIALOGUE

The usual practice at Child Hospital is to have a hospital-based, staff-only discussion after a child's assessment to discuss the findings. The medical report is also summarized in writing and made part of the record. After Arlo's assessment by the hospital-based team members was complete, they excused themselves for this brief discussion. While Arlo's mother and grandfather, the early interventionist, and the consulting psychologist waited for the hospital team to return, Arlo became fussy and the mother and grandfather left the room. When the hospital-based team members entered shortly thereafter, the family members had not yet returned. The following dialogue began after all professional team members were assembled, but before the family members had returned. The hospital pediatric fellow served as the team leader.

PEDIATRIC FELLOW: We finally received Arlo's birth history. He was born with aspiration pneumonia and intubated for 3 weeks before being weaned to room air. Routine lab work on the placenta and umbilical cord revealed abnormalities suggesting he had been in long-term distress in utero. Arlo's Apgar Score was 3 at 1 minute and 8 at 5 minutes, suggesting he was in immediate distress prior to his birth. When we last saw Arlo, at the gestational age of 10 months, he was beginning to roll over. In supported sitting he had very poor head control and exhibited generalized low muscle tone. We requested a number of routine tests, including an MRI of his brain, blood work, and various other tests to rule out muscular dystrophies of any type. All test results came back normal. Today's examination finds Arlo recovering well from his thoracic surgery and continuing to progress. (The pediatrician goes into some detail explaining the complicated surgery. None of the other team participants asks questions or comments during this explanation. Mother and grandfather enter the room during the final part of the detailed medical discussion.)

MOTHER: So will Arlo be okay now that he's had the operation? Why don't any of the tests show what his problem is?

GRANDFATHER: We want to know what's caused his problem.

PEDIATRIC FELLOW: He's making good progress now. He had some distress in utero that might have affected his growth and development. Sometimes it's hard to pinpoint the exact problem so we may want to do some more testing later. (To early interventionist and consulting psychologist) How are his developmental skills?

EARLY INTERVENTIONIST: He is a friendly, responsive baby, but he has some gaps in his social skills. In particular, development of his self-help skills seem to be hampered by his lag in motor skill development. His motor skills are improving now. He is able to get in and out of a sitting position independently. He's also beginning to crawl but can only go about 4 to 6 feet before he has to rest. When he crawls, he has a noticeable sway in his back and when sitting, he tires very quickly if he tries to use both of his hands to play with objects. He must rest his trunk by putting his arms down for support every 10 to 15 seconds and he can play for only about 5 to 10 minutes before he has to lie down to rest.

PSYCHOLOGIST: Arlo's performance on the Bayley Motor Scales indicated that he has significant delays, especially in gross motor areas. For example, although he is now able to move from a sitting to a creeping position, he is not yet able to pull himself to stand and all of his upright locomotor skills are delayed. He has difficulty rotating his trunk when he sits alone and this affects his ability to throw objects and do other coordinated activities. He is beginning to use partial thumb opposition but can't yet make fine coordinated movements such as putting small objects in containers. I agree that his balancing difficulties are hampering both fine and gross motor development, and of course, delays in motor areas affect how well he can demonstrate his social and cognitive abilities. His performance on the Bayley Mental Scales indicated that he was able to perform many of the tasks at his age level, such as building a two cube tower, putting block cubes in containers, looking for and retrieving toys, although his positioning for doing these tasks was not standard. He could also imitate words.

EARLY INTERVENTIONIST: His scores on the Battelle also indicated that he is making progress in cognitive and language areas. For example, he's playing with toys appropriately, following directions such as "give me the cup" or "put the ball in the bucket," and trying to say some words. He can roll cars on the floor, bang blocks together, and stack two blocks. He responds to games like "peek a boo." (To mother) He's showing a lot of interest in playing with you and his aunts.

MOTHER: Yes, he's getting to be fun!

PHYSICAL THERAPIST: He is continuing to exhibit ataxic movements, especially in the trunk. (To mother and grandfather) These are shaky and unsteady movements, resulting from the brain's failure to regulate posture and limb movement strength and direction. He should have some physical therapy for this. Where do you live? Is it possible for Arlo to get into physical therapy on a regular basis? Can he receive the therapy through the early intervention program?

GRANDFATHER: She lives about 40 minutes away from the program and there's no public transportation there. Since she doesn't drive, it would be hard to get Arlo to therapy.

EARLY INTERVENTIONIST: Are there any other family members who could arrange transportation for Arlo on a regular basis? Our agency doesn't provide home based physical therapy on an ongoing basis. However, we do provide a once-a-year evaluation.

GRANDFATHER: Maybe her brother or uncle could bring her for therapy once in a while. I had to take off work to bring her today and I can't keep doing that.

PHYSICAL THERAPIST: I don't think that it will be sufficient for Arlo to come only occasionally. He needs regular ongoing therapy so it's important that someone in the family be found to help with transportation.

MOTHER: I can try to get him to therapy but I'm not sure about getting there real regularly.

SOCIAL WORKER: Let me know if you can find someone to drive you. Then I'll help you get the appointments arranged.

PHYSICAL THERAPIST: What type of insurance does the family have?

SOCIAL WORKER: Arlo has a medical card and I understand that he may be covered under his father's insurance policy. (To the family) Are you sure just what this policy will cover? You'll be glad to know his medical card will pay for the therapy.

STAFF PEDIATRICIAN: We received a request from SSI (Supplemental Security Income) for information on Arlo's diagnosis. I dictated our information in a report last week. That office indicated that you applied for SSI.

MOTHER: Yes, I did.

GRANDFATHER: It was such a hassle. I went with her but even I got confused with all the forms to fill out. (To social worker) We couldn't have done it all without your help.

EARLY INTERVENTIONIST: I also received a request from SSI to send them Arlo's child-focused goals on his IFSP. This information was sent out last week. It's been about 2 months since it was initiated, so you should hear soon.

STAFF PEDIATRICIAN: I understand you've been confused about Arlo's birth history. We've talked a little about that today, but would you like the nurse to come to your house specifically to answer your questions?

MOTHER: Yes, that would be good.

GRANDFATHER: I'd like it to be at a time when I could hear it too.

CLINICAL NURSE: Now that we have a copy of Arlo's birth records, I'll be able to explain what happened at his birth. I'll call you and we will set up a time to do a home visit. Perhaps your sisters could be there, too.

EARLY INTERVENTIONIST: (To mother) It would be good if you had a tape recorder to record the nurse's session so you won't have to explain it all over again to other family members. I could probably lend you a recorder and show you how to use it.

GRANDFATHER: She also needs to find another pediatrician. The pediatrician we started with won't take a medical card.

CLINICAL NURSE: Let me call the pediatricians on the west side and see who is taking new patients and will also accept a medical card. I'll call you on Friday, before 10:00 A.M.

PEDIATRIC FELLOW: Okay, so what do we want for Arlo? Can we agree on some goals for the next 6 months? (He then takes the lead in stating recommendations, with which team members concur.)

RECOMMENDATIONS

Arlo continues to be eligible for the early intervention home-based program. The early interventionist and mother will continue to work on development of Arlo's motor, social, language, and cognitive skills. Possibilities for transportation for Arlo to and from physical therapy on a regular basis will be investigated and appointments will be set up, pending transportation decisions. The clinical nurse will make a home visit to talk more with the family to help them understand why Arlo may have developmental problems and to explain the results of the medical tests. The social worker will investigate which pediatricians take new patients with medical cards. Arlo will be evaluated again in 6 months by the same team to monitor his developmental progress.

QUESTIONS FOR DISCUSSION

1. What are the advantages and disadvantages of a two-stage team discussion (i.e., the hospital-based staff discussing the case before involving the rest of the professionals and the family)?

2. What seem to be the major concerns of each of the team members (including the family)? How do these concerns reflect their various perspectives? What were their reactions to issues raised by other team members? How effective was the pediatric fellow in leading the team discussion?

3. How will the team's ability to get the necessary services for the child be influenced by financial constraints, by service delivery coordination problems, and by transportation problems?
4. What seem to be the major concerns of the family? Were they adequately addressed by the team? Did the team show any behaviors that indicated they were aware of cultural values of the family that may influence how effectively the interventions can be accomplished? Could they have done more to involve the family in the goal setting?
5. Did the team discuss sufficiently the developmental and educational interventions that could be implemented by the family, the early intervention program staff, and the pediatric specialists?

chapter 3

Doris Bergen
Alex Thomas
Julie Rubin

PSYCHOLOGICAL ASSESSMENT PERSPECTIVES

The psychological assessment of children with suspected developmental disabilities began in 1905 with the work of Alfred Binet, who devised the first test of intelligence to predict which children would not be able to benefit from traditional schooling. Since that time, psychologists have been involved in assessment and identification of those children who are eligible for special education. Over the past century, child assessment has become a very important part of the psychologist's role, and many instruments have been designed to identify individual differences in cognitive development and learning potential. Although the assessment methods psychologists use have become increasingly refined and comprehensive in recent years, and their responsibilities often extend to include consultation and counseling, psychologists still spend a significant part of their time measuring individual differences in intellectual abilities and providing information needed for the determination of children's eligibility for special education services (Fagan & Sachs Wise, 1993).

The term psychologist includes school, clinical, and developmental psychologists, all of whom have expertise in assessing young children's developmental and learning abilities. Psychologists working with young children have had at least 3 years of graduate training, including a 1-year supervised internship. Psychologists may get their credentials from a state board of education or from a state licensing agency. Although each type of psychologist works in a different setting, all psychologists share common perspectives on appropriate assessment practices, professional ethics, and consultative roles when working with young children and their families (American Psychological Association, 1993).

UNDERLYING ASSUMPTIONS

Although psychologists bring to the early assessment process a variety of assessment skills, when the term psychological assessment is used most people immediately think of a process in which tests are used to determine the individual's intellectual abilities, achievement level, or mental health. This assumption is still common among the general public, but it is not the assumption under which present-day psychologists operate. Psychologists operate with the broad assumption that their task is to try to understand children's overall development and behavior, and to assess the child's functioning in relation to normative standards and common developmental principles and processes.

They conduct assessments for a broad range of purposes, using a variety of instruments. They continue to use the traditional standardized tests, which primarily measure intellectual and personality dimensions. These instruments allow for the comparison of a single individual to others of similar age and background and to the same individual over time (Anastasi, 1988). Psychologists may also use observational measures, criterion-referenced tests, play-based scales, and family interviews when doing a comprehensive assessment. They evaluate the child's performance and compare that performance with their knowledge of typical developmental stages and processes. This helps them decide if a child is delayed or developing in a nontypical manner, how severe a delay is, and what type of interventions may be useful.

Psychologists may be asked how a child has progressed. Comparisons over time require multiple sequenced assessments that look at factors such as rate of growth and changes that may occur in developmental patterns. Another question that psychologists may be asked is what the child's "fit" is within family and educational settings; these environmental concerns help determine the effectiveness of recommended interventions. With young children in particular, the family system and the child's role in that system must be considered (Bagnato & Neisworth, 1991).

Thus, another assumption that the psychologist makes is that the family members and the relevant school or agency personnel must be involved in the assessment process. Parents are the source of much insightful and in-depth information about their children. This information usually provides the context in which the psychologist decides on appropriate assessment measures, develops hypotheses about delay domains and reasons for delay, and evaluates which interventions may be productive. Psychologists try to give families the information they need to know—day-to-day and long-term information about diagnosis, treatment, and educational issues. Psychologists are particularly interested in assessing the family's ability to accommodate and meet the developmental needs of the child.

At present, the most frequent reason for referral to a psychologist is still to get answers to questions such as how a child compares to peers, whether there is a general developmental delay, or whether the child's development is different in specific ways from characteristic developmental patterns. This peer comparison or normative assessment is most relevant for diagnosis of the child as eligible for early intervention services and, indeed, the vast majority of psychological assessments in early intervention are for the purpose of determining eligibility for special services and for assistance in planning the nature of these services (Bagnato & Neisworth, 1991).

After a child has been enrolled in an educational program, the teacher and other educational and therapeutic specialists provide information to the psychologist that assists in furthering two objectives of assessment: (1) designing environmentally appropriate interventions and (2) monitoring developmental and learning progress. For intervention settings, the psychologist's role is to provide information about the individual child that will assist the early intervention or school-based program specialists in designing and providing appropriate educational experiences. Psychologists often act as consultants to educators and other intervention specialists. For example, they may collaborate to create a behavior management program that can be used to facilitate the child's physical skill development or to assist the child in gaining emotional control or social interaction skills. In particular, as children reach the transition period around age 3, when referral options for mandated public school sponsored programs are considered, social–emotional and behavioral problems often become a focus of psychological assessment and intervention, especially because they are likely to affect later school success (Barnett & Carey, 1992).

Other important assumptions on which psychologists base their work concern psychometric procedures. They stress that there must be excellent psychometric properties in their assessment instruments, and that the assessments should be conducted with appropriate and consistent methods. For example, reliability (the extent to which an instrument yields consistent scores for an individual on the same test given on different occasions) and validity (the extent to which an instrument yields scores that measure what it purports to measure) are needed in the instruments chosen for the assessment (Anastasi, 1988). Accurate interpretation of assessment results rests on adequate psychometric properties.

This issue is complicated by the commonly occurring situation in which the young child to be assessed is severely or multiply handicapped; there are few instruments with good psychometric properties designed for this population. Interpretation of assessment results are especially difficult when the young child has disabilities significant enough to affect the assessment performance (Anastasi, 1988). Because developmental sequences may not follow the paths or the rates found in typically developing children, great care is needed in interpreting observations of formal assessments of young children (Johnson-Martin, Jens, & Attermeier, 1990). Thus, prediction from early assessment results is particularly difficult.

A corollary assumption is that assessments are useful only if they promote better development, meaningful intervention, and appropriate education of young children. Psychologists are aware of interpretive problems that could affect determination of eligibility for services or types of intervention provided to children and families. When validity problems are apparent, they must guard against making errors of referring children who should not be referred or not referring children who should be referred. Sometimes the choice of assessment instrument or the type of disability the child has may affect the qualifying score level. This can result in the need for psychologists to decide which of two or more standardized instruments that purport to measure delay will give the most valid assessment of the child's abilities. For example, some instruments (e.g., McCarthy, 1972; Stanford-Binet IV; Thorndike et al, 1986) are more likely to indicate that the child is performing one or more standard deviations below the mean than are other instruments (e.g., Weschler, 1989). That is important if, for example, to qualify for early intervention services, the child must perform two standard deviations below the mean in one developmental domain or one standard deviation below the mean in two domains, as is required in some state guidelines (e.g., Ohio State Dept. of Education, 1991).

A number of corollary assumptions underlie every use of standardized assessment measures: (1) the nature of intelligence in infants is much like that of older children; (2) infant behavior is the same across settings, so performance in a clinical setting is representative of performance in other settings; and (3) the intelligence of children with a non-cognitive-related disability develops at a similar rate and pattern as it does for children without such a disability. All three of these assumptions have been called into question; thus, whether standardized tests present a valid picture is a matter of great debate (Sattler, 1992). However, psychologists generally believe that a well-designed standardized norm-referenced instrument is useful in assessing the development of young children, especially if used in conjunction with other assessment methods.

Another reality-based question that psychologists must consider is what the intensity level of intervention should be for a particular child. Usually psychologists develop some hypotheses concerning whether the developmental delay observed is a result of biological or established risk conditions (e.g., physical–sensory or other congenital problems) or to environmental risk conditions (e.g., familial, socioeconomic, or cultural situations). These conditions may differ not only in severity but also in their potential for improvement. Along with the individual assessment data, psychologists consider contextual factors, such as the motivation of the family, the educational programs available, and the community resources that are accessible when they make their recommendations.

METHODS OF ASSESSMENT

Psychologists have traditionally worked independently on referral questions. They would conduct the assessment, write a report on the results, and interpret the results to parents, school personnel, or referring agency, without consultation with other professionals who had knowledge of the child and family. School psychologists typically would focus on assessing comparative development, facilitating the process of designing educational interventions, and providing appropriate educational services, rather than on the medical or social conditions influencing children's development (Harrington, 1984). Clinical and developmental psychologists have also been concerned with applying their assessment information to educational intervention and service questions. However, they have usually given most attention to the etiology of the delays or differences in development and to the factors in the home and community environment that may be responsive to intervention (Egan, Schaefer, Chatoor, 1988; Fraiberg, 1980).

In actual practice, when the child is under the age of 3, it is difficult to separate individual, family, educational, and societal conditions when collecting and interpreting results and recommending interventions. Issues such as the role the child plays in the family, the social and educational interventions needed by the child, and the range of family, educational, and community support systems available to carry out these interventions are therefore relevant for all psychologists to consider (Bagnato & Neisworth, 1987; Slade & Bergman, 1988).

SPECIAL CONSIDERATIONS IN ASSESSING YOUNG CHILDREN

Whatever methods psychologists decide to use to assess infants and toddlers, they must keep in mind the special nature of the assessment process of a very young child. It is necessary to take into account such questions as when the best time of day is for a particular child to be seen. All infants, but particularly very young ones, are influenced by biological needs, such as hunger and fatigue, and they cannot be easily coaxed to delay satisfaction of these needs to comply with assessment demands. Flexibility in deciding the time of day and length of session is required, and more than one assessment session may be needed.

The child's social maturity can affect the assessment process also. For example, with infants less than 5 months it is usually not a problem if the psychologist greets the parent and child enthusiastically and quickly begins to present toys or engage in games requiring interaction. However, infants nearing 7 months are wary of strangers and must not be overwhelmed by demanding approaches before rapport is established. Rapport is often more easily established by putting an engaging toy in the child's view, smiling, talking softly to the parent, and casually inviting the child to begin to interact (Johnson-Martin, personal communication, Sept., 1985). It is very important to establish rapport if a reliable and valid assessment is to be obtained.

Young children are usually seen with the parent or caregiver in the room, often as they sit on the adult's lap. This position reassures the child and also facilitates the psychologist's job. Furniture should be the proper height for the adult to sit comfortably with the child at the work table. For children over 1 year, a chair with arms and a foot rest should be provided to make a relatively long sitting period more comfortable. It is important for the psychologist to be well prepared and organized. The appropriate materials should be in the room ahead of time, interesting toys should be available, and some food or drink at hand. The psychologist should do as much as possible to ensure that the child's best performance is being observed.

Psychologists should keep in mind that it is difficult to assess an infant's developmental status; even when the assessment is appropriately done, the information may not give a valid picture of what the child will be like in 3, 5, or 10 years. Psychologists must always remember that the assessment instruments vary in their psychometric properties, and adaptations that must be made to administer them to infants with disabilities or developmental delays may alter their validity (Harrington, 1984).

A TYPICAL ASSESSMENT BATTERY

There are a number of evaluative techniques that psychologists use in the assessment process. Although one prevalent view of psychologists has been that of a "tester," the realities of assessing young children and the need to tie assessment to intervention have contributed to the use of a variety of evaluative methods. Generally, the younger the child, the more likely the psychologist will be to employ non-test assessment strategies. Most assessment procedures include the following: (1) structured parent interview; (2) one or more standardized norm-referenced tests; (3) one or more criterion-referenced tests, if indicated by initial information; and (4) structured and unstructured behavioral observations collected during the assessment session and, if warranted and obtainable, across multiple settings and activities (home and educational settings; with family members, peers, teachers, and specialists).

Structured Parent Interview

Parents are naturally involved in interventions for young children and their participation is essential in the evaluation process because they have the greatest knowledge of their child. The interview with the parent(s) (preferably both, but usually the mother) should be done in a comfortable room set up for that purpose, not in a room with child-sized furniture only. It is usually done best in a room without an observation window. The interviewer must interact with the parents within a context of respect for the parents' difficult situation and help them to see that the interview is the first step in the process of helping their child. The psychologist must use the interview as the first step in helping to answer the questions that brought the parent to the assessment situation. The content of the interview should include:

1. Questions parents have regarding their child that may be answered by the assessment process. The questions may relate to the diagnosis or to services and interventions offered.
2. The parents' description of the child's problems.
3. The parents' beliefs about what caused the problems and what (if any) diagnostic labels they think describe the child.

To answer these questions it is necessary to elicit information about the child's medical, developmental, family, and social histories. Medical history includes information about prenatal influences, birth, delivery, course of hospitalization, accidents, medications, specialists involved, treatments received, and diagnoses formerly given. Developmental history includes such information as developmental milestones achieved, strengths and weaknesses in certain developmental domains, and unusual patterns of development. Family history includes information on family composition, financial resources, support system availability, and genetic background. Social history includes information on the social climate in the family, the child's relationships with siblings and peers, and the nature of the child's interactions with family members or caregivers. Some sample nonstandardized parent interview questions are included in Appendix A.

Frequently a standardized parent interview is given, such as the Vineland Adaptive Behavior Scales (Sparrow, Balla, & Cicchetti, 1984, 1985). The Vineland is a norm-referenced interview that provides a comparison of the parents' description of their child's behavior with descriptions other parents have given of typical children of similar age. The Vineland has four domains (communication, daily living skills, socialization, and motor skills). It is described further in Appendix B.

Whether the structured interview is norm-referenced or designed by the psychologist, gathering this information from parents is essential as a basis for understanding and interpreting results of other assessment measures. It is the "first line" of information the psychologist needs. In collecting these data, however, psychologists keep in mind that families who bring their very young children to be assessed are coping with deep emotions. They may have heard a number of opinions (lay and professional) about their child that cause them grave concern or they may never have spoken about their concerns, even though they have them, and thus have difficulty acknowledging the diagnosis.

Parents' concerns may include whether they are going to be able to cope with the challenges of caring for and educating their child, how this child will affect other children they have or were planning to have, and what the eventual outcome for their child and the family will be. Many of these parents are struggling with feelings of sadness, anger, guilt, frustration, worry, and despair. They want to hear the psychologist's opinion and yet they dread hearing it. These factors must be kept in mind by the psychologist when assessing the infant.

Standardized Norm-Referenced Tests

Although standardized assessment of infants and toddlers is made more difficult due to lowered reliability of measurement and the spurts of development characteristic of the early years of life, norm-referenced tests are frequently given by psychologists. Bagnato and Neisworth (1991) describe three purposes of norm-referenced testing: (1) to describe the child's functional skills in comparative terms; (2) to classify the degree of the child's deficits via a pre-existing diagnostic category; and (3) to predict the child's development in the absence of intervention or other major life changes.

The most frequently used standardized test for infants is the Bayley Scales of Infant Development, (BSID) which was first published in 1969. The BSID, second edition (Bayley, 1993), has new normative data from a sample of 1,700 children, representative of present-day child populations, including high-risk populations. Norm-referenced comparisons of children aged 1 to 42 months of age (the original covered 2 to 30 months) can be made on mental, motor, and behavior dimensions. Although the earlier BSID gave a good picture of young children at the time of testing, it was not a good predictor of later development. The revised version has incorporated items reported in research literature to be more predictive of

later abilities. However, longitudinal information on its predictive validity is not yet available. The Bayley and another norm-referenced tests
appropriate for toddlers, the Differential Ability Scales (DAS) (1990), are
described further in Appendix B.

Criterion-Referenced Measures

In addition to assessing intelligence or developmental progress, another purpose of an assessment is to determine if a child has attained a particular skill
commonly attained by children of a similar age. Criterion-referenced measures do not yield scores or percentiles, but describe the skills that a child
actually can display and assist the psychologists in making intervention recommendations. There are many criterion-referenced instruments available.
One frequently used for infants and toddlers is the Carolina Curriculum for
Handicapped and At-Risk Infants (Johnson-Martin, Jens, & Attermeier,
1990). This is a curriculum-based measure developed for use with children
in the birth- to 24-month developmental age range. It has an easy-to-use
format that assesses 24 developmental areas, with sequences of skills within
each area. It can be used for planning interventions and monitoring child
progress over time. A number of other appropriate criterion-referenced tests
are described in Chapter 4 and Appendix B.

Behavioral Observations

Two types of behavioral observation may provide information that adds to
the validity of the assessment conclusions: (1) observations made during
the formal assessment session by the psychologist and (2) observations
made in a natural (or simulated) educational setting, usually collected by
one or more of the assessment team members (Bracken, 1991).

Information gathered from observing the child's behavior during the
formal assessment process is an integral part of the psychologist's evaluation. During the various formal portions of the assessment, the psychologist incidentally observes the child's non-verbal communication, language
and other verbal communication attempts, social responsiveness, attention span, problem-solving approach, anxiety level, and general affect
(Bracken, 1991). The dimensions of observation may need to be especially
perceptive in evaluating young children with visual or hearing impairments, mental retardation, neurological impairments, or behavior disorders (Paget, 1991).

A structured behavioral observation frequently is included in the psychologist's assessment plan. A continuum of methods is used for this, ranging from anecdotal comments to time interval or event sampling. When
possible, it is useful to observe the child and caregiver during a natural

event, such as playing or eating; this can be noted while the family is waiting to be seen by the psychologist. It is helpful to have data collected in a
setting that is familiar to the child, such as at home or at a daycare or early
intervention setting. Observational instruments are described more fully
in Chapter 4 and in Appendix B.

A recent innovation in the methodology of assessment has been in
the design of play-based assessment models that use simulated environments, replicating those of early education programs (e.g., Linder, 1993).
This assessment approach draws on behavioral observations of skills and
developmental mastery levels that are demonstrated through a sampling
of behaviors in this environment. Play-based assessment models are
described more fully in Chapter 4 and in Appendix B.

Sattler (1992) describes the valuable functions served by behavioral
observations. They provide a picture of the spontaneous behavior of the
child in everyday settings, information about the child's interpersonal
behavior and learning style, a systematic record of the child's behavior
and that of significant others, verification of the accuracy of parental or
caregiver reports, and comparisons between the child's behavior in formal
settings and in natural or simulated settings.

INFORMATION EXCHANGE WITH FAMILIES AND
REFERRAL AGENCIES

Because psychologists want to provide answers to referral questions, they
must understand and use appropriate means for interpreting assessment
results to families and professionals working with young children. The psychological assessment is complete only after the results have been shared with
the parents and the referral source. The most common methods of convey-
ing assessment information include conferences or written reports. The conferences are typically held with the parents, either by the psychologist alone
or by the psychologist in conjunction with other team members. The written
reports are given to parents and, with their permission, to other professionals working with the child. Psychologists often use terminology that is precise
in communicating within their discipline, but it may be unclear or confusing to family members and teachers. A number of the basic terms commonly
used in reporting results of assessment are listed in Figure 3.1.

REPORTING TO PARENTS

The primary mode for reporting to parents is the interpretive conference.
In conducting the conference psychologists depend on the empathetic and

FIGURE 3.1
ASSESSMENT TERMS USED BY PSYCHOLOGISTS

Achievement	the amount of success children exhibit at a given task
Average	the most representative measurement or score (expressed as mean, median, or mode)
Developmental norm	age at which 50% of tested group successfully completes the task
Normative	measurement results within the average or typical range
Norms	typical scores on standardized measures representative of certain groups (e.g., age, ethnic, or local)
Psychometrics	measurement of human cognitive, motor, or affective behavior using a standard of performance
Reliability	the extent to which a test or observation shows consistent results
Standard scores	scores that are mathematically transformed so that results from different tests can be compared
Standardized tests	testing processes that use consistent methods, materials, and scoring procedures
Validity	the extent to which a test or observation measures what it is intended to measure

trusting relationship that they have built with the family during the assessment process. They answer questions that the family has, present assessment results and possible interventions, and assist parents in making plans to carry out recommendations (Shea, 1984). The interpretative conference provides a bridge between the assessment and intervention phases.

Parents are provided with information about community resources and with reading materials or references that are pertinent to the child's problems. The psychologist must explain the content in a manner that parents can understand and assimilate. Psychologists must also be able to deal comfortably with the intense and potentially negative affect that parents may express when hearing their child's diagnosis. Although expression of these feelings may be difficult for the psychologist to hear, it is important that parents have the opportunity to express their anguish and fears should they need to do so during the interview.

REPORTING TO PROFESSIONALS

Traditionally, psychologists have provided written reports to the interdisciplinary or multidisciplinary team once their assessment was complete. The traditional report was developed independently of the team and was one part of the total information set considered by the team, often without the psychologist being present. This report usually contained behavioral observations, a list of assessment instruments used, assessment results, interpretation of the results, a summary, and recommendations.

Increasingly, psychologists do not write a separate, individual report, but contribute to a team report that conveys a set of integrated information. When the psychologist participates in the team, the Individual Family Services Plan (IFSP) incorporates the psychological information into the team report. This facilitates the parents' understanding of the comprehensive assessment results and the development of the IFSP. If there is to be referral to other diagnosticians (e.g., a neurological evaluation), the psychologist may develop a technically detailed report, too.

The psychological report (or the psychological information in the team report) can serve a number of purposes: providing accurate written assessment data to a referral source, being a source of information for hypothesis testing and program evaluation, and serving as a record of the assessment and intervention plan (Sattler, 1992).

USEFULNESS OF A TRANSDISCIPLINARY MODEL

For a long time, psychologists have conducted their assessments separately from other professionals and have brought or sent their assessment reports to meetings where individual children's cases were discussed. Many psychologists now have had experiences working in inter-, multi-, and (more recently) transdisciplinary teams. The mandates of P.L. 99-457 promote greater team interaction in planning and providing early intervention programs.

From the psychologist's perspective, the strengths of this approach include:

1. Comprehensiveness, which occurs because children are assessed by professionals from a range of disciplines, resulting in a very thorough evaluation.
2. Mutual purpose, which creates camaraderie among professionals and increased knowledge of each other's discipline, resulting in increased professional understanding of the child being evaluated.
3. Collaboration, which allows the psychologist to know the scope of

services and expertise of other professionals intimately and thus to be more effective in recommending comprehensive services across disciplines.

Although the advantages are many, changes in the way professionals (including psychologists) work come slowly. Problems that remain include the following:

1. Significantly increased time commitment of each professional for each child's assessment, which could reduce the overall number of children that can be served.
2. Logistic problems concerning the scheduling of numerous multiple assessments and team meetings.
3. Cost factors, which are related to high cost of meetings attended by several professionals and methods of professional reimbursement for services.
4. Individual personality factors, which require team members to adapt to style differences, agree to role flexibility, and learn to commit to consensus decision making.
5. Status issues, which occur as professionals learn to respect each other's expertise and how to have professional cooperation in the service of team goals.

POLICY ISSUES

Assessment practices for infants and toddlers who have disabilities or who are at risk for developmental delay are driven by federal and state legislative mandates, accompanying rules and regulations, and local practice. States determine the lead agency that is charged with determining the rules regarding which populations are to be served and which procedures are to be followed. The promulgated mandates, rules and regulations in turn are influenced by the opinions of individual professionals and professional groups who express their views through communication with the responsible legislative or bureaucratic bodies. Because assessment practices are professionally and politically driven, there are often times when the best practices of the field are not reflected in governmental guidelines. As assessment teams become more established, it is essential that teams take the opportunity to share concerns and work toward having an increased contribution to policy decisions that affect very young children and their families. In a number of position papers, the National Association of School Psychologists (NASP) has stressed that assessment and intervention planning needs to be collaborative and interdisciplinary (e.g.,

NASP, 1987, 1993). The American Psychological Association (APA) has also addressed professional issues such as the ethical considerations to which psychologists must adhere (APA, 1993).

There are a number of local problems of practice that also need to be addressed in a concerted fashion to ensure that assessment services are provided to those families and young children who must be served. For example, the specific assessment practices of psychologists operating in school settings are influenced by local funding priorities, caseload size, and the degree of local support for early intervention. Also, the experience and training of presently employed school psychologists have not always prepared them to be experts in infant assessment or in team intervention approaches. Therefore, availability of inservice training can positively influence the quality of psychologists' contributions to early assessment and intervention.

Concurrently, although some psychologists in clinical or private practice settings may have had infant assessment as one focus of their work, the increasing demands for these assessments may be difficult for them to meet if they are to maintain other aspects of their practice. They must also reconcile medical payment restrictions or adjustments with the extent of early assessment services they can provide.

SUMMARY

Psychologists are interested in understanding children's overall development and behavior on a variety of dimensions and they conduct assessments for a broad range of purposes using an array of procedures and instruments. Traditionally, psychologists have worked independently with families and children and have provided their reports to parents orally and to early intervention teams as a written report. More and more psychologists are becoming integrally involved with planning interventions and working collaboratively with a team that incorporates professionals and parents. The transdisciplinary model holds promise for bringing the psychologists' perspectives into an integrated and comprehensive plan that can positively affect the developmental progress of young children.

QUESTIONS FOR DISCUSSION

1. What are the main advantage and the main disadvantage of psychologists working within teams rather than independently?
2. Of the procedures used for assessment described in this chapter (observation, interview, normative test, criterion-referenced test),

which combination would provide the most valid set of information about the developmental disabilities or delays of an infant of 9 months, 15 months, and 24 months?

PROBLEMS OF PRACTICE

Interview a clinical, developmental, or school psychologist who has had experience assessing infants or toddlers. Ask about state and local school system guidelines that influence what the psychologist does, how guidelines from other agencies affect psychological assessment, how most teams are constituted, and how psychologists integrate their activities with those of other team members. Finally, ask the psychologist what their most important contribution is to the team development of the IFSP.

SUGGESTED READINGS

Bagnato, S. J. & Neisworth, J. T. (1987) The developmental school psychologist: Professional profile of an emerging early childhood specialist. *Topics in Early Childhood Special Education, 7*(3), 75–89.

Fraiberg, S. (1980). Clinical assessment of the infant and his family. In S. Fraiberg (Ed.), *Clinical studies in infant mental health: The first year of life* (pp. 23–48). New York: Basic Books.

DIALOGUE

TRANSITION PLANNING FOR BRADLEY

GENDER, AGE, ETHNIC ORIGIN OF CHILD: Male, 36 months, Euro-American

OCCASION OR PURPOSE OF DIALOGUE: To provide information for an assessment by a school psychologist, which will lead to a transition plan determining the placement of Bradley into a public school program for 3- to 5-year-olds. Bradley has been receiving weekly hour-long early intervention home services during the past 24 months.

TEAM MEMBERS: The assessment data were obtained in the child's home by a team consisting of the early intervention specialist, an adapted physical education teacher, the child's mother, and the home care nurse. The team gathered for the dialogue include the school psychologist from the child's home school district, the early intervention specialist and adapted physical education teacher from the original team, the nurse and speech pathologist from the early intervention program who have been providing supportive services, and the child's mother.

SETTING: A conference room in a university developmental disabilities laboratory clinic.

OVERVIEW OF THE CASE

RISK CONDITIONS

Bradley contracted meningitis at birth, although this finding was only confirmed last Fall. He showed developmental delays at 4 months and was put on a ventilator at 10 months. He has had four MRIs of the brain, which all confirmed that there are no widespread areas of damage in the mid- or forebrain areas. His condition is presently labeled "static encephalopathy" with probable brain-stem damage that affects his ability to breath normally ("static" means it is not a progressive condition).

For a period of time Bradley was dependent on the ventilator for breathing 24 hours a day, but during the past 4 months he has been weaned from the ventilator and now requires manual ventilation only while sleeping. Ophthalmologic evaluation indicated that Bradley's visual impairment is due to optic nerve hypoplasia (failure of the optic nerve to develop normally in utero), resulting in constant eye dilation and poor visual acuity.

REASON FOR REFERRAL

Bradley falls between the birth- to 3-year services and the 3- to 5-year services. The home-based assessment information is to be used by the school psychologist and other team members to assist in the transition to appropriate placement. Objectives identified through the home assessment that will be discussed by the team include the following:

1. A transition plan will be written guiding the parents through the placement procedures for preschool. (Parent desires an inclusion program.)
2. The family will investigate buying a computer for Bradley to increase his communication skills and cause–effect knowledge. (This is a priority goal of the parent.)
3. Bradley will be given opportunities to socialize with typically developing peers on a regular basis.

BACKGROUND INFORMATION

Bradley's mother does not work outside the home and the employed father is home every evening. Currently, the father's insurance is paying for 24-hour nursing care in the home, but this funding terminates in Spring. At that time, the cost of Bradley's care will be switched to a state-funded program that permits children on ventilators or with tracheotomies to live at home. This program will provide 16 hours of nursing care, requiring the family to find other resources or provide the rest of the care themselves.

FAMILY STRENGTHS AND NEEDS

Strengths include a financially stable, close, intact immediate family, with competent parental skills and strong motivation to promote the optimal development of their child.

The expressed family need is that they be actively assisted in their efforts to facilitate Bradley's development. Another need, identified by the team, is that of broadening the family support system so that all the pressures of care are not on the immediate family. Although an extended family is in the region, the mother indicates other family members are not comfortable being with Bradley and provide no respite support. Because the mother does not wish to discuss possible ways to increase extended family support, gaining that support is not one of the identified family needs.

Sources of Assessment Information

Medical records and reports from hospital personnel are available. Assessment measures used by the team included Carolina Curriculum, Hawaii Early Learning Profile (HELP), Developmental Profile II, parent and nurse interviews, and observations during the home visit. During the assessment, the home environment was quiet and well lit, with no distractions. Based on the results from the assessment sources, Bradley's developmental status is as follows:

Social–Emotional Development

The parent interview and Developmental Profile II reveal that the family has some clearly defined social–emotional objectives for Bradley. For example, the mother wishes Bradley to engage in social interaction with his parents and siblings, and to facilitate these interactions, the family has set aside a time after dinner each evening for Bradley to interact with family members. To further the mother's wish to "normalize" Bradley's functional behavior, he is also being fed processed baby food, even though most of his nourishment comes from gastric-tube feedings.

The social–emotional section of the HELP showed Bradley's social skills to be scattered; his performance reached a ceiling at the 12- to 18-month level. He was able to establish eye contact, smiled when approached socially, and seemed to enjoy social play with adults. He also played ball cooperatively and demonstrated toy preference. Other social–emotional behaviors observed included gazing in the direction of persons who were speaking, smiling and waving when the assessment team came into the room, and expressing a range of emotions with his eyes and face. He did not exhibit stranger anxiety. The mother indicates that sibling interaction also occurs at times other than the family time.

Physical–Motor and Sensory–Perceptual Development

The Carolina Curriculum results and observational data indicate that Bradley is nonambulatory and still exhibits birth reflexes, especially when in the supine position. Because of these pathological extension patterns, he is unable to perform most gross motor tasks that would be typical for his age. A variety of positions was used during the assessment, with side-lying and sitting in a J seat (an adapted sling-support device) appearing to be his best, because they broke up his excessive trunk and leg extension. The side-lying position enabled him to bring his left hand to his mouth. He was able to roll to his back from his side when the nurse moved his leg to initiate hip rotation. In the J seat he showed capability of moving his head from side to side in response to auditory and visual stimuli.

With pillow support and in the prone position, he was able to prop himself with fists and attempt to look around and roll to his left side. In a sitting position he held up his head for about 2 minutes. All of these behaviors appear by approximately 3 months in a typically developing child. During the administration of the Carolina Curriculum, Bradley consistently moved his head to the left when presented with visual stimulation. This movement did not appear to be related to poor head control, but rather a deliberate head manipulation in order to gain greater visual acuity.

When performing fine motor tasks on the Carolina Curriculum, his muscle control fluctuated. In reaching activities, fingers fluctuated from open to tightly closed in a fist, and when activating toys with switches he used a poorly controlled sweeping motion, open fingers or clenched fist, and on one occasion an index finger. His fine motor skills generally fell in the birth-to-3-month level of typical development.

Cognitive–Language Development

The cognitive area of the HELP showed Bradley to be functioning in the 30-to-36-month range. Even with his visual impairment, he was able to match colors, pictures, shapes, and objects and to indicate objects that do not belong in a simple group by using a light-scanning box, stopping the light at the appropriate picture. He also demonstrated understanding of concepts such as "bigger," "under," and "longer" by stopping the light scan on pictures that illustrate these concepts.

Bradley was observed to be very attentive, to be able to wave "Hi" on request, and to vocalize "Hi" occasionally. He was not observed to say any other words. No formal measure of receptive or expressive language was given by the team. However, parent report on the Developmental Profile II indicated he can understand nonverbal gestures, recognize pictures, indicate "more," and use vocal sounds to indicate needs. He is not able to use expressive language above the one-word stage, however.

THE TEAM DIALOGUE

The team gathered to discuss the assessment results and determine what further information should be sought to enable an appropriate placement in an age 3 to 5 early intervention program (preferably in an inclusion setting). The early intervention specialist served as the team discussion leader.

EARLY INTERVENTIONIST: We gained a pretty good picture of Bradley's motor, social, and cognitive skills in the home assessment but since we didn't have a full team, we need to decide what else should be assessed before the placement decision is made.

PSYCHOLOGIST: It's clear that Bradley needs to be seen by an augmentative communication team. Is there one in this area?

SPEECH PATHOLOGIST: I think they have one at the cerebral palsy center at Child Hospital.

MOTHER: What would that team do?

PSYCHOLOGIST: This team would review all of your child's records and look at the various assessments that have been done. Then the physical therapist on their team would help determine the best body position for Bradley to be in for communication and the occupational therapist would determine his best mode of response (e.g., head, light, or hand switch) and position to make that response. The speech pathologist would evaluate Bradley's receptive and expressive skills, using some of these identified best positions to present objects and pictures. The psychologist would try to determine Bradley's level of cognitive development, using the communication adaptations recommended. For example, maybe Bradley needs a word board, a picture board, a computer, or an electronic communicator (to print messages or play back sounds). The communication technology options range from pointing to pictures pasted on cardboard to very sophisticated computers operated by eye gaze control. It is imperative that Bradley have this kind of assessment now so that the his optimal performance levels can be observed.

SPEECH PATHOLOGIST: I agree that a communication assessment is essential. (To mother) I can give you the phone number of the cerebral palsy center where the augmentative communication team is located.

MOTHER: I would like to have that done. I think Bradley is smarter than he appears to be because his poor movement abilities make it difficult for him to respond.

EARLY INTERVENTIONIST: Yes, our assessment certainly points to his needing this additional evaluation. There is also a special service in Center City where children with disabilities can have an evaluation to determine what kind of computer-assisted communication might be useful.

MOTHER: That's the place we heard about and wanted to try.

PSYCHOLOGIST: I think getting a computer should be a later step. Bradley may not be ready for a computer yet, but he does need the communication assessment. Because most assessment instruments are for children who can move well, we can't get a valid picture of his abilities from them.

His movements are limited; he can't talk and he can't point. Yet he seems to have communicative intent. The question is whether his sensorimotor level is sufficient for him to understand abstract symbol communication. That is necessary before a computer can be useful. One assessment method I'd suggest trying is the Uzgiris Hunt Scale. It specifically looks at sensorimotor response levels.

EARLY INTERVENTIONIST: He is still poor at activating switches, but he lets you know he wants to try. We had a communication board made for him. It's just a cassette box that has four lights on it. Every time he hits the switch it scans and he hits it again and the light stops. We put in photographs of his toys, books, and places in his house.

PSYCHOLOGIST: How does he use it? Does he initiate communication or just respond to questions? Could he tell you if he wanted a specific toy to play with?

EARLY INTERVENTIONIST: Yes, that is how we work with him. We say "Tell me what toy you want" or "Show me the book." He isn't good at being accurate with the switches so he indicates his frustration by waving his arms.

PSYCHOLOGIST: So the intent is there and he can make dependable choices! He needs to be able to use whatever skills he has to tell what he wants. It will be impossible to determine what kind of school placement he needs without this communication evaluation. He also needs an ophthalmology consultation to go along with that.

SPEECH PATHOLOGIST: A hearing evaluation would also be useful. We don't really have a good idea of his hearing abilities.

EARLY INTERVENTIONIST: Do you need to have one standardized test score to qualify him for a school program?

PSYCHOLOGIST: The state says you need to do a cognitive evaluation but it is clear that is a minor issue here. The big issue is that we cannot assess his cognitive abilities well without communication. Once we establish communication we could do a series of activities. Whether we get a full battery is immaterial. If he is able to do a number of tests at the 3-year-old level, that would show his relative cognitive strength. Whether psychometrically it is a score of 78, 95, or 110 doesn't matter. Perhaps a receptive language scale would be useful since he has the switch activating skill, and portions of the Bayley or DAS might be used. The skills he is reported to have are in the "twoish" range and he is 3, so he might be mildly delayed. However, there are some peak skills that make me think he may not be delayed cognitively. The reality is that he is dependent on others and his development may be hampered because he can't explore on his own.

NURSE: Plus he has spent almost 2½ years in and out of the hospital and that is not the most stimulating environment.

EARLY INTERVENTIONIST: His motor deficits really hamper him. He has no grasp at all. He is locked into the infant reflexes all the time.

PSYCHOLOGIST: So how does he press the switches?

EARLY INTERVENTIONIST: We have him sitting and have a support behind his shoulders to bring his shoulders in.

ADAPTED PHYSICAL EDUCATOR: We don't usually use the prone stander. The J seat and side-lying work best, but only when he is relaxed. Then he can push the button down to make the tape recorder play. His vision may also be obstructing his ability to use the switches. He always seems to tilt his head to the right, which may indicate he can see better that way.

MOTHER: Would you be able to improve his motor skills?

ADAPTED PHYSICAL EDUCATOR: Well, we could keep him in positions that would prevent him from going into those reflexes. When his nurse moved his leg over and rotated his hips he was able to roll over. That was a big success for him; he took pride in that accomplishment. I would continue to look for different positions and use toys that would give him the sensation of moving, such as bolsters.

MOTHER: Those sound like good ideas.

ADAPTED PHYSICAL EDUCATOR: I would highlight the positives. For example, Bradley has experienced social interactions with your family, so when he does get into a preschool program he may enjoy that atmosphere. He likes social interaction, music, and gross motor activities. He should also get in outdoor environments like lying in the grass and having other tactile experiences that he never gets inside.

EARLY INTERVENTIONIST: I would agree that he needs peer interaction. One of the things lacking in the social–emotional assessment we did was that there were no peers so we have no idea what he would do in a group. If we're thinking that this transition would put him into an inclusive placement like a preschool, we've got to know how he would interact.

PSYCHOLOGIST: My guess is that peers might be cautious at first. He doesn't talk or act like a 3-year-old. I think his interaction would be facilitated more by older peers than by peers his own age. Unfortunately, there is really only one public school placement option in his district and it is not an inclusion setting with typical peers. It involves mostly speech- and language-delayed children and it doesn't have many children with motor impairments. All of the children in the school district who qualify as developmentally delayed presently go to this same classroom. I know that the school district is moving toward an inclusion program, but it's not in place yet.

ADAPTED PHYSICAL EDUCATOR: Will Bradley have a nurse come to school with him?

NURSE: He's probably going to need a nurse or other health professional with him in school. This is another issue that still has to be resolved. He will also need the school to provide physical therapy, occupational therapy, and speech pathology services.

EARLY INTERVENTIONIST: There will be only 8 hours of home paid nursing care and the only way that will be available is if Mrs. Parent goes back to work. (To mother) You will also need some kind of support—respite care or something.

NURSE: It costs 52 dollars an hour to have a registered nurse in your home through respite care. It is 25 dollars for a practical nurse.

PSYCHOLOGIST: One major problem is that the expertise needed to help Bradley is beyond that of average school personnel. This is a very low incidence, medically involved case of a type rarely seen by school psychologists. (To mother) It's clear that the school system will have to work with you closely to find the right match.

EARLY INTERVENTIONIST: Ready School (private) does have an early intervention inclusion program that would meet his needs but right now they have only one opening so it may be that the school district will have to provide the placement. If the school district can't meet the child's needs then the district has to pay for appropriate education elsewhere.

MOTHER: The school district is obligated. I've looked into the law. If the district can't provide for my child's needs then we will take the problem to a due process hearing and push for the appropriate placement. We want what will be best for Bradley. He has a lot of potential.

PSYCHOLOGIST: I'm sure we'll find a good placement for Bradley. We agree with you that it's important to do what is best for your son.

MOTHER: We had to tell Dr. Smart what we wanted. We told him that we wanted to try to wean Bradley from the ventilator and he was against it. We just persisted and three months later Bradley was off the ventilator.

PSYCHOLOGIST: You seem to place a high priority on encouraging your other child's interaction with his brother.

MOTHER: Yes, that's why we have family time. We think it's also good for our 5-year-old, but sometimes we aren't sure.

NURSE: (To mother) I understand that your parents are not comfortable with the tubes and other technology that make it difficult to hold Bradley. Do you have concerns about their support?

MOTHER: It isn't a big issue. I think grandparents have a right to decide how much they want to be involved. If they don't want to do it, then they can't be forced.

PSYCHOLOGIST: The augmented communication could be a way to involve Bradley's grandparents. If they could communicate with him, they might be much more comfortable. Are you getting any kind of support group assistance or help such as counseling? It is usually helpful to have some ongoing contact with other people who are dealing with similar situations.

MOTHER: So far we're handling everything just fine.

EARLY INTERVENTIONIST: We've shared a lot of good ideas here. So let's state our recommendations. (Group agrees.)

RECOMMENDATIONS

Further assessment, especially in the area of communication, is essential in order to determine an appropriate placement for Bradley. Assessment of his communication capabilities should be conducted within the next two months and, if useful communication strategies are identified, a standardized psychometric test will then be given by the school psychologist. The parents should have the expectation that the school district will meet its responsibility to serve Bradley appropriately. After the additional assessments are complete, the school psychologist will provide placement suggestions, and the parents will visit those educational settings before a final decision is made. The parents are encouraged to get the financial and social resource support they need to continue their very effective management of Bradley's development.

QUESTIONS FOR DISCUSSION

1. This mother is an active participant in facilitating her child's development and in discussing options with the team. How did her presence and interaction style affect the team discussion? Were all of her concerns addressed?
2. What are the major problems the school district will face in trying to find an appropriate placement for Bradley, especially if further assessment shows his cognitive development to be only slightly delayed? What is the appropriate role for the school psychologist in this process?
3. How does the makeup of this team reflect the major areas of concern for Bradley? What professionals would have been good additions to the team? Why?
4. What are the methods of assessment that are presently being used to monitor Bradley's progress? Why were other methods suggested by team members?
5. Based on the assessment information, identified objectives, and team dialogue, what other developmentally appropriate strategies could be proposed to help the child and family?

chapter 4

Doris Bergen

Developmental and Educational Assessment Perspectives

Formal assessment of young children has traditionally been questioned, and often opposed, by early childhood educators (National Association for the Education of Young Children [NAEYC], 1988). Their knowledge of typical young children's developmental characteristics and their philosophical beliefs in "whole child" assessments, which include contextual variables and long-term "age/stage" progress interpretations of behavior change, have led them to favor repeated informal observation within the home or care setting as the most valid way to assess early development. They have held a "growth" perspective that presumes that most young children will achieve mastery over basic physical, cognitive, social, and emotional skills at each developmental stage as long as they have a moderately responsive and stimulating environment and opportunities for social interaction with caring, familiar, and responsive adults and peers.

Although early childhood educators usually do not believe it is necessary to focus on measuring specific skills or behaviors through standardized testing, they do have valid data on the developmental levels and skills of the children they see in home or school settings. However, these data are usually gathered over time using semi-intuitive qualitative methods rather than tests, and they are collected primarily for the purpose of individualizing and enhancing developmental goals rather than for identifying and categorizing children as developmentally delayed (Hills, 1993).

Special educators have often relied on normatively based psychometric assessments done by psychologists to determine the eligibility of children for receiving special education services. There are three methods of assessment that have been used by special educators themselves. They are all used within the home or school context and require repeated measures over time. One is criterion-referenced testing, which identifies the specific skills to be mastered. After testing, a curriculum is planned to further the learning of those skills. (Neisworth & Bagnato, 1986).

Another type of ongoing assessment used by special educators is behavior analysis, which focuses on observing a problematic behavior, planning a reinforcement to change the behavior, and then observing whether the new behavior is occurring on a regular basis (Wolery, Bailey, & Sugai, 1988). Special educators also use standardized subject-matter content tests in various academic areas to compare the learning of children with disabilities to that of typically developing peers.

In recent years, the new professional, the early childhood special educator (or early interventionist), who has drawn on both the developmental knowledge-base of early childhood education training and the behavior and skill-oriented viewpoints of special education training, has combined both of these discipline perspectives in assessment practice. The integration of these diverse approaches to assessment has begun to create a useful model; however, there are still questions about the extent of integration of early childhood "developmental theory" and special education "learning theory" approaches (Bailey & Simeonsson, 1988). A number of issues related to the collaboration of these two fields must be resolved.

UNDERLYING ASSUMPTIONS

Because this approach to assessment has been influenced by early childhood education and special education, the assumptions that influence developmental and educational assessment of young children with developmental risk conditions come from both of these disciplines. One assumption that is common to both early childhood education and special education is that families must be involved in their children's education, if that education is to be effective.

There have been many early childhood programs that included parents as teachers, in the classroom and at home, and also many in which parents play an important decision-making role. For example, Parent Cooperative Nurseries, which primarily serve children from middle-income families, and Head Start, which primarily serves children from low-income families, both stress parent decision-making and parent involvement as teachers (Powell, 1986; Pizzo, 1990; Raver & Zigler, 1991).

In special education, there has long been an emphasis on the importance of supporting parents in their roles of advocating, planning, and implementing educational services for their children (Featherstone, 1980).

Parents are present at meetings in which their child's assessment results and educational plan are discussed; and they must consent to the plan. Some parents have been extremely strong advocates for programs to meet the needs of children with disabilities or developmental delay and for more parent involvement in school decision-making processes.

There are a number of other assumptions, however, that are specific to either early childhood education or to special education.

EARLY CHILDHOOD EDUCATION

A basic assumption of early childhood educators is that young children must have developmentally appropriate educational experiences. Implicit in this assumption is another: that there must be careful observation of children's behavior in varied contexts in order to get the information needed to match planned educational experiences to children's developmental need level. Beginning in the 1920s and 1930s, numerous observational techniques were devised to study developmental milestones and characteristics, especially in physical, social, and play developmental domains. Today, similar methods continue to be used by early childhood educators to observe the development of young children's physical, social, emotional, play, and language abilities. In more recent years these and other observational methods have been used to observe cognitive abilities also (Schweinhart, 1993).

The majority of early childhood assessment techniques have been designed for natural rather than clinical settings. For infants and toddlers, the home has been the preferred environment for observation; however, day-care or other program settings have also been commonly used. Infants and toddlers are observed at play or in interaction with a familiar caregiver, usually the parent. Rarely have early childhood personnel conducted clinical observations in settings unfamiliar to the children being assessed. They have not generally used formal assessment instruments unless mandated to do so to meet a screening or eligibility demand (e.g., for Head Start handicapped requirement, for kindergarten readiness) or a program evaluation requirement (e.g., demonstrating that cognitive skills have increased in children in an early childhood program) (Bergan & Feld, 1993; Kagan, 1992; Meisels, 1993; Raver & Zigler, 1991).

This is because of a second assumption of educators in this discipline: that unfamiliar settings, one-time data collection, and narrowly structured instruments requiring a specific elicited response do not provide a valid picture of young children's developmental capabilities or potential (NAEYC, 1988). Assessment practice from this perspective favors repeated observations across time and settings, using general response categories rather than specific elicited responses as the measure of abilities, and focusing on best rather than first responses in assessing children's developmental level.

A third assumption of this discipline is that the teacher's role (or the parents' role in the home) should be facilitative rather than directive, and that assessment flows from this facilitative environment. That is, teachers (or parents) are expected to provide an environment with objects, persons, places, and events that children can act on to gain knowledge. Their actions and interactions with these "affordances" (Gibson, E., 1969; Gibson, J., 1979; Wachs & Chan, 1985) result in construction of knowledge appropriate for their developmental level. Teachers and parents who observe the choices children make and the interactions in which they engage make inferences about the children's approximate developmental levels. An appropriate match between children's developmental stages and the experiences provided in the planned environment is expected to enhance their developmental progress and result in optimal knowledge construction. This approach to learning and teaching has been called "developmentally appropriate practice" (Bredekamp, 1987).

The majority of early childhood educators hold a fourth assumption. They believe that children who are disabled or at risk for developmental delay can benefit from a developmentally appropriate practice environment as much as typical children can, as long as the environmental design is based on developmental and not age criteria. Because developmental principles apply to all children (see Figure 1.1), the processes of development are similar, even if specific domains are delayed in some children. Thus, early childhood educators have usually stressed the importance of assessment based on observation within the home or care setting for all young children and the inclusion of children who are disabled or at risk for delay in early childhood programs.

SPECIAL EDUCATION

The first special education law, P. L. 94-142 (U.S. Dept. of Education [1981]), required assessments to identify and categorize children who were disabled, and mandated the development of Individualized Educational Plans (IEP) for each identified child. These plans required a statement of objectives to be accomplished, including skills to be learned and behaviors to be changed, and an outline of the methods by which those objectives would be achieved. The IEP directed special educators' attention to assessment measures that could pinpoint deficits in skills and behaviors so that they could then be addressed in the objectives in the educational plan.

This perspective assumes that task analysis, which is the process of breaking down a learning task into a sequence of steps, can be an effective method for teaching and can provide criterion items for tests developed to measure the skills before and after teaching (Fredericks, Anderson, & Baldwin, 1979). Presumably, if the skill can be broken into its component parts, appropriately sequenced, and each component taught, the overall skill can be achieved. In a typically developing child, this careful attention to sequence may not be as necessary; however, special educators believe that the educational plan for children who have disabilities should clearly identify specific subgoals (or objectives) to be mastered if optimal learning is to occur.

A corollary assumption on which this assessment method is based is that a specific set of necessary skills that all children should learn can be identified, assessed, and taught. Another version of this approach is "process-oriented" assessment, which uses a test-teach-test paradigm (Bailey & Wolery, 1989). In these models, after testing, there is direct teaching of missing skills and repeated assessments until a criterion of skill mastery has been reached. This process has been called "dynamic assessment" (Feuerstein, 1979).

Although some special educators use assessment measures that incorporate milestones from the developmental knowledge-base, another assumption of this perspective is that it is less necessary to focus on developmental stages, such as level of thinking or knowledge construction, and more important to facilitate achievement of functional skills, such as practical self-care behaviors, or on academic readiness skills, such as labeling colors. Typical assessment items that might be on criterion-referenced tests used by special educators would address achievement of specific skills (e.g., holds spoon to feed self; points to named object) rather than achievement of stages outlined in developmental theory (e.g. has object permanence; uses differentiated action schema).

Because their experience tells them that the children they teach are unlikely to master basic skills through self-chosen activities or to respond to teacher-directed group instruction, a third assumption is that teachers should be active in directing learning and giving reinforcement to children's learning attempts in one-on-one or small group settings, and that parents should also use these teaching techniques at home. This approach is believed to be most effective in helping children with disabilities to achieve at their potential. Thus, the IEP is very specific as to the learning objectives that will be taught in interaction with an adult, either the teacher or parent.

Special educators also hold the assumption that *learning* can be defined as *observed behavior changes* and thus they try to demonstrate that their educational methods have resulted in a positive change in the child's behavior—that is, in learning. For example, they would expect the effects of providing positive reinforcement for a child's practicing of reading skills to be evident in changed behavior (e.g., fewer errors in reading). They use behavior analysis to observe behavior changes over time (Wolery, Bailey, & Sugai, 1988). For example, by keeping track of a child's reading errors and showing a decrease in the amount over time, they can document learning progress. With older children, the IEP objectives have typically focused on academic objectives and on school-defined expectations for social competence. However, behavior analysis can also be used to document the achievement of developmentally appropriate early childhood objectives, such as increased child-initiated interactions with the objects in the environment, children's expanded ability to choose appropriate activities, or increased positive social interactions with parents or peers.

CONFLUENCE IN EARLY CHILDHOOD SPECIAL EDUCATION

In 1986, Public Law 99-457 expanded the services that were to be provided to special needs populations by requiring assessment and intervention services for young children and their families. This law provided grants to states to identify infants and toddlers who had disabilities or who were at risk for developmental delay and set the parameters for models of assessment and intervention. Assessments were to include:

1. Review of medical and health records.
2. Multifactored assessment of cognitive, language, psychosocial, self-help, and physical (including vision and hearing) domains.
3. Use of a team approach by professionals from a range of disciplines.
4. Development of an Individual Family Service Plan (IFSP), which expanded the IEP concept to specifically include the family in the assessment and intervention process.
5. Culturally and racially non-biased procedures, including presentation of test items in native language or preferred communication mode.

In addition, the law specified that "qualified" personnel should conduct the assessment and required that the states define the personnel preparation standards for how to become qualified.

Many of the assumptions about assessment that early childhood special educators hold can be derived from the mandates of P. L. 99-457 and a subsequent revision, P. L. 100-146. However, they have also integrated the assumptions of early childhood educators and of special educators who work with children of a wider age range in designing the models of assessment and intervention that are being used in this field. Other influences on early childhood special education practice have come from the medical, therapeutic, and support service disciplines, discussed in other chapters.

One basic assumption is that a team approach results in a better assessment of infants and toddlers than an assessment by one professional. Because most instruments used by professionals from all disciplines have poor reliability and validity, a case can be made that the varied perspectives on the child's developmental disability or delay gained by having a team with members from a number of disciplines serves as a reliability and validity check. It also is assumed to provide a more comprehensive picture of the child's strengths and needs.

A second assumption is that active family involvement is a crucial component in both the assessment process and the intervention plan development. Because family influences are especially important during the first years of a child's life, any plan developed to guide the intervention process must have the strong investment of the family. Thus, assessment of the needs and strengths of the family and participation of the family in assessment and intervention planning are seen as vital to overall effectiveness. Three corollary (but often unacknowledged) assumptions that are derived from early intervention law are that (1) most members of the child's family have the best interests of the child in mind, even if they are not initially aware of what they can do to help; (2) either the immediate family or the extended family has both the ability and willingness to take *primary* responsibility for the child's long-term welfare; and (3) support services must be available to assist the family in meeting the psychological and financial responsibilities that result from a family- and community-centered rather than an institution-centered approach to early intervention.

A third major assumption is that, even if the young child has some very salient developmental problems in one or two domains, the assessment is not complete unless a range of developmental domains (at least the five mandated in the law) are evaluated. This is an especially important assumption when assessing young children because in the early years all of these domains are closely interfaced. For example, first words, pretend play, understanding of the word "no," stranger anxiety, walking, and object permanence all occur within the same few months in typically developing children. Delays in development in some of these domains or general delay across all of these domains can be diagnostic in determining the child's level of overall or specific disability or delay.

A fourth important assumption is that a better understanding of the child's disabilities and strengths can be obtained if a range of assessment methods are used, including those derived from early childhood (e.g., developmental observations of play and social interactions); special education (e.g., criterion-referenced tests, behavior analysis); psychology (e.g., norm-referenced tests, interviews); medical personnel (e.g., physical and health assessments); and therapeutic and family specialists, (e.g., family interviews, samples of spontaneous language). The context of the assessment is noted and an attempt is made to observe the child at home and in a school or clinic setting.

Finally, there is an assumption about the levels of assessment that are needed. Three levels are judged to be essential: (1) screening; (2) comprehensive assessment; and (3) progress-monitoring assessment (sometimes called evaluation). Because of eligibility criteria that must be met in early intervention programs, screening assessments, in which a few criteria are used to determine which children are likely to have needs for which a full assessment should be done, compose the first phase of the assessment process. These may be done by medical or psychological personnel, with referral to the comprehensive assessment team, or the early intervention team may do screening and full assessment procedures. After a comprehensive assessment has been done, the IFSP is designed. Then, repeated assessment of developmental progress during the early intervention program is conducted and the family service plans are revised as needed.

METHODS OF ASSESSMENT

Because of the requirements of P. L. 99-457, all early childhood special education programs are now using some form of multidimensional team assessment. However, the instruments used in these assessments, the composition of the teams, and the extent of interaction of the teams varies greatly. The assessment perspective of the early childhood special educator is still evolving, with newer methods that have been used in research or practice still being tested. Unfortunately, not all methods being used have been evaluated thoroughly for reliability and validity standards, and often no normative data are provided (Meisels, 1987). Although some adaptations of existing assessment measures for children with motoric, sensory, or perceptual disabilities have been made, often their concurrent validity with the nonadapted measure has not been demonstrated.

SPECIAL CONSIDERATIONS IN ASSESSING YOUNG CHILDREN

Given the cautions with present instruments, there are six important aspects of the early childhood special education perspective that are crucial to an effective assessment. It should:

1. be based on a combination of developmental theory and learning theory and use integrated methodology derived from both sources
2. clearly convey respect for the active role of family members in

assessing and planning for their child's educational experiences
3. involve team members from all relevant disciplines along with family members
4. use a variety of instruments and procedures
5. include all developmental domains
6. result in data that are useful for planning curriculum goals and intervention strategies in home-based and group-based inclusion settings, and that enhance child developmental progress and developmentally appropriate family–child interactions.

In a review of current assessment practices in this field, Fewell (1991) discusses two primary approaches that are being used by early childhood special educators, one that could be called the "multitest multidomain model" and one that she named the "one-test multidomain model."

MULTITEST MULTIDOMAIN MODEL

This model draws on a "team of experts," who assess different developmental domains using measures familiar to team members from particular disciplines. The "team-of-experts" model has the advantage of being a comprehensive, in-depth assessment that draws on the range of skills of a wide variety of professionals. A full team may include an early intervention teacher, speech pathologist, occupational therapist, physical therapist, social worker, family educator or coordinator, psychologist, and nurse. It may also include a physician; however, often the medical report is available, but the physician is not present at team meetings. In some early intervention settings, an adapted physical education teacher is part of the assessment team to give information on child-initiated motor action in gym and playground settings (Porter, 1993). Although the parent is considered a participant on every team, the actual level of family participation may vary greatly. The "team-of-experts" model may be intimidating to families, although an effort is usually made to make family members aware that *they are the primary experts* with valuable information about their child to share with the team.

The extent of actual teamwork in the assessment process and in the IFSP development also varies, depending on the makeup of the team and the climate of interaction that has been established. Some members may continue to function primarily at the periphery of the team, as information providers rather than as on-site team participants. Teams often start out as inter- or multidisciplinary and move toward a transdisciplinary model. This model incorporates a wide range of assessment methods, with team members determining the appropriate instruments to be used. They also decide how much of the assessment will use an "arena" approach, in which the team observes as a group while one member is eliciting responses through interaction with the child, and how much information will be collected by individual team members working independently with the child and parent. One version of the arena format is shown in Figure 4.1.

Standardized Assessment Measures

In this model, standardized assessment measures familiar to various members of the team may be used by those professionals within the team setting, or they may designate one professional to conduct the formal part of the assessment while other team members observe. For example, to assess cognitive development, the team psychologist may use a norm-referenced instrument, such as the mental scale of the Bayley Scales of Infant Development (BSID) (Bayley, 1993). (The recently revised Bayley Scale is discussed in Chapter 3 and in Appendix B). Other normative psychometric instruments (e.g., the DAS [Elliot, 1990]) may be used by the psychologist. Standardized criterion-referenced instruments that include cognitive assessment (e.g., Battelle Developmental Inventory [Newborg, Stock, Wnek, Guidubaldi, Svinicki, 1991]) may also be used by the psychologist or by other team members.

FIGURE 4.1

TRANSDISCIPLINARY ARENA ASSESSMENT AND PROGRAM PLANNING MEETING

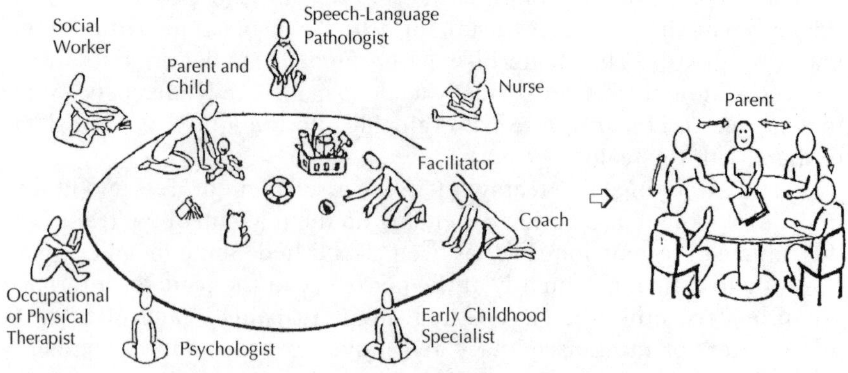

Source Note: Graphic idea adapted from PROJECT KAI, Brighton, MA, with permission.

In addition, an instrument based on cognitive developmental theory may be used to assess the child's sensorimotor stage. The Piagetian theory-based Ordinal Scales of Psychological Development (Uzgiris & Hunt, 1975) provides this type of assessment. The term "ordinal" indicates that the seven areas of sensorimotor ability to be demonstrated are listed in order of attainment; thus, successful performance at one level implies that all lower levels in that domain have been mastered. It has been revised for use with children with disabilities (Dunst, 1980), and concurrent validity of the scale with psychometric instruments has been demonstrated (Hefernan & Black, 1984). It may be used either as a supplement to a psychometric measure or as the only measure. It is described further in Appendix B.

If the entire BSID is given, it will also assess motor development (Bayley Motor Scales). Another instrument often used for motor development assessment is the Peabody Developmental Motor Scales (Folio & Fewell, 1983). This is often used by physical and occupational therapists. It is described further in Chapter 5 and Appendix B. Speech pathologists may use a parent interview measure, Receptive Expressive Emergent Language Scale (REEL-2) (Bzoch & League, 1990) or a structured observation measure, Preschool Language Scale-3 (Zimmerman, Steiner, & Pond, 1992). One member of the team may collect a spontaneous language sample, to be analyzed for language features (see Chapter 6 and Appendix B).

For psychosocial and self-help skill assessment, one standardized parent or teacher interview measure, the Vineland Adaptive Behavior Scales (Sparrow, Balla, & Cicchetti, 1984, 1985) is often used (see Chapter 3 and Appendix B). Another method of assessing social–emotional domains is with parent and teacher responses on structured interviews or rating scale measures. For example, the Child Behavior Checklist for Ages 2–3 (Achenbach, 1988) asks parents or caregivers to give their opinions on a sample of children's social and emotional behaviors. Overall assessment of development often involves the parents; for example, the Developmental Profile II (Alpern, Boll, & Shearer, 1984) can be used as an interview instrument or given to the parent to complete in writing, and the Early Child Developmental Inventory (Ireton, 1988) asks parents to rate their child's developmental skills. These instruments may be used by a variety of the team members, but are most often used by the early intervention specialist or the social worker or family coordinator. They are described further in Appendix B.

Structured Play-Based Procedures

Recently, many early childhood special educators have promoted the use of structured play-based team observational procedures to assess play development and parent–child interactions. In these methods, play is observed for the purpose of evaluating the developmental level of the child's play skill and for assessing other developmental domain levels that are revealed by the child's play behavior. Parent–child interactions in play or caregiving are observed either in natural settings or in simulated settings. These can be especially relevant for understanding the social context of the child's experiences.

A number of play-based models have been developed (e.g., Fewell, 1986; Linder, 1993; Westby, 1980). These approaches are all designed to provide assessment information in settings that draw on the child's own interests and choices of activity and, therefore, give a picture of "best performance." They lend themselves well to administration in arena assessment settings.

For example, the Linder Transdisciplinary Play-Based Assessment model is conducted in a playroom, preferably one with an observation room. A team conducts the assessment and, after the assessment session, the team discusses their recorded observations, usually with the parent present. A videotape is often made to be used for review and documentation. In the Fewell assessment model, young children are observed in interaction with specified toy sets that are designed to elicit a range of skills. There are two conditions with this model: first, spontaneous play and then, elicited play. The Westby method involves collection of both spontaneous play and language data. Play-based assessment instruments are described further in Appendix B.

Other Measures

Depending on the team plan, a variety of nonstandardized measures may also be used in the assessment. For example, there are usually informal and formal observational procedures used in the home, classroom, or simulated environment, as part of the overall team assessment process. Informal observational techniques are valuable for understanding processes, such as adult and peer interactions with the child, and for evaluating behaviors, such as play, humor, or aggression, which may be difficult to elicit through standardized methods. They are also useful for monitoring specific areas of developmental progress related to planned interventions (Wolery, 1989a, 1989b). Team members may design their own observational tools to gain specific kinds of information or they may use ones reported in the literature, such as the Two-Dimensional Play Observation Form (Bergen, 1988). Some observational formats are described in Chapter 7 and in Appendix B.

Ecologically focused procedures have also been designed to assess home, community, and school or agency environments. These probe systematically the contexts in which young children develop. This method is described further in Chapter 9 and in Appendix A. Information from measures given at other times (e.g., pediatric evaluations) may also be included in the comprehensive assessment.

Although the System to Plan Early Childhood Services (SPECS) (Bagnato & Neisworth, 1990) is not a specific measure, it provides an innovative way to structure a comprehensive team assessment and organize data for decision making, which involves clinical judgment rather than use of test scores. This is described further in Appendix B.

ONE-TEST MULTIDOMAIN MODEL

Because of the time-consuming nature of the multitest type of team assessment, another model of assessment has been widely used, which Fewell (1991) calls the "one-test, multidomain assessment." When this approach is used, the early intervention unit decides on one test that has subtests in all domains, such as the Battelle Developmental Inventory (Newborg et al., 1984); the Brigance Diagnostic Inventory of Early Development-Revised (Brigance, 1991); the Carolina Curriculum for Handicapped Infants and At-Risk Infants (Johnson-Martin, Jens, & Attermeier, 1990); or the Hawaii Early Learning Profile (Furono et al., 1979). Team members may each use various portions of the same test or the test may be given by one team member, such as the early intervention teacher, who communicates the information to the team for follow-up testing in specific domains. These are described in Appendix B.

Fewell (1991, pp. 169–170) cites a number of advantages of this approach, such as that these tests are relatively inexpensive, they can be administered by staff who are not psychometricians or specialists, and they usually have sequenced items in each domain that are also tied to curriculum. This latter aspect is especially appealing to early interventionists because the items failed can then form the basis of objectives to be included on the IFSP. The tests can be used repeatedly to chart developmental progress. If the screening assessment is done by the early intervention unit, this test often is used, with follow-up in domains of concern.

Although there are many appealing aspects to the one-test approach, especially when teams must assess many children repeatedly, Fewell (1991, p. 170) points out numerous flaws in this method. Some of the tests are not psychometrically or theoretically sound, having been formed by taking items from a variety of other developmental tests, without collection of further validity data. The age equivalents are frequently taken from developmental schedules rather than from normative samples; there are often uneven numbers of items in each domain or at various age levels; and the age ranges are not always equivalent. They often lack standardization, have no standard scores to use in comparisons of change, lack a typical child comparative group, and may have more than one scoring option, which raises another validity question. Furthermore, because the items are supposedly tied to curricular goals, they may lend themselves to "teaching-to-the-test" approaches.

In spite of the problems with the one-test method, it has become increasingly popular because of its cost, time, curricular, and personnel advantages. One advantage not mentioned by Fewell is that teachers often feel that testing a child in all domains themselves gives them more information than does reading someone else's report. They like to be able to test children on the range of skills that they will be teaching. Another advantage of this approach is that it does lend itself to a transdisciplinary team model, although the team may consist of members from a narrow range of disciplines. Because they are usually housed in the same facility, however, the team members can gradually develop a trust level that facilitates role release and integrated implementation of the educational and family service plan.

INFORMATION EXCHANGE WITH FAMILIES AND REFERRAL AGENCIES

As the assumptions and practice of early childhood special education professionals would indicate, information exchange with families is a major strength of their assessment approach. Families are involved in determining their own needs and strengths, in providing information about their child, in developing the IFSP that is to serve the family and child, and, usually, in implementing that plan. When the model is working well, it provides an integrated information exchange because both the family and the early intervention team are giving and receiving information, discussing potential action, reaching consensus on the plan, and periodically evaluating and revising the plan.

Similarly, the expectation of the model is that referrals to other agencies will be smooth because these agencies will have strong working relationships with the early intervention unit, and some of the team members may act as ongoing liaisons with the agencies or may even be employees of these agencies. Since the model assumes that a case manager or service coordinator will facilitate service delivery to the families, these services are likely to be provided in a timely and cost-effective manner.

Like most models, however, information exchange with families and with agencies is not always accomplished smoothly. Much depends on family motivation, agency staff roles and responsibilities, time commitments of team participants, and early intervention staff commitment to information exchange. Although the conceptual model is not always realized in practice, most early intervention units are making good progress toward reaching this goal of effective information exchange.

USEFULNESS OF A TRANSDISCIPLINARY MODEL

From the standpoint of early childhood special educators, the primary strength of the model is clear: It results in improved service to young children and their families and, therefore, in increased effectiveness of early intervention. The weakness is also clear: It takes time and effort to work effectively in a team approach and to gain the commitment of professionals from other disciplines to give up their "individual expert" mind set and embrace an "team-of-experts" perspective. If the team members are all part of the early intervention staff, this perspective is facilitated; however, few program units can employ all of the personnel needed for a full discipline perspective. Designing models that facilitate interaction of a full compliment of team members is an important challenge for early intervention practice.

Another issue is that of increasing the skills of professionals in early intervention to enable them to work confidently with families in this team relationship. In a recent study, many early intervention professionals expressed concern about the impact the change to a more family-centered model would have on their own profession, on their work with families and children, and on their work with other professionals. Educators and therapists rated themselves as possessing less family-oriented skills than did social workers and nurses (Bailey, Palsha, & Simeonsson, 1991). Personnel preparation in these and other early intervention related fields will be affected by the move to a transdisciplinary team approach.

POLICY ISSUES

A number of levels of policy affect early childhood special education assessment practice: federal, state, and local. At the federal level, the legal mandates are broadly stated and thus are subject to a number of interpretations, which has resulted in variations in policy implementation at the state level. State agency personnel have had the responsibility of defining how federal mandates can be carried out in a cost-effective and politically acceptable manner. Because the climates and resources vary from state to state, the range of methods for meeting the mandates also varies, with some states providing excellent models and others falling behind.

There have been variations in local policy interpretation, depending on the stakeholders involved in early intervention services in each community. Fewell (1991), citing Wolff's (1989) critique of present practice, indicates two issues relevant to local practice: 1) "early intervention practitioners' unquestioned acceptance of popular practices that may be diametrically opposed to theories they espouse regarding child development and assessment" (p. 167); and 2) "practitioners' quickness to refer and serve at-risk or what he [Wolff] called marginally handicapped children" (p. 168).

Although federal law indicates that young children who are "at risk" for developmental delay may be included in the tracking, assessment, and intervention services each state provides, in practice, each state has defined the group to be served somewhat differently, using broad or narrow parameters. For example, in Ohio, the agency responsible for the birth to age three programs (i.e., Department of Mental Retardation and Developmental Disabilities) has defined the population primarily in terms of biological and established risk categories, but environmentally at-risk children are not excluded, if places are available. This has resulted in local decisions to include young siblings of preschool children with manifest delay, if there is also evidence of environmental risk factors. Whether this policy results in inappropriate inclusion of children who are only marginally at risk or in appropriately giving the opportunity to avoid developmental delay to children who come from conditions where probability of risk does exist is a matter of present debate.

There are many other decisions that early interventionists must make within the policy guidelines of federal and state agencies. In addition to decisions about practice–theory congruence and which risk levels to include, local policy must address issues of selection of reliable, valid, and representatively normed tests; appropriate team composition and participation levels; allocation of case management responsibility; movement toward inclusion and integration of programs; and level of family involvement.

In general, early childhood educators and early childhood special educators are strongly in support of the basic policies in the field. This is clear from the number of professional associations that have endorsed the importance of early intervention, family-centered practice, inclusion, and well-prepared professional educators. These include the Association for Childhood Education International (ACEI, 1993), Association of Teacher Educators (ATE/NAEYC 1991), Division for Early Childhood/Council for Exceptional Children (DEC/CEC, 1993), National Association for Early Childhood Teacher Educators (NAECTE, 1991), and the National Association for the Education of Young Children (ATE/NAEYC, 1991). Three of these organizations have recently issued a joint position statement on preparing personnel (ATE/DEC/NAEYC, 1994).

Early intervention professionals, however, still indicate that there are many barriers to a truly family-centered transdisciplinary approach (Bailey, Buysse, Edmondson, & Smith, 1992). These include *family* barriers, such as lack of knowledge, attitudes toward participation, and time constraints; *system* barriers, such as state and local administrative policies, lack of funds and other resources, and inflexibility of patterns of practice; *professional* barriers, such as lack of knowledge, attitudes toward participation, and attitudes toward families; and *testing* barriers, such as lack of reliable, valid, and practical instruments.

A broad policy question for American society, however, is whether young children and their families should even have to demonstrate "eligibility" for services. If these services were available to all young children and their families, one-shot assessment screening to determine eligibility for services could be eliminated, and classroom observation could be the first level of identification of children with delay. This would require an increased level of public funding initially, although, in the long term, it may result in less societal cost. Many advocates assert that it is imperative to provide comprehensive, early, and effective services for all children and families who are at risk, especially if that risk results from poverty (Zigler, 1993).

SUMMARY

Developmental and educational perspectives have arisen from the disciplines of early childhood and special education; each have somewhat different theoretical views and educational practice. However, these have been integrated in early intervention and this integrated perspective forms the basis of early assessment and intervention practice. Federal mandates and state interpretations of these mandates have also been influential in determining the required components of assessment and intervention. At the present time, most professionals coming from this perspective are in support of team collaboration, multiple measures, family involvement, and comprehensive domain assessment models recommended by legal mandates and theoretical constructs. However, a number of problems in the realization of this approach have been identified, and further development of effective models is needed.

QUESTIONS FOR DISCUSSION

1. How would the results of a "multitest multidomain" model and a "one-test multidomain" model differ in relation to the IFSP developed?

2. What could be done to reduce the problem of time constraints so that an early intervention team could function more effectively?

PROBLEMS OF PRACTICE

Attend an arena assessment and observe how the members of the team interact during the assessment and intervention planning process. Identify which professional performed the service coordinating and primary testing roles, which additional assessments other team members conducted, and how the parent was involved in the assessment process. Analyze the strengths and weaknesses of this assessment approach for the particular child and family you observed.

SUGGESTED READINGS

Fewell, R. R. (1991). Trends in the assessment of infants and toddlers with disabilities. *Exceptional Children, 58*(2), 166–173.

Bredekamp, S. (Ed.) (1987). *Developmentally appropriate practice in early childhood programs serving children from birth through age 8* (exp. ed.). Washington, DC: National Association for the Education of Young Children.

DIALOGUE

GENDER, AGE, ETHNIC ORIGIN OF CHILD: Female, 33 months, African American.

OCCASION OR PURPOSE OF DIALOGUE: Final IFSP review before transition into a an age 3 to 5 program; to discuss developmental progress and the transition plan (to either another program in the early intervention setting or a program in the school district). Carly has been receiving services in a self-contained classroom containing five children with developmental delays, ages 18 to 36 months. Twice-a-month home visits by the early interventionist are also conducted.

TEAM MEMBERS: An occupational therapist, speech pathologist, and early intervention specialist, all of whom have been part of the intervention team, and the child's mother.

SETTING: A conference room in the early intervention center.

OVERVIEW OF THE CASE

RISK CONDITIONS

Carly was diagnosed with Down's syndrome at birth. She has subsequently undergone two surgeries on her sinuses, and ventilation tubes have been inserted in her ears twice. She has also had her adenoids removed. There is a hole in her heart that is reported to be closing slowly. Her physician has recommended that treatment of this condition be postponed for 2 years. Carly currently wears glasses.

REASON FOR REFERRAL

Carly's progress during the past 6 months needs to be assessed and objectives developed for her transition to an appropriate age 3 to 5 program. Objectives identified at the last assessment, which must be evaluated at this session, follow:

1. Carly will increase the use of sign and verbal language, especially at meal times and bed time.

2. Carly will increase her cooperative behavior at school and home.
3. Carly will demonstrate the ability to drink from a cup (no lid) without spilling.
4. Carly will demonstrate the ability to use a spoon to feed herself with little spilling.
5. Carly will demonstrate understanding of "table manners." (This is an important parent-identified objective; they would like to be able to take Carly out to restaurants with the rest of the family.)

BACKGROUND INFORMATION

Carly comes from a stable, intact family. She has two older brothers. The father works in a lab at a hospital medical center. The mother is at home full time. The parents are both participants in the Down's Syndrome Association. They are also active in a number of African-American groups in the city in which they reside. Carly started in the early intervention program when she was 3 months old.

FAMILY STRENGTHS AND NEEDS

Strengths include parents who are able and willing to attain necessary services (and to be assertive in getting them). The father has a stable income and good insurance. Although the family has had many needs at various times in the past, including a period when the father was out of work, at present they have not identified any major need. There are a few neighbors who provide respite support for the family and a large group of friends with common interests. They have an emotionally close extended family, but they must rely on neighbors and friends for day-to-day support because the other family members live approximately 800 miles away.

SOURCES OF ASSESSMENT INFORMATION

These measures include those collected in the early intervention program (Brigance Diagnostic Inventory of Early Development (Revised), Preschool Language Scale-3, parent interview, school and home play observations). Updated standardized testing by the school psychologist is being arranged, but has not yet been administered. There is not presently a plan to have a hearing assessment conducted. Based on the results from the assessment sources used, Carly's developmental status is as follows:

Social-Emotional Development

Carly follows directions and makes transitions more easily than she did in the first year in the program. She engages in practice and pretend play along side (and occasionally with) peers and her social skills are appropriate for play situations (e.g., beginning to share toys). She exhibits both affection and assertiveness toward adults and peers. Her self-help skills have also improved. On the Brigance inventory, her performance was at the 28- to 30-month level in social and emotional development and at the 24- to 25-month level in self-help skills.

Physical–Motor and Sensory–Perceptual Development

Carly showed delays in achieving many physical development milestones. For example, she sat at 10 months, crawled at 20 months, and walked at 24 months. She continues to show immature and somewhat uncoordinated walking and running patterns. However, there is no great concern over her gross motor abilities. Her fine motor skills have also improved. For example, she is able to hold a crayon well and draw scribbling pictures, put small objects into containers, and use the pincer grasp on her eating utensils. She is not yet drinking without spilling, however. Her scores on the motor portions of the Brigance indicate that her skills are scattered, ranging from 24 to 29 months in gross and fine motor skills and behaviors.

Cognitive–Language Development

In early testing, Carly was assessed as having an approximate 1-year delay on most cognitive and language measures. For example, at 24 months she could correctly point to pictures of familiar objects, but she could not name pictures of the objects. She could build a tower of 4 cubes and imitate actions; she could not build a tower of 6 cubes and imitate words. Carly's cognitive scores have maintained the pattern of approximately a 1-year delay. Her general knowledge and comprehension was at the 22-to-24 month level on the Brigance tasks. (A cognitive assessment is also to be conducted by the psychologist of the school district where Carly will be enrolled.) In her language development, Carly has made some progress. She used one-word signing almost exclusively until age 2½, but now she uses some spoken words, too. The signing reduces as she gains greater verbal facility. The clarity of her speech could be improved. She continues to have problems in articulation and vocabulary, but her pragmatics are relatively strong. She scored at the 2–0 to 2–6 level in auditory comprehension on the Preschool Language Scale–3. Her expressive language score (including signs) was at the 1–6 to 1–1 level, indicating that her expressive language is less well developed than her receptive language. Her performance on the Brigance speech and language tasks was congruent with the PLS–3.

THE TEAM DIALOGUE

The team is gathered to review the IFSP objectives and determine what progress has been made, to write new objectives for her final months in the birth to age 3 program, and to begin transition planning for the age 3 to 5 program. The early intervention teacher is the team discussion leader.

EARLY INTERVENTION TEACHER: First, let's review the objectives we had for Carly and see how she has done on them.

SPEECH PATHOLOGIST: The first objective for Carly this year was to increase her use of both verbal and sign language. We really encouraged her to use basic signs and many single words and two-word sentences. She has developed very well in this past year.

MOTHER: She's almost completely verbal now. She even uses simple sentences. You've done a good job encouraging her to speak.

SPEECH PATHOLOGIST: She is phasing out the signing all by herself. We were somewhat surprised at how fast that has happened.

MOTHER: Do you think we should just let the signing go? She is just not using it. She doesn't seem to need it. My boys are sometimes signing more than she is!

SPEECH PATHOLOGIST: Our objective was to have her increase both her sign and verbal vocabulary. She has chosen to increase her verbal vocabulary and to use verbal communication more than sign communication. This is what we were hoping would eventually happen; however, it has happened earlier than we thought it would. She hasn't had a hearing test for a while though; it might be good to have another assessment to be sure she hasn't had any hearing loss from the infections she'd had previously.

TEACHER: That would be a good idea. Do we agree that the first objective—increasing Carly's communication skills—has been accomplished?

MOTHER: Yes, I'm pleased about it. I think speech is real important. In fact, it's the most important thing to me. I want her to speak well. I think that will help her to have friends. How is she getting along with the other kids? Is she talking to them and getting along better?

TEACHER: That was our second objective. As far as we're concerned, even though she is into a little bit of the "power trip" that comes along with verbal language, she does show much improved cooperation since last

Fall. It's even more than she showed since our 90-day review in January. She gives you a "no" every once in a while just to assert herself, but even then she follows through with what you have asked her to do. Sometimes she needs a prompt of putting out our hand or helping her get up. What are your main concerns at home? Are you getting a lot of resistance at meal time?

MOTHER: No problem. Carly does want to show her independence. She wants to "do it herself." There are times when she finishes eating before we do, but usually she is slower. As long as we let her eat by herself she is okay. That's true of a lot of other things, too. It took a while for me to get used to it because I'd always done so much for her. But now I see it as a really good sign of progress.

TEACHER: In class our criteria was that she would complete activities and cooperate without having physical prompts. I would say she definitely has accomplished this. She moves from activity to activity, accepts the rule that materials should stay in their activity area, and she doesn't try nearly as much to walk away with the toys she likes best. She even cooperates in the gym. In the beginning she only liked the swing and that was all she'd do. Now she tries many things. We're just hoping that you see this change at home.

MOTHER: Oh, we do.

TEACHER: So that objective has been accomplished. What about the improvement in her eating habits? The plan was for you to try letting her eat independently using a sectioned bowl. We also agreed to have her eat independently at school.

OCCUPATIONAL THERAPIST: We also wanted her to eat slowly enough and with small enough bites so that she wouldn't choke and to drink from a cup without a lid.

MOTHER: At home it is just so much more convenient to give her a cup with a lid on it. She usually sits on the floor when she gets a drink. She'll tell me she wants a drink, then sit on the floor, and either hand me the cup or throw the cup onto the counter. I know I need to get her drinking from a regular cup. . . .

OCCUPATIONAL THERAPIST: Don't worry about it. I'm sure that she will pick up that skill soon. At school she is able to drink from an unlidded cup, with just a little help.

MOTHER: She sometimes picks up the boys' drinks and drinks from their glasses.

OCCUPATIONAL THERAPIST: Does she? Well that's good. The reason we can have her drink from the regular cup here is we can do it on a one-to-one basis.

MOTHER: It's definitely not one-to-one at home.

OCCUPATIONAL THERAPIST: Even if you just try once or twice a week to get her to drink without using the sipper it would be good. She can just take a drink out of your cup or glass. Just put a little bit of pressure on her lower lip, pushing it up against the cup, to keep her from dribbling. I let her do whatever she wants with the upper lip. She puts her tongue on the lip of the cup, but she still is able to get quite a bit down.

TEACHER: Even though she's not demonstrating this behavior all the time, I think we are satisfied with her progress.

MOTHER: Definitely.

TEACHER: Carly seems to be eating independently now and only needs occasional reminders about the amount of food in her mouth or to hold the spoon correctly. You also wanted her to realize when the meal was over and to stay seated until the rest of the family was finished so that you could go to a restaurant occasionally. We made the plan that the adults should give Carly a warning in advance that the meal was coming to an end and help her transition to the next activity by giving her a prompt, such as "One more bite and then we will go outside."

MOTHER: That is going really well. She used to scream all the time and still borders on doing that. If you ask her to wipe her mouth, she always says "no" before doing it because she's afraid you're going to say "now we're finished."

TEACHER: That's why it's important to have her wipe her mouth a number of times during the meal so she doesn't always connect it with the end of the meal. Have you eaten out any more?

MOTHER: Oh, yeah. More than we did at the beginning of the year.

TEACHER: You can practice more during the summer. Maybe you can take her without the boys so they don't have to suffer through her transition. Then, if she is being difficult, you can just take her out of the restaurant and the whole family doesn't have to go through it.

MOTHER: Another problem is that she is getting real picky about what she eats. Just lately she's started the bad habit of handing you her plate about twenty times during the meal to say she is done. I usually just wait her out. I gave her cereal in place of the other food a few times but I cut that out. She just has to realize that if she doesn't eat she'll be hungry.

TEACHER: Since it isn't an issue of getting enough nourishment, you don't need to be concerned about her expressing food preferences. There are a number of options to deal with her "pickiness." You can just take her plate and put it in the sink if she gives it to you. When she asks for it back, tell her she said she was finished. Another option would be to excuse her from the table when she says that. It shouldn't turn into a game for you. If it was something she used to like but now won't eat, then you can just figure she doesn't need it that badly. It seems that Carly has made progress on the table manners objective, even though you might like to see more changes.

MOTHER: Yes, she is certainly better than she was.

TEACHER: Now let's talk about Carly's transition to preschool. Have you heard any more from the psychologist about the multifactored evaluation?

MOTHER: I called him last week and they sent me some notes to sign but I haven't signed them. I'm pretty confused about what the school district is doing.

TEACHER: What plan is there other than the fact that we are going to have a meeting with the school psychologist?

MOTHER: I don't even know if that is planned. I think that they are thinking Carly will stay in your preschool program next year. I'm also observing the program they have in the school district. It's supposed to be one combined with Head Start and I don't know if I like that or not until I see it. I have an appointment next week to see that. The psychologist plans to do the testing some time after that.

TEACHER: When you visit the psychologist, tell him that you need to have the testing done in the next 2 weeks if it is to be done before our term is over. Remind him that he said he would see her at least twice before the actual testing so that she will be familiar with him. I think the recommendations we make today will also be helpful to the school psychologist. (Group agrees on recommendations.)

RECOMMENDATIONS

Carly has shown progress in all areas addressed by the most recent IFSP. Carly seems to be experiencing a "learning spurt" at the present time. She will be eligible to begin a preschool program in Fall and could probably function quite well in an inclusion program. She should continue to receive speech therapy to improve her vocabulary and speaking clarity. She should have an occupational therapist's evaluation as part of the multifactored testing to determine if further therapy is needed in this area. An audiological evaluation is recommended. The comprehensive psychological testing should be accomplished within the next few weeks. After the psychological evaluation, the team will meet again to make a decision as to whether Carly will attend the age 3 to 5 program at the early intervention center or the school district Head Start inclusion program.

QUESTIONS FOR DISCUSSION

1. Carly is presently exhibiting behaviors that are often seen in typically developing children between the ages of 18 and 30 months. Which of the parent and teacher concerns are specific to her disability condition and which are "typical," given the fact that her overall development is

delayed by approximately 1 year? What were the behaviors Carly exhibited that the participants identified as signs of growth, even though there were some problems with the way Carly was exhibiting them?

2. Which of the goals for Carly that were discussed were primarily meeting family or school needs and which were primarily meeting Carly's needs? What concerns of the mother about Carly's future (e.g., having friends, eating out with family) reflected the concerns of many families who have children with disabilities? Were they adequately addressed by the rest of the team?

3. What could have been added to this team discussion if the psychologist from the school district and an audiologist who had tested Carly's hearing had been present at the meeting? What information could each of them have provided that would have assisted in the transition planning?

4. Which type of preschool program would probably be better for Carly, given her particular developmental status? What could Carly's family do to collaborate with that program to further a smooth transition?

5. How did the early interventionist facilitate the mother's full participation in the discussion? Did her interaction style reflect any awareness of cultural values that the family might have that are different from dominant cultural values?

chapter 5

Doris Bergen

PHYSICAL AND OCCUPATIONAL THERAPY ASSESSMENT PERSPECTIVES

Physical therapists and occupational therapists play important roles in the assessment of very young children. Many neonates with identified disabilities, biological risk, or environmental risk exhibit difficulties in maintaining basic survival skills. Usually these problems are related to dysfunctions in their physical attributes or to health factors. For example, neonates may have difficulty feeding, moving their head to prevent suffocation, or breathing independently. Even after they survive the crucial first days of life, infants may continue to have such difficulties and, in addition, often have muscle tone problems, fine and gross motor skill delays, and sensory processing disorganization or distortion. Physical therapists and occupational therapists, working closely with medical personnel and with other early intervention specialists such as speech pathologists and early childhood special educators, can have a positive effect on the developmental problems during these children's first 3 years.

The developmental domains addressed by physical therapists and occupational therapists sometimes overlap; the differentiation in their roles is often unclear to parents and professionals of other disciplines. This is partly due to the historical tradition of these two fields, which both arose in response to the needs of adults who had physical or sensory-based problems that interfered with occupational and adaptive life skills. The initial distinctions made in their roles with adults have not carried over clearly to their work with children, partly because of differences in the needs of children but also because the disciplines have both evolved to be more inclusive and integrative. Also as new knowledge of brain functioning has been amassed, information about the systemic nature of motor and sensory problems has contributed to an integration of the perspectives of these disciplines.

The term "physical therapist" refers to the physical modalities used to intervene in treatment. These involve heat and cold, including diathermy (i.e., electromagnetic wave-generated heat), ultrasound (i.e., high frequency sound waves), light, electrical stimulation, and water, all of which are used as treatment modalities by physical therapists. They work on the body to relieve pain, prevent deformity, and restore functioning, and are concerned with problems such as range of motion, posture and mobility, and gross and fine motor functioning, especially as related to functional mobility and transitions. They also are concerned with assessing neurological phenomena such as *muscle tone*, which is related to elasticity and tension (i.e., the timing of movement and the level of activation of muscles).

The term "occupational therapist" arose from the functional goal of these therapists, which was to assist disabled workers to return to their previous occupation or to develop adapted occupational skills for both out-of-home jobs and work in the home. Their focus was often on improving the fine motor skills that many occupations require, and their method of treatment included craft-related activities and, in the case of children, play-related activities, since play has been interpreted to be the child's "work." In their assessment of children, they have primarily been concerned with sensory processing (including visual problems) and fine motor skill development, giving attention to analysis of how environmental modifications such as appropriate toy selection, equipment adaptations, and spatial organization can foster motor and sensory development.

Current early intervention practice varies in the breadth of the roles of these two groups of therapists. Much of the variation depends on the graduate training specializations of each, which may include a focus on neurodevelopmental treatment, sensory integration theory, Feldenkrais method (i.e., movement awareness), cranio-sacral therapy (i.e., working with fascial systems [fibrous tissues] and deep fluids), manual therapy (i.e., manipulation and mobilization), or infant–parent massage (i.e., deep tissue work).

If only one therapist is present in a particular setting, that therapist may observe across any of the developmental domains that are crucial to child survival or effective physical functioning. They also consult with pediatric associates and other therapists. When both therapists are present in a setting, they may seem to be doing similar activities; however, both are assessing, facilitating, inhibiting, or challenging the child with a perspective unique to their discipline. Thus, although they work in a collaborative manner because of their overlapping expertise and interests, they also respect the specialties of each discipline. The involvement of an occupational therapist, physical therapist, or both depends on the age of the child and on the nature of the physical or sensory disability.

UNDERLYING ASSUMPTIONS

A number of assumptions are shared by these therapists and provide the basis for their assessment and intervention practices. The first is the conviction that it is important to start as early as possible to identify and address problems in physical–motor and sensory–perceptual developmental domains. Because the first years of life encompass so many physically-based developmental milestones (e.g., visual inspection, head control, eye-hand coordination, rolling, grasping and releasing objects, feeding self, sitting alone, standing, walking), every day that goes by without problems being identified and help being provided may result in reduced ability of the child to interact effectively with the environment. Young children find ways to accomplish independence by using compensatory patterns that may not be the best choice, if they do not have therapeutic intervention.

The value of independent functioning (or of as much independence as is possible) is a second assumption. Although not all children will be able to function without social or equipment assistance, these therapists try to enable children to function effectively in as independent a manner as their disabilities will permit, and at their fullest potential level, especially in regard to basic life skills and social or occupational abilities. This is why they give attention to positioning to enable best functioning; to providing visual, auditory, tactile, olfactory, and other types of sensory stimulation, or to limiting such stimulation to reach an optimal sensory balance; and to environmental adaptations or the use of adaptive equipment and braces that can give children with physical disabilities a sense of control and mastery. Because young children search and understand the world through physical–motor and sensory–perceptual modes, the ability to be actively engaged will affect all their domains of development. The more independent these children can be, the easier they will be to care for and the more likely they will be to function effectively and have a purposeful life style in society, which has also been a traditional goal of these disciplines.

Because not all children will have independence without assistance, the importance of active adult attention to environmental intervention is thus a third assumption under which these therapists operate. However, these interventions should approximate natural experiences that occur in typical children's lives. For example, because an infant with neurological impairments may not respond in the same way as a typical child during early parent–child interactions, therapists may focus on improving that child's ability to take an interactive role. They are often involved in helping parents know how to engage successfully in feeding, bathing, dressing, diapering, toileting, quieting, and sleep-inducing activities with infants who have motor or sensory-based problems. These interactive experiences are closely tied to attachment processes, social referencing, and other developmental domains, and are thus crucial for the development of both parents and children. Parental feelings of competence can be greatly affected by therapists' interventions that promote successful interactions in caring and play situations.

A fourth commonly held assumption is that, because there is individual variability in developmental progress, expectations for individual children should be at a higher level of expectation than that of minimal performance. Even among the group of young children who have significant delay or disabilities, many children's progress exceeds minimal expectations. Thus, it is essential that therapists maintain their commitment to the systematic and persistent effort that is often needed to promote developmental progress. To the uninformed observer, the extent and timing of motor or sensory change processes are often hard to discern, but to the therapist, these small changes can make a significant difference in developmental progress and eventual functioning.

One distinction often made between the roles of physical and occupational therapists is that the occupational therapist does fine motor and the physical therapist does gross motor assessment and intervention. Because fine motor skills are closely tied to visual abilities, the occupational therapist has been most likely to be concerned with visual acuity and distortion effects on development. Although this separation of fine and gross motor domains and assignment of each to different therapists is often used as a guideline in selecting a consulting therapist, in actual practice this distinction may or may not be especially useful because there are many motor development processes that depend on both good posture, mobility, and gross motor coordination and on good sensory integration and fine motor skills. According to Weeks & Ewer-Jones (1991), "perception and motor behavior (gross or fine) are inextricably linked" (p. 261). Thus, both occupational and physical therapists are often concerned with whole body sensory and motor coordination issues.

One assumption that has been more characteristic of occupational therapists in the past is that naturalistic, play-based assessment and intervention is a preferred mode. The occupational therapist has typically used observation of children at play as an assessment method and has stressed play and craft-like intervention activities, many of which incorporate fine motor skill development. Physical therapists have typically had a more task-oriented approach, sometimes working on certain skills or using intrusive interventions (e.g., in sports medicine or cardiac rehabilitation). With young children, however, most physical therapists agree with the assumption that natural, playful approaches to assessment and intervention are more successful, especially if children are more likely to repeat the desired behavior at other times if it is incorporated in play. Thus, therapists from both disciplines who are working with young children are likely to use play-oriented approaches.

Similarly, a characteristic of physical therapists is that they have traditionally accepted many assumptions of medical models, including having a taxonomy of precise terminology to label deficits and a focus on physiological and neurological interconnections with behavior. These terms have enhanced and simplified communication among professionals. However, physical therapists have also needed to learn the skill of communicating this information in nontechnical ways to educators and parents. Although occupational therapists have had more focus on identifying enjoyable activities that could improve motor and sensory functional skills, they have also moved toward a more "medical-scientific" approach and developed a set of precise terminology for describing child deficit characteristics. Examples of the terminology often used to describe child motor and sensory characteristics are listed in Figure 5.1. Because these disciplines have worked so closely with medical personnel, they share some of the terminology of medically-oriented disciplines. Their methods of assessment have often had a clinical component and been done in conjunction with medically based personnel.

METHODS OF ASSESSMENT

Physical and occupational therapists are interested not only in assessing whether there are developmental delays or major deficits in sensory and motor areas, but also in evaluating the quality of movement and movement transitions and sensory responses exhibited by the children being assessed. The quality of movement transitions and sensorimotor processes are of special importance because they can often point to the areas of development that may be in jeopardy over the long term. In assessing young children, these therapists have typically used a combination of methods that range from clinical judgment to standardized testing.

CLINICAL EVALUATION

Clinical judgment includes determining whether intervention is needed or whether there is a likelihood the problem can be resolved without intervention. In such cases, the developmental picture may indicate that diag-

FIGURE 5.1
MOVEMENT TERMINOLOGY

Term	Definition
Prone	Lying on stomach
Supine	Lying on back
Lateral	Pertaining to the side
Abduction	Movement away from the midline of the body
Adduction	Movement toward the midline of the body
Extension	Straightening a body part at the joint
Flexion	Bending a body part at the joint
External rotation	Rotation of a joint that moves a body part away from the midline
Internal rotation	Rotation of a body joint that moves a body part toward the midline
Symmetry	Equal development of both sides of the body in size and shape or same position of both sides of the body while assuming postures and performing movements
Asymmetry	Unequal development of one side of the body from the other in size or shape or different position of one side of the body from the other while assuming postures and performing movements
Rotation	Twisting of the body along the body axis or movement between the shoulders and pelvis (trunk rotation), needed in all volitional and transitional movements (moving from one posture to another)
Dissociation	Ability to isolate and use only those body parts and muscles needed to perform independent movements
Weight bearing	Symmetrical posture, with weight evenly distributed over weight-bearing joints or body parts (e.g., prone on forearms or extended arms, sitting, kneeling, standing)
Weight shift	Shifting the weight of the body from a position of equal weight bearing in an antigravity posture to one side of the body to free a body part to perform independent movements; a weight shift precedes every volitional movement

Source Note: Reprinted with permission from Smith (1989).

nostic evaluation should be conducted at a later time, but that no inter-vention is needed immediately. If it is determined that there should be intervention, the type of treatment, whether it should be short- or long-term, and when it should be started are other clinical judgment issues.

With medically fragile neonates, therapists usually draw on the information provided by medical personnel who have identified through clinical judgment those children who are at risk because of prematurity or low birth weight for gestational age and those who have established risk conditions, such as cerebral palsy, spina bifida, visual impairment, Down's syndrome, and limb loss or other physical anomalies that may make basic survival and typical functioning problematic. These children usually require further assessment and immediate services from the ther-apists.

Therapists also are involved in assessing young children who are referred because they appear highly disorganized, hypersensitive, hyper-active, delayed in development, autistic, or motorically clumsy. Children who have experienced a trauma, such as severe burns, which can affect motor and sensory functioning, are also evaluated. Clinical judgment may include assessing posture, mobility, muscle tone, auditory and visual responses, or motor coordination and determining the treatment needed to increase purposefulness and quality of movement.

Therapists use clinical judgment to observe the qualitative aspects, types, and levels of severity of sensory or movement problems before determining intervention procedures. That is, they are concerned with evaluation of "process" characteristics, such as motor control and quality of sequence of actions (Williams, 1990). They may observe informally, not-ing these characteristics, or they may use a checklist of some type to record systematically these process components.

The following areas are evaluated clinically to assess oral–motor and respiratory–phonatory problems: movement of each part of the oral–motor mechanism during natural activities, such as feeding; influence of postu-ral tone, movement, and sensory stimulation on functioning; coordination of respiratory functioning and oral functioning; and uses of communica-tion modes (Alexander, 1990).

Motor assessment dimensions usually addressed in neuromotor eval-uations include judgments concerning muscle tone (elasticity and tension), muscle strength (force generating ability), postural reactions (equilibrium, righting, protective responses), and structural mobility and integrity (skele-tal and muscle relationships) (Gallagher & Cech, 1988).

Aspects of muscle tone that should be evaluated include underlying (at rest) and predominant (in action) muscle tone along with the distribu-tion of tone throughout the body. Presence or absence of primitive reflexes and automatic postural reactions, such as self-righting, maintaining equilibrium, and extending limbs to prevent falling, are assessed. The quality of volitional movements, such as walking and grasping, and of transitional volitional movements, such as pulling to stand and moving from a prone to a sitting position, are also evaluated clinically (Smith, 1989).

Clinical assessment procedures usually involve handling the infant (e.g., holding and repositioning); eliciting movements and sensory responses (e.g., touching); presenting objects to track visual pursuit and observe grasping responses); and observing spontaneous behaviors of the infant (e.g., synchronic and asynchronic movements during parent–child interaction; coordinated and uncoordinated play with an object). Traditional assessment procedures have relied more heavily on the first two of these—handling and eliciting; however, therapists are now placing more emphasis on spontaneous observational data than they did in the past.

STANDARDIZED ASSESSMENT MEASURES

Standardized assessment instruments are used to gain a comparative perspective on the child's abilities and disabilities. However, standardized tests rarely assess the qualitative aspects of motor and sensory development that are of major importance in therapists' clinical evaluations. Although there are a number of standardized instruments designed specifically to judge motor or neuromotor development (e.g., Folio & Fewell, 1983), broadly based standardized instruments that are used for overall developmental assessments often provide the basis for interventions in motor and sensory areas. For example, normative instruments, such as the Brazelton, Bayley, and Denver, provide motor and sensory assessment data as do criterion-referenced instruments, such as the Carolina and HELP. Sensorimotor behaviors may also be assessed with Piagetian-based instruments, such as the Ordinal Scales of Psychological Development (Uzgiris & Hunt, 1975). Data for these normative assessments of motor development may be obtained by the physical and occupational therapists or they may use data collected by other trained members of the assessment team.

Instruments such as the Peabody Developmental Motor Scales (PDMS) (Folio & Fewell, 1983) have been designed specifically to assess gross and fine motor development of young children, between birth and 7 years. It includes measures of grasping, hand use, eye–hand coordination, manual dexterity, reflexes, balance, nonlocomotor, locomotor, and receipt and propulsion, but does not assess quality of movement. It is designed to assist in intervention planning and assessment.

Another instrument specifically designed to assess neuromotor development is the Movement Assessment of Infants (MAI) (Chandler, Andrews, Swanson, & Larson, 1980). This is a nonstandardized test designed to assess muscle tone, primitive reflexes, automatic reactions, and volitional movement during the first year of life. Because it is graded, having levels of movement behaviors that lead to the later behaviors, it can be helpful in establishing a base from which intervention methods can be planned. More information on these motor assessment measures is found in Appendix B.

Chandler (1990) indicates that four factors may make neuromotor assessment results have reduced sensitivity (accurate detection of movement dysfunction) and specificity (accurate detection of no movement dysfunction):

1. Infant state and behavior variability at the time of testing
2. Extensive variations in normal movement patterns
3. An environment different from that in which the instrument was designed
4. Questions of reliability and validity common to all instrumentation

These factors should be kept in mind when using assessment results to determine intervention recommendations.

INFORMATION EXCHANGE WITH FAMILIES AND REFERRAL AGENCIES

Once the assessment data have been evaluated by the physical or occupational therapist, and a determination of the extent of sensory or movement problems have been made, an intervention plan is developed and communicated to parents and teachers. This is an important step because the effectiveness of the intervention is related to the effectiveness of the initial communication.

PARENT SUPPORT AND EDUCATION

In their communication with families, physical and occupational therapists try to give very clear factual information about the child's sensory and motor functioning, but they also try to convey a supportive and hopeful attitude that will give family members the incentive to be engaged actively in assisting their child to improve developmental and functional skills. Finding the right balance between encouraging the family and enlisting their efforts without giving false expectations can be difficult to achieve, but it is essential if the development of the child is to be facilitated. If a severe problem that threatens the child's health has been identified at birth, the therapist's role is often to give clear information about the clinical reasons for the feeding, respiratory, or muscle problem; to outline some immediate practical steps that are being taken to address the problem; and to work with the parents on techniques that will help them cope with the problem when the child is discharged from the hospital.

When the child is not referred to the therapist until a later age, the therapist usually starts with a discussion of the parents' concerns, wants, and needs regarding the child. For example, the therapist may discuss the parents' perceptions of the reason for the referral, their understanding of the problem, and their motivation to work with the therapist to benefit the child. Parental information is very helpful in making the clinical assessment. It is essential that the therapist be a good listener, hearing not only the words of the parents but also their emotional tone.

Families may vary a great deal in their responses to the needs of a child with motor or sensory problems. Some appear very anxious and express great concern, others do not show much anxiety or express their concern. Some seem to be very conscious of the potential delays these problems may cause, others seem almost unaware that problems exist. Some parents may wish to expend a lot of energy observing, stimulating, and working with their child in structured sensory or motor activities, others may prefer an intervention focused primarily at the early intervention program. There may be many other stresses in the family situation that leave parents and other family members little energy to cope with the child's disabilities. The therapist tries to develop a plan that will get the most positive results with the least stress to families.

One technique that may be used by therapists is to give the parents some things to observe as they are caring for the child. For example, they may be asked to note whether the child's head always turns to the right when being fed or diapered. If the parents can observe the problem that exists, then the therapist and parent can identify helpful actions to carry out in the home setting. In deciding which types of parental involvement may be appropriate, the therapist considers how that level of parental involvement could affect the family system as a whole.

Families need to have the option of not doing any structured intervention themselves. Their role is often one of maintaining the consistent methods demonstrated or suggested by the therapist as they engage in routine care and play activities with their child in the home. Most families are eager to help their child, and a low-key approach that gives suggestions in a relaxed way ("Let's see how that works") is usually helpful. It is best to keep professional jargon out of the conversation with parents. Parenting is a unique role that has its own set of activities and responsibilities, and it is most important that the therapist build on family strengths in determining how parents can be best involved in intervention activities. Respect for the values of families from diverse cultural backgrounds is also essential in planning appropriate interventions.

Within the early intervention program setting, the family can gain support from observing the therapist's involvement with their child and can thus learn appropriate models of interaction to use at home. Therapists usually try to communicate to parents the reasons why they are engaging their child in certain procedures. Sometimes, in the presence of the "experts" parents may feel inadequate. The therapist's support of the parents' confidence in their abilities to provide experiences at home that will enhance the experiences gained by the child in the early intervention setting is essential. It is especially important in working with families of young children who have severe sensory or motor disabilities that the family members are truly part of the early intervention team, whether or not they are actively engaged in structured activities with their child.

SUGGESTING INTERVENTIONS

In the hospital, intervention techniques may be suggested to improve the infant's ability to be fed effectively by the parent; in the home, plans for helping the parent learn effective stimulation methods for a visually impaired child may be initiated; and in the early intervention program, teachers may be taught to position the child so that fine motor activities can be provided successfully.

Recent studies in inclusion programs indicate that motor development can be enhanced by neuro-behavioral intervention targeted on specific motor skills (e.g., reach and grasp, head control) that can then be generalized to other settings (Horn & Jones, 1992; Martin, Davis, & Brady, 1992). The presence of peers seems to enhance social responses and motivate children with severe physical disabilities to increase motor responses.

The therapists may suggest adaptive devices to enhance independent movement and prescribe exercises to improve muscle tone or coordination and variety of movement. They may also provide techniques for mobilization (i.e., manipulation of joints), neuromuscular re-education, and modification of tone, and for improving daily living skills (e.g., dressing methods, chairs for feeding, bath seats, appropriate food textures) and for assisting developmental skill areas (e.g., rolling, sitting). Often, these interventions involve working closely with family members. Development can be greatly enhanced by consistent, systematic, and responsive parental interactions and by parental involvement in the design of a safe home environment in which the child can function as independently as possible. The therapist must present parents with a clear and integrated program of interaction suggestions.

REPORTING TO PROFESSIONALS

Physical and occupational therapists usually work very closely with hospitals, educational facilities, and agencies because their expertise is often required. Their reporting methods vary from written reports giving medical and technical information to informal oral reports given directly to physicians, agency personnel, or other interventionists. Thus, their reporting methods are flexible, depending on the level of specificity and technical information desired. Although precise terminology is useful, it is important to determine what level of technical detail is appropriate and to avoid a reporting manner that is confusing or incomprehensible to those not familiar with the terminology of the field.

USEFULNESS OF A TRANSDISCIPLINARY MODEL

For physical and occupational therapists, the transdisciplinary team model can provide a number of advantages that may enhance their services for children and families. Foremost among them are the flexibility of the team approach and the ongoing collegial interaction that can enrich the overall assessment and intervention process. For example, in a team assessment, the therapist may fill the role of team coordinator when the child's primary problems are of a sensory or motor nature. Also, the data collected by early childhood special educators, psychologists, and other team members from their normative or criterion referenced instruments usually contain a good sample of motor and sensory behaviors; this information may be useful to the physical and occupational therapists in conjunction with their clinical assessments. An advantage of an arena assessment in which the parent participates is that parent–child interactions may be observed by the therapists. Knowledge of these interactions may assist the therapists in planning home activities for the child.

In non-team assessment approaches, members of each discipline may not be able to gain knowledge of the other professionals' goals, perspectives, skills, or individual styles. In ongoing team approaches, therapists are able to be knowledgable about the skills of members of other disciplines; this knowledge may be useful in enabling therapists to decide which aspects of their intervention plan can be supported through "role release" of intervention techniques to teachers and other team members. For example, the therapists and the early childhood special educator can work closely together to maintain motor coordination and sensory integration intervention opportunities within the regular program day. This sharing of knowledge about each others' disciplines and collaboration in intervention is present in many interdisciplinary and transdisciplinary team approaches. Therefore, some therapists question whether the team approach needs to be a transdisciplinary one in order to accomplish these goals.

In order for teams to work well, however, time must be spent in coordinating and communicating. Mutual respect and understanding the technical language of each profession does not occur immediately. Thus, the stability of the team over time is very important. Stable, integrated teams are often seen in special projects housed in hospital, school, or private practice settings, where a close working relationship between the project team members is facilitated over time. In such cases, the discipline barriers between the occupational, physical, and speech therapists' roles may be broken down as they work together with children who have feeding and other basic survival problems. Some educationally based early intervention teams are beginning to develop these close working relationships and, as team members continue to work together, the integrative team approach should be enhanced.

There are a number of problems that concern therapists who participate in transdisciplinary team models. One problem is that the team approach requires a lot of time, but it is often not possible to bill the time spent in team interaction rather than direct therapeutic service. Another problem is that the membership of a team is not always stable and, if stability is lacking or some members of the team are less committed to attending and participating, the team effort can be impaired. A third problem is that administrative structures sometimes undermine team approaches, especially if administrative rules do not allow time for team meetings or count that time as part of the staffs' paid duties. A fourth problem is that, because they fulfill a specialist's role, these therapists may have to serve on numerous assessment teams and, therefore, they may not become well integrated into any of the teams. Finally, it is often difficult to blend varied philosophies and personalities and to get the right mix of role sharing. If there is too much overlap, it may become hard to distinguish the distinct disciplines of team members.

Therapists also have differing opinions about the value of arena assessments. Although this type of assessment may enable the therapist to observe the child's sensory and motor capabilities in action in a somewhat natural setting as various tasks or play activities are presented to the child, in actual practice, separate one-on-one assessments must usually still be conducted by the physical and occupational therapists. For example, in an arena assessment the occupational therapist may need to prompt the core assessor to be sure that all tasks related to block stacking are presented. Usually there will be gaps in the assessment tasks that have to be filled in later if the therapist is not the one presenting the tasks in the arena assessment. Because of state and professional requirements for use of standardized methods, many therapists do not believe that they can collect valid data simply by observing other team members' assessment of the child. Another concern expressed by some therapists is that observation by so many professionals at one time may be intrusive and result in poor child performance, especially for children with severe motor or sensory problems.

As there is more and more recognition of the importance of assessing all aspects of the child in context, the usefulness of team approaches may be more clearly delineated. Physical and occupational therapists already see their professional roles connected to those of other disciplines and they usually are supportive of team approaches. However, they generally see more collaborative benefits in intervention teaming rather than in assessment teaming.

POLICY ISSUES

In addition to the policy issues related to local administrative structures that may hamper team assessment practices, occupational and physical therapists are concerned with policies concerning the broad societal policy issue of long-term commitment to providing support for sensory and motor impaired children. National, state, and local governmental policy statements indicate that persons with these types of disabilities are priority concerns; however, neither the funding levels nor the support structures are in place to give families the kind of long-term supportive assistance they need for their children. For example, some children with severe sensory or motor impairments need closely monitored, long-term, 24-hour care; others need intensive and consistent therapeutic services; still others could function relatively independently if their families had the financial means to provide appropriate adaptive equipment and educational resources. The need for respite care and social–emotional support is also very great. One of the major tasks in coordinating services for children whose families do not have financial resources to foster optimal development is to find community and other resources to meet these needs.

Although progress is being made, there is still a narrow range of options available to families who do not have sufficient financial means to provide for their children's developmental progress and who do not qualify for public assistance. A wider range of options should be available for these families. For example, parents who must work could be given the option of staying home with pay to care for their child or to have care while they are working; a governmental fund could be made available to pay for adaptive equipment needs of children whose assessment results indicate that they require such equipment; and applied research to develop and improve methods of communication for children with sensory or motor problems could be made a funding priority.

Another policy concern related to professional practice is that of clarifying and, if necessary, reconciling the professional standards of the discipline with team approaches to assessment. For example, in some states (e.g., Ohio), physical therapists can do assessments only on referral of physicians or other approved medical personnel. Therefore, they cannot participate as a team member in an initial screening assessment that is not supervised by medical personnel. This rule is not in practice in all states and even in Ohio it applies only to physical, not to occupational, therapists.

The American Physical Therapy Association (APTA) Task Force on Early Intervention, Section on Pediatrics, has outlined competencies for physical therapists who are working in early intervention (APTA, 1991). This document indicates that physical therapists can assist in team assessment, program development, and implementation of IFSPs, and can also serve as case managers or service coordinators. The guidelines support the role of physical therapists in collaborating with the family and other team members in providing coordinated services to infants and toddlers.

According to the occupational and physical therapy guidelines in most states, however, only licensed professionals can conduct motor and sensory assessment procedures and make intervention recommendations (e.g., Ohio Revised Code, 4755.01, 4755.40). That is, they cannot participate in "delegation of tasks to unlicensed persons." If these professionals must meet such standards, they will have to designate clearly how much "role release," a feature of transdisciplinary team practice, is appropriate in an assessment situation. This problem is not unique to these professional disciplines, but applies to all of the licensed or certified specialist groups (i.e., psychologists, speech pathologists, audiologists, and social workers) who are being asked to be part of early intervention transdisciplinary teams.

SUMMARY

Although physical therapists and occupational therapists each have specific and complex areas of expertise, they often work collaboratively and share many similar assumptions regarding assessment and therapeutic practice. They use clinical judgment and standardized measures to assess young children's motor and sensory developmental levels and they are very concerned about the quality of movement processes. Because these therapists often work in conjunction with hospital or pediatric settings, their collaboration with medical personnel is usually great. However, they also have close interaction with the families of children with physical, motor, and sensory problems. Their involvement on early intervention teams in educational settings provides an important perspective. However, there are also some constraints on the roles they can take in team assessment and intervention practice.

QUESTIONS FOR DISCUSSION

1. On what aspects of development would a physical therapist be most likely to focus an assessment for an infant with suspected cerebral palsy? How would that compare with what an occupational therapist might observe in the same child?
2. What would a physical therapist suggest for family and professional team interventions for a toddler who has gross motor delays and sensory processing disorganization? How would that compare with what an occupational therapist might suggest?

PROBLEMS OF PRACTICE

Observe a diagnostic assessment being carried out by a team that includes a physical and an occupational therapist. Note what instruments and clinical procedures each of them uses in evaluating the young child's development. After the assessment is complete, ask them to explain why they used the specific methods observed, especially in relation to the particular child's potential problems. Sit in on the team meeting in which the therapists express their views and tie their conclusions to the information you collected about the assessment practices they followed.

SUGGESTED READINGS

Chandler, L. S. (1990). Neuromotor assessment. In E. D. Gibbs & D. M. Teti (Eds.), *Interdisciplinary assessment of infants* (pp. 45–62). Baltimore: Paul H. Brookes.

Smith, P. D. (1989). Assessing motor skills. In D. B. Bailey & M. Wolery (Eds.), *Assessing infants and preschoolers with handicaps* (pp. 301–338). New York: Merrill.

DIALOGUE

INITIAL ASSESSMENT AND IFSP FOR DOLLY

GENDER, AGE, ETHNIC ORIGIN OF CHILD: Female, 10 months, Euro-American.

OCCASION OR PURPOSE OF DIALOGUE: Initial evaluation of Dolly; to develop the first IFSP. No early intervention program has yet been recommended.

TEAM MEMBERS: A pediatrician, social worker, physical therapist, occupational therapist, psychologist, early intervention specialist, the child's mother, and the maternal grandparents.

SETTING: A hospital-affiliated clinical center for developmental disabilities.

OVERVIEW OF THE CASE

RISK CONDITIONS

Dolly was born 5 weeks prematurely, weighing 3 pounds, 5 ounces at birth. Neonatal urine tested positive for cocaine and alcohol. A diagnosis of Fetal Alcohol Syndrome (FAS) was made by the medical staff. Dolly required full ventilator assistance during her first 3 weeks of life, but she was weaned to no assistance by her 6th week of life. She required oxygen during sleep for an additional 3 months. She had Respiratory Distress Syndrome (RDS) as a result of the premature development of her lungs. Dolly had difficulty sucking and keeping food down while in the Neonatal Intensive Care Unit (NICU), thus making her weight gain very poor. She was hospitalized until she was 9 weeks, having reached 5 pounds, 5 ounces in weight by that time.

REASON FOR REFERRAL

Because of the diagnoses of RDS and FAS, Children's Services was contacted by the hospital staff. Based on their social worker's evaluation of the case, the decision was made to place Dolly in the grandparents' home when she was released from the hospital at 9 weeks. Dolly was enrolled in the hospital-based tracking program by the grandparents. Monitoring of her developmental progress by hospital clinic staff and public health nurse home visitations was recommended. Since that time, the family has participated in the tracking program services only sporadically. For example, Dolly has only recently had her first health check-up and received the first of her immunizations at the well-child clinic associated with the hospital. Referral for an assessment of developmental delay was based on the clinic's report of Dolly's continuing poor development and low weight gain. At the time of her discharge from the hospital, Dolly's mother was enrolled in drug abuse counseling services. Although the mother attended the prescribed counseling sessions for 6 months, her attendance was sporadic after the first 2 months and she dropped out completely a month ago. She was living with friends until that time, but has since returned to her parents' home. Thus, she is now participating in Dolly's care.

BACKGROUND INFORMATION

Dolly's mother is an unmarried parent, aged 18 at the time of Dolly's birth. She is an admitted alcoholic who acknowledged drinking routinely on a daily basis and using cocaine 2 or 3 times a week during her pregnancy. She states that she was unaware that this would be harmful to her unborn child. She does agree that her nutritional intake was probably poor during the pregnancy, although she does not really remember what she ate. Until she was 7 months pregnant, she was able to hide the pregnancy from her parents by wearing loose-fitting clothes and reducing her weight by eating very little. At 7 months, her parents suspected the pregnancy and demanded she see a doctor and that is when she began prenatal care. Although the parents urged her to give up the baby for adoption (she wanted to keep the baby), they agreed to have Dolly placed with them until such time as Dolly's mother was drug-free and capable of caring for Dolly.

FAMILY STRENGTHS AND NEEDS

The mother's parents work outside the home and provide a relatively stable but low-income environment. They have never been dependent on welfare. The grandparents are concerned about Dolly's development and are willing to provide support and care until their daughter is able to function on her own. They state that they are very concerned about their daughter's drug dependency and support her efforts to overcome it. However, the grandfather has a history of alcohol abuse, which is presently under control through his participation in Alcoholics Anonymous. The child's mother asserts that she would like to be a good mother for Dolly and would like to conquer her dependency on alcohol. She reports that she no longer uses cocaine.

Family needs are primarily related to the daughter's inability, so far, to discontinue her alcohol-dependent behavior. Her parents report that she has been involved with the "wrong sort of kids," which resulted in her dropping out of high school in her senior year. They feel frustrated in their attempts to help her. She has not returned to school and does not have a General Equivalency Diploma (GED). Thus, the family needs now focus on the child's mother being helped to overcome her alcohol dependency and gain the ability to go back to school or to work and on gaining early intervention services that will assist Dolly's development.

SOURCES OF ASSESSMENT INFORMATION

Information from a series of medical tests (including an MRI) are available, along with parental and grandparental interview data obtained during the initial disposition of the case. Assessment measures used by the present team include home observation, physical manipulation tests and clinical observations of Dolly's natural movements, family interview, the Bayley Scales of Infant Development, the Receptive–Expressive Emergent Language Scale (REEL), and the Developmental Profile II.

Social–Emotional Development

Dolly was very irritable at birth and remains irritable and extremely sensitive to new stimuli, sleeping erratically and having difficulty comforting herself or being comforted. This behavior has resulted in some disruption of the typical relationship of child and caregivers, particularly because the family must face this irritability day and night. Dolly still cries often, without reasons that are discernible to the caregivers, although she is beginning to self-quiet and to quiet when picked up. She regarded faces at 2½ months and smiled spontaneously before 6 months. Although her present social play periods are short, Dolly is beginning to smile and respond to turn-taking, even laughing during these episodes, which are conducted primarily by the grandmother. Social–emotional assessment measures, adjusted for prematurity, indicate that Dolly is approximately 3 months delayed overall, with some out-of-sequence and aberrant behaviors. For example, even at 10 months she seems unusually fearful and timid, extremely sensitive to stimulation, and noninitiating of activity. Her behaviors in interaction with mother and grandparents (e.g., her preferences for comforting) indicate that her attachment to the grandmother is more secure than to the mother, which is not surprising since the mother has not been living in the home until recently. The mother is presently the caregiver when the grandparents are at work. Dolly's self-help skills and social functioning are at the 5- to 6-month level on the Developmental Profile.

Physical–Motor and Sensory–Perceptual Development.

Dolly is still very small for her gestational age; she is in the lowest quadrant of weight for her size and age. Her physical coordination is also delayed. She can pick up her head while prone and immediately rolls over on her back by extending her head. She does not roll from her back to stomach or to either side. In supported sitting, Dolly is beginning to gain head control and can hold her head for 15 to 30 seconds to look at a face or object. She still has newborn reflexes, including the grasp, rooting, and asymmetrical tonic neck reflexes. She moves her hands away from any tactile stimulation and keeps hands fisted. She cannot yet voluntarily hold an object in either hand. Coordination of respiratory functioning and oral functioning is poor, causing difficulties in feeding. Her physical developmental age on the Developmental Profile was 2 to 3 months. Her hearing and vision appear to be within normal limits, although neither has been tested by specialists. On the Bayley Motor Scale, Dolly's Psychomotor Development Index Score, adjusted for prematurity, was below 50 and her Behavior Rating for Motor Quality was not optimal.

Cognitive–Language Development

Dolly reacts by looking for sources of sound and shows interest in the various sounds of objects. She moves her arm when a rattle is placed in her hand. She watches people move across the room and stares at the television for short periods. However, if the volume on the television is high, she cries. The grandparents report that there are differences in her cries and that they can tell if she is hungry, tired, or frustrated. She also is beginning to vocalize her wish to continue social play. However, she gives no other indications of communicative intent. According to the Developmental Profile II, she is functioning at the newborn (0- to 6-month) level on both the academic and the communication scales. Her Bayley Mental Development Index Score, adjusted for prematurity, is 56. Her raw score is 53, which is congruent approximately with a 6-month level of development, adjusted for prematurity. Her Behavior Rating on both orientation–engagement and emotional–regulation is non-optimal. On the REEL, Dolly's receptive language was at the 4- to 5-month level, her expressive language at the 2- to 3-month level, adjusted for prematurity.

THE TEAM DIALOGUE

This is an initial evaluation to determine eligibility for services and thus most team members had not observed the child until they conducted this assessment. The social worker has been working with the family as case manager. The pediatrician from the hospital clinic, who is familiar with Dolly's medical history, is the team leader for the evaluation.

PEDIATRICIAN: As background, let me review the initial medical report on Dolly. Her birth was 5 weeks premature and she was under 3½ pounds in weight. Based on neonatal testing, a diagnosis of Fetal Alcohol Syndrome was made. Her MRI supports this diagnosis, showing asymmetrical brain tissue development and a small brain size. She has decreased brain matter mostly throughout the cortex and cerebellum. Her ventricles are enlarged due to decreased brain matter, not hydrocephalus. (Ventricles are fluid-filled cavities inside the brain where cerebral–spinal fluid is produced.) After the initial alcohol and cocaine withdrawal, Dolly progressed relatively well. She is completely off supplemental oxygen and, although her RDS continues to cause increased secretions in her lungs, she seems to be handling them all right on her own. She no longer requires suctioning, and all other medical tests are within normal limits. However, Dolly has a fairly pronounced developmental delay according to our observations. I strongly recommend that an early intervention program be provided for Dolly. (To mother and grandparents) The early interventionist is trained in enhancing development in young children with delays and I understand the county has a free program that would enable the early interventionist to come to your home on a weekly basis.

GRANDPARENTS: That sounds good. We could certainly use some help. (To daughter) What do you think, Mira?

MOTHER: Do they let you know when they're coming or do they just drop in?

EARLY INTERVENTIONIST: We schedule a regular time for our visit and we try to bring toys and do play activities that will help Dolly develop her skills.

MOTHER: I guess that it would be okay. We could use some ideas to help her be a good baby. She really is hard to take sometimes.

PEDIATRICIAN: Can the team members give us some information about Dolly's present developmental condition?

PHYSICAL THERAPIST: Based on my initial assessment, I'd say Dolly has generalized hypertonia (exceptionally high tension in muscles) throughout her body. She exhibits all her newborn reflexes, which makes purposeful movement difficult. She has limited extensibility (range of motion), and her posture is too tightly flexed and asymmetrical. (To pediatrician) There are a number of methods that could be recommended for dealing with Dolly's hypertonia. What do you think about muscle relaxants to help reduce some of this tone?

PEDIATRICIAN: I don't think so. I prefer not to medicate her with any muscle relaxants because it might interfere with her breathing function. I would rather wait until her RDS improved.

PHYSICAL THERAPIST: I understand. The best plan would be to have her enroll in the hospital clinic program so that the treatment methods can be carefully chosen and closely monitored. I recommend that Dolly get physical therapy on a regular weekly basis at the clinic. (To grandparents) How have you been dealing with Dolly's movement difficulties until now? Have you observed that she does better when you hold her in certain ways?

GRANDMOTHER: She's hard to hold at all because she is so tense. That's part of the reason it's hard to comfort her.

PHYSICAL THERAPIST: One advantage of having her in the physical therapy program is that you will be able to learn some positioning techniques that will help break up Dolly's reflexive movements and thus make her easier to handle. The therapist will also give you ideas to use at home that will help Dolly have a greater range of motion so she can play better. The physician and therapist may also recommend some equipment that will help you continue the therapy methods of the hospital clinic at home.

GRANDMOTHER: What equipment will we need?

PHYSICAL THERAPIST: The therapists will decide that after Dolly begins the program. We can then order the prescribed equipment through our OT/PT department here at the hospital.

SOCIAL WORKER: (To grandparents) Can you drive her to therapy? Do you have health insurance to pay for it?

GRANDMOTHER: I could probably drive her there if the appointments could be in late afternoon. We have insurance, but Mira isn't covered under our policy. We just finished paying for her delivery bill. We can't afford to pay for Dolly's medical expenses. They are over 200,000 dollars already. We can never pay that much. We'll never make that kind of money in our lifetime.

SOCIAL WORKER: We're trying to get a medical card for Dolly. The application has been submitted. We're also working with the hospital to see if we can get some of Dolly's bills reduced. There are several agencies that help out in situations like this.

GRANDFATHER: We've never accepted charity in our lives, but I guess we'll have to because we have no other way of paying this debt.

PEDIATRICIAN: What about Dolly's development in other areas?

OCCUPATIONAL THERAPIST: I'm concerned about Dolly's sensitivity to touch.

Her hands seem especially sensitive. I would like to see her receive weekly OT sessions to address this tactile sensitivity. Also, she is having some problems with oral functioning, especially in coordinating her feeding and breathing movements. She needs to improve her poor feeding skills. She seems to be doing okay on the bottle, but it is time to move onto stage one baby food and I know she has been having difficulty with this. I recommend that Dolly be evaluated by the hospital's feeding team to assess her feeding capabilities. (To grandparents) They will be able to give you suggestions to help her learn these skills.

GRANDFATHER: A whole team just to work on her eating? Will that cost more?

SOCIAL WORKER: Yes, but it could be included in the services that are paid for by Medicare.

PEDIATRICIAN: How are Dolly's communication and skill learning progressing?

PSYCHOLOGIST: Her main way of communicating is still through crying, but she is beginning to vocalize when she is being played with. Her cognitive development is progressing very slowly. She can show visual preferences, follow moving objects, and play with a rattle, but she isn't yet reaching for toys or looking for fallen objects. Her skills seem to be scattered. For example, she does smile when she sees her image in a mirror and is beginning to imitate sounds. (To family) I think that the early interventionist could show you some ways to play with her that would help her gain more language skills.

EARLY INTERVENTIONIST: (To family) We could have that be one of our first objectives. I can help you learn how to do that when I visit. (To grandparents) I understand that your daughter is now living with you and Dolly. How is that going?

GRANDFATHER: Not too well. Mira won't take much responsibility for Dolly. She always wants to be with her friends. She thinks life is one big party.

MOTHER: I do not! I've been taking care of Dolly all day when you're not home. I need to get out sometimes in the evening. I can't stand to be cooped up all the time. I really need my own apartment. I can't stay with my friends and I don't want to stay with my parents. If I had my own apartment, I could take care of Dolly and be a better mother. I'd really like to have my own apartment.

EARLY INTERVENTIONIST: Besides having your own apartment, what other kind of help do you need to be a better mother?

GRANDPARENTS: She needs to stop drinking! (They comment simultaneously with mother's next comment.)

MOTHER: I don't know.

SOCIAL WORKER: (To mother) Do you think your drinking problem is getting in the way of your caring for Dolly?

MOTHER: I don't really think it's much of a problem now. I only drink when I go out with my friends. Dad won't allow booze in the house.

SOCIAL WORKER: (To mother) Perhaps you should think about getting rid of your alcohol dependency problem for good. I can investigate a treatment program for you. Certainly you would need to conquer your drug problem before you could get an apartment of your own and be able to have Dolly with you. There are residential programs that have you stay for the treatment period and ones that you just go to on a day-to-day basis. Would you prefer to have an outpatient program or to be in a residential unit?

MOTHER: If I tried to do it, I'd need to get away. My friends really enjoy drinking so when I'm with them I want to do it. The counseling I had just didn't cut it. Especially because I was staying with my friends then. But, I don't know if I want to be put in such a place. It sounds like a jail.

PEDIATRICIAN: I understand there is a new residential treatment center that incorporates both the drug treatment program and classes toward a GED. It's about 45 minutes from the hospital and is really a pleasant environment. If you do well there, I think they might even let you have your baby with you later on. What do you think of that?

MOTHER: Maybe they won't have room for me. I don't know yet if I want to try it. I know I do want to get my own place, though.

SOCIAL WORKER: (To grandparents) If Mira were accepted into this program, would you be able to find care for Dolly during the day and to take care of her yourself at night?

GRANDMOTHER: We could try. We had a sitter part of the time and took Dolly to our other daughter's house the rest of the time when Mira wasn't living at home. I guess we can do that again. We'll do just about anything to see that Mira gets the help she needs. We could use some suggestions for somebody to take care of the baby though. We can't keep asking Joan (other daughter) to do it.

EARLY INTERVENTIONIST: I think I could give you some ideas about finding other caregivers. We usually have that type of information available at our office.

SOCIAL WORKER: She may also qualify for some home nursing care. I'll check into that, too.

PEDIATRICIAN: Well, I think we have made some progress here. It seems we have identified a number of recommendations and objectives and are ready to do the IFSP.

RECOMMENDATIONS

Dolly will be enrolled in an early intervention home visitor program, and activities related to furthering her cognitive, language, motor, and social development will be initiated by the early interventionist. The medical–financial resources will be investigated, and a medical card application will be initiated. Once the card has been obtained, Dolly will begin weekly OT and PT treatment, the hospital feeding team will evaluate her feeding skills, and the therapy equipment needed for the home will be ordered when it is prescribed. The social worker will give Dolly's mother more information about the residential drug treatment program and, if she decides to enter it, will assist her in enrolling. If the mother's drug dependency problem is overcome, planning for eventual placement of Dolly with her mother and the movement of her mother to an apartment will begin. Dolly's developmental progress will be monitored by the early intervention program in which she is enrolled.

QUESTIONS FOR DISCUSSION

1. What are the biological risk factors and the environmental risk factors in this case? What predictions can be made about the child's long-term development if the environmental risk factors continue to be evident and if the recommended PT and OT therapy cannot be obtained?
2. How did the presence of the family members add to the knowledge-base needed to make effective recommendations?
3. What is the likelihood that the family understood the professional's comments on the child's developmental status? Should these have been made clearer or is it not necessary for the family to understand all the details? Did the OT and PT give the right amount of information for the family to absorb at the present time?
4. What are the delivery system factors that must fall into place in order for the team recommendations to be carried out? How may the mother's motivational and the family's interpersonal problems affect the success of the plan?
5. How can the complexity of problems this family faces be addressed in the long term? Are broader interventions needed than those that can be met through early intervention services? If so, what are they?

chapter 6

Doris Bergen
Kathleen Hutchinson
Elizabeth Johnston

SPEECH PATHOLOGY AND AUDIOLOGY ASSESSMENT PERSPECTIVES

Language delay is a commonly identified problem among at-risk young children. However, hearing loss often remains unidentified because poor language production or comprehension and auditory inattention problems may be attributed to other established, biological, or environmental risk conditions. For example, disturbing reports persist of typically intelligent, hearing-impaired persons found after years of placement in programs for the mentally impaired .

Speech pathologists and audiologists are usually part of a team of early intervention specialists who deal with speech and hearing-impaired children. These professionals need knowledge of normal and disordered speech and hearing abilities and a wide range of clinical experiences before being permitted to practice. Standards for educational and professional practice have been established by the American Speech–Language and Hearing Association (ASHA). ASHA recommends, and most states maintain, that speech pathologists and audiologists should obtain an undergraduate degree in both disciplines and an advanced degree at the master's or doctoral level. Students are also required to obtain several hundred hours of practice in each specialty to receive ASHA certification and state licensure.

UNDERLYING ASSUMPTIONS

There are four major assumptions on which assessment and intervention in the disciplines of speech therapy and audiology are based. First, the recognition that normal hearing plays a major role in the development of language production and comprehension and that distortions or loss of hearing can result in numerous types of developmental delay. One of the etiologies that accounts for most language disorders in young children is hearing-impairment based. There are two primary types of childhood hearing impairment:

1. *Pervasive middle-ear syndrome* is a chronic infection that can render the child hearing-impaired during the first few years of life, often without the family recognizing the problem. Even if it results in no long-term hearing loss, the child will have missed cognitive information, language models, and family interaction opportunities that may result in language delay and delays in general cognition, social skills, and pragmatic functioning.

2. *Sensorineural hearing impairment* prevents the child from receiving all or most of the language input available to children with normal hearing. These children must be diagnosed as early as possible so that hearing augmentation can be provided, if appropriate.

There are a number of factors influencing how detrimental the effects of hearing loss will be, such as age of onset, severity of the loss, range of sound frequencies lost, and presence or absence of other disabilities. Hearing impairment is a broad classification from mild to profound. The greater the hearing loss, the more difficult it will be for the child to acquire vocally produced language. While children with mild losses are only likely to be language delayed, those with severe and profound losses may fail to acquire language without hearing amplification and may display disorders of articulation, voice, and rhythm in their speech. Figure 6.1 describes the categories of sound loss and the likely effects on language and cognition.

Children who acquire language before the onset of a hearing loss have a better prognosis than those who experience the loss earlier. The infant or toddler who receives early assessment and intervention will fare better because of early use of visual, manual, and auditory enhancements. Although reduced hearing for speech sounds and delayed expressive language skills are clearly the most obvious results of hearing loss, they may also lead to other communicative and cognitive impairments. The cognitive potential of hearing-impaired children is no different from that of normally hearing peers; however, they score less well on tasks requiring rule learning, logical operations, and sequential memory. Most studies show no differences on tasks requiring only visual skills (Holm & Kunze, 1969). While thinking processes may be affected by language learning problems, often these children's thinking may be more limited by their being given less exposure to the stimulating experiences from which most children learn.

A second assumption is that numerous other variables besides hearing impairment can influence language acquisition and development. In

FIGURE 6.1
CATEGORIES OF SOUND LOSS AND EFFECTS ON LANGUAGE AND COGNITION

Mild Hearing Loss (15–30 dB HTL)
- Vowel sounds are clear, except for voiceless consonants such as "s" (*lost* may be heard as *loss*).
- Hearing of short unstressed words and less intense speech sounds are inconsistently perceived.

Moderate Hearing Loss (30–50 dB HTL)
- Most speech sounds at conversational levels are lost, but with amplification can be heard.
- Sounds of low energy and high frequency, such as fricatives, may be distorted or missing (*stroke* may be heard as *soak*).
- Short unstressed words are not heard.
- Difficulty learning abstract concepts, multiple word meanings, and development of object classes.

Severe Hearing Loss (55–70 dB HTL)
- Only loud environmental sounds and intense speech at close range can be heard.
- Language does not develop without amplification.
- Vowel sounds and consonant group differences can be heard with amplification.
- Development of grammar rules and abstract meanings is delayed or missing.

Profound Hearing Loss (75–90 dB HTL)
- Not even intense speech sound can be heard without amplification.
- Hearing does not have a major role in language acquisition, without amplification.

working with young children who are having problems in effective communication, the clinician or team of professionals must consider a wide variety of other variables, some of which are more specific to certain types of disabilities or at-risk conditions, and must analyze the interactions between these variables. They include the following:

1. *Cognitive–developmental delay* is usually accompanied by language delay. It appears that language can develop no faster than the cognition that supports it.

2. *Physiological–neurological problems,* such as cleft palate, specific developmental childhood aphasia or apraxia, or pervasive communication disorder (i.e., autism) affects language acquisition in ways that are

specific to the disability. For neurologically impaired children, language problems are magnified by inability to organize and access cognitive processes needed for effective communication.

3. *Social–emotional problems* may be the basis for many language disorders. Social–emotional problems may make children less motivated to use language and less able to access communication systems. Their language is likely to have more characteristics of language deviance than delay.

4. *Environmental conditions* may also affect language acquisition. For example, family communication patterns may provide limited language stimulation, and various cultural groups may give models of different or mixed linguistic systems. Conditions of abuse or neglect are often accompanied by delays in language acquisition, perhaps because the caregiver–child interaction is disrupted. Although it is often difficult to specify the relationship between language delay and environmental risk, language delays are commonly reported in these children.

A very important third assumption for assessment and intervention is that, because the development of language follows a universal pattern and sequence, language acquisition in young children who are at risk can be described, evaluated in relation to these universals, and assisted through planned intervention strategies.

Language is composed of a set of arbitrary symbols, systematic in nature and mutually agreed on by a speech community as its means of transmitting experience. Study of language acquisition has identified the presence of a number of language universals—elements so basic that they must be present for a language to exist (Berko-Gleason, 1985). Cultural and language backgrounds determine the language children acquire. If they have learned the sound (phonemic) system, the set of structural rules (syntax and morphology), the vocabulary and its meaning relationships (semantics), and the conventions of speech (pragmatics) of their language family, they can communicate effectively in that society. This is a difficult task, but very young children seem well attuned to it and appear to accomplish it effortlessly.

Children learn language primarily through interaction with caregivers, who typically use an interaction pattern called "caregiver talk" or "motherese" (Nelson, 1993; Nelson, 1985; Owens, 1988). This interactive process provides infants with important early interpersonal experiences, and teaches social communication rules (pragmatics), such as vocal and verbal turn-taking, eye contact, and joint reference. It also teaches how to interpret words in meaningful relationships (semantics), how to use accepted word order (syntax), the use of word affixes (morphology), and the sounds used in a particular language (phonemics).

Two types of problem occur when language acquisition is not proceeding normally: delay and deviance. Language delay occurs when aspects of language are developing in normal order, but are significantly later than the norm. For example, a child with cognitive delay may have the language patterns of a younger child. Language deviance is seen when a profile has some aspects very delayed and some average or advanced, thus producing a disordered effect. For example, a child with developmental childhood aphasia may have language that is disorganized and expressed in a way that cannot be understood. It is important to recognize that language delay can become language deviance when specific areas remain delayed while others advance. Communication problems may generate social and emotional problems that complicate the original language problem.

A fourth assumption on which intervention is based is that the development of early language is vital to later school success. Young children who have no oral language capability are at risk for developmental delay in academic content learning. Bess and McConnell (1981) indicate that if the onset of hearing loss occurs after oral language has been achieved, children are more successful in inclusion programs. However, they also found that factors of speech intelligibility and high socioeconomic status were associated with great inclusion success. There is predictive evidence of relationships between language problems in the 3- to 5-year range and problems in later reading and writing (Cooper & Griffith, 1978; Lahey, 1988). Because success in school is cumulative, it is axiomatic that language problems contribute to problems in reading, writing, and other academic areas. Moreover, lack of ability to use pragmatic rules affects general communicative competence and social skills. Thus, improving language skills is an important goal in the education of hearing-impaired children (Scholdroth, 1988).

METHODS OF ASSESSMENT

The importance of hearing to language comprehension and production suggests that assessment of hearing should be conducted at an early age. By toddler age, speech and language evaluation should also be conducted, if delay in understanding or producing speech is evident.

AUDIOLOGIC EVALUATION

When parents observe a lack of response to sound in their infant or toddler, they usually are referred to an otologist, a physician who specializes in measurement and treatment of ear disease. The physician usually refers to an audiologist, who is trained to evaluate the degree of loss, speech components involved, and type of hearing impairment, for an audiologic evaluation.

In order to understand hearing assessment, some knowledge of the basic elements of the acoustic spectrum is essential. Hearing is the result of sound vibrations that reach the ear as air particles adjacent to the vibrating source become displaced and propel waves of disturbance in the surrounding air. These sound waves of pressure are distinguished by the number of vibrations each second (the *frequency*, measured in hertz [Hz]) and the force of the sound wave (the *intensity*, measured in decibels (dB)). Speech sounds have a combination of frequencies between 50 and 4,000 Hz and intensities between 30 and 80 dB. Examples of sound pressure levels are shown in Figure 6.2.

Most speech sounds are complex events made up of multiple frequencies with accompanying resonances. The intensity of a voice varies with the amount of air pressure exhaled and speech sound wave form varies with the speaker's individual characteristics, dialect, gender, stress pattern, and the context. Definitions of these speech elements are described in Figure 6.3.

The criterion used to define normal hearing has typically been the lowest decibel (dB) level perceptible to the listener across a range of frequencies, measured in hertz (Hz). This lowest sound intensity necessary to stimulate the auditory system is the Hearing Threshold Level (HTL) (Martin, 1986). Classification of normal hearing is traditionally based on the HTL average across different frequencies that comprise speech sounds. Hearing thresholds of 25 dB HTL or less, which is equivalent to a softly dripping water faucet, is the standard of normal hearing (American Academy of Otolaryngology [AAO], 1979). Hearing impairment is defined as a loss within the range of 15 to 85 dB HTL, and profound loss (deafness) is a loss greater than 90 dB HTL. However, recent evidence indi-

FIGURE 6.2
EXAMPLES OF DIFFERENT SOUND PRESSURE LEVELS

Decibel	Stimulus
20	Forest
30	Whisper
60	Conversation
80	Average street traffic

FIGURE 6.3
DEFINITIONS OF SPEECH ELEMENTS

Voiced sounds	Produced by flow of air from the lungs causing the vocal chords to vibrate ("u" as in cup). All vowels are voiced sounds.
Voiceless sounds	Produced by flow of air without vibration of the vocal chords ("p" as in pit; "f" as in fun).
Fricatives	Consonants produced by rapid changes in pressure constricted through air passage cavities. They come in voiced or unvoiced pairs ("z," "s").
Plosives	Consonants produced by brief obstructing of vocal track so sound comes in quick bursts. They are also paired ("p," "b").
Nasals	Voiced consonants in which sound passes through the nose *(man).*

cates that a loss at even the 20 dB HTL may interfere with normal language acquisition (Northern & Downs, 1984).

To assess basic hearing capabilities a specialized electronic instrument called an audiometer, which produces calibrated tones at several frequencies (Hz) at precise intensity levels (dB), is used. The frequency and intensity parameters and the audiometric threshold methods are defined by the American National Standards Institute (ANSI, 1969).

The most common audiometric test is done with *pure tones* from single, specified frequencies, presented separately using earphones (or for infants, in a sound field with loudspeakers) at several frequencies. Each ear is tested separately, and responses are recorded on a graph called a audiogram. Appendix A shows an audiogram, with the numbers across the top denoting frequencies (Hz) tested, and the numbers on the vertical showing intensity levels (dB).

The use of noisemakers and sound field tonal signals has been a traditional initial observational tool for young children. The tonal stimulus is presented through a loudspeaker in a soundproof room. In a sound field, visual reinforcement is often used to maintain attention. Light-rigged toys on or near the loudspeaker are first flashed on simultaneously with the presentation of the tonal signal. This initially brings the child's attention to the loudspeaker. After the training period, the tonal stimulus and child's response precede the reinforcement of the flashing toy. The lowest levels of auditory reactions are termed "minimal response levels." Signal presentations for a hearing-impaired child may seem quite loud to an observer with normal hearing.

A pure tone threshold does not necessarily indicate how well the child understands speech and distinguishes between speech sounds. The audiologist administers speech tests to estimate this. A common *speech audiometry* test requires the child to repeat single-syllable words, such as "bear" or "neck," or to point to pictures of such words. This word identification test is given at a comfortable loudness level through the earphone or loudspeaker. The percentage of presented words correctly identified is the speech discrimination score. The test provides knowledge of the degree of difficulty understanding speech, which speech sounds are perceived or distorted, and which part of the ear is disordered. Children who hear speech but do not understand words usually have a loss in the cochlea or auditory nerve (sensorineural).

For various middle-ear disorders, *immittance audiometry* provides an accurate and easy method by comparing the sound pressure level (SPL) flowing in the ear canal with the amount reflected back from the eardrum. A high amount of reflected sound is measured when a disorder causes the eardrum to be stiffer than normal. Immittance audiometry is valuable for detecting middle-ear disease that may not otherwise be observed, especially in children without symptoms of hearing loss. Otitis media, a common childhood disease and a frequent cause of hearing loss and language delay, can be identified by this method. This test uses a physiologic response and requires no response cooperation from the child.

If a hearing impairment is discerned, an *amplification assessment* is made. The hearing aid is chosen with the child's environment in mind. For example, if the child is in an early intervention program classroom, the aid should accommodate that environment. After purchase of the hearing aid, there should be an electroacoustic analysis and behavioral measurement of the aid and the classroom amplification system.

The *behavioral evaluation* of a hearing aid or classroom amplification system provides the most valuable information for estimating the benefit of the device. It enables the audiologist to determine the best aid for auditory threshold improvement, speech awareness, and word discrimination. The evaluation compares unaided and aided tonal responses in the sound field with the child's ability to be aware of and understand speech with and without the hearing aid. Informal methods can also be used, such as having the child follow simple commands, point to familiar toys, or indicate the presence of sounds in the Five-Sound Test (Ling, 1976). The five sounds (ah, i, oo, s, sh) represent a range of low- and high-frequency speech components.

Tremendous insight into hearing and speech behaviors can be obtained from parents, through a medical history that records probable onset and degree of loss, and from parent behavioral observation reports. Care should be taken, however, in interpreting parent answers. Because parents provide facial expressions and visual cues to enhance communication, and hearing-impaired children respond to these cues, parents may mistakenly believe that the child is hearing. They may also be able to interpret the child's speech even though voice quality and articulation are distorted. All of the described procedures may be needed to get a complete picture of the child's hearing over time; thus, parents should know that the pediatric hearing test is a continuous, age-dependent activity, and that, as the child matures, more accurate measures can be gained.

Problems of testing include those common to assessing all young children. Although noise makers, such as squeeze toys, are used in some evaluations, the lack of frequency and intensity control limits this technique. Audiologists can make frequency spectrum tests to define these components. Too often, children with hearing impairments exhibit inconsistent auditory responses in the structured testing settings. Establishing a comfortable relationship with parents can help the child relax and cooperate. In testing, behavioral responses to auditory signals must be time-locked to the stimulus presentation. Limitations of behavioral observations include young children's rapid habituation of response, a lack of consistency in determining which behaviors constitute an acceptable response, and subjective decisions by audiologists as to whether the response was made.

SPEECH–LANGUAGE EVALUATION

Speech–language evaluation is conducted using interview and observational methods, along with standardized tests. Measures of language production and comprehension are based on observing the child's performance in four areas that are all essential for effective communication: the child's presentation mode, language structure, ability to convey and gain meaning from speech, and ability to use social communication rules.

All languages have a *presentation mode*, which typically takes the form of orally produced sounds (speech) and, later, writing. However, individuals with disabilities may also use presentation modes of gestures, sign language, or augmented means of communication, such as computer-assisted speech. All languages have *structure*, which determines appropriate word order (syntax) and word endings (morphology) and all have *meaning*, the formal semantic elements, which include vocabulary, linguistic concepts, and meanings that exist between words in various semantic relationships. Communicative competence also requires the ability to use *social communication rules* (pragmatics) that make the language understood by others in the way the speaker intended. These context-specific verbal and nonverbal linguistic interactions provide signals that help speaker and listener understand each other (Johnston & Johnston, 1984).

The most useful speech–language diagnostic information should be comprehensive in scope, derived from more than one type of measure, and include input from parents and from other professionals. In addition to having a measure of hearing, it should address the oral peripheral mechanism (i.e., bone and soft-tissue structures) needed for speech production, an inventory of the sounds the child produces, an estimate of the child's mean length of utterance (MLU), and a sample of the words and sentences the child produces. It should also include comparisons with cognitive development and with play development.

With the young child, the information base usually comes from reports of parents. *Parent report* scales, such as the Receptive Expressive Emergent Language Scale (REEL-2) (Bzoch & League, 1991), are often used. This scale scores observations in receptive and expressive categories and yields language age and quotient scores of receptive language age (RLA), expressive language age (ELA), and combined language age (CLA). Another parent report scale is the Rossetti Language Communication Scales (Rossetti, 1990). Comprehensive criterion-referenced measures, such as the Hawaii Early Learning Profile (HELP) (Furuno et al., 1988) also include language assessment sections. Both the HELP and the Rossetti scales combine parent report with clinician observation of spontaneous and elicited behavior. Many less formal, clinician-generated parent report scales are also used (Raver, 1991).

While parent report measures provide a base for clinician elicited observations, there are few *standardized tests* for infants and toddlers. The Preschool Language Scale-3 (PLS-3) (Zimmerman, Steiner, & Pond, 1992) yields normative data for children as young as 2 weeks; it is in general use among speech–language pathologists. The parent reports and standardized tests are described further in Appendix B. Many psychometric tests also include language evaluations (e.g., Denver, Bayley).

The paucity of standardized language tests for very young children is probably desirable, given the nature of young children's language. There are so many variables and so few absolutes or commonalities, even in the language of children considered to be developing normally, that standardized norms are unreliable. Thus, the clinician or team must gather data from a variety of sources, including the spontaneous language of the child in interaction with parent, team members, and peers.

Clinical observations of *parent–child language interaction* are employed when the child refuses to respond in a customary fashion to clinician or team members. It is also used when the parent–child interaction dimension is judged important to analyze. This information can lead to intervention suggestions that help parents and caregivers elicit child language and respond more appropriately to language attempts.

Spontaneous language of the child can also be measured by recording all the child's free conversation that can be elicited in a 10- to 15-minute play setting with trusted adults or peers. (This can be modified for very young children.) The clinician places great importance on analysis of spontaneous language because it is an indicator of the natural conversational language the child exhibits in a familiar context. There are numerous ways of analyzing this expressive language, including analysis of phonemes, syntax, semantics, and pragmatics. Mean length of utterance (MLU) is often calculated (Brown, 1973). The MLU estimates the number of meaningful elements in child sentences.

In typically developing children it is assumed that all developmental systems are at mental age level. Thus measurement of *cognitive and play capabilities,* which are closely tied to language, are also useful. The Westby Play Scaling System (Westby, 1980) enables clinicians to assess children's developmental level across cognitive and play areas as well as language. This scale does not provide scores, norms, or other statistics, but it does provide a baseline for comparing these three dimensions. It is described further in Appendix B. When children's language is below their cognitive and play development, the implication of specific language disorder is clear. On the other hand, the presence of depressed play in comparison to language and cognition signals the possibility of a social or emotional disorder. Children typically do not have either language or play behavior levels more advanced than their level of cognition.

There are a number of factors that make accurate assessment and identification of language problems difficult. One of the most obvious is that young children's language reactions in strange testing situations may not accurately portray their abilities. Another is that parent report measures may include parents' idiosyncratic interpretations of the questions, inability to recall accurate information, or desire to portray their child and themselves in an ideal manner. Hence, it is important to obtain multiple measures of language competence when assessing very young children.

INFORMATION EXCHANGE WITH FAMILIES AND REFERRAL AGENCIES

It is often the speech pathologist or audiologist who must inform parents that they have a hearing-impaired or language-delayed child. It is best to have had parents observe the child's responses in the evaluation situation so that they can see for themselves that the child does not hear or speak typically. Good practice requires that parents are told what the test battery will entail, that results of initial tests be conveyed to parents, and that the complete diagnostic plan be explained. The conclusion of the discussion should synthesize the finding for parents and aid them in obtaining referral sources.

PARENT SUPPORT AND EDUCATION

Although parents may have had a strong suspicion of a problem, verification of their fears may still be very difficult for them to accept. However, attempts to minimize the actual problem are harmful to the acceptance of the reality of the situation. A sympathetic attitude and understanding of parents' feelings of anger and loss will help. Parents usually want to find out everything regarding present and future functioning of the child; however, clinicians must be prudent about the level of detail they provide and how firmly they state their prognosis for progress. It is important to convey that parents have a positive role to play and that no one can predict what a child can attain with appropriate training.

SUGGESTING INTERVENTIONS

From the initial diagnosis, a plan for intervention is made with the parents (Gargiulo, 1985). Often the diagnostic and referral process includes assembling a team with expertise to plan for the child's needs. If further referrals are needed, parents are informed and assistance provided. If the child is not placed in an early intervention program, a schedule for monitoring development and a plan for follow-up assessment should be developed.

There are a number of interventions to which referral may be made. Individual therapy, which is most appropriately used in combination with a group experience, is sometimes suggested. More often, language group therapy, which enrolls children for 6 to 8 hours per week and is modeled after typical language-rich early childhood programs, is a preferred model. Clinicians interact in the setting, planning and manipulating the curriculum for the specific needs of the children. If a language disorder is the only common element, the child–child interaction provides models of many other forms of desirable behavior (Johnston & Johnston, 1984).

Another widely used intervention is placement in one of the early intervention classrooms provided under the mandate of P.L. 99-457. This is a highly effective model, in which the speech pathologist works with children in collaboration with the early intervention teacher, using therapy materials that are part of the typical materials of the classroom. These classrooms may have other children who are not language delayed or disordered, and thus peer language models are available.

Children often attend one of these group programs and also attend an inclusion program primarily composed of children who are typically developing. A great advantage of the inclusion setting is that a wide range of rich language models are provided by the typically developing children. Usually, consultation with the teacher is provided by the speech pathologist.

Another type of intervention is an intensive short-term program during summer vacation or on some other special basis. These programs have a limited focus, but can provide specific language interventions (Leighty-Troester, Doubledee, Deakin, and Ruder, 1981). Finally, intervention may be in the form of mother–infant dyad repair (Johnston, 1992), which combines ongoing diagnostic work with intervention. In this approach, the clinician interacts with mother and child, providing diagnostic insights and modeling appropriate interactions, planning activities with the parent, and evaluating and giving ongoing feedback. Over time, parent and child learn new ways of interacting, and thus the parent–child relationship is strengthened.

REPORTING TO PROFESSIONALS

Audiologists and speech pathologists provide written reports to other professionals. However, speech pathologists are more often on-site members of early intervention teams, and thus they usually engage in ongoing dialogue with other team members and gain diagnostic information from the arena assessment or other team assessments. They also engage in role sharing by participating in the early intervention classroom and by suggesting techniques to be used by the classroom teacher. The audiologist usually serves in a consulting role to provide suggestions, rather than as a member of the on-site team. More involvement of audiologists on teams could have benefits, especially for children who may have hearing loss but whose language or behavior problems were not initially identified as hearing-related.

USEFULNESS OF A TRANSDISCIPLINARY MODEL

In the past, when young children were identified as having hearing or language problems, the family was asked to purchase services from a variety of professionals: pediatrician, otologist, audiologist, and speech–language pathologist. Although decisions made by these individual professionals might have been in the best interest of the child, the decisions might not have been consistent with each other, thus disrupting the coherence of the intervention and burdening and confusing the family (Able-Boon, Sandall, Stevens, & Frederick, 1992).

Traditionally, the approach to delivering service focused on identifying and remediating the child's deficits, while "educating" the parent and child. Current approaches focus on developing systems that recognize parents and professionals as equal partners, with clinician and parent working together to determine goals and activities for the child. These changes reinforce the focus on family intervention, which emphasizes the enhancement of the whole child within the context of the family.

Scharfenaker, Snelling, and Ferrer-Vincent (1987) recommend that a multidisciplinary team of clinic personnel assess, treat, and manage hearing and language delayed or disordered young children. In many states the services established by P.L. 99-457 are accessed through a mental health board or other agency that offers identification and remediation assistance by a team of providers. The early intervention unit provides the collaborative forum that results in the development of the IFSP.

A great strength of a transdisciplinary team approach is that a better assessment of the child's potential may be gained from analysis of the observations of a number of professionals, and the intervention plan may be more integrated and congruent with family and professional intervention goals. Also, this team cooperation enables many language-based intervention strategies to be incorporated into the ongoing classroom activities.

The primary weakness of transdisciplinary assessment (as compared to interdisciplinary assessment) from the perspective of audiologists and speech pathologists is that, because the American Speech–Language and Hearing Association (ASHA) regulates and provides clear guidelines about who can perform services and which services can be provided, there are limitations to what other team members can do. This problem is one that a number of licensed or certified professions face when they are asked to release aspects of their assessment and intervention role to other team members. Thus, the transdisciplinary team model of selecting one team member to do the overall assessment is not usually realistic.

It is difficult to give other team members sufficient information to understand the fine points of speech–language and audiologic work. If they are not adequately trained, there is a great possibility that they could miss or misinterpret important observations and fail to find the factors contributing to the problem. They could even do harm by contraindicated management. Therefore, it is essential in transdisciplinary teamwork that the speech–language and audiologic specialists be active in the assessment process, in the interpretation of the assessment results, and in the intervention planning.

POLICY ISSUES

There are a number of policy issues arising from the mandates of P.L 99-457 that have implications for assessment practices related to infants and toddlers with hearing or language impairments. Some of these mandates attempt to alter materially their traditionally independent clinical approach to assessment and to redefine the role of these professionals who work in early intervention. Although their assessment practices and intervention planning may be affected by transdisciplinary team requirements, ASHA policies do not yet reflect a commitment to this team approach. In fact, their policies seem to be moving in the opposite direction (i.e., toward increased specialization), which may result in dilemmas for specialists working in early intervention where policies emphasizing transdisciplinary teaming are promoted.

There are debates about what constitutes appropriate placements for these children. In particular, questions that remain to be answered include whether inclusion models are preferable to separate programs; how much support from speech and hearing consultants must be available for an inclusion program to be effective; and what the role of the speech pathologist should be within these regular classrooms, if language development is to be facilitated.

Another controversy concerns the best intervention method (i.e., sign language, lip reading, or a combination of both) for deaf children whose hearing ability cannot be improved sufficiently to permit normal development of speech. Some studies show that hearing impaired young children who are exposed to signing begin using referential signing at about the same time as hearing children begin to use vocal symbols (e. g., Folven & Bonnevillian, 1991). Differences of opinion exist over whether "total communication," using all methods simultaneously, is more advantageous than using only one. Decisions regarding how many communication modes should be encouraged are often made by early intervention professionals on the basis of their own practical experiences, because there is not yet a strong body of research to indicate whether an "either–or" or "total" method is best.

Some early intervention personnel recommend teaching signing to hearing children who have diagnosed cognitive delay (e.g., Down's syndrome) as a first communication modality. Recent research confirms early studies that show communication in the gestural modality can be initiated slightly earlier than in the verbal modality (Goodwyn & Acredolo, 1993). However, these researchers indicate that the same cognitive processes of memory, categorization, and symbolization underlie communication abilities in both modalities, and thus the requisite cognitive skills must be present for full development of either communication mode.

With the advent of technologically based augmented communication devices, the possibilities for their use are only beginning to be realized. It is possible that many children (e.g., those with severe cerebral palsy or autism) who have not been communicative will be able to use these devices. Policy decisions about the use of these costly methods compared to more traditional approaches will also have to be made.

For language delayed children whose primary language is not English, differences in viewpoints about bilingual and multilingual approaches are a recurring policy question. Often, the child's native language is also not well developed. Whether the native language should be enhanced first or the young child should begin learning English is sometimes a matter of debate, especially if the parent is not proficient in English. Although research indicates that the native language system must be well developed if the English language system is to be effectively learned (Cummins, 1980; Harley, Hart, & Lapkin, 1986), there are still policy controversies over this issue. There is some evidence that young Spanish-speaking children who are taught English during preschool years gain in their ability to use private speech, which Vygotsky (1962) has stated is essential for developing internalized thought and cognitive abilities (Diaz, Padilla, & Weathersby, 1991).

SUMMARY

The importance of normal hearing in the acquisition of language cannot be overemphasized. Therefore, early assessment of hearing capabilities and remediation of hearing loss, if possible, are vital to language acquisition. Cognitive, physiological–neurological, social–emotional, and environmental conditions also have an effect on young children's language production and comprehension; these factors must be considered when language delay begins to be evident. If intervention does not occur early, there may be language deviance along with delay. The assessment methods of audiologists and speech pathologists are designed to gain an accurate early evaluation of hearing and language problems and to provide information that promotes effective intervention plans for language development. The team assessment model has many strengths; however, there are still a number of policy issues related to standards of these professions that may make it difficult for professionals to engage in the "ideal" transdisciplinary team discussed in the early intervention literature.

QUESTIONS FOR DISCUSSION

1. Within a comprehensive performance test battery, what should a speech–language and audiologic evaluation include for a child aged

under 2 years and between 2 and 3 years?
2. Why is it important for the parent or caregiver to observe the speech–language or audiologic evaluation?

Problems of Practice

Observe a clinical speech–language or audiologic evaluation of a young child and note the measures used and the methods that were effective in getting valid child performance. After the observation, ask the evaluator whether the same information could have been obtained in a team assessment having a number of professionals present. Find out what the speech–language or audiologic professional thinks about the values of a transdisciplinary team approach and the problems of such an approach.

Suggested Readings

Nelson, N. W. (1993). *Childhood language disorders in context.* New York: Merrill.
White, S. J., & White, R. E. (1987). The effects of hearing status of the family and age of intervention on receptive and expressive oral language skills in hearing impaired infants. In H. Levitt, N. McGarr, & D. Geffner (Eds.), *Development of language and communication skills in hearing impaired children* (ASHA Monograph No. 26, 2–24). Washington, DC: American Speech–Language and Hearing Association.

DIALOGUE

INITIAL ASSESSMENT, IFSP, AND
TRANSITION PLANNING FOR EUN

GENDER, AGE, ETHNIC ORIGIN OF CHILD: Female, 33 months, Asian American.

OCCASION OR PURPOSE OF DIALOGUE: An initial assessment of Eun, who has just moved to the state; to develop the IFSP for the remainder of the year; and to discuss the transition plan for an age 3 to 5 program for the Fall. Prior to this meeting, the family service coordinator had completed an in-home intake session with the family to determine eligibility for services.

TEAM MEMBERS: Early intervention specialist, family service coordinator, speech pathologist, occupational therapist, nurse, school psychologist, and child's mother and father.

SETTING: Conference room at the early intervention center.

OVERVIEW OF THE CASE

RISK CONDITIONS

Eun is the first child of her mother, who has had three pregnancies, two of which resulted in miscarriages. Eun was born by emergency caesarean section due to decreased fetal heartbeat. Anoxia (loss of oxygen) occurred during the birth period. Eun's birth weight was 5 lbs 6 oz. At 1 month, audiometry brainstem-evoked-response (ABR) revealed a severe to profound hearing loss. Pure tone assessment conducted by an audiologist when Eun was 12 months indicated that her loss was sensorineural and bilateral. Eun has had chronic otitis media, which led to pressure equalization (PE) tubes being inserted at the time of the audiometric pure tone assessment. Seizures were also noted during Eun's first year of life, although they have been under control with medication for the past year. Because of her middle-ear and seizure problems, which may have affected the ABR readings, the results may need further confirmation. Eun now has a vibro-tactile hearing aid. There is no family history of medical or learning problems.

REASON FOR REFERRAL

Eun had been receiving services in another state. Her paternal grandmother contacted the early intervention program in her county when she learned that Eun and her family were returning to this state, because she was aware that Eun would need to receive early intervention services. No referral was initiated by the early intervention program in the other state. However, on request, Eun's records were provided by the physician, audiologist, and early intervention staff in that state.

BACKGROUND INFORMATION

The family has resided in the state for 1 month. They presently live with the paternal grandmother while the family is looking for housing and the father is getting settled in a new job. Eun has been in an early intervention program that focused on children with hearing impairments since she was 6 months of age. The program was affiliated with a hospital in that state.

FAMILY STRENGTHS AND NEEDS

Eun has a caring and committed family who are devoted to gaining the best in educational experiences for Eun. Although their recent move has resulted in the loss of previous support systems, the presence of the paternal grandparents in this area and the family's prior experience in gaining access to needed resources are strengths. The parents identified only one need: Eun needs to be enrolled in whatever program will be most beneficial for her continuing development.

SOURCES OF ASSESSMENT INFORMATION

Sources include previously collected medical and audiometric data and the IFSP documents from the state in which Eun had been residing. Assessment methods used by the present team included the Battelle Developmental Inventory, Vineland Adaptive Behavior Scale, Linder Play-Based Assessment Scale, Preschool Language Scale-3, observation of communication in home and school setting, and informal interview with the parents. Eun's developmental status was evaluated based on evidence from these sources.

Social–Emotional Development

Eun is a social child who interacts with peers using signs and gestures. For example, she asks for toys, makes comments about the play, and calls attention to her activities through signing. In the assessment setting, with a peer, she exhibited some frustration because the other child did not understand all her signs. The out-of-state early intervention records indicate that she participates in both group and solitary play and demonstrates the ability to pretend, using objects in transformed actions (e.g., giving the doll a bath in a dishpan; putting on a hat and taking a purse to go shopping). In her pretend play she has been observed to combine as many as four schemes. In the team arena assessment, she demonstrated simple pretend play, awareness of routines, and direction-following when they were given in sign language. She is also conscious of the facial expressions of others and appears to be beginning to read lips. Her mother reports that she is aware of gender identity and is beginning to choose her friends based on that criteria. She spontaneously greets adults and peers and comforts peers who are in distress. Her personal–social level on the Battelle is 36 months, and her adaptive behavior level on the Vineland is 32 months.

Physical–Motor and Sensory–Perceptual Development

Eun uses her sight to scan and explore her environment. She can attend for long periods to social stimuli and activities when motivated to do so. Her motor skills are age appropriate. For example, she walks up and down stairs with minimal assistance, runs avoiding obstacles, jumps forward, climbs on gym equipment, and goes down the slide. Her gross and fine motor coordination is smooth. She uses a spoon and fork, serves herself food, drinks without spilling, dresses with only slight help, uses scissors to cut paper, opens doors by turning the knobs, and can execute tasks such as putting rings on a post. Her gross motor level on the Battelle was in the range of 30 to 35 months; her fine motor level in the range of 39 to 43 months.

Cognitive–Language Development

Eun exhibits ability to match primary colors, circles, squares, and triangles; put together 4-piece puzzles; follow 3-step directions (signed); identify big and little shapes; and point to objects (signed requests). She enjoys looking at picture books and signs the names of the pictures. Her Battelle scores indicated a cognitive level of 34 months. She was unable to respond to the

Preschool Language Scale-3, because of her hearing loss. Therefore, her language performance is based on team members' observation and parent report. She uses over 200 signs to comment, request, answer questions, and name common objects and pictures. She has recently imitated 2-word sign phrases and combined noun and adjective signs occasionally. She uses gestures with peers (e.g., shakes fingers, uses facial frowns) to protest, deny, or express possession. She can identify body parts and demonstrates knowledge of numbers up to 4. She also uses vocalizations at home to attract attention and has occasionally used a 3-word sign. Vocalizations were noted during the free play observation; they were primarily vowel sounds.

THE TEAM DIALOGUE

After completing the arena assessment, the team has gathered to review the information, to set up an IFSP for the next 3 months, and to discuss the transition plan for preschool placement in Fall. The family service coordinator is the leader of the team discussion.

FAMILY SERVICE COORDINATOR: Now that we've completed our assessment, we need to discuss Eun's IFSP for this year and begin the process of decision-making for Eun's preschool placement. (To parents) I think you've met all the team members, but let's all introduce ourselves again before we begin our discussion of what we observed. (Introductions are made.) (To parents) We talked in general about goals for Eun when I visited you at home. Now we want to review Eun's developmental status and discuss priority goals with the whole team. (To early interventionist) Jane, why don't you start with an overview of Eun's development?

EARLY INTERVENTION TEACHER: The team observed Eun during the arena play-based assessment and administered a number of instruments as part of the assessment. The assessment indicates that, within all of the domains of development, except speech, Eun is performing at the developmental level that is appropriate for her age. Her fine and gross motor skills are age appropriate and she seems very well coordinated. In the cognitive domain, her understanding of symbolic play and ability to use symbols to represent pictures and ideas indicate that she has a beginning grasp of concepts. Other evidence of this comes from her ability to demonstrate discrimination between big and little, colors, and shapes. Using the medium of signing, she has a well developed expressive and receptive communication system. She is using signs and gestures for social communication and is developing peer interaction skills. We observed her sign "pretty girl" and "hug Anna" when she was in the room with her peer.

MOTHER: She will go anywhere with anybody! She says "Hi" to adults with her sign and she really likes playing with other kids. I've noticed lately that she's beginning to choose to play mostly with girls. Is that typical for her age?

TEACHER: Yes, we often see that happening around age 3. Most of her adaptive skills are also within typical age range. She dresses herself and eats independently. She isn't yet toilet trained, but seems to be getting interested.

MOTHER: That's an important area to work on. I have not been pleased that I haven't yet had success in getting her toilet trained. It's one of the things she's been resistant about.

FAMILY SERVICE COORDINATOR: Overall, does the team see any major developmental concerns, with the exception of those that relate to her hearing loss? (Most team members answer "no" or indicate with head shaking that there are no major concerns.)

SPEECH PATHOLOGIST: One point to note is that she seems to be performing at a higher communication level at home than what we have observed in our assessment. In the next few months, we might focus on helping her to use 2- and 3-word signs and on increasing her vocalizations at school. Some direct experience in language building that is clearly related to receptive input would also be useful. Through experience therapy we could improve her receptive language and increase her number of size and spatial concept words. For example, we could work on words related to concepts of "over," "under," and "behind."

MOTHER: That's what we're working on now. We're trying to get her to sign things like "big blue ball."

SPEECH PATHOLOGIST: That's good, but that type of phrase is not as important as phrases like "ball roll," "my ball," "no ball," and "I roll." We want to emphasize production of meaningful sentences. It's also important for her to answer and ask more what, where, when, why types of questions. From the assessment, it is difficult to sort out which of her responses are just concrete-level reactions to visual stimuli from those responses that demonstrate a true understanding of the concepts. Usually, children with profound impairments don't do this well. I really think she needs another audiological assessment to determine whether that original diagnosis of the extent of hearing loss was correct. If she is really doing this well in concept development, she may have more hearing than was originally indicated.

FAMILY SERVICE COORDINATOR: Does anyone else have a comment about that suggestion?

SCHOOL PSYCHOLOGIST: I think that it is absolutely essential to have her hearing re-evaluated, if we are going to determine the best placement for her.

TEACHER: I agree. (To parents) You also mentioned you were interested in increasing her social skills, such as participation in group activities and ability to take turns.

FATHER: That's important because she doesn't get that experience at home. Everyone waits on her at my parents' house. She needs to learn to be part of the group.

MOTHER: We also want to work on her paying attention. She seems to "turn us off," especially around the family at home. It's probably easy for her to do that, but we don't like that behavior. She can be really stubborn. That's one of our main concerns. We consider obedience important.

TEACHER: Some of that behavior may be age appropriate, but I can understand your desire to have her pay attention to your wishes. She seemed to attend to the team when we were asking her to focus on tasks. But we can certainly work on helping you provide a structure that will foster her attention and motivation to follow your directions.

OCCUPATIONAL THERAPIST: She is very motivated to be successful when she is manipulating materials. Her fine motor skills are highly developed and, as long as they provide the right amount of challenge, she will attend for long periods to those tasks.

NURSE: Now that she is off her seizure medicine, have you noticed any changes in her attention or behavior?

FATHER: I haven't. (To mother) Have you?

MOTHER: No, but maybe it's true that her not paying attention is age related. This behavior seemed to be more noticeable lately.

NURSE: Have you obtained a medical card for this state yet? If she needs another audiological assessment and possibly new hearing aids, you will want to have that paid for.

FATHER: We have applied for it. Another thing we want to know is whether we can be reimbursed for travel to speech therapy and the early intervention program. The drive is over 14 miles one-way.

FAMILY SERVICE COORDINATOR: If the necessary forms have been filled out, that shouldn't be a problem. I'll check on where they are in the process.

SCHOOL PSYCHOLOGIST: I assume she will be wearing a hearing aid when she starts the preschool program. Is that likely?

MOTHER: Yes, although we really don't know whether it is doing any good. She doesn't seem to act differently whether it is on or not. The speech therapist we had before we moved here recommended she have a hearing exam and a new hearing aid before she starts preschool. She's been in a growing period and her present hearing aid doesn't fit well.

SCHOOL PSYCHOLOGIST: Next year, if she goes to the preschool connected with the early intervention program, she could use the auditory trainer. It's hooked into the central system. Do you want me to check out which preschools in this county have such systems?

MOTHER: Yes, that would be important. However, we haven't really had much success in getting her to wear her present hearing aid. She needs to be motivated to use it. Maybe if she got one in a high-fashion color she might like it better.

TEACHER: If she stays in the preschool program here, she might be more motivated to wear it because we can put her in a class where a number of the children wear hearing aids.

MOTHER: She's starting to read lips and is really trying to talk. She says "hot," but there is no voice to the "h" or the "t." It comes out "ah."

SPEECH PATHOLOGIST: If the hearing aid can help her to hear even minimally, that will help her talking.

SCHOOL PSYCHOLOGIST: Are you checking any other private preschools that focus on hearing impaired children?

MOTHER: We haven't looked into anything except the early intervention one so far. I would really like a specialized program such as she went to in the state where we lived. When she is 5 I definitely want her to go to a school that focuses on children with hearing impairments. There's a good one in this region. One of the reasons we moved back here was so that she could go to that school. But we don't know if the school district where we will end up living will pay for that.

SCHOOL PSYCHOLOGIST: There are guidelines that tell what will be paid for by the school district. I will get you a copy of those. When she is closer to 5, the school psychologist in the area where you live will help you evaluate the options. I think we need to know how she does in the hearing-aid augmentation environment of the preschool first.

FATHER: I think we will probably have her stay with this early intervention program for the preschool, at least for the next year. We want to see how she does here for the next few months before deciding definitely, though. We plan to live in this county so Eun will be able to come to this county program.

TEACHER: Eun can probably make some good progress in the next few months here. We have Head Start programs also in this building and so she can have the opportunity to be with those peers as well as with other children who have hearing aids and are signing.

FATHER: We want her to be ready for kindergarten. It's especially important to us that she keeps her motivation for learning. Eun did so well during her first few years because she had comprehensive services in the state we lived in. We want to make certain she will have everything she needs here. We were concerned that there wouldn't be as good a linkage to these services.

FAMILY SERVICE COORDINATOR: Well, you've both done a good job with Eun and we'll try to help her continue her progress. I think we have our recommendations in mind so let's review them once more. (Team reviews and agrees on recommendations.)

RECOMMENDATIONS

Eun will participate in the early intervention program for the next 3 months, and goals related to cognitive, language, and social skills will be the major focus for her development. The parents and early intervention staff will also work on increasing Eun's motivation to attend to and follow parental directions and increasing her interest in gaining toileting control. Her parents will schedule an audiological evaluation after they have their medical card and, depending on the results of that evaluation, a hearing aid decision will be made. With the assistance of the family service coordinator, they will also seek other comprehensive services that are needed. In 90 days, another IFSP review will be held, at which time a decision will be made about the preschool program that provides the best option for Eun.

QUESTIONS FOR DISCUSSION

1. How did the parents and early intervention staff try to coordinate the transition from a program in another state to the one in this state? Were there any ways that they could have improved on the process?
2. What seem to be the parents' short-term and long-term goals for Eun? Are their goals typical of most parents or are they influenced by the family's culture of origin? How may those goals differ from those of the early intervention staff and those of the psychologist from the county?
3. Did the team members effectively use the data from all of the assessment sources in determining Eun's developmental progress? Would any other information have been useful to include?
4. How did the family service coordinator define her role in coordinating Eun's case? Would another member of the team have been more effective in that role? If an audiologist had been part of the team and assigned case management responsibilities, would the management of the case have been different?
5. What is the value of having the county school psychologist become involved in the team discussions at this early stage? How could later psychological assessment procedures be affected by the psychologist knowing more about what the parents and early intervention staff are doing for Eun?

chapter 7

Doris Bergen

SOCIAL WORK AND FAMILY EDUCATION AND COORDINATION ASSESSMENT PERSPECTIVES

Because the very young child is so embedded in the family context, the effectiveness of any type of early intervention is always mediated by the individuals in the family. Thus, professionals who work with young children have always recognized that their responsibilities included establishing linkages with the children's parents and others in the family (e.g., siblings, grandparents) and involving these family members in educational, therapeutic, or care processes. Parent involvement in the form of educational or decision-making experiences have been integral parts of most specially funded early childhood pilot projects (e.g., Lazar, Darlington, Murray, Royce, & Snipper, 1982); a required component of Head Start since its inception (Raver & Zigler, 1991; Zigler & Black, 1989); and a mandated requirement of special education law (P.L. 94-142).

Social workers have traditionally had the most clearly defined role as facilitators of service delivery to families and as communication and advocacy links between families and social agencies. However, many other early childhood professionals have positions that include responsibilities for working with families. Family liaison and coordination roles may be those of home visitor, family educator, family counselor, case manager or service coordinator, and family advocate.

These roles are often performed by professionals from nursing, early childhood education, and therapeutic specialties as well as from social work. However, in many professional training programs there is minimal emphasis on family issues (e.g., one course). Even when there is a course in family theory and practice included in personnel preparation programs in education, health, or therapy, it rarely has a focus on families with infants or toddlers or requires in-field practice involving work with families (Bailey, Simeonsson, Yoder, & Huntington, 1990).

Since the mandate of P.L. 99-457, the emphasis on family involvement has become more extensive and intensive. This law requires that family members not only be involved in hearing about assessment and intervention decisions and giving their approval, but also must be an active part of all assessment and intervention activities (Turnbull, 1991). The family is to be a full participant in all aspects of the early intervention team process. In the Individualized Family Services Plan (IFSP), not only child-focused intervention goals are to be identified, but goals for the family, which address family needs and strengths in relation to the child, are to be identified and implemented. The support services required by the family to reach these goals are to be made accessible through improved delivery of services and comprehensive case management. Even for those professionals who in the past have engaged in communicating with families, providing family education, or involving families in decision-making, this new emphasis requires a change in perspective. It also requires families to change their ideas about their own roles in helping their young children who have disabilities or risk for delay. There are still discrepancies between what is stated in federal- and state-level policies regarding family-centered assessment and intervention practices and what is reported as actual practice by professionals in the field who are providing services to families and children (Dunst, Johanson, Trivette, & Hamby, 1991).

UNDERLYING ASSUMPTIONS

One of the major assumptions of this perspective is that child assessment cannot be isolated from the family because the child is an integral part of the family system (Turnbull, Summers, Brotherson, 1984). Family systems theory states that, because of the interrelated linkages among the members of the family, socially interactive processes among members of a system are affected when a change is instituted in any part of the system (Bailey, 1988; Barnard & Corrales, 1979). An intervention that changes the child (e.g., increased language) may affect the other family members' behavior (e.g., talk more to child). An intervention with another family member (e.g., mother becomes more confident in handling child) may affect the child (e.g., positive behavior changes) and other members (e.g., father spends more time with child). Family interactions with the community (e.g., getting food stamps) also may affect the child and other family members (e.g., better health and growth).

A second assumption is that the family is an excellent source of information about the child and thus can provide reliable and valid assessment data. Parents can report detailed information that is useful for determining the child's levels of functioning and styles of interaction. The information provided also sheds light on the social context, as parents describe settings, antecedents, consequences, and their interactions with the child. While this information by itself might be incomplete or biased, it adds to the overall data set and gives valuable clues to the assessment team as to which domains should be observed carefully and which developmental issues are crucial to the family members. Observation of the child's interaction with parents and other family members can also give professional team members good insights into the dynamics of their own interactions with the child that may affect developmental progress.

A third assumption is that the crucial needs of families take priority and must be identified and addressed if intervention with the child is to be effective. For example, if the electricity bill cannot be paid, that must be resolved before the parents will have the energy to learn to play games with their young child. A stronger version of this assumption is that the intervention outcomes for the family are as important or even more important than the outcomes for the child (Bailey & Simeonsson, 1984). A corollary assumption is, of course, that if family needs are met, the child's needs are more likely to be addressed.

The assumption that all families have strengths and needs is of great importance. Often, special educators have operated from a deficit perspective that has not acknowledged the strengths the family has at hand to cope with their child's disabilities (Dunst, 1985). By helping the family members to identify their strengths, the professional team members can help them mobilize those strengths to meet the challenges their child and family situation present. A corollary assumption is that the support provided by early intervention can begin the process, but that, ultimately, the family must develop its "natural" support system in the community, with full ability to access the community resources needed to sustain the development of the child over the long term.

Other assumptions that influence this perspective relate to family motivation and cooperation. If the family members increase their understanding of their child's needs, they will be more comfortable with the intervention options proposed, more motivated to seek identified resources, and more willing to perform the roles they must play to help their child. Initially not all families have a high level of trust with professionals, and thus the time spent to build trust and understanding can be vital in the intervention process. Superficial interaction with the family rarely helps to achieve the child's developmental goals. It is assumed that the process of developing a trusting relationship takes time, particularly with families who have had prior negative experiences with professionals (e.g., families who have been involved with the children's protective services system). In these cases, it takes more effort and more time to develop a working relationship.

Another assumption about family motivation is that the family has the right not to be served, even if important needs of the child have been identified. The most important difference between early intervention and later schooling that may not be understood by all professionals who work with families is that, although states are mandated to provide certain services for young children, families are not required to use them. Family participation in early assessment and intervention activities is voluntary, not mandatory. This reality of family choice is often difficult for professionals to accept, and there are times when they wish that families could be required to participate. If the relationship between the professional and the family is developing well, refusal of services does not usually become a problem. However, there may indeed be a point at which the family's right to refuse services must be weighed against the child's rights for health and safety.

There will be times when the child's right to be protected must take precedence over the family's rights to privacy and control and, at such times, referral to a child protection agency may be necessary. Such families may be cited for abuse or neglect, and court-ordered participation in early intervention or other services may be required. However, most professionals believe that, if the family is involved in all aspects of the assessment and intervention process, they are likely to want their child to have the assistance provided by the early intervention program. In many cases, if relationships with the family are developed through regularly scheduled home visits that are focused on enhancing the child's strengths and addressing development delays, the family will respond positively. One of the reasons why active family involvement in the assessment process is judged to be so important is that it is also likely to increase family motivation to meet their child's needs.

METHODS OF ASSESSMENT

Although a number of standardized interview methods have been developed to gain information about families, the typical method used by social workers and family educators and coordinators to gain initial assessment data is that of informal, open-ended interviewing. Of course, a number of basic informational forms must also be completed and signed in the course of the assessment. Most experienced professionals in family assessment believe that the collection of information should be low key, and that it should be preceded by a general discussion in which rapport with the parents is established.

INFORMAL ASSESSMENT PROCESSES

Initial family assessment contact is typically made after referral from a medical or psychological source has indicated that a particular child and family may be eligible for early intervention services. These sources are usually hospital personnel, public health nurses, primary care physicians, psychologists, or social workers. If an early tracking program is in place for neonates who are at risk, a systematic set of referrals may be made, including home nursing care, well-baby clinic, therapeutic services, or early intervention program evaluation services. Although there are some self-referrals by parents, most states require an "official" referral before a screening assessment to determine eligibility for services is conducted.

An appointment is set up by phone or mail, and one member of an assessment team—usually the social worker or family educator or coordinator—conducts this screening. This is to prevent the parents and child from being overwhelmed by the presence of many unfamiliar professionals. It is most often held in the home, although it may also be held in the early intervention setting. It begins with an explanation of the program and the answering of general questions and then proceeds to questions related to family needs and strengths and to child developmental progress or delay. In order to help families learn to trust the professional, it is important for the professional to stress the issue of confidentiality. Family members need to know that what they say in the interview cannot be repeated without their consent and that they will have an opportunity to review the information that will be relayed to other professionals.

The interview usually follows a relatively standard format, but it is adapted depending on how articulate the parents are in defining their concerns and needs, the nature of the child's disabilities or delays, and the extent of services needed by the family. During the course of the interview, the home-setting characteristics, the interactions among the child and other family members, and the obvious physical and economic needs of the family are also observed unobtrusively. Usually, few written notes are made during the interview, but, after leaving the home, the family assessment professional completes forms and summarizes observational and interview information. Forms requiring signatures are also completed with the family members.

If immediate access to services are needed (e.g., financial assistance, food supplies, home nursing care), the family assessment professional may initiate those services after or even during the interview. There can be a first "informal contract," such as an agreement as to immediate needs of the family and which part of the task to meet those needs will be done by the professional and by the family (i.e., even if it is a minor task that is part of a larger need). The professional can then make a definite time commitment as to when the task will be accomplished and when the professional will get back with the family regarding that need.

From this practical example, families usually learn that they can trust the professional. Because their earliest experiences may have been disjointed (e.g., hospital team assessment and intervention, but no follow-up services; information about some services but no specific directions about gaining access to the services), the presence of the case manager or family educator or coordinator may be welcomed by the family to provide a "secure base" of contact.

The congruence of parental reports about their child's development with observational or standardized assessment results is fairly high, especially for screening purposes (Diamond & Squires, 1993). However, parents are more accurate in reporting current skills than past skill levels and frequently observed rather than seldom-observed behavior. Also, a recognition format rather than a recall format is more useful (e.g. "Does your child say these words?" rather than "What words does your child say?"). Of course, if parents are required to respond to a written questionnaire, they must have the requisite reading, writing, and comprehension skills to be able to answer accurately (Diamond & Squires, 1993). An approach that involves mothers in completing an infant monitoring questionnaire, in which infant development was described at 8 time periods, from 4 months to 36 months, seems to be effective in improving mothers' evaluations of infant developmental status (Squires & Bricker, 1991).

STANDARDIZED ASSESSMENT MEASURES

Some interviews are supplemented by survey forms or rating instruments that are standardized, technically sound, and appropriately normed. According to Bailey (1988), advantages of using standardized measures include the following:

1. A common set of stimuli to which all families respond permits comparisons among families.
2. Responses are elicited that might not have been spontaneously addressed by family members.
3. Inadvertent omission of important data is avoided.
4. Variability due to individual characteristics of assessors is minimized.
5. Periodic administration of standard measures assists in program evaluation.

Ostfeld and Gibbs (1990) state that those who question the use of standardized approaches have done so on the following grounds:

1. Some of the instruments that have been developed are intrusive and not respectful to families.
2. The use of a test-like "diagnosis" instrument may increase the barriers between the family members and the family service educator or coordinator.
3. Family members may have reading or comprehension problems or may have emotional concerns that interfere with their ability to respond.

If a standard instrument is used, its purpose must be clear and the information collected must be useful to the early intervention staff. Ostfeld and Gibbs (1990) suggest that parents can be told they may omit questions that are of concern to them and debriefing should be used if the experience seems stressful to the family. To overcome concerns with some questions on standard interview forms, some early intervention professionals have designed structured interview guidelines for their own use or for their agencies (Pitzer, 1992).

In spite of concerns with standard family assessment measures, a wide variety of instruments designed to evaluate needs and strengths have been used by early intervention professionals. For example, there are measures of family stress (e.g., Abidin, 1986; Stein & Jessop, 1982); of family functioning and adjustment (e.g., Olson, Portner, & Lavee, 1985); and of coping styles (Hymovich, 1988). Many of these are primarily research tools and have not been used extensively in early intervention practice. One example of a general needs assessment survey is the Family Needs Survey (Bailey & Simeonsson, 1988), which measures family perception of their needs in six areas (e.g., information, social support, community services). The authors recommend that this structured approach be combined with an open-ended solicitation of needs.

Two measures by Dunst and colleagues also evaluate needs and perceived support. They are the Family Support Scale and the Family Needs Scale (Dunst, Trivette, and Deal, 1988). The first identifies possible support resources for the family in terms of availability and desirability. The second explores the family need for basic resources, such as financial help and transportation assistance. These family needs assessment measures are described further in Appendix B.

Methods of assessing the home environment and parent–child interactions have also been developed, and some have been widely used by specific professional groups. For example, nursing professionals often use the Nursing Child Assessment Satellite Training instrument (NCAST, 1978a, 1978b), originally designed to find factors that predict developmental risk. This instrument is now being used by other home visitor professionals. There is a scale for feeding situations (NCAFS) and teaching situations (NCATS). Research shows that high-risk parent–child dyads usually have lower scores on the interaction measures than low–risk dyads (Huber, 1991). Because of the lack of normative data on high-risk families, however, caution must be used in drawing conclusions about interaction quality with only one administration. Some portions of the NCAST are based on the Home Observation for Measurement of the Environment (HOME) (Caldwell & Bradley, 1979), which measures parent–child interaction and the home physical environment, and which has demonstrated predictive validity for later cognitive performance (Bradley & Caldwell, 1976). These are described further in Appendix B.

There are numerous interaction scales that have been used primarily for research purposes but that have applicability to early intervention assessment. For example, Greenspan, Leiberman, & Poisson (1990) developed an observation method for assessing newborn, infant, toddler, and 3-year-old interactions with caregivers, using coded videotaped play interactions. They have been particularly concerned with social–emotional and attachment development, which this scale is designed to measure. However, it is complicated to use and has not yet been published in a final version. It is described in Appendix B. Although these interactive dimensions of parental behavior are important to assess, there are no reliable and valid measures that are also easy to use.

During the home visit, informal observation of the child's development is conducted and a standardized developmental instrument is used to assess the child's level of developmental delay. This is likely to be an instrument, such as the Denver II, Developmental Profile, Child Developmental Inventory, that can be administered in a relatively short time with the parent reporting information on child performance in addition to the evidence obtained from child observation in the home.

PLANNING THE INDIVIDUALIZED FAMILY SERVICES PLAN

After the various measures have been reviewed, a judgment as to whether the family and child are eligible for a full assessment leading to an Individualized Family Services Plan and to subsequent early intervention services is made by the family assessment professional. For those children and families judged eligible for services based on the screening, a full team assessment is conducted and the IFSP written within 45 days, as required by federal guidelines. In some states, children at environmental risk may be enrolled in an intervention program without a specific eligibility diagnosis in order to be able to observe over time whether delays qualifying the child for services are present.

For the development of the IFSP, the parents are invited to be participants and the other relevant members of the team are identified. Parents are usually willing to be present, but their level of participation in team observation and discussion varies greatly, depending on their comfort level and personality characteristics. If the assessment is to be conducted in the home, the team will be small, with perhaps the social worker, speech pathologist, occupational therapist, and early intervention teacher, or some subset of this group conducting the assessment. If the assessment is to be conducted at a clinic or program site, the team may be larger, but not all team members will interact intrusively with the child. The discussion of findings results in the identification of family and child needs and strengths and agreement on priority goals to be addressed by the team. The service coordinator (i.e., case manager) is also identified. An example of an IFSP format used by one early intervention program is shown in Appendix A.

INFORMATION EXCHANGE WITH FAMILIES AND REFERRAL AGENCIES

Social workers and family educators and coordinators spend a lot of time communicating with family members and coordinating access to the services of agencies that focus on families and children. They often begin this parental contact while the child is in the intensive care unit of the hospital. A number of hospitals now provide parent–child units that focus on needs of the entire family (Reiser, 1992). The professionals whose role involves work with families are usually knowledgable about information exchange processes, and they often measure their effectiveness in terms of how successfully they have coordinated the delivery of services and engaged families in seeking access to resources that will meet family-identified needs. Information exchange occurs informally (e.g., phone calls, casual chats) and formally (e.g., parent education meetings, referrals to agencies).

In particular, these professionals communicate with and prepare parents for IFSP meetings, organize and lead parent support and education groups, and make educationally oriented home visits, often on a regular basis. They also suggest contacts or even make the contacts with community agencies that can provide family resources, respite care, financial assistance, food supplements, counseling, and other services identified as needed by the family.

THE INDIVIDUALIZED FAMILY SERVICES PLAN MEETING

In preparing for the IFSP meetings, these professionals usually help parents identify the goals that they might have and give them a sense of what the agenda will contain. They can help the parents to focus on concrete family-centered goals for inclusion in the IFSP, such as taking a class in parenting, setting aside play time with the child and siblings, or going out with friends. During meetings with other professionals, the family-oriented team members often serve as clarifiers or expanders of parental comments and interpreters of the information reported by other members of the team. For example, they may accompany the parents to a meeting at a hospital and take an active role in helping the parents interpret the technical reports of physicians or therapists. They may ensure that the parents have had the opportunity to express their ideas when a number of professional team members are reporting their results of assessment or recommendations for intervention.

Because they are very knowledgable about the community resources available to assist families, they often expedite emergency services, help families understand which services certain agencies can provide, give suggestions when initial efforts are not successful, and smooth the way by making initial contacts or being a supporting presence as parents make these contacts. They also make follow-up calls and visits to ensure that the necessary services are being delivered.

The family-oriented team members must be especially sensitive in finding the balance between respecting family values and cultural practices and promoting access to services that will be most beneficial to the child and family. Not all parents know what questions they need to ask to help their child and themselves, and they can not always identify the important services they should receive. A good starting point is to help the parents make a "wish list" of tangible items, such as access to a Women and Infant Care (WIC) nutritional program or Supplemental Security Income (SSI) funds, transportation to the doctor, a person to provide respite care, or a walker or other piece of equipment for their child.

PARENT SUPPORT AND EDUCATION

Another important way that information is exchanged is in parent support or education meetings, either formally set up on a regular (e.g., once-a-month) basis or the result of collecting a number of parents who are visiting classrooms during the program day. If the parents have been observing the classes, they may meet to discuss the developmental issues surrounding what they have observed and to gain ideas for supporting their children's development at home. Some of these group meetings include topics of general interest to parents of children with disabilities, often topics that the parents have identified. Speakers on such topics as legal rights, financial planning, or family advocacy are sometimes invited. Speakers can be especially helpful if they are from agencies that provide needed services, because parents can get acquainted with the persons they may eventually need to contact. Some groups evolve into serving primarily a supportive function for the parent members. The typical pattern is that they are more educationally oriented early in the school year and become more support oriented as the members become better acquainted.

Because many services for infants and toddlers are provided in the home, the role of the home visitor is of special importance to the education and care of the child and to the needs for education and support of the parents. The two types of professionals who primarily provide ongoing home services are nurses and early intervention teachers. Public health nurses are often the first line of contact with a family after hospital discharge. During their weekly or intermittent visits, they provide initial education on caring for children who are medically fragile or disabled, and often are a supportive presence during the first few months of the child's life.

Nurses (usually a licensed practical nurse [LPN]) also provide intensive long-term home care for young children who have severe disabilities that require life support systems or other major medical interventions. These professionals find that their role includes not only caring for the physical and social–emotional needs of the child, but also providing a listening ear and informational support for the parents. These nurses provide respite for parents from the demanding task of caring for their child. They often accompany the parent when the child must be taken to medical or therapy appointments and may at times take the child to these appointments when the parent is unable to do so. When the nurse spends many hours in the home, a bond can grow with the family; this can result in positive gains for all family members. On the other hand, especially if the mother is working out of the home, the nurse must be careful not to become indispensable to the child and disrupt parental attachment. The nurse must also be cognizant of the stress a non-family adult in the home for extended time periods can put on other family members.

Home visiting teachers may face similar problems because they visit on a consistent basis, often weekly. However, the length of their visits is usually 1 to 2 hours. The expected role of the home teacher is to provide educational experiences for the child and to encourage the parent to interact with the child in playful, developmentally appropriate ways. Often the teacher finds, however, that parental needs to discuss their own life crises or concerns about the child's health or development must take precedence over the activities related to the child's educational plan. The home visitor may also provide information about child development and community resources, specialized procedures, and home activities to facilitate the child's development (Sandall, Able-Boone, & Speirer, 1992). Home visitors encounter a range of situations and must be resourceful, confident, and tolerant and convey a respectful and optimistic tone to the family. Most early intervention center-based programs include a home visit component, which helps teachers to understand the children in the context of home as well as in the group environment. For many parents, especially young single mothers, the home visit may be crucial in solidifying the linkages with the early intervention team.

CONDITIONS AFFECTING FAMILY–PROFESSIONAL INTERACTIONS

The developmental life stage of parents and the environmental risk conditions encountered by the family may influence parents' motivation and ability to participate in the assessment process. These factors may also negatively affect their ability to provide nurturing, stimulating, responsive, and developmentally challenging environments for their infants and toddlers, and may influence their interactions with the professional team members. Thus, professionals with family-oriented roles must be especially cognizant of such conditions.

For example, when working with adolescent parents, knowledge of developmental issues they are encountering can be helpful. The cognitive stage of adolescent parents may be that of "egocentric idealism" (Elkind, 1976), during which they think they are the center of everyone's attention and feel that their experiences are unique. This thinking pattern may account for the commonly seen adolescent sense of invulnerability, which promotes a high level of risk-taking behavior (e.g., fast driving, alcoholism, multiple sexual experiences, pregnancy) (Anderson et al., 1993).

Adolescent parents may entertain glowing fantasies about the child-to-be and then be disappointed by reality after the child's birth, especially if the child has developmental problems. They may interpret typical infant behaviors, such as crying, as evidence that the infant is trying to annoy them instead of interpreting the cry as evidence of the child having needs that must be met. Their own needs for developing identity, independence, or intimacy may make them less able to attend to their child's needs.

Adolescents also face peer pressures that differentially affect males and females from various ethnic, cultural, and religious backgrounds (Spencer & Dornbusch, 1990; Thorton & Cambrun, 1989; Xiaohe & Whyte, 1990). These pressures may have an effect on the age of their first sexual encounter and, therefore, their first pregnancy, the decision to bear or raise the child, and the commitment to caring for a child with disabilities or delays.

Developmental issues are not confined to adolescent parents, however. Erikson (1963) suggests that adults may experience developmental crises concerning intimacy (i.e., forming close, stable relationships) and generativity (i.e., showing nurturing and giving behaviors), especially if they did not experience those conditions when they were younger. Marital state at any parental age influences parent–child and parent–professional interactions. For example, if the male parent is not physically or emotionally available, intimacy needs of the female parent may not be met and generativity will be affected. Responsibility for care of young children usually rests on the female parent (and possibly her female parent, too). The benefits of caring fathers have been demonstrated in longitudinal research (Snarey, 1993). However, father–child relationships are affected more strongly by unmarried or divorced states than are mother–child relationships (Dunn, 1993). If early intervention professionals hope to involve fathers positively with their young children, they must be aware of the factors that promote and diminish those relationships (Fike, 1993).

Severe parental crises and resulting behaviors can also interact negatively with child development needs. For example, parental mental illness is associated with child mental or behavioral disorders, although the presence of one healthy parent may ameliorate the risk to the child (Constantino, 1993). Maternal depression is associated with marriage problems, strains due to inadequate social support, and having children with difficult temperaments (Goodman, Radke-Yarrow, & Teti, 1993). Because infants are in tune with their mothers' emotional tone, if the mother is depressed, the infant may display a depressed interactional style and have a reduction in competence, positive affect, and preference for mastery of challenging tasks (Redding, Harmon, & Morgan, 1990).

Health and mental health problems affect parents' motivation to participate in the early intervention program. They may even feel alienated from or subtly rejected by the social systems designed to help them. For example, Woodruff (1993) asserts that mothers and children infected with the human immunovirus (HIV) have often been neglected and marginalized by social agencies. Early intervention professionals who take into account adult development factors may be more successful in finding ways to include these adults as participants on the early intervention team.

USEFULNESS OF A TRANSDISCIPLINARY MODEL

From the perspective of the social worker and family educator or coordinator, the transdisciplinary team can provide excellent support to reach the goals of family involvement that they are encouraging. Especially if the family members are given the opportunity to be full participants on the team, the experience can be very empowering of the family. The identification of one team member as the case manager or service coordinator can be helpful in making the plethora of information less threatening. The commitment of the team to discuss the recommendations for the child with the family rather than simply reporting their own decisions to the family can make the entire process more understandable and relevant.

Unfortunately, the presence of too many team members can also be overwhelming for family members and the process may take more time than many families can give, especially if they have work roles to fulfill. Many families, especially those from nondominant cultural groups, may not be comfortable taking the role of "equal" team members when surrounded by professionals. Thus, in actual team situations they may defer to the other team members, which results in the IFSP meeting appearing more like an IEP meeting, in which the child's status is reported to, not interactively discussed with, the parents.

Some teams try to solve this problem by having one team member discuss potential recommendations with the family on a one-to-one basis in the home before the IFSP meeting. Whether this results in more participation by the family, makes the meeting go more smoothly, or enables the family to have a sense that their views were heard has not been evaluated systematically, although it does make common sense.

The aspect of coordinated service delivery among agencies is another strength of the transdisciplinary approach and, when it is working well, families usually report a much improved process for gaining access to services. Many professionals from disparate agencies find that they are enjoying a closer working relationship and learning more about the needs of the families they serve because they have these close linkages and consistency of handling with the service coordinator, who is often the social worker or family educator or coordinator. In order for collaborative models to work effectively, however, there are some policy issues that must be addressed.

POLICY ISSUES

When families need assistance, these needs are often immediate and extensive, covering a range of services provided by a separate agency or funding source. Each of these agencies has its own set of paperwork, guidelines, and time sequences that must be addressed, if the services are to be received. Whether this bureaucracy is essential for responsible financial management or agency protection is doubtful. Professionals working with families know that many family members become discouraged or even defeated by form-filling requirements, time-consuming application processes, and confusing guidelines. Professionals and family members frequently report encountering officiousness and rudeness on the part of agency personnel, perhaps arising from a negative attitude toward persons eligible for certain entitlements. Often, the family professional must perform an active advocacy role, taking the time to help family members to complete paperwork requirements or to pursue phone contacts. They may at times have to serve as buffers or barrier demolishers before services can be received.

A policy decision to develop flexible procedures that would permit help to begin while the documentation is being completed could result in improved services to families. For example, the 45-day timing deadline for IFSP completion may be appropriate in theory, but it is dysfunctional in practice. To arrange for the full team to participate, sufficient time must be available to get those participants to arrange their schedules to attend. Policies that permit an initial agreement regarding services to be provided—with a longer time frame to develop the IFSP—may enhance both the service delivery time frame and the comprehensive plan designed for the child and family.

Of course, agencies do need to have procedures that demonstrate their accountability and effectiveness. However, these procedures should be reviewed to determine those required as part of routine practice and those necessary for effective service delivery. The current movement toward coordination and integration of services will be positively accomplished only if procedural issues are also part of the negotiations. As part of the integrative efforts, there should be common information formats that prevent duplication of paperwork and avoid repetitive information-giving efforts by families and by the family professionals who coordinate and manage their service delivery. The family-centered approach challenges present service providers to rethink policies and procedures that do not serve families. As Kaufmann, Hurth, and Johnson (1991) remark, "Traditional agency-centered approaches to the IFSP process that are designed to meet the needs of agencies rather than the people they serve are not an adequate response to this challenge" (pp. 79–80).

Another policy question that could be raised about integrated collaborative services is whether families are actually best served by a unified agency approach. Would opportunity for alternative choices within the service system be an advantage in meeting the needs of culturally or economically diverse families? For example, a small private agency with similar religious or cultural perspectives to those of the family may be preferable to a large "mainstream" governmental unit. Whether all potential service sources would be more effective if joined in one large, complex, system is at least a matter of debate.

It is also debatable whether the family assessment models presently being advocated, which suggest comprehensive assessment in all areas of family functioning, are really best for children and their families. Slentz & Bricker (1992) propose an alternative that they call "family-guided" rather than "family-centered" because they stress that the emphasis should be on the child rather than on the family, and that the IFSP goals should focus on the child rather than casting the family in the role of "needy."

Even with the press for coordination and cost-effectiveness of services, the presence of some overlapping agency responsibilities may be valuable. For families to feel a sense of control over their child's future, they should have some choices to make among reasonable alternatives. Although families who have children with disabilities are in all income and cultural groups, there is a high proportion of children at risk for delay in the less powerful groups in our society—the poor, the minority, and the recent immigrant populations. Policies have often resulted in their surrendering control in order to get needed services. Professionals who work with these families can have a positive effect on their lives by helping them to learn how to gain access to the present systems and what methods they can use to affect future decisions about early intervention policy.

SUMMARY

A cornerstone of early assessment and intervention policy and practice is the view that young children cannot be isolated from the family context. Thus, the family is to be involved in all aspects, including screening, diagnosis, and intervention planning, and the needs and strengths of the family and child are to be assessed and considered in the service delivery plan. Professionals who work closely with families, especially those who visit homes, must operate from this base of beliefs and demonstrate a respectful and helpful orientation.

While there are some situations in which family and child welfare is not congruent, close involvement with the family usually results in increased understanding of the child and a more effective plan for enhancing the child's development. Family involvement is also empowering, and may have long-term effects on the family's capability of providing the care and educational experiences needed by the child. The support systems that enable the family to meet their child's and their own needs must be in place, and access to the services of such systems must be facilitated by the early intervention team as a whole. Because social work, nursing, and educational personnel typically serve as the major contacts with families and provide the connecting links to the early intervention team, their role is especially important to the success of a transdisciplinary team approach that exemplifies family involvement.

Questions for Discussion

1. What are the advantages and the disadvantages of having a family-centered approach to infants and their families and to toddlers and their families?
2. What assessment and intervention methods would be useful with families whose ability to focus on their child's needs is being affected by adult developmental issues?

Problems of Practice

Interview a social worker or family educator or coordinator and determine which of the roles discussed in this chapter are part of that person's job description. Using that information as a guide, interview three families who are receiving services from the agency or school where that professional is employed. Find out which services the families think have been especially valuable and what they need that is not presently being provided. Make a recommendation based on these findings.

Suggested Readings

Bailey, D. (1988). Rationale and model for family assessment in early intervention. In D. Bailey & R. Simeonsson (Eds.), *Family assessment in early intervention* (pp. 1–26). Columbus, OH: Merrill.

McGonigel, M. J., Kaufmann, R. K., & Johnson, B. H. (Eds.) (1991). *Guidelines and recommended practices for the Individualized Family Service Plan F* (2nd ed.). Bethesda, MD: Association for the Care of Children's Health.

DIALOGUE

INITIAL ASSESSMENT AND IFSP FOR FERRIS

GENDER, AGE, AND ETHNIC ORIGIN OF CHILD: Male, 22 months, African American.

OCCASION OR PURPOSE OF DIALOGUE: An initial assessment of eligibility for services; to provide information for development of the IFSP and to begin transition planning for entry into the center-based toddler program next Fall. The program service model is that of a once-a-week visit by the early intervention home visitor, who also provides service coordination. The toddler program is available for children when they reach 24 months.

TEAM MEMBERS: Early intervention home visitor and child's mother.

SETTING: The living room of the child's home.

OVERVIEW OF THE CASE

RISK CONDITIONS

Ferris has cerebral palsy, seizures, and hydrocephaly. Ferris's mother received ongoing prenatal care and the delivery of her child was without incident. However, developmental problems were evident at birth. Hydrocephaly was diagnosed at that time, resulting in the child's placement in the neonatal nursery. Seizures began at 1 week and the suspected cerebral palsy was confirmed at 4 months by the hospital pediatric specialist. Because of the nature of his disabilities, Ferris has spent three periods of 10 to 12 days in the hospital. He has already undergone two surgeries for shunt inserts and will undergo surgery during the summer to reform his skull. He is on phenobarbital for seizure control.

REASON FOR REFERRAL

Initial referral to public health was initiated through the hospital where Ferris was born. He was referred to the early intervention agency by the public health nurse, who regularly visits the home. This evaluation by the early intervention home visitor is to begin the development of the IFSP that will be designed by the full team within the 45-day required period.

BACKGROUND INFORMATION

Ferris is an only child who lives with his parents. His father is attending law school and his mother works in a retail store 3 days a week. The parents interact on a daily basis with Ferris. However, Ferris spends time with a caregiver in her home while his parents are at work. There have been three different "regular" caregivers during Ferris's short life. Because of the part-time nature of the mother's work and the student status of the father, the family is presently of low-income socioeconomic status.

FAMILY STRENGTHS AND NEEDS

Strengths include parents who are very willing to seek resources for Ferris and to follow through on suggestions from specialists and physicians. The mother is working part time so that she can be with the child some of the time and, because the father is in college, his hours have some flexibility, enabling him to spend time with Ferris, too. He also has a part-time job, however, and needs a great deal of study time. There is an extended family in the area who offer occasional caregiving and other supportive assistance, such as driving mother and child to the physician's office. The child's health needs are funded by a health insurance plan through the mother's employer.

The family need identified by the mother is to have the early intervention home visitor, the speech pathologist, and the physical and occupational therapists provide services for Ferris. Currently, the only service the family is receiving comes from the public health nurse. Although finances are tight, conditions are stable, and the family has never been on public assistance.

SOURCES OF ASSESSMENT INFORMATION

Medical records and reports from hospital personnel are available. Other measures used by the early interventionist include home observation, informal parent interview, Early Intervention Developmental Profile, and the HELP. The following information about Ferris was obtained during this assessment period in the home (before and during the dialogue with mother).

Social–Emotional Development

Ferris enjoys interactions with parents and other familiar people. He responded reciprocally to the interaction attempts of the home visitor. His mother reports that he loves attention and that he displays toy preferences. His social–emotional developmental age is in the 9-to-12-month range (EIDP/HELP).

Physical–Motor and Sensory–Perceptual Development

As measured by the EIDP and HELP, Ferris shows a fine motor developmental age of 9 to 12 months and a gross motor age of 2 to 7 months. He is able to turn the pages of a book, hold crayons and bring them to paper, transfer objects from his right to his left hand, and show preference for the left hand. He can bear weight on his feet, sit for short periods using his left hand to steady himself, and right himself when tipped to the left side. The effect of his cerebral palsy is evident in his asymmetry of movement, with less well controlled movement on the right side of his body.

Cognitive–Language Development

In the area of cognition, Ferris shows an age range of 11 to 15 months. He pats pictures in books, attends to the pictures, and attempts to label them. He identifies himself in a mirror, tracks disappearing objects, and shows surprise when objects have incongruous actions. He enjoys games such as peek-a-boo and gonna-get-you, and laughs at "silly" actions. His language comprehension and performance ranges in the 13- to 21-month period; his comprehension being more highly developed than his production. He says six words or holophrastic phrases ("Hi," "Thank you," "Bye-bye," "Mama," "Go," and "Upper" [meaning he wants to be picked up]). He repeats and imitates words and sounds. However, he usually cries to get attention instead of using words.

THE TEAM DIALOGUE

The early intervention home visitor and the parent are seated on the living room floor, near Ferris, who is in his adapted seating device.

HOME VISITOR: Those are nice books in the Easter basket. Did you get them at a bookstore?

MOTHER: No, they came from the supermarket. I looked for some books and toys to buy because I didn't want to get all candy for Easter. I really like them because the covers are hard and he can't eat them. He's chewed up some of the cloth books I bought.

HOME VISITOR: These are really nice for his small hands, and you are right about this type of book lasting better. (She pauses in conversation to hold a book up to Ferris, turning a few pages and commenting on the pictures, before beginning the "business" of the visit.) I'm here today to observe Ferris's behavior and have you tell me about his skills. But first we have to get the rest of the basic information we need to help us determine what services should be provided. I will be able to fill out a lot of the information from our observation and discussion, but we'll go through everything on the IFSP form and make sure we have everything that you and your husband would like to see worked on. Do you have any questions about the cover page?

MOTHER: No.

HOME VISITOR: The goals are going to be generated by you, but I will give my input on what I've observed and what I feel Ferris should be working on. I went ahead and put down the information on programs and contact persons. I wasn't sure who the caregiver is for Ferris during the day. Would you mind giving me that information in case I need it to go to her house to observe?

MOTHER: Not at all. The sitter lives very close and wouldn't mind if you visited.

HOME VISITOR: What days is he with her?

MOTHER: Every week day except Wednesday.

HOME VISITOR: Are there any other resource people that you or Ferris are in contact with?

MOTHER: The only other person I can think of is the nurse that comes out from Human Resources and tells us about services in the area.

HOME VISITOR: Here is a brochure from one of the agencies that is concerned about parent education and parent information exchange. The agency has a weekly program covering topics that parents have expressed an interest in. They operate on a rotation, so if you can't make one week, the same topics will be covered in another week. It's also a great support group because all of the parents, including the woman who started the program, have children with disabilities.

MOTHER: Thank you. We'll look this over.

HOME VISITOR: I also brought some financial information that you expressed interest in when I called you. Does Ferris get SSI?

MOTHER: No, not yet, but we did apply for it; we just haven't heard yet.

HOME VISITOR: If there are specific things that you want information on that I haven't covered, let me know and I'll try to get you in touch with the right people.

MOTHER: I would like to know more about play programs. I might want to take him to something like that.

Home Visitor: Okay, I'll see what I can find out about those. We also need to do the medical information. I've listed the doctors I know he sees. Anyone else?

Mother: He does see Dr. Nervus (neurologist).

Home Visitor: Any concerns about his upcoming surgeries?

Mother: He goes in at the end of May for 4 days to have tests and observations, and they'll probably schedule his first surgery for his skull reconstruction in June. I'd like to have most of his surgeries completed this summer, before he starts the toddler school.

Home Visitor: I think that's a great idea. That way he won't miss a lot of school days and will get more consistency in his program. After we finish the observation and assessment procedures, we will fill in those parts on the IFSP form and list some of the areas that we feel Ferris should be working on as goals and which services he needs. Is there anything right now that you would like Ferris to be getting that he's not?

Mother: The only thing I can think of is physical and occupational therapy. How should I go about getting those services?

Home Visitor: Your best bet is to go through Child Hospital for physical therapy. You may be able to have the sessions covered by insurance. We can provide a consultative service for occupational therapy. Also, when Ferris starts the toddler program he will get regular occupational therapy and physical therapy there. Getting therapy in your home is a problem because there aren't many independent consulting therapists or agency services of that type. I'll bring you information on the therapy program at Child Hospital and the name of the person you can contact there, though.

Mother: I'll have to check with my insurance company to see if that will be covered for sure, and how much. Although we have some coverage, because I'm part time, I don't get full benefits.

Home Visitor: I'll also find information on some other agencies to see if you can get financial help through them.

Mother: That would be great; we'll also probably need help with the wheelchair I think he should have.

Home Visitor: We'll make a note to discuss that in our goal section. Now I'd like to observe Ferris and see what kinds of skills he has. (Conducts the observational portion and asks mother for reports of skills in areas not observed.)

Home Visitor: Now we'll work on the skill sheets and I'll get your input. The first area is motor skills. Is there anything in that area that you would like to see worked on?

Mother: He uses his left hand much more than his right. Maybe he should do some more activities with his right hand. He can feed himself with finger food and tries with a spoon, but it doesn't get to his mouth.

Home Visitor: I've noticed he can hold on to his toy spoon. A goal our occupational therapist may want to work on when she's here might be getting Ferris to feed himself with a spoon. We can also consult with the occupational therapist about whether the goal of using his right hand in reaching and holding on to things would be appropriate. If she agrees, I can set up activities where he will have no other choice but to use that hand. Anything else with motor goals?

Mother: His doctor says there is nothing wrong with the reflexes in his legs, but he just doesn't seem to realize they are there, or what they're used for. I'd like to see him use his legs, but I'm thinking that because of his problems with his head (deformation), the pressure on his brain may not allow him to use his legs right now. We may have to wait until after the surgeries and see what happens. With his head being so big, it's hard enough for him to concentrate on keeping his head up and balancing himself.

Home Visitor: I think you might be right as far as use of his legs. But we can work on awareness of his lower body. We'll wait until the next review period to talk about goals for using his legs, which will be after the surgeries are complete. Anything else?

Mother: No, I can't think of anything.

Home Visitor: I've talked with our speech pathologist and she will be conducting an assessment when she visits you to determine whether Ferris needs speech therapy. She will be making consultative visits about once a month. Also, I can work on language activities when I come on Wednesdays. It might also be a good idea for him to have another hearing and communication evaluation after his surgery is complete.

Mother: He seems to understand a lot, but I'd like him to be able to tell us what he wants—like what toy he wants to play with, or when he's hungry. The words he says now aren't enough for that. I'd like him to name some pictures in his books, too.

Home Visitor: That's an excellent goal! I noticed that when he wanted our attention today he cried or threw something. I'll be bringing in different toys and games for Ferris to manipulate to encourage his language and cognitive development. Is there anything you'd specifically like written down as a cognitive goal?

Mother: No, I think that when Ferris is given something he usually figures out how to use it with time. He enjoys looking at things and manipulating things as long as someone is doing it with him.

Home Visitor: How about social skills? Anything you'd like worked on specifically?

Mother: No. I think he's very social. He likes being around adults and kids and is very friendly to everyone. He loves to talk to people, even though they can't understand most of what he is saying.

HOME VISITOR: Let's read over the goals we have decided on. (She reads the goal statements and the mother agrees to the way they are stated.) I'll go back and write these goals up on the outcome sheet. I'll also fill in the parts about my assessment results. Other team members will also review the assessment. We will add anything else we think might be useful. Then I'll bring it back next week and you can go through it, add anything else that you want, and then you can sign it. This will be our initial IFSP. Is there anything else today that we didn't cover?

MOTHER: I'm working on getting him a wheelchair. I've already contacted his orthopedic doctor and he wants a physical therapist's evaluation also before he prescribes it.

HOME VISITOR: We can do that kind of evaluation at our school as a consultative session. If you'd like that, I will have one of the physical therapists from our program contact you.

MOTHER: Okay, that would be great. I'd like to get this done as soon as possible so that we can order it in time for him to get it before school starts.

HOME VISITOR: Here's information about the transition plan for the toddler program. I stated that Ferris will be 28 months old in September and eligible in Fall for our toddler program. The following year he can attend the preschool in your school district. He'll need to be tested by his home school district before he can be placed there, though. I'd encourage you to observe at a number of preschools during the next year to help you decide what kind of program you want for Ferris.

MOTHER: The school district said they'd do the testing when he is 3. I would just need to sign their form. I'm waiting to see when the surgeries will be completed before I plan for this Fall. I think Ferris would like the toddler program because he likes to be around other kids. The sitter he has now doesn't take care of any other children, but the first two did and he enjoyed seeing them.

HOME VISITOR: You've been doing a great job getting things going for Ferris. You're really well organized. Let me know if there is anything else I can help with. Do you want to tell me who you might like to have receive copies of the IFSP?

MOTHER: Why don't you just make some copies for me and I'll give them out if a doctor or therapist requests it. Will Ferris also get an IFSP when he goes to preschool?

HOME VISITOR: No, this is for younger kids. He'll have an individual educational plan, called an IEP, when he goes to preschool. It will be similar, but it focuses more on child goals than family goals. In the toddler program he will still have an IFSP, which includes the family goals.

MOTHER: Is the IFSP only for kids with problems?

HOME VISITOR: Yes. It's to help us do the best planning to enable Ferris to reach the developmental goals that our team identifies through the assessment. Let's review the recommendations to be sure we agree on what the IFSP will say.

RECOMMENDATIONS

The initial IFSP will focus on helping the family gain the information and services they have identified as needs, which include occupational and physical therapy, and financial assistance for purchasing a wheelchair, if the therapist's evaluation indicates one is needed. The home visitor will work with Ferris's family on improving his motor skills and on developing more precise communication methods to make his needs better known. The speech pathologist will also make an assessment and provide consultative service for the family. Ferris will be eligible for the toddler program in fall. His developmental progress will be monitored and the IFSP goals reviewed after his surgery is completed. The parents will continue as co-service coordinators with the early intervention home visitor. The IFSP will be reviewed in 90 days, as mandated by law.

QUESTIONS FOR DISCUSSION

1. What might have been problems in the service delivery system that resulted in Ferris receiving his initial IFSP at the age of 22 months, even though his disabilities were evident in the first months of his life? Would an earlier referral have made a difference to Ferris or his parents? How will the home visitor's knowledge of and coordination with outside services now be able to help Ferris and his family?
2. What were some of the data that Ferris's mother provided that helped in the assessment of Ferris?
3. Ferris's mother seems to be more competent, articulate, and assertive than many parents. What happens in situations when parents do not take such an active role in finding services for their child? What happens when health insurance is not provided for part-time employees?
4. Is an IFSP that is first developed by the early intervention home visitor and the parent as useful as one that is initially developed by a full team? What are the advantages and the disadvantages of this approach?
5. What skills did the family or home visitor exhibit in engaging the parent in a meaningful dialogue? Did she display any behaviors that explored the acculturation level of the family or the cultural values they may hold that could influence the assessment and intervention process?

chapter 8

Doris Bergen
Susan Mosley-Howard

ASSESSMENT PERSPECTIVES FOR CULTURALLY DIVERSE YOUNG CHILDREN

In the period between 1980 and 1990, the population of the United States increased by only 9.8%, which was the lowest increase in 200 years of census taking. During the same period, the change in the composition of the population was the greatest since the immigration wave period at the turn of the century (Outtz, 1993). The US Census Bureau projects that, as a result of immigration and birth patterns, by early in the 21st century, one-third of all Americans will be from Hispanic, African, Asian, Pacific Island, or Native American cultural backgrounds, with Hispanic Americans replacing African Americans as the largest minority population (14%). According to Outtz, "we are a multifaceted society. It was true before, and it is even truer today . . . full participation of all sectors of our diverse population is increasingly vital to the survival and growth of this nation" (p. 6). To ensure that this full participation will occur, young children from every cultural group must be enabled to reach their developmental achievement potential.

The concept of cultural diversity has been examined from many perspectives, depending on the definition of culture used in those perspectives. Specific cultural groups have been defined both narrowly and broadly, ranging from those groups demarcated by geographical boundaries, historical traditions, or religious value systems to those groups who share common attributes, values, and behaviors within the same boundaries, traditions, or systems (Frisby, 1992; Geertz, 1973). Because culture is a pervasive construct, used to explain and describe processes and products, it must be defined carefully when it is being used to explain how it influences the assessment of young children and to describe what its effects will be on the contexts in which assessment occurs.

In this chapter, culture is defined as the patterns of behaving, thinking, and feeling of a particular group, which may be either geographical or ethnic in origin, that are transmitted during the socialization of young children who are members of that group. This socialization process creates deeply rooted and often intuitive scripts for action, thought, and emotional evaluation of experiences. These scripts interact with developmental processes, such as cognitive, language, and social-emotional competencies, and affect the ability of young children to demonstrate those competencies in an assessment situation. If assessment and intervention is to be effective, it must be planned to take into account knowledge of relevant cultural differences and it must acknowledge cultural realities that have an impact on the lives of culturally diverse young children.

Because many states have developed early intervention eligibility guidelines that require administration of at least one standardized normative instrument in their multifactored assessment process, the use of such instruments continues to be an integral part of early assessment practice. Norm-referenced assessment is often promoted as essential not only for determining eligibility but also for monitoring children's developmental progress and evaluating how well the planned objectives for children and families have been met.

For most young children who are part of the Eurocentric culture, norm-referenced measures may be useful because they permit comparisons with other children from that culture, even though questions about the technical properties of these tests remain. These instruments have many reliability, validity, and interpretation limitations when they are used with non-dominant groups, such as children who have developmental risk conditions that inhibit their ability to perform in the standardized manner. When the tests are used to assess young children from culturally diverse backgrounds who may be at risk for developmental delay, the limitations are even more problematic.

As these problems have been recognized, alternatives to traditional assessment, such as use of portfolios (Gardner, 1983, 1993), observations of play (Linder, 1993), and multifactored assessment procedures (Meisels, 1987) have been proposed. The importance of explicitly recognizing the effect of culture on assessment has also been stressed (Hale-Bensen, 1986). In the light of the identified problems with assessment methods and the lack of a substantial knowledge-base regarding the specific development of culturally diverse young children, it is essential that appropriate assessment contexts and multifactored instruments be used to increase the amount of accurate information about the development of these children.

UNDERLYING ASSUMPTIONS

A basic assumption of this perspective is that not all children and families who bear a certain cultural label bring the same level of dominant culture awareness or test-taking sophistication into the assessment setting. Much research has focused on issues of cultural "world views" or what could be called the level of acculturation to the dominant culture (e.g., English, 1983; Myers, 1988; Nobles, 1980, 1986; Schiele, 1991). A family's level of acculturation into the dominant culture determines the extent to which the members expose their children to the culture of origin and to the acquired dominant culture and mediates their interactions within both cultures.

Some families from non-dominant cultures are sufficiently acculturated to Eurocentric viewpoints that they are able to use that viewpoint when it is necessary to achieve a particular goal. These "transitional" families (Saracho & Hancock, 1983) may begin to convey some dominant cultural ideas to their children during infancy. Even with this level of acculturation, however, young children from non-dominant cultures still do not interact extensively with the dominant culture. For example, fewer than one in four minority children below age 4 attend out-of-home educational programs (Fradd, 1987).

Other "traditional" families, especially those who are first-generation immigrants, who grew up in rural areas, who are isolated from mainstream economic success, or who hold strong non-dominant religious or moral values, may have made explicit to their young children the behaviors and values only from their culture of origin. Moreover, they may exclusively use their language or dialect of origin in the home or they may use an undifferentiated mixture of their language and dialect and the dominant language.

Achor (1978) studied acculturation in Mexican-American families and described four levels of acculturation: accommodation to the majority, insulation from the majority, mobilization and interaction with both cultures, and alienation. Children whose families fit into these different categories of acculturation differ greatly in their familiarity and ease with the dominant cultural expectations integral to most assessment methods and in their ability to demonstrate best performance in assessment situations.

Even for cultural groups who are not recent immigrants, there are acculturation differences. For example, the extent of an Afrocentric world view among African-American families varies greatly, and the degree to which African-American families adhere to culture-of-origin views can have a great effect on the developmental levels that their children demonstrate in a testing situation. Ogbu (1988) points to the "caste" level of African Americans as influencing their access and exposure to the resources of the dominant culture. That is, African Americans with high levels of education and income tend to be more able to acculturate when they desire to do so. He also points out that the childrearing practices of parents reflect their views of what competencies their children need to survive and be successful in the society (Ogbu, 1981).

A corollary assumption is that the diverse socialization processes of these various cultural groups affect the response style and characteristic thinking patterns exhibited by their young children. Hale-Benson (1986), Boykin (1985), Hilliard (1987), and others suggest that children's cognitive style is influenced by what world view has been part of their earliest experiences. For example, if children are immersed in an Afrocentric view, which values global and relational thinking, field-dependent reasoning, functional perspectives, cooperative endeavors, and affective orientations, they use this thinking style in interactions with others, including assessment team members. Familiarity and good rapport with the test giver has been shown to affect positively the cognitive performance of African-American children, while it does not affect the performance of European-American children (Zigler, Abelson, & Seitz, 1973).

In a discussion of the "self-sufficiency" perspective, which is an accepted cultural value in modern industrial societies, Feinman (1991) asserts that a developmental achievement for infants in American society is to be able to function while "being alone." He contrasts this with the cultural expectation in many African, South American, and Asian societies that mothers and infants be almost inseparable. When separation from the mother occurs in these cultural groups, the infant is not expected to be alone, but in the company of other familiar people. In contrast, the Eurocentric perspective encourages manipulation of objects and provides relatively long periods of time when the infant is alone, engaged in object manipulation.

For example, Young (1970) has noted differences in object orientation between dominant-culture infants and those from African-American families, in which there is a greater focus on interpersonal interactions than on object interactions. Delpit (1988) indicates that adults in these two cultures provide different language and social interaction models, with African-American adults giving commands and rules in a more direct style than European-American adults. Both of these cultural differences can affect young children's test performance.

Other examples of socialization factors that may affect children's performance in assessment situations can be drawn from studies of Asian, Eskimo, African-American, Appalachian, Native-American, and Hispanic families (e.g., Briggs, 1970; Chan, 1986; Boykin, 1985; Fernald & Morikawa, 1993; Govle, 1982; Grosman, 1984; Iwacha, 1983; Laosa, 1977, 1982; Ruiz, 1981; Ruiz & Padilla, 1979; Steward & Steward, 1973), which indicate that the various cultural groups differentially socialize for obedience and respect for authority (Asian, African-American, Hispanic); harmony and cooperation (Asian, Hispanic, Native-American); spontaneity, active movement, and emotional expressiveness (African-American, Native-American); independence and emotional restraint (Eskimo, Appalachian); and family loyalty and respect for elders (Asian, Hispanic, Appalachian).

The timing of socialization also differs, with many cultures being indulgent of infants and stringent in teaching prosocial behaviors after the first year. Expectations for the developmental achievements of boys may be higher than for girls (e.g., Hispanic, Appalachian), and having a child with disabilities may be difficult to accept in some cultures (e.g., Asian) and more easily accepted in others (e.g., African American). A recent study of parents and toddlers in four cultures (US, Guatemala, India, Turkey) indicates that cultural and demographic factors influence whether parents actively guide toddlers' participation in the social group, have academic or social developmental goals, and take responsibility for toddler learning by structuring teaching situations or give that responsibility to the toddlers (Rogoff, Mistry, Goncu, & Mosier, 1993).

Another assumption is that even those assessment measures that have documented reliability and validity in assessing the development of young children from Eurocentric homes must be examined closely before they can be judged suitable for evaluating culturally diverse young children. These measures may not evaluate the range of skills, abilities, or acquired knowledge common to these children. They are often not able to note subtle developmental changes and culturally influenced patterns of change that are part of the children's repertoire of behaviors. Numerous studies have documented problems with traditional measures (e.g., Hilliard, 1987; McAdoo & McAdoo, 1985; Santos de Barona & Barona, 1991). According to Santos de Barona & Barona, because development often presents itself in an uneven fashion, maximum levels of performance may fail to be measured. Further, the external validity of the instruments is questionable, especially when used to assess culturally diverse children.

For many of these tests, the lack of normative samples from diverse cultural groups makes valid comparisons impossible; interpretations of the meaning of test results may be affected by the assessment teams' lack of knowledge of specific group cultural differences; and test-taking behavior may be negatively affected by culturally based socialization factors (e.g., girls should not act assertively). Although an increased number of children of culturally diverse backgrounds is now being included in normative groups, the process is still flawed. For example, culturally representative normative groups were collected for the Kaufman Assessment

Battery for Children (Kaufman & Kaufman, 1983); however, there was a greater representation from families in the non-dominant group who had high educational levels than is proportionally true for that total population group (Bracken, 1985).

Unless norm-referenced measures have norms that accurately represent each cultural and socioeconomic group for which comparisons are to be made, the results may not give a useful comparative picture of these young children's development. Furthermore, even if tests are normed with representative groups, if the test has been conceptualized and constructed from a Eurocentric perspective that focuses on analytical and logical functions, it may not adequately assess children whose culture promotes other thinking patterns.

Similarly, criterion-referenced tests may reflect biases in the test developers' determination of the specific test items to be used to demonstrate competence in various developmental domains. For example, certain self-care skills that are valued in one culture may not be taught by parents in another, and the child who has not been taught that type of self-care will not be able to demonstrate that skill. Also, many developmental achievements are assessed with the use of blocks. Those children who are not familiar with blocks may be less able to demonstrate their cognitive, motor, and language abilities when given commands to perform using blocks. Tests must be designed to permit a variety of objects, some of which are familiar to children of each culture, to be used to demonstrate performance in a particular developmental domain.

Because most standardized tests focus on linear thinking, field-independent reasoning, abstract symbolic perspectives, individual endeavors, and analytical orientations, children whose acculturation is only to their culture of origin may be less effective in meeting test demands. This factor is especially important in the period from birth to age 3 because, during that period, the family environment is preeminent in the socialization process.

The assumption that other culturally related environmental factors affect performance is also important to consider. For example, low socioeconomic level, which is often related to non-dominant culture status, has an effect on the resources families can use to encourage children's developmental progress and thus may negatively affect their development. While it is not always the case that behaviors caused by poor socioeconomic conditions are manifested in the testing situation, because many at-risk children from non-dominant cultures come from low-income families, this factor cannot be overlooked in making inferences about assessment results.

Other culturally related environmental factors, such as family composition, size, and presence of extended family members, also affect the development of children and their ability to demonstrate skills. In addition, the manner in which a particular cultural group is treated in the society has an effect on children's emotional development, and the social status of the cultural group has an effect on the social behaviors that are expected and learned by their children. When interpreting test results, this ecologically interactive perspective must be taken into account.

Thus, another strong assumption is that the presence and active participation of the families of children from diverse cultural origins are essential in the assessment process, if it is to result in an accurate evaluation. Families must be given an important role and their participation as experts regarding their children must be valued. Much of the learning of the very young child is idiosyncratic and based on experiences within a small circle of family and community members. For example, families may use different words for similar concepts or objects (e.g., use of the word "dolly" or "baby" when referring to a doll) and have different pragmatic rules for appropriate communication (e.g., do not look in the eyes of an adult when the adult is talking to you). If assessment team members do not have a knowledge of a particular culture, they need family members to help plan the assessment and to participate in eliciting the child's most effective performance. They also need advice about the linguistic or dialectical modes that will be most helpful in gaining evidence of child competence.

Familial involvement should occur in the pre-assessment, initial assessment, and ongoing assessment phases. In pre-assessment, family members can be interviewed to obtain developmental, cultural, and educational information, as well as information about family needs and linguistic status (Correa, 1989). One way to involve family members in initial assessment is to use a participant–observer technique in which the family members and the assessment team members observe and create anecdotal records of the child's behaviors. In ongoing assessment and interpretation phases, family members can serve as consultants when collected data are being interpreted.

A final assumption, often overlooked in conducting assessments, is that assessment team members each bring their own cultural perspectives to the assessment process. There is an interaction of their views, the assessment measures, the family's attitudes and beliefs, and the child's cultural experience in the testing situation. Because the team members' views of the child's abilities are mediated by their own world views, the conclusions they draw may reflect those world views. They must examine their own cultural biases and attempt to set them aside when testing children from diverse cultural backgrounds. Unless the assessment team members are aware of their own cultural perspectives and the potentially different thought patterns or social behaviors resulting from children's culture of origin that can affect their performance in a testing situation, the team will not be able to make valid inferences regarding the children's developmental status.

Although an ideal assessment team would have at least one member from the cultural group of the child being assessed, this is often not possible in practice. Even team members who are well versed in another culture or linguistic system are not experts in all cultures or languages. Therefore, the team should try to locate written information and community informants who can assist them in understanding the cultural context and the interaction style expected by members of the child's culture. For example, even among cultures that appear to be very similar (e.g., Vietnamese, Cambodian, Laotian, and Hmong), there are differences in the structure and use of names (Morrow, 1989), and the use of a "disrespectful" address may hamper the assessment and intervention process. It is particularly important for the team members to be aware of their own cultural perspectives and to avoid stereotypic assumptions in interpreting assessment results.

METHODS OF ASSESSMENT

When assessing young children from diverse cultures, a range of methods can be useful, as long as the assessment results are interpreted within the context of the cultural milieu. A single standardized measure may provide some useful information; however, a culturally sensitive, multifaceted assessment is the preferred mode.

STANDARDIZED SINGLE-INSTRUMENT ASSESSMENT

A typical method for assessment of young children has been the administration of one normative- or criterion-referenced assessment measure that is focused on "typical" developmental milestones (i.e., normative for Eurocentric populations). Although infant assessment measures have included a strong emphasis on motor skills, toddlers require a demonstration of processes that tap logical and linguistic problem-solving skills. They also require independent rather than collaborative demonstrations of abilities. For example, no items require the young child to demonstrate the ability to work cooperatively on a task with the parent.

In comparison to measures for preschool and school-aged children, assessment instruments for infants and toddlers have usually shown less disparity in results between culturally diverse children and dominant-culture children. There are a number of explanations for the initial similarity of performance and the gradual increase in diversity of performance with age. This result may indicate that the measures used with very young children capture more accurately the breadth of skills culturally diverse children can demonstrate. It may also indicate that the patterns of development for culturally diverse children increase in variability from typical patterns at later ages. Cultural factors and genetic and other environmental influences may have an increased effect over the course of children's development.

The concept of "canalization" may be relevant here (Shonkoff, Hauser-Cram, Krauss, & Upshur, 1992). This term refers to the narrow developmental path that many characteristics take during the early years of life. For example, motor skills such as sitting and walking and basic social and cognitive behaviors do not appear to differ greatly in timing of appearance, even under relatively extreme environmental deprivation (Kagan, 1984). The range of variation in human performance seems to widen as environmental experiences interact with individual and cultural differences.

The greater differences at older ages could be caused by culturally diverse children's later negative experiences within the dominant culture, which make them less likely to demonstrate their capabilities in testing situations. The increase in the range of differences can also be a result of the ongoing development of culturally different thinking styles, affective responses, and linguistic patterns. Although this question has not been systematically studied, it is likely that the cumulative effect of person and environment interactions contribute to the greater range of individual performance differences at later ages (Bronfenbrenner, 1993). The culturally sensitive assessment process, therefore, should include information from numerous sources embedded within the relevant cultural context. As part of the process, the information obtained should be interpreted in light of the acculturation level of the family and child and the socialization practices appropriate in that culture.

COMPREHENSIVE, MULTIFACTORED ASSESSMENT

The suggestions given in earlier chapters that pertain to successful ways to get optimal infant and toddler performance during assessments are also pertinent here. The assessment team should be especially sensitive to the use of assessment approaches that draw the highest levels of performance from young children who are not members of the dominant culture. These techniques of sensitivity apply to the assessment of children from all non-dominant cultural groups. However, assessment team members should also prepare themselves to work with the specific cultural groups who are most likely to be included in their assessment population by reading some of the literature on culturally diverse socialization processes (e.g., Saracho & Spodek, 1983; Hilliard, 1987; McAdoo & McAdoo, 1988).

The increasingly typical assessment method preferred for all infants and toddlers is a multiple assessment approach that has the parent or primary care provider as a full member of the assessment team. The assessment procedures for culturally diverse young children do not differ in overall structure from those for all young children, but special attention should be placed on their comprehensiveness and relevance. In the initial interview, there are some specific questions that are especially important to ask families from diverse cultural groups. Ramirez (1991) has developed a 57-item traditionalism and modernism inventory to determine acculturation level. Although his inventory is used for therapeutic purposes, questions of similar types can provide contextual information to guide the assessment by identifying the acculturation level likely to be exhibited in child performance. Some examples of questions that can be asked to determine acculturation level are listed below in five categories.

1. *Prenatal and Neonatal History*
   - Was prenatal care provided by a physician or by another culturally sanctioned person? What month was it begun and of what did it consist (e.g., special diet, physical check-ups)?
   - Were there any unusual prenatal or birth circumstances relevant to the ethnic or racial group, such as presence of a genetically based syndrome, illness, length of gestation, difficulty of birth, use of medication or other substances?
   - Are there particular medical or psychological practices before, during, or after birth that the family's culture expects to have carried out (e.g., circumcision)?

2. *Sociodemographic Context*
   - What is family's length of time in the US? If they are recent immigrants, what circumstances surrounded the immigration and resettlement experience?
   - Is the family part of a certain "caste level" (e.g., educational, socioeconomic, religious) within their cultural group?
   - Does the family live in a neighborhood with diversity of cultures or entirely with members of the same cultural group?
   - Does the family have strong ties to a religion common to their cultural group?
   - Is there an extended family in the same living space or in the local area? What is their role in relation to the child?
   - What is the socioeconomic level of the parents and of other family members?
   - What is the educational level of the parents and of other family members?

3. *Linguistic Context*
   - What language(s) is/are spoken in the home?
   - Which family members speak which languages?
   - What language(s) is/are used in interaction with the child?
   - Are non–English-speaking members of the family engaged in learning English?
   - Is the English language or the culture of origin language seen or heard on television or radio?

4. *Family Socialization*
   - What are the living arrangements of the child's parents (separate or shared)?
   - How often do the mother, father, and extended family members interact with the child (e.g., on hourly, daily, weekly, monthly basis)?
   - Is a family member expected to be with the child most of the time (e.g., is child routinely carried as the adult goes about daily activities)?
   - What are the values of the family that most or all family members strongly support (e.g., mother staying at home, breast feeding)?
   - What are the behaviors that the family expects to see in all children at certain ages (e.g., toilet trained by a certain age, respect for adults)?
   - How do family members characterize the strengths and needs of the child (e.g., style and rate of learning, adaptive behaviors)?
   - Are the neighbors expected to support the family socialization system? How do they do that?
   - Are the family's friends primarily from the same cultural group?
   - Are there primary caregivers other than family members?
   - Has the child had exposure to out-of-home care or education? How successful have those experiences been?
   - Has the family received help from social service, health, or other community agency personnel? How successful have those experiences been?

5. *Cultural Commitment*
   - Does the family adhere to all or some of the customs, beliefs, and traditions of the culture of origin?
   - Does the family express knowledge of and pride in their cultural history?
   - Do family members identify with their culture or race?

Before using any standardized assessment methods, determination of primary language use and functional language use should be made. Decisions about whether English, the home language, or a combination should be used must be made prior to the assessment; ideally, the team should have a member with both English and the home language. On standardized measures, for children from non-dominant linguistic backgrounds, instruments that have been designed in the language of origin or that have been translated and back translated to be sure of accuracy are preferred to instantaneous informal translations of English language tests (Vazquez Nuttall, Romero, & Kalesnik, 1992).

After the preliminary information has been gathered as the ecological context for the assessment, a transdisciplinary team assessment that includes the following components should be conducted:

1. Naturalistic observation in varied settings, including adult–child, peer–child, and sibling–child interactions with familiar partners
2. Parent, caregiver, or significant other observations and ratings
3. Relevant norm-referenced instruments
4. Relevant curriculum-based instruments
5. Sample of child's spontaneous language
6. Samples of child products, if age permits (e.g., drawings, block structures)

Information from physical–motor, sensory–perceptual, cognitive–language, social–emotional, and play domains should be collected. Most assessment batteries used with infants and toddlers include a standard, norm-referenced instrument that measures psychomotor, physical, cognitive, and social domains. The tests created for this purpose historically excluded children from culturally diverse backgrounds when technical standards were being determined. In recent years, test makers have begun to include culturally diverse populations in developing their normative samples and to design measures appropriate for non–English-language speakers. For example, the revised Bayley Scales (1993) includes representative samples of major cultural groups in the US, and the Denver II is now available in a Spanish language version. Evans (1985) and Patton (1992) have given suggestions for instruments to be used with culturally diverse young children because of their higher level of sensitivity to cultural factors and to young children. Even though the instruments still do not reflect all of the important aspects of diverse learning styles, they do assess more accurately than some other norm-referenced instruments. Some instruments that have features making them more culturally sensitive are the Denver II, Preschool Language Scale–3, Uzgiris-Hunt Scales, Bayley II, Home Observation of Environment, and Vineland Adaptive Behavior Scales–Revised. These are described further in Appendix B.

Standardized instruments and informal measures must be sensitive to the variety of attributes that have cultural relevance, and the team must give attention to uncovering skills that may not be part of typical assessments. For example, the ability of the infant to cooperate in turn-taking social play with an adult has recently been recognized as a vital skill that all infants should possess (Bruner & Sherwood, 1976). Because of the emphasis in many non-Eurocentric cultures on family–social interaction, these infants may have especially well developed skills in this domain.

Assessment methods should include those that can add to the team's understanding of family dynamics, structure, interaction, and acculturation level; analyze culturally influenced cognitive and language style; determine family–child relationships and adult–child social interaction patterns; assess psychomotor skills; and evaluate affective tone and orientation. (Many examples of these methods are discussed in chapters 2 through 7.) Care should be taken to include tests that can point out skills based on cognitive and language style components of the culture; for example, those that draw on both "left-brain" and "right-brain" skills. Torrance's (1990) Tests of Creative Thinking and Hilliard's (1976) The "Who" and "O" Checklists can provide this type of information. A balanced collection of information should be sought and interpretation of results should come from an holistic view rather than a fragmented perspective. Play-based assessment approaches are also very useful, especially if play can be observed both in the home and in an intervention program setting. They are described in Appendix B.

EVOLVING ASSESSMENT METHODS

A number of assessment models that take cultural considerations into account are now being developed. One model, the Program Aptitude Competence Test System (PACTS) approach (Savage and Adair, 1980), uses a team composed of a variety of experts and significant others from the child's environment to qualitatively assess affective, cultural, cognitive, behavioral, and social variables. Another approach, recently proposed for African-American children by Hamilton, Oscar, & Atkins, (1993), advocates the use of the *Optimal Performer Locator,* which is designed to tap into optimal performance. The theoretical base is derived from Hilliard (1987), who asserts that optimal performance can be attained by all children, and sub-optimal performance can become optimal through practice.

Hamilton et al. (1993) state that a *person by environment* perspective is the foundation of the assessment process. The *Optimal Performer Locator* introduces the child to materials that are culturally relevant and the tasks tap into all modes of functioning (e.g., tactile, kinesthetic, cognitive). If the child's performance initially fails to match desired outcomes, behaviors are modeled and the child is then reevaluated to determine if the skills have been acquired. This approach is congruent with Vygotsky's (1962) suggestion that the "zone of proximal development" be assessed. Another method drawing on cultural strengths is that of Mercer (1989), who designed a System of Multicultural Pluralistic Assessment (SOMPA). The assumptions of this method are:

1. There are many normal curves of behavior.
2. People of different cultural groups can not be validly compared.
3. Multiple measures are necessary.
4. A multicultural perspective is essential.

Although these approaches have focused on the assessment of children aged 3 and older, they can give guidance to the design of assessment for culturally diverse young children also.

After the assessment information has been collected, the team should examine the variety of developmental indicants and discuss what inferences should be made, given the family and child's level of acculturation and socialization context. The IFSP planning team should include not only professionals with a wide range of assessment skills but also members of the child's family and possibly other members of the cultural group. Using the rich data that have been obtained from the comprehensive assessment approach, the team should develop the IFSP through a consensus process.

INFORMATION EXCHANGE WITH FAMILIES AND REFERRAL AGENCIES

Especially for young children from diverse cultural groups, it is critical for the family to be involved in the assessment process from its inception. It is important to gain meaningful and useful information about infants and toddlers and to obtain ideas for the best ways to communicate with families. Historically, there has been a schism between the agencies of the dominant-culture and culturally diverse families (Neighbors, Jackson, Bowman, & Gurin, 1982). To close this gap there may be a need to use as conduits indigenous community people within the subculture; to learn to recognize the "chain of command" within that family structure; to know whether the family prefers gaining information face to face or in written form; and to understand the cultural barriers that prevent "reasonable" requests from being honored.

There may be a level of mistrust and intimidation felt by the family and by the professionals. An important goal is to assist families in becoming empowered. If they can experience their empowerment and their potential for influencing their child's developmental achievement, they are likely to become more involved in the implementation of activities that further the educational goals for their child. Sometimes professional team members must be aware of and work on their own mixed feelings about family empowerment. They need to see the empowerment of culturally diverse families as adding to the strength and ability of the entire team to affect the children's lives rather than as a potential loss of their professional expertise and overall control.

USEFULNESS OF A TRANSDISCIPLINARY MODEL

The transdisciplinary approach offers a comprehensive look at the child's developmental status, including assets and deficits; gives the professional team members an in-depth and dynamic view of the child's culture and the significant people in the child's life; and permits the entire team (family and professionals) to work together to enhance the child's development. In order for it to be effective, however, the professionals involved in the team must be aware of, truly knowledgable about, and sensitive to the unique cultural dynamics that interact with the needs of the child.

There are few professional training programs that prepare students sufficiently to perform effectively in this role. Professionals need to have indepth and extensive knowledge backgrounds and practical experiences with culturally diverse children and families in order to feel comfortable as a member of a culturally diverse transdisciplinary team. They must also learn to be confident in challenging the "system" (i.e., schools, preschools, daycare, physicians, hospitals), if that is needed to gain the resources for appropriately assessing and planning educational experiences for culturally diverse young children.

Although this approach provides the information-rich context in which to gain a valid picture of the child within the family, there are two practical disadvantages: It requires more time than traditional assessment approaches and it relies on the ability of the team to achieve consensus on the child's developmental status, taking into account the knowledge base drawn from the child's culture of origin. Given the many diverse cultural influences in American society, this is not an easy task. It is, however, a necessary one, if the potential of all young children is to be understood and fostered.

POLICY ISSUES

Many of the concepts already discussed in this chapter are embedded in policy issues that the whole culture must address. The effects of the increased numbers of culturally diverse groups on the dominant Eurocentric paradigm of assessment and educational planning and implementation have only begun to be explored. An important issue is in the definition of "at-risk" populations. How this phrase is defined will have implications for who is assessed and served in early intervention, what resources are devoted to this age level, and what level of empowerment the families of these children will be allowed to achieve.

For example, state departments that oversee intervention services may define eligibility differently. Some states include environmental risk conditions that have been related to developmental delay (e.g., low socioeconomic status, substance abuse) in determining eligibility for early intervention services. Other states require evidence that performance is 1 or 2 standard deviations below the mean on standardized norm-referenced tests for a child to qualify for an early intervention program. Young children who come from culturally diverse backgrounds may be over-represented or under-represented in early intervention programs in various states, depending on how eligibility criteria are defined and interpreted.

Another policy dilemma concerns access to and cost of transdisciplinary team services. Many families from non-dominant cultural groups do not know how to access services, and they may perceive that they are being discouraged from seeking these services. Access-promoting policies and committed financial resources must be available for assessment and early intervention services to reach the children who need them. The information on availability of services should be clearly designed and widely communicated. However, if family empowerment is to be maintained, services must be provided in a manner that increases the family's sense of control and independence, enabling them to become effective seekers of resources throughout the life of the child, if needed.

A team-related policy issue is that of determining what the role of indigenous persons of the culture should be in the assessment process. In the past, and often still today, assessments by professionals have been conducted without the involvement of culturally knowledgable persons because they often do not possess the professional skills thought to be needed by team members. Even in assessments of children from linguistically different backgrounds an indigenous person has not often been present. Inservice training of indigenous persons to be team participants and preparation of professionals who are members of varied cultural groups are essential if culturally diverse children are to receive appropriate assessment and placement.

SUMMARY

In assessing young children of diverse cultural backgrounds, it is essential that the assessment team have knowledge of the diverse cultures of the children they assess. They should use flexibility in selecting assessment procedures, including ethnographic and naturalistic modes of assessment along with standard measures, and they should interpret the assessment data in the light of the ecological interactions relevant to the particular cultures of the children. They should always be aware of the influence of their own cultural perceptions and experiences and monitor their assessment and intervention decisions within the context of their knowledge of their own culturally based perspectives.

QUESTIONS FOR DISCUSSION

1. What aspects of the transdisciplinary assessment process are likely to be useful in gaining a valid assessment of a young child from a non-Eurocentric cultural group? What aspects are likely to be problematic?
2. How can the assessment team use knowledge of the family's level of acculturation to plan and carry out the assessment and intervention tasks?

PROBLEMS OF PRACTICE

Observe a team assessment or an IFSP meeting for a child whose culture of origin is Asian, African-American, Appalachian, Native-American, or Hispanic. Focus in particular on the role of the parents or other family members who are present, noting the amount of participation, questions or comments, leadership taken, and affective responses to the child (if present) or team members (if present). After the observation, interview the family members to get a sense of their understanding of the process and their perceptions of the teams' interactions with themselves and their child. Evaluate the validity and effectiveness of the early intervention assessment or plan for the child.

SUGGESTED READINGS

Saracho, O. N., & Hancock, F. M. (1983). Mexican-American culture. In O. N. Saracho & B. Spodek (Eds.). *Understanding the multicultural experience in early childhood education* (pp. 3–15). Washington, DC: National Association for the Education of Young Children.

Hale-Benson, J. (1986). *Black children: Their roots, culture, and learning styles*. Baltimore, MD: Johns Hopkins University Press.

DIALOGUE

IFSP Review and Transition Planning
for Gamal

Gender, age, ethnic origin of child: Male, 36 months, Middle Eastern American.

Occasion or purpose of dialogue: Final IFSP review before transition to an age 3 to 5 program; to discuss developmental progress. Gamal has been receiving services since he was 4 months old. He had a home-based program until 18 months; since that time he has been in the toddler center-based program. The center program includes monthly home visits.

Team members: The early interventionist, occupational therapist, physical therapist, speech pathologist, adapted physical educator, family service coordinator, and the child's father.

Setting: Conference room of the early intervention center.

OVERVIEW OF THE CASE

RISK CONDITIONS

Gamal is the product of a pregnancy complicated by premature onset of labor, for which sporadic hospitalizations occurred in the last trimester of the pregnancy. He was born following a 32-week gestation period. Birth weight was 4 lbs 2 oz. His right foot was outwardly rotated and a physical therapist evaluated the problem during the 2 weeks he remained in the neonatal nursery. It was determined that the rotation was due to the placement of the foot within the womb, rather than a physical abnormality. Before discharge, the foot placement had self-corrected. Gamal's medical record after that time has included a history of asthma and otitis media. At the age of 2, he had an insertion of pressure equalization (PE) tubes. A hearing screening performed last Fall indicated that Gamal had difficulty hearing pure tones in his right ear. No further diagnosis or intervention has been conducted.

REASON FOR REFERRAL

Because of Gamal's prematurity and the fact that his two older siblings were premature and exhibited developmental delays, Gamal was referred to the early intervention program when he was 2 months old. The referral was made by the hospital social worker who routinely visits the families of premature infants. The early intervention program social worker then made a home intake visit, and Gamal began receiving early intervention services when he was 4 months old. At the last IFSP review, the following objectives were identified and they will be evaluated at this meeting:

1. Gamal will increase his receptive and expressive language usage in English.
2. Gamal will engage in pretend play and other social interactions with peers.
3. Gamal will participate in group activities.
4. Gamal will dress and undress himself independently.
5. Gamal will improve his fine motor coordination and balance.

BACKGROUND INFORMATION

Gamal's parents immigrated to the US 7 years ago from a Middle Eastern country and still speak the language of origin in the home. Gamal's two older siblings both attended the early intervention program. His initial referral was based on biological and environmental risk conditions. The father is employed in a local industry and he is able to converse adequately in English. The mother is a full-time homemaker who does not speak English.

FAMILY STRENGTHS AND NEEDS

Both father and mother are very concerned about the development of their children. The father carries the primary participation role, attending all early intervention team meetings. The mother has carried out activities in the home that were suggested by early intervention personnel but, because no one on the early intervention staff speaks their native language, the father has had to act as the translator. The parents do not have an extended family support network in this country, having left most of their family members in the native country. The father does have one younger brother who is studying at a college within the state. However, he is not usually available as a support resource. They have a number of friends from their religious group who have provided respite assistance on occasion. Their greatest strength is their desire to facilitate the development of their children. Access to a stable support system remains a need, especially because the language barrier does not permit the mother to make friends easily in the majority culture neighborhood in which they live.

SOURCES OF ASSESSMENT INFORMATION

The review assessment included a structured interview with the father, observation of the child in the early intervention classroom, and testing with the Battelle Developmental Inventory, the Peabody Developmental Motor Scales, and the Preschool Language Scale–3 (PLS–3). Because the PLS-3 does not have a version in the child's language of origin, it could be used only to indicate the child's English level. A spontaneous language sample was therefore also obtained and analyzed for phonetic, syntactic, semantic, and pragmatic quality. Based on the results of the team assessment, Gamal's developmental status was determined.

Social–Emotional Development

Gamal's parents report that he is much more socially interactive in the home than he is in the program setting. They indicate that he interacts with his siblings in play and uses both his native language and English. In the early intervention setting, he separates easily from his parents, engages in some interaction with peers, is able to share toys, and participates as a group member during activities. He shows enthusiasm, expresses affection toward peers, shows pride in his work, and responds to his name when in the group. He also engages in pretend play, often taking the role of father or other adult. He rarely makes requests that require adults to be resources; rather, he waits for his needs to be noticed. On the Battelle, his personal-social skills were at the 38-month level; his social skills requiring language are the least well developed. His self-help skills are at an appropriate age level (34 months on the Battelle). He serves food to himself, obtains a drink from a water source, and uses a spoon and a fork. He is also able to put on his coat, hat, and other simple articles of clothing. He moves independently and avoids common dangers.

Physical–Motor and Sensory–Perceptual Development

Gamal has many age-appropriate fine motor skills, such as folding paper, turning door knobs, using scissors to cut paper, stringing beads, and imitating writing strokes. He can remove a cap from a bottle by twisting it, wind a toy, build a tower of 10 cubes, and reproduce a 4-piece block design. He was unable to reproduce a circle or cross and needed assistance in tracing a line. He demonstrated a right-hand preference and mature grasp patterns with objects, but he had difficulty with movements that require isolated finger use. According to the Peabody Motor Scales, Gamal is exhibiting an average performance for his age level. His only difficulty seemed to be in some eye–hand coordination skills.

In the gross motor area of the Peabody, Gamal showed a scattering of skills from the 17-to-35-month level, with an age equivalent of about 20 months. He uses the railing to go up and down stairs, climbs on the gym set, jumps in place, and goes down the slide. He can throw and kick a ball, but cannot catch. He is beginning to use the balance beam, can squat and recover, walk sideways, and walk on a line. He cannot jump from a height or stand on one foot with control. His muscle tone appears slightly low, but range of motion is within functional limits. Gamal often sits in the "W" position (on knees with legs spread out), but he can change his position if asked to do so. He runs flat-footed.

Cognitive–Language Development

Gamal matches primary colors and similar pictures, and he can sort objects according to color. He can complete 4-piece puzzles, label objects, follow directions, attend to tasks alone and within the group, and focus on a task while being aware of others. His cognitive age level score on the Battelle was 26 months; however, the test validity is suspect because of his lack of facility with English. For example, he could find hidden toys, but could not repeat a 2-digit sequence; he could reach around a barrier to obtain a toy, but could not always label the toy; and he could match shapes, but not name them. He is, however, responsive to verbal commands that include adverbs and prepositions, and he demonstrated the beginnings of an English vocabulary (10 to 20 words). Although Gamal was able to identify pictures, body parts, and verbs in context on the PLS–3, he could not give spatial–concept or quantity–concept labels, nor could he identify actions and objects by function. His score, which indicated an English language age equivalency of 20 months, reflects the fact that English is not the primary language spoken in the home. Similarly, Gamal's English language age on the PLS–3 expressive language section was also 20 months. He could repeat one word, name objects, use "my," use question inflection, and produce a series of single words. He had difficulty combining words in spontaneous speech, naming pictures, using plurals, answering "wh" questions, and using present progressives. In the spontaneous language sample obtained through observation in the classroom, Gamal primarily used nonverbal communication to request, inform, and greet. He used jargon when playing, which seems to be a mixture of English and native language words. Because no measure of Gamal's ability in his native language was taken, no valid evaluation of his overall language ability is available from this assessment.

THE TEAM DIALOGUE

The professionals on this team have worked with Gamal's family for the past 2 years. They have participated in recurring dialogues with the father concerning Gamal and his siblings. The team is gathered to review Gamal's developmental progress and make transition plans for his entry into the age 3 to 5 program. The early intervention teacher serves as the team leader for the discussion.

EARLY INTERVENTION TEACHER: We're glad you could come in tonight to participate in Gamal's IFSP review.

FATHER: I appreciate your having these meetings in the evening so that I can attend.

TEACHER: We would like to go over the results of our latest evaluation of Gamal's progress with you. Then, if you have particular questions, we can discuss those further. In the social–emotional area of development he seems to be pretty much within his age level and our objectives from the last IFSP have been reached. One of his achievements is that he plays cooperatively with other children in pretend play. He's doing a good job of sharing toys and participating in group activities, too. His adaptive behaviors are about at age level so that objective has also been reached. He has learned to dress himself and is learning to remove his clothing for swimming time. He needs some help with fasteners, though.

FATHER: You teach him to dress wrong! (Using a joking tone, he is referring to the way the teacher lays out the coat so it can be reversed when pulled over the child's head.)

TEACHER: (Smiles) That method works well for most children. (Her response also has a joking tone.)

OCCUPATIONAL THERAPIST: If he gets his clothes oriented correctly, he gets them on correctly! (Also in a bantering tone.)

TEACHER: One self-help skill he hasn't mastered yet is toileting. If he doesn't learn that over the summer, we'll decide whether we need a toileting goal in Fall.

FATHER: I hope he learns over the summer. My wife doesn't seem to mind looking after him; she's very patient.

OCCUPATIONAL THERAPIST: We think Gamal still has a few fine motor coordination skills to learn, although he has made progress on this objective. He still has difficulty with large buttons. We aren't expecting him to use zippers or snaps yet, but it might be good to help him practice buttoning.

FATHER: I know he has a hard time doing that. Sometimes it's easier just to do it for him, especially when we're in a hurry. I'm not so concerned about these skills, but what about his language. Is he learning English?

SPEECH PATHOLOGIST: I gave Gamal the same English language test I gave to your daughter. His score on the test wasn't valid for his overall language development, but it did tell something about his English use. He isn't using English at a 3-year-old level yet. There are a number of things he can do well. For example, he could identify pictures when I gave the English names and he could produce a series of English words. However, he isn't using his English consistently in class, so we can't say that this objective has been accomplished. He either communicates nonverbally or uses a combined jargon of English and Arabic.

FATHER: He's a completely different type than his brother, who likes to joke and have fun. Gamal is very serious most of the time.

SPEECH PATHOLOGIST: Do you think that makes him less talkative?

FATHER: Yes, he only talks a lot when he's very comfortable.

SPEECH PATHOLOGIST: I have some questions about whether Gamal is hearing everything. Are his tubes still in place?

FATHER: One fell out.

SPEECH PATHOLOGIST: He only passed the pure tone screening in one ear. You probably should have the doctor examine him again and decide if the tube needs to be replaced.

FATHER: I know it should be checked. He gets sick so easily and his hearing seems to depend on how his asthma is.

SPEECH PATHOLOGIST: That could be a factor. His Eustachian tube is not yet well developed and the fluid is not draining. You should really keep having it checked because if he isn't hearing well that could keep his language from developing. This may be why the objective of increasing receptive and expressive language hasn't been achieved. For whatever reason, Gamal isn't choosing to use his English language at school. He understands he needs to communicate, but just doesn't do it.

FATHER: I think he uses more English that he did at 2 years. At home he says, "I want juice" and "I want ice cream."

SPEECH PATHOLOGIST: That's a good sign!

TEACHER: He usually says less at school. He talks a lot more at home. I've noticed that when I make my home visits.

OCCUPATIONAL THERAPIST: I haven't heard a sound from him when I've been in the classroom. When I assessed his motor development in a one-on-one setting, I was surprised to realize how much language he does have.

SPEECH PATHOLOGIST: It is important to encourage him to use English at home because it is true that he doesn't talk much here.

FATHER: Isn't that just because he's shy? All my kids have that problem. They are shy.

SPEECH PATHOLOGIST: That may be a contributing factor. When he gets into preschool in the Fall, he may use his language more. Do you have any other questions?

FATHER: I don't know of any right now.

SPEECH PATHOLOGIST: Be sure to let us know about the tubes. He got the original ones a year ago, right?

FATHER: Yes.

TEACHER: (To the occupational therapist, physical therapist, and adapted physical educator) Gamal has made some progress on his motor development goals also, hasn't he?

PHYSICAL THERAPIST: Yes, although his gross motor development is still delayed in certain areas. He isn't as delayed as his sister was at his age. He can throw and kick a ball, stand on the balance beam, and go up and down the stairs. He still has difficulty walking sideways on a line and he wavers when he tries to stand on one foot. So our objective of improving his balance is partially, but not completely, met. He doesn't need physical therapy, but it would be helpful for him to have adapted physical education. The adapted physical educator will plan strategies that will help him increase his ability to move confidently through a variety of gross motor activities.

ADAPTED PHYSICAL EDUCATOR (APE): (To father) I'll be glad to tell you more about the play activities we do and explain how Gamal will benefit from participating in these. Perhaps you or your wife might like to come and observe when Gamal is participating in these activities.

FATHER: That sounds good, but I don't know when I could do it and my wife doesn't go out much.

OCCUPATIONAL THERAPIST: I'm pleased with how well Gamal's fine motor skills have progressed. He is operating close to age level. The skills he needs work on are probably ones that he hasn't had as much experience with. For example, he needs practice in cutting, copying, buttoning, and drawing lines and scribbles. These are the kinds of activities you can do with him at home as well as at school.

FATHER: My wife will be glad to do that. She has the house all arranged for the children's activities.

OCCUPATIONAL THERAPIST: In order to draw a circle Gamal will need to do motor planning. That is, he needs to think about the sequence of actions in the task. It's not just a motor skill, but also a planning skill.

FATHER: A lot of the time I think Gamal is older than 3. He seems ahead of where the other two were at this age.

OCCUPATIONAL THERAPIST: Well, he is doing some motor skills above his age level and he really doesn't need occupational therapy.

FATHER: It seems like our main concern should be his language. (To speech pathologist) Do you think he'll stay mixed up between the two languages? He understands both languages. I can ask him something or tell him what to do in either language and he will do it, but he won't talk.

SPEECH PATHOLOGIST: Children can usually learn more than one language at a time, but it may take a while for them to sort them out. It's a good sign that he seems to understand directions in both of them. You should probably encourage him to talk by doing play activities where talking is needed, sometimes English and sometimes Arabic, but keeping it consistently one or the other.

OCCUPATIONAL THERAPIST: Yes, that could help. I saw an example when he was playing a computer game and was hearing questions from the animals' voices. He answered those questions in English.

FATHER: My two younger children don't talk as much as the older one. They aren't like him. He's very funny and always has something to say.

TEACHER: The younger ones will talk more in one-to-one situations. They also like being in small groups with a few peers. That might be the best situation in which to encourage his English speaking.

FATHER: I can see Gamal doing better in school than either of my other two. Maybe that's because he's been healthier and was bigger when he was born.

TEACHER: Those might be factors. Now, I've written down some tentative objectives for the new IFSP. When you get home, look over the list with your wife and if you have questions or want changes, let us know. Have we agreed that Gamal will come to our preschool 4 days a week next year? (To father) Didn't you say you wanted him to come to the afternoon session?

FATHER: Yes, in the morning he's lazy. I'll talk to my wife to be sure though. Let me check before we decide.

TEACHER: Okay. Your wife is welcome to come along to these meetings or to visit at school. You did say that she is beginning to speak English.

FATHER: Yes, she is going to a class. If she learns, that should also help Gamal to learn.

TEACHER: Right, and it will be good for you, too. Let's summarize our recommendations now. (Group agrees.)

RECOMMENDATIONS

The early intervention staff and the parents will work on a set of objectives related to Gamal's increasing his ability to dress himself, gain toilet control, do circle drawing, improve cutting skills, use English sentences, identify concepts labeled with English words, and improve gross motor coordination. Gamal's father will plan to have his hearing checked again to see if new PE tubes are needed. The transition plan for Gamal is for him to attend the preschool at the early intervention center for 4 half-days (probably in afternoons). The priority objective will be to encourage Gamal to talk more both at home and at school.

QUESTIONS FOR DISCUSSION

1. It is evident that living in two language worlds has had an effect on Gamal's developmental progress. What other strategies could the team have tried to help Gamal deal with this situation? How might the family's cultural values and traditions (e.g. appropriate roles for women, expectations for child achievement, valued learning styles) have had an effect on the concerns expressed by the father? Did the team members seem aware of these and respond appropriately?

2. Were the concerns expressed by the team members about the validity of the assessment measures appropriate? How did they attempt to counter any cultural biases in the assessment methods?

3. How did the roles played by the various team members during the meeting reflect role specificity and also role release? Did the behavior of this team give evidence to the fact that they have been working together for a number of years? Were there parts of the dialogue which showed that team members were not operating as effectively as they could have in their listening and responding?

4. Were there any ways that the team members could have prepared themselves to be more knowledgable about the family cultural values? If they had more knowledge or assistance from a native language speaker, could the discussion have been more supportive of the acculturation level of the family?

5. Why did the team focus so exclusively on developmental objectives for Gamal rather than on identifying health issues (e.g., Gamal's asthma) and other needs of the family (e.g., social support) that they might have addressed? If they had asked the father to discuss family needs, what would his response have been?

chapter 9

Doris Bergen
Caroline Everington

ASSESSMENT PERSPECTIVES FOR YOUNG CHILDREN WITH SEVERE DISABILITIES OR ENVIRONMENTAL TRAUMA

The phrase "severely disabled" generally refers to those infants and children who have conditions that make their developmental progress very delayed or distorted, especially if these conditions have severely limited their ability to engage actively in examination and manipulation of objects in their environment or to initiate and respond to social interactions with caregiving adults.

Often, these children are labeled as trainable mentally retarded, multihandicapped, autistic, deaf or blind, or emotionally disturbed (Falvey, 1989). Children labeled "multihandicapped" usually exhibit severe to profound mental retardation and one or more significant sensory or motor impairments or special health care needs (Orelove & Sobsey, 1991). Characteristics of these children can include skeletal deformities, seizure disorders, severe impairments in hearing or vision, and restricted or dysfunctional movement patterns. Not all children with severe impairments have accompanying cognitive impairments; however, they may still have delays in cognitive development because of the other disabilities.

Because these disabilities affect how the children respond to standard assessment procedures, early intervention personnel must consider their effects on valid assessment during the planning and conducting phases of assessment. For example, adaptations must often be made in the

216

presentation of stimuli to accommodate sensory or motor deficits, and acceptance of varied response modes by children with impairments may be essential. Children who live in environments where they have encountered severe abuse (e.g., drug, physical, mental, or sexual), extreme neglect (e.g., abandonment, lack of basic nutrition or care), or intense trauma (e.g., gang war or other pervasive violence) may have severely delayed or distorted development and aberrant methods of response when assessment procedures are tried. Initial assessment of these children using standard procedures is unlikely to provide a valid picture of their potential because of the effects of trauma on their social–emotional and behavioral response patterns.

Issues of environmental trauma are very relevant to professionals working with children who have severe disabilities. Extreme abuse or neglect often cause disabilities in children (e.g., head injury, broken bones, or lead poisoning) and they also are accompaniments to disabilities (e.g., children with severe impairments may be subject to maltreatment). Although the exact numbers are not available, professional experience with children who have severe disabilities indicates that they are very vulnerable to abuse or neglect.

UNDERLYING ASSUMPTIONS

Because of the difficulties in gaining valid results from typical measures, one assumption is that children who have severe or profound cognitive delay or multiple disabilities will benefit more from an assessment based on an ecological inventory strategy than on the traditional approaches using norm-referenced instruments. This view is supported by a well-documented line of research with severely cognitively delayed individuals, which indicates that they have significant problems in generalizing learned material to new settings, persons, and situations (Stokes & Baer, 1977). Thus, they may be unlikely to demonstrate their skills in an unfamiliar situation.

For example, information such as color or shape identification, which is standard on many tests, may not be readily transferred to new settings or used in appropriate problem-solving situations by children with severe cognitive delay. Rather, in situ assessment and training for what are termed "functional skills" is believed by many to be a very effective method of promoting skill acquisition, retention, and generalization.

The ecological inventory approach requires an initial inventory of the environments (e.g., home, school, and neighborhood) in which the child interacts and a catalog of the present level of skills considered by primary caregivers as most important for functioning in those environments.

When the children are very young, this approach is even more important and fully congruent with accepted early childhood practice. It is also very compatible with the early intervention emphasis on considering family and community setting variables in the assessment process.

Another assumption, which is also congruent with early intervention practice, is that multifactored assessment is especially important when evaluating children with severe impairments that may restrict their ability to perform in a formal setting. Therefore, it is important to gather information from norm-referenced assessment of children's acquisition of basic skills in language, motor, cognitive, and other developmental domains. Proponents of the ecological approach have tended to discount information from traditional measures as being irrelevant to the needs of persons with severe disabilities (Brown, Nietupski, & Hamre-Nietupski, 1976). However, over- or under-estimation of cognitive abilities can result in lack of knowledge acquisition or in behavioral difficulties when a skill is being taught (McClennen, 1991) and, thus, even a rough estimate of cognitive abilities can be useful.

Over-estimation (i.e., presenting experiences beyond the child's abilities) can result in characteristics often observed in children with severe disabilities: high dependence, task avoidance, and failure expectancy. Under-estimation (i.e., continuing to present experiences that the child has mastered) can result in boredom and behavior problems. For example, language acquisition is enhanced when the child's present language, cognitive, and social skill levels are used as a foundation, targeting the next sequential steps to be encouraged (McLean & Snyder-McLean, 1978).

Given the complex needs of these children, assessment must incorporate both developmental and ecological approaches. In order to do this, assistance is needed from professionals in a variety of specialized disciplines so that the adaptations and accommodations that maximize responding are provided. This leads to another assumption: That the adaptations made to increase the possibilities for appropriate responses must be carefully planned and documented as part of the assessment report. For example, a physical therapist may determine that certain positioning will permit greater responsivity or that an electrical device may facilitate the child's ability to answer. In reporting assessment results, the nature of these adaptations must be described.

Children who have had extreme environmental trauma also need ecologically sound and multifactored assessment from early intervention personnel who know both typical developmental stages and processes, as well as the behaviors that might be present in children who have been subjected to severe abuse, neglect, or other trauma. A major assumption in assessing children who have experienced environmental trauma caused by adults is that the best interests of the child must be served in the assessment, even if that results in a negative evaluation of the primary or extended family environment. Therefore, early assessment practices attempt to describe all aspects of the environment, including those that define family needs and possible environmental problems. The assessment team typically does not make explicit judgments on the quality of the environment, but they may suggest referrals to other agencies for further evaluation.

Because early intervention personnel are strongly in support of family involvement and believe that families are a primary positive influence on young children, it is sometimes difficult for them to reconcile this view with indications that abuse or neglect may exist. During the process of assessment, however, if indications of abuse or neglect are detected, it is the professional's responsibility to report such suspicions to the appropriate agency. If not reported, the professional is liable. After investigation by the appropriate agency, a determination is made as to resolution of the situation. If the family is judged to be motivated to change these behaviors, the early intervention team members may be involved in assisting the family in improving the environment. For example, they may provide alternative discipline techniques for the parent to use or get the parent in contact with needed nutritional services.

ASSESSMENT OF YOUNG CHILDREN WITH SEVERE OR MULTIPLE DISABILITIES

Assessment of these children must incorporate ecological and developmental approaches and address accommodations for specific conditions of disability. An appropriate model of assessment includes an ecological inventory and a comparison of those findings with data from norm-referenced measures. Assessment adaptations that can be made to get children's best performance are also necessary, although the validity of the measure for comparing with normative samples is reduced.

ECOLOGICAL INVENTORY

For severely disabled individuals of older ages, the ecological inventory typically includes community, domestic, leisure, and vocational domains (Falvey, 1989). For infants and young children, the first three of these are included. Within each domain, the environments that have the most important impact on the child's development are identified. Of course, for young children the home is the most crucial domestic domain, although there may be extended family settings that are also relevant. In the community domain, young children may spend much of their time in a child care or early intervention setting; however, the church, the doctor's office or hospital clinic, and the grocery store may also be relevant settings in the community. For young children, the leisure domain consists of the play settings in which the child interacts with toys, peers, or adults. For example, the park, swimming pool, or various community events can be observed. Often, parents with children who have multiple disabilities do not engage in leisure or community activities or even take their children with them when shopping or doing other routine activities. An advantage of the ecological inventory assessment is that the process may be used to encourage them to begin including this child in a broader range of life activities. Further description of an ecological inventory is in Appendix A.

Participation of the primary caregivers and interactors in each environment (parents, teachers, caregivers, pediatrician, hospital personnel) in observing and assessing the child's skills and needs is essential. Once the critical environments have been identified, sub-environments are identified and critical activities within those environments are monitored, using a task analysis that is constructed for each of these critical activities. The skills possessed are noted and a discrepancy analysis is performed that provides information on the child's abilities relative to the skills needed for each activity designated as critical. Those skills then become the focus of curriculum in order to close the gap between present developmental level and desired level.

For example, in the home the sub-environments of kitchen, bedroom, bathroom, living room, and porch may be identified, and the activities may be bathing, dressing, self-feeding, or playing with siblings. For each of these, the sub-skills are identified, such as holding a spoon, putting food on the spoon, bringing the spoon to the mouth, putting the spoon contents into the mouth, and swallowing the food for the self-feeding activity. The discrepancy analysis may identify that the child can hold the spoon and bring it to the mouth, but could not yet scoop the food. Learning to scoop with the spoon would then be the focus of learning for the child.

When the ecological inventory has been completed for the relevant settings, the child's overall performance is analyzed to determine strengths and weaknesses across environments and to note what performance-eliciting characteristics of one setting may be developed in others. For example, a hearing impaired child may sign in 2- or 3-word sentences and vocalize at home, while only signing 1-word sentences and never vocalizing at the early intervention program. This may be identified as a skill to be encouraged in the program environment.

As with any form of assessment, the results may generate a bewildering array of needed skills. Because of the intensity of intervention required for skill development with these children, making priorities is necessary. The skills can be prioritized by a variety of criteria, such as frequency of use across environments, importance of a particular skill to the parent, caregiver or teacher, importance for long-range functioning in future environments, and interests of the child. For example, the parent may want the hearing impaired child to vocalize at school, while the teacher may be more concerned about the child's ability to interact with other hearing impaired peers through signing. These differing perceptions can then be discussed at the IFSP meeting and a priority of skills can be developed.

NORM-REFERENCED ASSESSMENT

Information from norm-referenced assessments must also be integrated with the ecological inventory information. A number of these instruments have been discussed in chapters 3 through 8. Although the results taken alone can be misleading for children with severe disabilities, the comparison of these results with the ecological results is very useful in determining priority objectives for the child. For example, the ecological inventory may indicate the child needs to indicate preferences at mealtime, greet the early intervention teacher, and indicate the need to use the toilet. The assessments of the speech pathologist and the psychologists may indicate that the child is functioning at the sensorimotor stage of cognitive development, uses no formal language (either sign or verbal), and does not use sounds or primitive gestures to demonstrate communicative intent. Further, the child demonstrates turn-taking in a simple game of patty-cake, and imitates gross gestures such as a hand clap. The physical therapist indicates that fine motor skills are progressing typically.

The conclusion of the team may be that, because of the level of cognitive development and the fact that no communicative intent has been demonstrated, it is too early to begin training the child to use a formal symbol system (verbal or sign) and the use of pictures is too abstract. An appropriate language goal would be to help the child learn conventional gestures to communicate a "vocabulary" of simple needs such as "eat," "help," and "wet." Vocal imitation and refinement of gestures into conventional signs would continue to be encouraged.

A second example provides an illustration of the integration of information from the physical therapist. An ecological inventory may indicate that a child with severe cerebral palsy lacks control for functional use of limbs in any of the settings observed. However, the child does gaze at objects of interest at home and in the early intervention setting. For this child, initial communication may be accomplished through the use of directed eye gaze. The norm-referenced instruments show the child is functioning at sensorimotor level; thus, a communication device using pictures or abstract symbols would be inappropriate. In addition, because no symbol system use is being demonstrated (gesture or word), encouraging yes and no responses is not appropriate. For this child, learning to direct eye gaze to select desired objects may be the best initial approach, because it is a concrete task appropriate to the sensorimotor stage.

ADAPTATIONS FOR ASSESSING SPECIFIC IMPAIRMENTS

For many children with severe problems in sensory, motor, or communication areas, adaptations need to be made in the stimuli and response requirements for assessment and in the subsequent design of programs. Often, a physical therapist, occupational therapist, speech pathologist, or audiologist is included in the determination of adaptations to be made in the assessment process. Children for whom adaptations need to be made include those with sensory deficits, motor control or coordination problems, pervasive communication disorders, or some combination of these.

In a standardized testing situation, any change in the procedures affects the validity of the results, and these results can then not be used comparatively with the normative reference group. Some tests, such as the Developmental Activities Screening Inventory (DASI II) and Battelle, describe adaptations that can be made; this standardization of adaptations is helpful. Instruments with adaptations are described in Appendix B. Many of these tests have not yet provided representative norm groups for adaptive administration of the instruments and thus they still can not be used for making comparisons.

Sensory Adaptations

Children with deficits in vision, hearing, or both present unique problems. Assessment of some skill areas, such as visual or auditory pursuit of stimuli, may need to be abandoned. Another domain that will be affected is expressive and receptive language. However, the lack of visual or auditory abilities may not adversely affect demonstration of motor and self-care skills, unless child movement opportunities have been restricted by caregivers because of the vision loss.

For children who have been diagnosed as deaf and blind and who display no overt reaction to environmental stimuli, it is necessary to develop conditioning of a voluntary response that could function as a signal for important actions or needs. Van Dijk (1986) suggests that tactile and olfactory signals can be used to provide an initial foundation for communication. For example, a tactile symbol, such as an earring, can be used to symbolize the teacher or a particular scent paired with a certain activity can symbolize the activity. In the assessment process, careful observation of the relationship between nonverbal behaviors, such as gestures or facial expressions, and the contexts in which these behaviors occur can provide information about modalities and routines that can be used to establish communication. For children with some vision or hearing, use of visual or auditory aids (e.g., magnifiers or auditory trainers) or enhancement of stimuli through modifications of materials (e.g., large pictures or print or reduction of distraction in the environment) may be sufficient to make use of a traditional assessment measure possible. Of course, if a hearing aid or eye glasses can improve the child's responses, those should be provided before the assessment of other domains.

Motor Adaptations

Children with limited motor abilities or problems with muscle tone and postural development present other unique challenges for assessment and programming (Bobath, 1980). After the physical and occupational therapists have answered basic questions about techniques and optimal positions for normalization of muscle tone and motor performance, primitive reflexes that may inhibit performance, and range of motion that can be expected, adaptations to permit response capability can be determined. For children with extremely limited movement, alternative response methods, such as using an eye glance to substitute for pointing to pictures or objects, are possible (Carpignano & Bigge, 1991).

In assessing young children with atypical posture and movement patterns, the application of appropriate positioning and handling techniques is essential (Campbell, McInerney, & Cooper, 1984; Finnie, 1975; Rainforth & York, 1991). The early intervention specialist must work closely with the occupational or physical therapist to determine optimal positions for normalization of muscle tone, postural control, and maximum movement. Therapeutic adaptive equipment, such as specialized chairs, balls, bolsters, and side-liers, can help to inhibit abnormal reflex patterns and encourage normalized tone and control. For infants and very young children, many effective adaptations can be made with pillows, bean bags, or rolled towels (Finnie, 1975), thus minimizing expense. Because too much support is potentially dangerous if it limits opportunities to develop external control (Rainforth & York, 1991), such adaptations must be done in consultation with relevant therapists.

There is an array of mechanical and electronic adaptations to facilitate self-care skills, communication, and ambulation (Orelove & Sobsey, 1991). These devices can vary from simple adaptations using materials in the home or work environment (Burkhardt, 1981) to sophisticated computerized adaptations for environmental control and communication. It is important for the early intervention specialist to work closely with the speech pathologist, physical therapist, and occupational therapist in selecting and adapting such equipment.

Communication Adaptations

Communication adaptations are often needed for young children who exhibit pervasive communication disorders (e.g., autism). These behaviors include, but are not limited to, abnormally high rates of self-stimulatory behavior (e.g., hand flicking, rocking, or humming), self-injurious behavior (e.g., head banging, hair pulling, hand biting), lack of or extremely distorted language (e.g., referring to self in third person, echolalia), social withdrawal (e.g., inattention to pronounced social stimuli, focus on object world), or inappropriate or nonexistent emotional reactions to others (Smith & Luckasson, 1992). It is especially important to determine what adapted methods or devices can be used to facilitate communication with these young children because their pervasive communication disorders affect all aspects of their development and learning.

Behavior change for these children is usually attempted either by (1) remedying behavior deficits in social and language skills through training the child to exhibit more appropriate social and communication behaviors or (2) decreasing behavior excesses through reduction of frequency and magnitude of inappropriate behaviors, such as head banging (Haney & Falvey, 1989; Sternberg & Taylor, 1988). Because there is often a relationship between deficits and excesses, the most effective interventions address both (Haring, 1987; Sternberg & Taylor, 1988).

One significant contribution in this area has been in the analysis of the communicative function of aberrant behavior, such as self-stimulation or self-injury (Donnellan, Mirenda, Mesaros, & Fassbender, 1984; Iwata, Dorsey, Slifer, Bauman, & Richman, 1982). In this approach, children are observed in the context of their environment and the communicative function of the aberrant behavior is determined. For example, Iwata et al. (1982) found that self-injurious behavior usually served one of three functions: gaining attention, receiving sensory input, or escaping from an unpleasant task. Once the function being served has been determined, the intervention can focus on helping children learn appropriate ways to get their needs met (Cipani, 1990). This approach has had more success with changing severe behaviors than has typical behavior management.

Another emerging trend that has implications for assessment of children with autism is the use of facilitated communication (Biklen, 1991). This approach differs from that of other adapted communication methods, which enable children to act independently to communicate needs and thoughts, by having an individual physically assist the child, holding the child's hand or arm and typing out or pointing to letters on a typewriter or communication board. Numerous first-person narrative accounts have reported the claim that individuals who had previously been diagnosed as severely impaired now are displaying advanced language and literacy skills.

Although not widespread or systematically documented, the approach may result in increased appreciation for the potential for individual change. However, because constant participation of the facilitator is required, validity can be compromised (Wheeler, Jacobson, Paglieri, & Schwartz, 1993). That is, there is the risk of inadvertent cueing from the facilitator. A review of recent empirical studies using double-blind methodology indicates strong support for the notion that facilitators are exerting control over the messages supposedly produced by the children with severe disabilities (Green, 1993), which raises doubts about the usefulness of the approach for assessment.

ASSESSMENT OF YOUNG CHILDREN WITH SEVERE ENVIRONMENTAL TRAUMA

Because of the effects that severe environmental trauma have on young children's ability to perform at their optimal level, an appropriate model for assessment should combine an ecological inventory with results from norm-referenced measures. Adaptations of these measures may also be necessary to solicit the child's best performance.

ECOLOGICAL INVENTORY

The ecological inventory method is very useful in assessing children who may have suffered from severe abuse or neglect, although families vary in the extent to which they will cooperate in such an assessment. Research indicates that young children's attachment problems, uncontrolled aggression, poor self-concept, hypervigilance, extreme passivity, or object rather than social orientation are associated with chaotic home environments and child maltreatment in the early years (Cicchetti, 1985; Susman, Trickett, Iannotti, Hollenbeck, & Zahn-Waxler, 1985). Children with disabilities or developmental problems are often likely to experience parental abuse or neglect, especially when they are in multi-risk families (Cicchetti & Toth, 1987).

According to Susman et al. (1985), abusive parents are more authoritarian, use anxiety and guilt induction, have inconsistent discipline, are overprotective, encourage child dependency, and show more negative affect. They often do not respond appropriately to their infant's cries or smiles (Frodi & Lamb, 1980). These interaction patterns may also affect child attachment (Beckwith, 1985). However, research also shows that these parents are usually under great stress (Daniel, Hampton, & Newberger, 1983; Hughes & Barad, 1983) and often are social isolates themselves (Oden, 1988). They may have less realistic expectations of developmentally appropriate behavior and so may expect young children to show greater maturity than is possible, given their age or disability (Kravitz & Driscoll, 1983).

If an ecological inventory is conducted, which involves the family members in providing information about their child's level of skills and in helping to decide what next steps can be taken to further skill development and behavior change, parents and other family members may become more realistic about and more aware of the abilities of their child. They may also become invested in assisting the child's development and may learn more appropriate techniques of discipline and teaching.

The ecological inventory can also draw on whatever support system is available to the family, such as a church, doctor, neighbor, or social agency, and the perspectives on the child that come from these sources may make a difference in parental perceptions of the child and in parental behavior. Most agencies are committed to helping children stay with their families. The ecological inventory can be one of the major resources for pinpointing the practices in the home that have negatively affected the child and for opening the way to positive behavior changes within the family.

NORM-REFERENCED ASSESSMENT

It is equally important for these children that a comparison of their developmental level with that of typically developing children be made. Because distortions in their behavior or development can be due to a variety of etiological factors, the relative weight of conditions caused by biological risk (i.e., medical or health-related) or established risk (i.e., identifiable disability category) and those caused by environmental risk should be assessed, so that appropriate interventions can be planned and implemented.

For example, language delay and behavior problems are often exhibited in children who live in conditions of severe environmental trauma, such as abuse or neglect. However, these problems may also be the result of identified risk conditions such as autism or hearing impairment. Although much information on etiology can be established through social and medical history data collection, standardized assessment instruments administered by the audiologist or speech pathologist and the psychologist on the team can make explicit the character of a language deficit or inappropriate behavior pattern and, by ruling out biological or established risk conditions that could be the cause, can clarify useful environmental intervention approaches.

Further validation of the findings from normative instruments may be obtained by evaluating the child's play behavior with structured observations or rating scales, and by determining whether the profile of behavior is consistent with severe environmental risk conditions. Play-based observation is an important assessment component for children who have had environmental trauma, because play development is usually disrupted when children are under great stress. Often the child is suspicious and wary, extremely distractible, and has boundary problems (either overcontrolled or undercontrolled) that make sustained play impossible (Kaplan-Sanoff, Brewster, Stillwell, & Bergen, 1988). The themes of play may also be precocious, with sexual or violent language and behavior being predominant. Even at toddler age, "failure-to-thrive" children can repeat their unconscious memories of their mother's inadequate nurturing in "exacting detail" during play with dolls (Haynes-Seman & Hart, 1987). Observational analysis of child play behaviors can suggest insights into child motivation, interests, and thinking, which will assist team members in making intervention plans. Play observation methods are described in Chapter 4 and Appendix B.

One important difference between evaluations of children in this category and all other assessments is that, if severe abuse or neglect are suspected, the procedures used in the assessment must be available to serve as documentation, if the suspected abuser is to be legally charged. While this is not the goal of assessments in early intervention, team members should be prepared to have the best interests of the child in mind, to use procedures that are objective, and to report findings that may need further investigation (Tyler & Gregory, 1992).

Adaptations for Assessing Specific Trauma Conditions

In cases of suspected abuse or neglect, child behavior in routine assessments is often symptomatic, giving indications of these conditions and making it difficult for the child's best performance to be assessed. Adaptations may be needed during the assessment, such as giving the child a long time to become familiar with and trusting of the adults before conducting the assessment, doing the assessment in a "safe" place (i.e., without the suspected abuser being present), reassuring the child frequently that his or her behavior is acceptable, and providing tangible reinforcements for performance. Because it may be necessary to document the case for legal authorities, the role of the psychologist often becomes crucial in providing the basis for the charge. Every member of the team should be well aware of ethical and legally correct procedures to be used, however, because many "leading" questions and unfounded assumptions can be unfair to the family and can bias legitimate cases. They must also be prepared to work closely with agencies such as children's services, providing assessment information and carrying out recommended interventions.

INFORMATION EXCHANGE WITH FAMILIES AND REFERRAL AGENCIES

Because the families are closely involved in developing ecological inventories and in discussing their children's strengths and needs, early intervention personnel's information exchange with families of children who have severe disabilities is usually ongoing and detailed. They are usually in touch with medical and support service personnel from the time of their child's birth, and thus those communication linkages are strong. There may be delivery of nursing services in the home, repeated hospitalization for medical procedures, and a constant stream of specialists in contact with the family. Whether this results in good or poor information exchange depends on the specific personnel involved and on the case manager who is facilitating referrals to agencies.

In the case of suspected abuse or neglect, information exchange with families may be disrupted at the point where a problem is uncovered, or the family may have been withholding of information from the start. In fact, perceived gaps in the information given by families is often symptomatic of the problem. Team members should try to find the balance between open discussion of the child's needs and developmental delay conditions and the family's reticence to discuss negative information that may be relevant. While the team should highly respect family need for privacy, they should also know when the problem should be referred to other agency personnel, and they should make those referrals when warranted.

USEFULNESS OF A TRANSDISCIPLINARY MODEL

The transdisciplinary model is especially useful for assessment of children with severe disabilities. It provides the multidomain and multisetting information needed to plan interventions for these children and the intense involvement of professionals from a range of disciplines is really required if families are to gain the support they need to assume the long-term comprehensive care responsibilities that their children demand. The team model is also very useful in assessing and intervening for children who have experienced abuse or neglect because it provides a base for validity checks and support for the family in making appropriate changes.

While the ecological inventory outlined in this chapter provides an extremely comprehensive understanding of the child's skills and needs in relevant areas and demonstrates the benefits of family involvement, the data collection and analysis process is extremely time consuming. The full process, which includes the integrated norm-referenced information, provides such a wealth of information on skill deficits and strengths that all of these cannot be addressed at one time. Developing the priorities for intervention from these data can also consume the time and effort of the assessment team.

Another problem with the transdisciplinary approach is that professionals from most other disciplines often have not been exposed to the model, even though the early childhood special educator may have had this training. Professionals from some disciplines (e.g., therapists or medical personnel) may have difficulty releasing any part of their role expertise to teachers or parents and, especially in the intense intervention model that is often used with children who have severe disabilities, the efforts of teachers or parents to perform those additional roles may be extremely stressful for them.

For children with severe disabilities, the transdisciplinary team model can be so facilitative of their optimal development that every effort should be made to solve the time and training problems. For children who have had traumatic life experiences that result in disabilities or developmental problems, this model is also especially helpful because access to community resources and service agencies is more readily available from team members.

POLICY ISSUES

Infants and young children with severe disabilities are not only more susceptible to environmental abuse, neglect, and exploitation, but also tend to be "devalued" or viewed as "expendable" by society, and are frequently marginalized. Two policy issues of concern for early intervention team members working with children who have severe disabilities are: (1) rights to medical treatment and educational services and (2) inclusion in educational and community settings.

The first issue, right to medical treatment for infants and young children who have life-threatening conditions, continues to present moral and ethical (and ultimately, policy) dilemmas (Lusthaus, 1985). While treatment decisions are typically made by parents, other family members, or guardians, in many cases decisions for non-treatment are made without adequate information on the prognosis or expectations for development for children with a particular condition. For example, in the past, life-saving medical intervention was often questioned or not provided in cases that involved infants diagnosed with spina bifida or Down's syndrome. Non-treatment decisions were even made when necessary surgery was of a routine nature. Now there is evidence that the prognosis for further development and generally satisfactory quality of life is quite good for children who have either of these conditions (Smith & Luckasson, 1992).

The amount of information given to parents and the manner of the presentation—optimistic versus pessimistic—can have a marked influence on parental decisions. The early intervention specialist can serve a vital role in providing the parents and family physician with accurate information on the condition, along with the medical, therapeutic, social, and educational services available for family and child. Because of the increasing costs of health care, it is reasonable to assume that families and children will continue to face right-to-treatment issues. A number of professional organizations has addressed these issues in policy statements (e.g., American Association of Mental Retardation [AAMR], 1983; The Association for Severely Handicapped [TASH], 1989). The consensus from the statements of both AAMR and TASH affirms the right to equal medical treatment for all infants.

A related issue concerning children with severe disabilities is "educability" (Noonan, Brown, Mulligan, & Rettig, 1982; Sternberg, 1988). Questions are raised about whether these individuals really can learn and whether it is wise to attempt to educate children who will be a "burden on society" (Baer, 1981). Especially in times when societal resources are limited, the question of whether money should be spent on individuals who may never be totally independent is often asked. These issues continue to be debated by legislators and tax payers who are concerned about the rising costs of special education, particularly for those individuals with severe disabilities who require many professionals to give them adequate services. Certainly, there is little question of the beneficial effects of early intervention. This message may not have reached all policy decision makers, however. Early intervention team members may need to be prepared to provide additional information on the necessity and effectiveness of intervention for children with severe disabilities. Because the progress of these children is often slow and difficult to observe, the maintenance of accurate and appropriate monitoring systems to record children's progress is essential, if communication with policy makers is to have an effect.

Another policy concern that has received recent attention is that of access of individuals with severe disabilities to inclusive educational and community settings. While one of the basic premises of the original Education for All Handicapped Act in 1975 (P.L. 94-142) and subsequent reauthorizations is the concept of "least restrictive environment," practice over the past 18 years has indicated that these individuals continue to be excluded from many functions of mainstream society, and that considerable stigma is still associated with individuals who have disabilities.

The movement to educate children with disabilities in neighborhood schools and preschools, in general education classrooms, and in community settings has been gaining momentum at local, state, and national levels (Thousand & Villa, 1993). For example, the Council for Exceptional Children (CEC, 1993) and other professional organizations (e.g., TASH, 1989), have developed policy statements in support of inclusive schools and community settings; a number of states are providing funding for inclusion demonstration programs in public schools.

Such efforts do not diminish the importance of having personnel who have specialized training to work with children with disabilities, but invite a collaborative team approach to the education of all children. While segregated settings (e.g., special centers for persons with disabilities) may have the advantage of providing centralized services, increasing numbers of programs are documenting equally effective service delivery and learning in integrated inclusive settings (Thousand & Villa, 1993).

Finally, there are policy issues that surround conditions of severe environmental trauma that must be addressed, such as whether there are "rights of the child" to be considered when the child's welfare seems to be at risk or whether "rights of the family" to decide the child's future always take precedence. In American society, the rights of families to control their children's lives has traditionally been upheld by the courts (e.g., Meyer v. Nebraska, 1923; Pierce v. Society of Sisters, 1925; Stanley v. Illinois, 1971) and has been made explicit in laws giving parents choice over care and educational decisions.

This view is commonly held even when children's access to health or educational services is jeopardized by parental decisions, such as parental failure to provide immunizations to protect from disease or parental decisions for attendance at private schools with uncertified teachers. Other issues, such as biological versus adoptive parental rights as they affect child rights to stable attachments, mandates to keep families together even in situations of documented child abuse or parental drug use, and policies that result in repeated separations without resolution of custody issues all need to be addressed further.

Because of the vulnerability of these child populations to exploitation and marginalization, it is critical that early intervention team members act as thoughtful advocates for children and their families within the context of these policy issues. There may even be occasions when they should give public voice to their concerns and provide information to inform policy makers and the general public about the needs of children who have severe disabilities or who have been subject to severe environmental trauma.

SUMMARY

The importance of a multifactored assessment within appropriate ecological contexts cannot be overstressed for young children who have severe disabilities or who have experienced severe environmental risk. These are often the children who have been judged to be "untestable" with conventional methods. An approach that includes an ecological survey of the range of skills the children can exhibit in varied environments and a comparative evaluation using adapted standardized instruments is most likely to provide the comprehensive data needed for intervention planning. The transdisciplinary team approach holds great potential for facilitating developmental achievements for these populations of children because it incorporates methods that are sensitive to the complexities of the developmental problems and the dynamics of interaction that affect their development. However, there are many issues of practice and policy that can also influence how effectively assessment and intervention can be provided for these children by the early intervention team.

QUESTIONS FOR DISCUSSION

1. What is the most useful combination of assessment methods that a team could design to get an accurate picture of the abilities of a visually impaired infant of 9 months, a toddler of 22 months who is exhibiting behaviors symptomatic of autism, and a 30-month-old child with severe cerebral palsy?
2. What factors must be kept in mind in conducting an ecological and standardized assessment of a young child who has experienced severe trauma, such as physical or sexual abuse?

PROBLEMS OF PRACTICE

Conduct an ecological inventory for an infant or toddler who has severe disabilities and who also comes from a home with at least one environmental risk indicator. Observe the young child and family in at least three different environments (e.g., at home, at the early intervention program, and at a church nursery, social service setting, extended family gathering, or other mesosystem environment). Plan to observe the child's demonstration of the same developmental skills in all three settings, noting in which setting they are most facilitated by adults and in which setting they are least often demonstrated. Make an evaluation of the interactive factors in those three settings that contribute to or detract from the child's ability to demonstrate his or her optimum performance level.

Suggested Readings

Brown, L., Nietupski, J., & Hamre-Nietupski, S. (1976). Criterion of ultimate functioning. In M. A. Thomas (Ed.), *Hey, don't forget about me! Education's investment in the severely, profoundly, & multiply handicapped* (pp. 2–15). Reston, VA: Council for Exceptional Children.

Cicchetti, D., & Toth, S. L. (1987). The application of a transactional risk model to intervention with multi-risk maltreating families. *Zero to Three, 7*(5), 1–8.

DIALOGUE

IFSP REVIEW OF HARRY

GENDER, AGE, ETHNIC ORIGIN OF CHILD: Male, 27 months, Euro-American.

OCCASION OR PURPOSE OF DIALOGUE: Second review of Harry, 3 months after initial IFSP was developed; to assess developmental progress. Harry has been receiving services in a self-contained classroom with 4 children in the age range of 15 to 36 months. The teacher, instructional aid, and most of the children's mothers are present for the 2-hour session. Other support personnel also engage in interactions within the classroom setting. Once a month, home visits by the early interventionist are conducted.

TEAM MEMBERS: The early interventionist, instructional assistant (teacher aid), physical therapist, occupational therapist, speech pathologist, and the child's mother.

SETTING: The classroom of the early intervention program, after child session.

OVERVIEW OF THE CASE

RISK CONDITIONS

Harry was developing typically until the age of 3 months. He contracted an ear infection at this time, which was accompanied by a high fever. He began having severe and repeated epileptic seizures, which medical team personnel were initially unable to control. The precipitating cause of the seizures remains undocumented. However, there is the possibility that a secondary bacterial infection occurred in the brain, leading to status epilepticus, with permanent brain damage. The seizures continued during the next 17 months as the medical team attempted to find the proper medication and dosage level to control the condition. An MRI indicated damage to the visual and language areas of the brain. For the past 7 months Harry's seizures have been sporadic, but generally under control. However, Harry has severe and multiple problems, including visual, physical, language, and cognitive impairments.

REASON FOR REFERRAL

Harry's mother actively sought the early intervention program through self-referral. He has continued to see a neurologist and pediatrician from the hospital where his illness was treated, and, until recently, had been receiving occupational therapy and physical therapy from the hospital. A visual impairment specialist from the Association for the Blind also visits Harry once a month at his home. However, the mother desired a comprehensive educational program for Harry. She requested his evaluation by the early intervention staff. He has been in the early intervention program for 3 months; this is the 90-day review. Objectives identified in the first IFSP development, which will be evaluated in the meeting, included the following:

1. Harry will sit independently and participate in play with siblings and peers.
2. Harry will play with a variety of toys and increase his level of play skills.
3. Harry will bear weight on lower extremities with good alignment.
4. Harry will increase vocal interactions and communicate his wants, needs, and preferences through gestures and using tactile speech strips—textures placed on switches that activate loop tapes.
5. The family will obtain equipment as needed to facilitate positioning at home and at day care.

BACKGROUND INFORMATION

Harry's mother had an uncomplicated pregnancy and delivery. Videotapes taken during the first 3 months of Harry's life show evidence of a typically developing child. After the seizures, Harry was treated at Child Hospital, receiving physical and occupational therapy in addition to physician care. He also received an assessment of hearing and vision. His hearing was judged to be normal, but he was found to have a severe visual impairment. He wears splints on his curled feet to flatten them and to support his ankles when being given weight-bearing exercises and continues to receive medication prescribed by the hospital pediatric staff.

FAMILY STRENGTHS AND NEEDS

Strengths include parents who are able and willing to access needed resources, a cooperative extended family support system in the immediate area, and parental involvement in agency service systems (e.g., respite care resources and financial aid resources to purchase visual impairment equipment). The mother is the director of a day care center that Harry is able to attend when not in the early intervention program. The parents (especially the mother) are strongly motivated to help their child in whatever ways possible. They are willing to follow through with activities in the home.

Family needs identified by the parents include continuation of respite care, and consultation on long-range planning to provide for Harry's needs as he grows older (e.g., methods of transporting him and educational options). The mother has also requested suggestions for a support group in which she could participate and ideas for activities that can be done at home to promote Harry's development.

SOURCES OF ASSESSMENT INFORMATION

Medical records and reports from hospital personnel are available. The Association for the Blind has also evaluated Harry's visual potential. Assessment measures collected by the early intervention staff include the Carolina Curriculum, Hawaii Early Learning Profile (HELP), parent interview, play-based assessment, and school and home observations by teacher, parent, and therapists.

Social–Emotional Development

Harry shows ability to demonstrate his emotions. He smiles and laughs in response to adult vocal play, tickling, and other "rough housing." He squeals when happy and cries when upset. He smiles and occasionally vocalizes in response to peer voices. He is not initiating of social interaction, however. He definitely has likes and dislikes, which he communicates through facial, vocal, and body tension responses. His developmental skills are scattered, with his performance on the HELP being in the 4- to 8-month range, although he exhibits a few higher level responses.

Physical–Motor and Sensory–Perceptual Development

Harry rolls from either side (primarily from left), sits with support for short periods, and actively extends to change position. Protective responses to the sides and front when sitting are beginning to be demonstrated. His head position in sitting and prone is primarily extended, but in the past month he has demonstrated ability to bring his head to the middle of his body and hold it there for 1 to 4 minutes. His hearing is excellent, but his vision is limited to seeing light and black and white. He does not reach out for or explore objects. He can clap his hands and he tolerates tactile stimuli for short periods of time. During periods when he is not engaged in interaction with an adult, he engages in self-stimulating behaviors, especially rolling back and forth. His hands are clenched at times, but not as often as they were 3 months ago. Now he keeps them open most of the time. He can bite off pieces of food and is beginning to move food in chewing motion when eating. His HELP motor skill performance is also scattered, with an age level range of 2 to 6 months.

Cognitive–Language Development

Harry does not spontaneously reach for, explore, or play manipulatively with toys and other objects. These abilities may be difficult for him to demonstrate because of his limited vision. He does show interest in novel sounds and he will orient to search for their source. When presented with switch-activated toys, he will interact for several minutes. However, he does not continue to initiate actions when the toy response occurs. It is unclear whether he understands the cause–effect relationship between his action and the response or whether he interacts with the adapted switch as an end in itself. He is able to activate the adaptive switches with his full left hand or with his right middle finger. When prompted, he reaches to relocate a switch for continuation of interaction with the adapted toys. He pats adult hands to request "more" of an activity, or signals to continue by tapping his leg with his hand.

He inconsistently participates in vocal play with adults. His vocalizations consist of vowel sounds and a limited variety of repetitive syllable consonant and vowel combinations (mother reports "Dada" and "Mama," but these have not been observed in the early intervention setting). The HELP communication profile is in the 2- to 6-month range. He does seem to have communicative intent, attempting to draw the attention of the caregivers when they are busy elsewhere, and using gestural or vocal means to gain their attention.

THE TEAM DIALOGUE

The team is gathered to review the initial IFSP, to determine what progress has been made, and to make a revised IFSP based on this review. The early intervention teacher is the team leader for this discussion.

EARLY INTERVENTION TEACHER: (To mother) I understand Harry is no longer being seen by a private physical or occupational therapist. Can you explain why Child Hospital canceled these services?

MOTHER: They said if he was getting services in another county, he no longer needed theirs. It didn't make sense to me because I think he still needs them and I liked going to that place. I don't really want to start at another place.

PHYSICAL THERAPIST: They do provide those services in our county also. I suggest you call the Developmental Services Center to inquire about getting him into their therapy program. The center is affiliated with the hospital.

TEACHER: Can you also give me the number of the therapists you were seeing? I can ask them to reconsider Harry's need for their program.

MOTHER: Thanks. I'll call the center to ask what they have. I'd rather stay with Child Hospital though. Will you let me know what you find out? How do you think Harry is getting along in the program? I've seen you working with him on the goals we set, but I don't think he's making much progress, at least at home.

PHYSICAL THERAPIST: I feel that Harry is at a crucial point now. Either he will increase his self-stimulation behavior or he'll work through it. Any external stimulation he can get is good for him. He doesn't care for some types; for example, he doesn't care to be moved in space at all. He has let us all know that! We also know he loves the water and the moving car.

TEACHER AID: At least he is letting us stimulate him more than he did back in September. (To mother) We couldn't get near him without your holding him. His favorite activity now is the music box. He gets a lot of positive reinforcement from hearing that.

TEACHER: We are still seeing a lot of crying behavior at the school. Has that continued to be a problem at home?

MOTHER: I don't think it has gotten much better. It's really frustrating for him to show or tell what he wants.

TEACHER: We talk to him while we go through activities and give him options to be happy or not, but he doesn't seem to be interested or motivated to be active. Although he's slightly increased the amount of time he interacts with toys, his play skills haven't really increased much. (To mother) We've found that the best ways to get him to stop crying are by letting you hold him or by playing his music box. He does love music so that may be the best "entry" spot.

MOTHER: Do you think the medication he's on could cause him to be irritable? I think that the seizure medication isn't helping and the dosage is too strong for him. I want to see about changing the dosage.

PHYSICAL THERAPIST: Why change this now? The "meds" are not knocking him out and the seizures are controlled. Last Fall he seizured every time we moved him! It seems to me that the medication is working most of the time.

TEACHER: It might be good just to check with the doctor to determine if the medication (Phenobarbital) could be a factor in his irritability, though.

MOTHER: I'm not going to do anything now; I was just thinking about it. Is Harry doing any better with his sounds? At home he is able to make his wants known a little better.

TEACHER: I don't think our objective in this area has been reached, although he's increased his vocal interactions somewhat. As far as expressive language goes, I have only noticed one time where he's repeated sounds (ba-ba-ba for bounce-bounce-bounce). I've heard no inflection; I can't get that at all. His understanding of language is also hard to judge. We are trying to provide opportunities for him to learn vocal turn taking by touching his mouth and cueing "Your turn, Harry." So far, this strategy has been slightly successful; we've gotten him to take up to 3 turns, but he seems to be imitating more than communicating. He still needs the tactile stimulation cues in order to respond.

MOTHER: I haven't heard him use any inflections either, but he has responded to my talking to him sometimes by making ba-ba type sounds.

SPEECH PATHOLOGIST: Because his communicative attempts are so limited, I brought in some loop tapes to the classroom for him to use with the music and with the lights. How's he doing with those? (The classroom has a light board. Loop tapes are cassette tapes that, when activated, play the same message over and over).

TEACHER: I'm not sure he can make a distinction between the choice of playing with the lights or the music. I know that loop tapes work well with older children, but maybe we need to continue focusing on increasing his vocalizations and gestures.

SPEECH PATHOLOGIST: We're going to have to observe him to see if it's the tactile stimulation that he doesn't like, the kind of music, the lights, or what. If he does not actively seek using the loop tapes at school, do you want me to send some loop tapes home?

TEACHER: I'd prefer to send home something that is part of the family routine so they do not have to feel that they must do something more or learn something else for Harry. (To mother) What do you think, Madge?

MOTHER: I'm willing to try them, if they can help him. He does like sounds so he might use them, especially if my older children do it with him. He likes to have them play with him.

TEACHER: That's a good suggestion. (To physical therapist) I think he's also going to need new splints soon; his toes are already hanging out of the present ones.

PHYSICAL THERAPIST: I'm looking more to give him a stable base to support on; some toes hanging out when he's in the prone stander won't hurt. I can dip and stretch the splints.

TEACHER: I had him up in the prone stander today and his right foot was barely touching, but his left foot looked good. (She demonstrates posture.)

PHYSICAL THERAPIST: Harry has made some progress on the objectives of sitting and bearing weight on his lower extremities. However, he really hasn't achieved these objectives completely. About the best sign I see is when he's getting into a spread-legged, on-his-knees position. It's the only time that I see him weight-bearing. Defensiveness on the soles of his feet doesn't help. The use of the brushes should reduce this defensiveness. (The brushes are surgical scrub sponges with soft plastic bristles. Therapists use them for 10 seconds on each extremity and on skin to increase tactile stimulation.)

OCCUPATIONAL THERAPIST: He has usually accepted the brush on his soles as well as hands. In fact, he is responding to this activity by holding his hand out with palm up to indicate "more."

PHYSICAL THERAPIST: The ability to sit is there; he's choosing not to do it by actively getting out of the position.

TEACHER: So we need to find a reinforcement for sitting. Half the battle with him is if he's in a good mood or not. I think we need to find out more about what will reinforce him for sitting, playing, vocalizing, and gesturing. I also think we need to know more about his cognitive skills. I plan to try the Uzgiris-Hunt Scales to see how he responds to means–ends and causality problems and to find out more about how his sensorimotor schemes are developing. Perhaps we need to get some more information by doing a ecological inventory. We could learn more if we saw his behavior in a wider variety of settings.

PHYSICAL THERAPIST: We need to give him lots of opportunities to sit, bounce, and balance himself. (To mother and early interventionist) You could start him on your lap and bounce him so that he feels a sense of support. Then, slowly bounce him away from you and off your lap until he accepts independence gradually.

OCCUPATIONAL THERAPIST: He's not reaching and holding. There's no spontaneous reaching at all to indicate that he wants anything. He does reach when prompted by tactile stimulation.

TEACHER: But sometimes he withdraws from tactile stimulation and sometimes he seems to finds it by accident. He will pound on the table more often if he's in the prone stander. The most indication of wanting something that I've seen is by a head turn or if he stops crying.

MOTHER: His brother can sometimes get him to show what he wants better than I can. Especially when he is in his new corner chair. (An adapted chair has recently been purchased; this fulfills the objective related to positioning equipment.)

TEACHER: (To mother) Is there anything else we can suggest for home to help you and your family with Harry?

PHYSICAL THERAPIST: What about a wheelchair? You need to start thinking of it because he's getting too big and heavy to carry. Plus, he doesn't always want to be carried and he arches himself back. You aren't going to be able to hang onto him when he gets much bigger. He could easily throw himself out of your arms.

MOTHER: I'm not sure I want a wheelchair. I'd rather wait with that until we see how much progress he makes in the next few months. He's beginning to roll and sit up, so maybe he'll be able to start moving around by himself before long. I'd like to try the loop tapes, though, because I want him to be able to play by himself.

TEACHER: Well, when I come for my home visit, I'll observe Harry there and we'll talk about how we could find out more about the behaviors and skills he demonstrates in other settings. Do you take him to church, to your other children's school, or to the supermarket? We could decide on some behaviors that you could notice in every place. For example, we could find out where and when he is most likely to be contented, to be trying to vocalize, or to be interested in the objects around him. One place to start would be with the sound environment. We could note what sounds in his environment elicit what types of behavior. Then at our next meeting we could talk about whether we could create the environments that seemed to bring out the highest levels of his skills. (To mother) Are you interested in trying an ecological inventory?

MOTHER: Yes, and I think my older boys would enjoy keeping track of Harry's behaviors, too. We all might see that he is doing things we haven't noticed before.

TEACHER: I'll draw up a plan and show you how to collect the information. Then we'll try to follow the same plan here at school to be able to compare his behavior here with that shown in other settings. (To teacher aid) Do you think this inventory is something that we can have the time to do?

TEACHER AID: Yes, there are usually enough adults here to have one person observing. Some of the other parents might be willing to be observers part of the time, too.

TEACHER: Did you find out any more about the parent support groups in this area? Did you call Mrs. Leader, the coordinator of the parent group in town, or the developmental services center parent education director, Miss Nursely?

MOTHER: Yes, neither group met over the summer, but both will be starting in September. I plan to go to one of them, or maybe I'll try both and see what the meetings are like.

TEACHER: (To mother) I think our co-leadership of service coordination is working well. Do you agree?

MOTHER: Yes, I am pleased with this arrangement.

TEACHER: Are we ready to make our recommendations? (Group agrees.)

RECOMMENDATIONS

Harry continues to be eligible for the early intervention program and will remain in the two-afternoon-per-week session. The role of service coordination leadership will continue to be shared by the early interventionist and the parents. Harry will receive physical therapy, occupational therapy, speech therapy, and adapted physical education in the early intervention setting, and access to private physical and occupational therapy will also be explored. The team members will continue their interventions, monitoring, and ongoing assessment of Harry's development, with particular emphasis on vocal and verbal play interactions, reinforcement for sitting and mobility attempts, and provision of adaptive equipment to encourage his reaching for and activating toys. His sensorimotor development will be systematically assessed and a plan for conducting an ecological inventory will be developed and a similar set of information on Harry's behavior (crying, vocalizing, playing, listening) will be collected in a variety of environments. Progress will be monitored daily with formal review in 90 days by the team. Harry's mother will select a support group and begin participation. Discussion of the need for a wheelchair will continue, in consultation with Harry's physician.

QUESTIONS FOR DISCUSSION

1. This mother is an active participant on the team. How did her presence and interaction style affect the team discussion?
2. What appear to be the team's major areas of focus for Harry? How does the makeup of the team reflect that focus? How is the team handling what appear to be some differences of opinion about the intervention objectives?
3. Would the presence of additional team members have added other useful perspectives (e.g., personnel from the children's hospital, adapted physical educator, psychologist, or visual impairment specialist)? If input of those professionals is desired, how could the team set up a collaborative two-way communication process with them when they are not regular members of the team?
4. What are the methods of assessment presently being used to monitor Harry's progress? Are these sufficient at this time? Are there specific areas that need to have a sharper assessment focus? Would the proposed ecological inventory be useful in expanding the range of behaviors and settings in which Harry's capabilities can be noted?
5. Based on the assessment information, identified objectives, and team dialogue, what other developmentally appropriate strategies could be proposed to help the child and family?

chapter 10

Doris Bergen
Sharon Raver-Lampman

Implementing and Evaluating Transdisciplinary Assessment

The concept of transdisciplinary assessment involves the mutual collection and sharing of assessment results with professional participation that crosses traditional discipline boundaries (Bennett, 1982). The transdisciplinary model was originally used by personnel in programs that needed to provide comprehensive services, but which faced limited staff resources and less than optimal facilities. By collaborating in the assessment process, early intervention professionals believed that staff and facilities could be used in a time- and cost-efficient manner. As the model became more established, the role of family members as full team participants was elaborated, and the practices of role release and arena assessment were made explicit. Problems in implementing the model were also identified and variations that met the needs of particular early intervention programs were designed. The ideal model is described in numerous publications (e.g., Foley, 1990; Raver, 1991; Woodruff & McGonigel, 1988); however, it has been difficult to put the model into practice in its ideal form. Earlier chapters have explained why professionals from a wide range of disciplines see both promise and problems in using the model. A review of the qualities of the ideal model and of some of the recent evaluations of family and professional experiences with the model may serve to make explicit the present status of its implementation. From these evaluations (and those discussed in other chapters), it is clear that effective implementation requires the development of skills in communication, conflict resolution, and team building. Professional preparation programs for all of the involved disciplines must prepare their graduates to use such skills at both preservice and inservice levels.

AN IDEAL TRANSDISCIPLINARY ASSESSMENT MODEL

In an ideal transdisciplinary approach, professionals from many disciplines (e.g., child development, counseling, psychology, early childhood, family life studies, health and physical therapy, nursing, nutrition, pediatrics, social work, special education, and speech pathology and audiology) work as an interactive team, with the direct guidance of families, to develop unified and integrated Individual Family Service Plans (IFSP). The plans are then implemented, monitored regularly, and revised as needed by the team members.

UNDERLYING ASSUMPTIONS

One assumption of this approach is that early assessment must closely involve the young child's family because the family is a major influence on early development and learning. Thus, an ecological perspective that includes the immediate and also the greater family circle is advocated, if assessment is to be valid and intervention is to be successful. In practice, the immediate family (and often only the mother) have been the pre-eminent figures, taking most of the responsibility for the child's care.

A second assumption is that a group of professionals working together with the family in a team approach can provide a cost-effective, accurate, and educationally sound assessment and result in a consensus-derived developmentally appropriate intervention method that captures the best of the expertise of each discipline. In theory, the congruence of team viewpoints gained from multiple perspectives can enhance the validity of the assessment. In actual practice, the differing perspectives may result in the need to resolve conflicting views and to compromise on intervention plans.

A third assumption is that the services that are provided will be respectful and supportive of families, while at the same time providing an atmosphere that will make the family feel in charge of their child's future development. By validating the family as expert, the approach can foster family independence. In practice, however, some families are more able to function well as team members than are others.

Finally, there is an assumption that collaborative approaches can be demonstrated by a wide range of professionals, even those who come from disciplines where independent work rather than cooperative endeavors has been the norm. In practice, little experience in group co-operation has been given to students in most professional training programs and, therefore, there is a wide range of effectiveness demonstrated by these professionals. Two essential elements of this approach are role release and arena assessment, which have not been stressed in traditional professional preparation programs in the involved disciplines.

ROLE RELEASE

Professionals involved in transdisciplinary assessments have many respon-sibilities. They conduct assessments with the team and with the guidance of families. They develop service plans as a team, again guided by families' priorities and collaboration. In the transdisciplinary model all team mem-bers are responsible for how the primary service provider, a team member authorized by the team to work directly with the family, implements the team's plan with the family. This exchange of roles is the process that sep-arates transdisciplinary teams from other models.

Role release is the sharing of responsibilities, usually across profes-sional disciplines, by more than one team member. Intervention in infancy demands that personnel function as generalists as well as specialists (McCollum & Hughes, 1988; Bruder & Nikitas, 1992). Role sharing requires that professionals teach their discipline-specific skills to other team mem-bers who have different discipline backgrounds. For example, therapists (e.g., speech–language or occupational and physical) may train family members and other professionals on the team in strategies and techniques they could offer a child if they were providing the services directly. Through this process, professionals learn to rely on the expertise of their colleagues, as well as on family members (Bailey, Simeonsson, Yoder, & Huntington, 1990; Johnson et al., 1992; Woodruff, 1980).

There are some constraints, however, on the extent of role release that should be practiced in these teams. Because of codes of ethics and profes-sional standards, professionals involved in role sharing must clearly state when it is appropriate or inadvisable to share discipline skills (Drew & Turn-bull, 1987). This is best handled by establishing explicit guidelines for skills that are shared, as well as clear mechanisms for follow-up on released skills. Since professionals sharing skills are responsible for the quality of services ultimately received by families, role release requires continuous training and retraining among team and family members. It also requires the building of a trust level among all team participants, which permits the team to feel comfortable in collaborating on arena assessments.

ARENA ASSESSMENT

With children under the age of 3, transdisciplinary assessment ideally takes the form of arena assessment. In an arena assessment, one professional does the testing while other team members, including family members(s), observe (Wolery & Dyk, 1984). Professionals may sit on the floor around the child and parent(s) (or alternatively, in an observation area) and observe while one professional acts as the prime "facilitator" during the assessment. The facilitator engages the child in activities selected to demonstrate the child's developmental strengths and weaknesses (Woodruff & McGonigel, 1988).

Before an arena assessment is conducted, team members meet and identify for the facilitator behaviors they would like to have elicited for their individual discipline-specific evaluations. If all behaviors to be assessed are not observed during the arena assessment, parent reports may be used (when appropriate) or further assessment time may need to be arranged. Because of the play-oriented nature of arena assessments, only criterion-referenced instruments are suitable. Professionals experienced in arena assessments report that, with training as a team, they are able to observe what they need for discipline-specific evaluations, while also having the experience of seeing the "whole child."

Immediately following arena assessments, team members meet to share observations, evaluate their meaning, and set goals, guided by the family's priorities and observations. The cross-disciplinary nature of arena assessments encourages team members to seek and select integrated strategies and interventions that can serve the child's developmental needs in more than one domain.

According to arena assessment proponents, this approach can yield benefits for families, children and team members. For example, Beninghof & Singer (1992) and Woodruff (1980) have outlined some of these benefits. First, families may benefit from arena assessments in these ways:

1. The process communicates to families that they are fully functioning members of the teams.
2. It prevents different professionals from asking families similar questions repeatedly.
3. The process of helping young children is viewed as a series of problem-solving experiences that the team and family address rather than as a one-time decision-making experience.

Second, children may benefit in the following ways:

1. All assessment information is gathered at one time, rather than at separate times for each domain.
2. Children are able to demonstrate both strengths and weaknesses in a natural setting.
3. The assessment may result in increased access to services, consistency in education, and an integrated and comprehensive program. When team members show each other strategies they would use if they were providing services, children may be able to receive therapy or other services consistently, not just when the professional of a particular discipline is in their home or classroom.

Third, arena assessments may provide teams these advantages:

1. The team can provide more integrated assessments.
2. The team can share knowledge of the child from observations collected during the same time period, which leads to easier and more valid consensus.
3. The team members both receive and share expertise and this expands their knowledge, especially because they are getting their own perspective and that of others simultaneously.
4. The team intervention strategies will be more comprehensive and effective.

In practice, the extent of role release and the exact nature of arena assessment vary widely in existing early intervention programs. Research on what families, as well as professionals, see as positive and negative aspects of present early intervention practice is beginning to be reported and, as this accumulates, it will inform future practice. It has been of two types: family evaluations and professional evaluations of the transdisciplinary model.

FAMILY EVALUATION OF TRANSDISCIPLINARY ASSESSMENT

Federal law and early intervention literature strongly stress that families are to be full participants on early intervention teams, both during the assessment phase and in the intervention planning and evaluation phases. Although data are still sparse, a number of studies have looked at parents' views of the services they are receiving and, in general, those parent samples indicate satisfaction with the services. For example, one study (Angell & McWilliam, 1992) indicated that 97% of families felt professionals gave them opportunities to make decisions and supported their decisions, 83% found it was easy to get services, and 93% perceived that interagency collaboration was working. Good experiences seemed to be related to the personal characteristics of individual professionals and to the benefits the children seemed to be receiving. Bad experiences were related to poor professional attitudes or lack of therapeutic services.

In another study done in conjunction with a medical center project (Haring, Sterling, & Myse, 1992), however, parents identified a number of concerns related to poor communication by medical personnel, who often lack information about referral services and understanding of the effect having a child with disabilities has on a family system. Bonding may be interrupted when there is a medical crisis at birth, families are separated, and there is extreme anxiety about the child's survival and prognosis. Families often seem unaware of the services available for them and they do not understand the Individualized Family Service Plan (IFSP) or their role as a primary member of the early intervention team.

In a study of parents' participation in the IFSP process, Able-Boone (1992) found that the IFSPs were more child-centered than family-centered, although most IFSPs noted family resources and strengths. The amount of family participation varied in relation to families' styles of communication, with only 7 out of the 25 planning conferences showing parents talking more than professionals. However, professionals often encouraged parental participation by asking questions and many professionals expressed interest in developing strategies to increase family participation levels. Able-Boone concludes that there must be sensitivity to the family's preferred role, because some family members prefer to be team leaders and others prefer to take a passive role.

Another parental view of early intervention services comes from evaluations of parent groups (e.g., Krauss, Upshur, Shonkoff, & Hauser-Cram, 1993), which have shown mixed results as to positive and negative outcomes. In this study, parents reported that they received social support, but those with higher levels of participation felt the groups created more stress because they encountered the experiences of other parents with children with disabilities and sometimes felt forced to confront feelings for which they were not prepared.

Fathers and mothers do not always have the same impression of program helpfulness. Upshur (1991) reported that both parents felt home visits were more beneficial than parent groups, but that fathers indicated that services overall were less helpful and that they needed more assistance in learning how to be an advocate and how to meet other family members' needs than did mothers. Although both mothers and fathers felt the program was beneficial, they agreed that the benefits to mothers was greater than to fathers.

Narrative reports of a number of families' experiences, gained in interviews conducted by the author, also suggest that the integrated and equal participation discussed in the literature is not always evident in practice. These data show that, although families of children at risk for developmental delay do encounter many helpful professional individuals during the first few years of their child's life, their experiences with both individuals and team members also include being "closed out" of participation in crucial early assessment and intervention decisions and "left stranded" without knowledge of how to meet their own and their child's needs. There is still apparently wide variation in how much early intervention professionals convey a respect for parental concerns and expertise, with some professional groups being more responsive than others.

The data collected from these interviews with parents point to four problem areas that make early assessment and intervention processes less helpful for families than the literature suggests. Problems that families report include:

1. having limited and poor quality *initial* information provided to them about their child's condition, especially in medical trauma situations
2. having to deal with unclear directions, complex procedures, and uncoordinated service delivery systems that make gaining access to services difficult
3. finding gaps in effective linkages between teams who work at different sites (e.g., hospitals, pediatric settings, early intervention programs, and home care agencies)
4. encountering attitudes of some professionals that parental concerns or expertise need be only minimally considered during assessment and intervention planning.

These concerns show that the feelings of family empowerment and active control over their child's destiny, which supposedly arise from the "ideal" team approaches described and advocated in early intervention literature, are not yet present in the experiences of all families. Instead, the feeling of many parents may be one of helplessness, especially during the time when their child is being initially assessed in the hospital. Families also may feel helpless when they lack information about available services and do not know which professionals to contact for the information. Some parents continue this "learned helplessness," others react by increasing their own resolve to help their children.

If parents do become strong advocates for their children and are successful in eventually obtaining the information and services needed, they may have attained empowerment in spite of, rather than because of, the professionals who are involved in assessing and determining interventions for their child. As awareness of the importance of family empowerment grows among early intervention professionals, the experiences of families may reflect the increased participatory perspective that advocates of family-centered team approaches have described so eloquently in the literature (Bailey & Simeonsson, 1988; Dunst & Trivette, 1987; Turnbull, Summers, & Brotherson, 1987).

PROFESSIONAL EVALUATION OF TRANSDISCIPLINARY ASSESSMENT

It should not be concluded that highly trained and specialized professionals find it easy to work collaboratively. Problems with the transdisciplinary assessment process are well documented (Bailey, DeWert, Thiele, & Ware, 1983; Bailey, Palsha, & Simeonsson, 1991; Crisler, 1979; Fordyce, 1982; Gilliam & Coleman, 1981). The most common complaints found are:

1. Differing levels of participation by different professional groups
2. Lack of meaningful discussion in team meetings
3. Lack of training and guidance in the team process
4. Inability of professionals to work together in a truly integrative fashion

In fact, recent evidence reveals that professionals serving infants, toddlers, and their families continue to express serious concerns about cross-discipline collaboration (Bailey, Palsha, & Simeonsson, 1991). A survey of supervisors and administrators of infant and toddler programs in six states ranked competence in interpersonal skills (e.g., focusing on abilities such as conflict resolution and communication with parents and colleagues) as one of their top three skill needs (Johnson, Kilgo, Cook, Hammitte, Beauchamp, & Finn, 1992). Successful transdisciplinary assessment appears to hinge on skills in team communication, skills for handling conflicts, and skills in team building.

However, there is some evidence that, even with these problems, a team of professionals may be more effective than individual professionals in assessing family needs. In a comparison of family needs assessed by mothers, individual professionals, and interdisciplinary teams, Garshelis and McConnell (1993) found that individual professionals were able to match only 47% of mother-identified needs, while teams matched 57%. Mothers' most frequently cited needs were for information on services, reading material about how other parents cope, more time for themselves, and help locating respite care. The researchers concluded that teams were more effective than individual professionals, but that even teams do not do very well. They suggest that teams do more follow-up discussions after they have used a needs survey.

GUIDELINES FOR SUCCESSFUL TEAMWORK

Clearly, role and responsibility sharing among family and professional team members is not always easily attained. The approach demands flexibility, tolerance, and understanding among those involved (Garland, Woodruff, & Buck, 1988). Team members need to share a "common mission" and to work systematically to reach the team's goals.

TEAM COMMUNICATION TECHNIQUES

Transdisciplinary assessment is built on professional collaboration. However, successful collaboration does not always occur as planned (File & Kontos, 1992). First, team members must acknowledge that they need each other to accomplish their goals and re-examine their personal views of the validity of the contributions of persons from a range of disciplines.

Second, they must actively work to control personal variables that may interfere with rewarding teamwork. A self-awareness of the positive and negative potential effects of one's own interpersonal interaction style must be fostered in every team member. If continuing problems in this area occur, training sessions or individual conferences may be used to improve these skills. For personal events that impinge temporarily on team members' effectiveness, a climate of support among the team may help to keep the problems in perspective and minimize these effects on team operation.

Third, team members must agree on how families will be involved in all aspects of service delivery (Raver, 1991). Differences in individual beliefs about the "mission" of a program can easily overlap with team functioning and lead to interpersonal tensions. Some communication problems occur when staff and administrators do not share similar perceptions or language. Discipline-specific jargon can jeopardize communication among team members and families. It is not uncommon for team members from different disciplines to embrace quite different "missions." These differences can hinder communication, unless they are discussed openly with mutual respect.

Team members and team leaders need to foster a climate of mutual trust and to have the ability to communicate their commitment to making the transdisciplinary model work (Woodruff & McGonigel, 1988). Team meetings should be a place to share openly with colleagues and to gain assurance that every point of view will be respected, even during disagreement. The transdisciplinary assessment approach cannot function effectively without high standards of communication and collaboration.

CONFLICT RESOLUTION

Conflict resolution strategies are essential tools for handling the disputes that will inevitably arise when collaborative decisions must be made. Conflict resolution requires team members to be able to state the conflict as explicitly as possible, generate several means of resolving the conflict, and then conscientiously agree to follow team-generated solutions. For conflict to have positive outcomes, it must be actively confronted and managed by the team through a process of consensus building. Generally, conflicts are best confronted immediately, openly, and directly, rather than by behind-the-scene indirect negotiations. In fact, the most efficient teams devise a system for decision-making and handling disputes before they occur (Raver, 1991). Interestingly, some programs report that involving families as full members of the transdisciplinary team reduces professional conflicts and discipline loyalties because the team becomes unified by addressing the families' priorities.

TEAM BUILDING ACTIVITIES

Transdisciplinary team members are responsible for organizing regular staff development meetings for teaching their discipline skills to team members as well as for sharing discipline-specific information. These activities are called team-building activities because they develop the team's cohesiveness and improve functioning. Garland and Linder (1988) suggest these common team-building activities:

1. Observations of other team members
2. Discussions or consultations
3. On-site demonstrations of skills with discussion by the team
4. Workshops on specific techniques with hands-on practice
5. Role play or simulations of techniques
6. Courses on team building approaches or techniques

Administrators are important in supporting transdisciplinary teaming because they can structure time for the team to plan, practice, and critique their work together. Administrators should regard "teaming time" as part of a strategy that ensures quality services (Garland & Linder, 1988). Successful transdisciplinary teams acknowledge that rewarding teamwork is not a given, but the result of good communication, sound problem-solving mechanisms, and structured team-building skills. These ultimately result in good experiences for young children and their families.

PROFESSIONAL PREPARATION

Many early intervention professional programs are striving to improve preparation across relevant disciplines. They are beginning to include an emphasis on cross disciplinary linkages for assessment and intervention services (Hanson & Lovett, 1992). Professionals have indicated a need to know more about the terminology used by other disciplines and the expertise held by other professionals. They have also identified the need for consulting skills and knowledge of procedures underlying team building and group process (Bailey et al., 1990). These types of concerns do not seem to differ as a function of the discipline surveyed (Bailey et al., 1991).

Although there are some effective models that have been developed in various parts of the nation, the foundations for transdisciplinary assessment are just now being laid. Research on early childhood special education professional preparation programs reveals that the majority of these programs have separate assessment courses with a practicum component. Assessment topics receiving the greatest emphasis are instructional assessment for programming, appropriate assessment procedures, use of observational techniques, and communicating and interpreting test results (Stayton & Johnson, 1990). Experiences with team methods are not a major focus of most early assessment and intervention courses.

Because it is difficult for students to differentiate the transdisciplinary model from other assessment models simply by reading, experiences with such models are needed (Beninghof & Singer, 1992). Not only are personnel preparation programs weak in providing team assessment experience, they typically provide relatively little training specific to the population from birth to age 3, even when the focus is on cross-discipline training (Hanson & Lovett, 1992).

If the transdisciplinary assessment model is ever to be fully implemented in early intervention, personnel preparation programs will have to make collaborative cross-disciplinary experiences in assessing infants and toddlers a core requirement in such programs.

SUMMARY

The ideal model of transdisciplinary assessment has been described in detail in early intervention literature. However, it has yet to be fully implemented in practice. Some models developed using transdisciplinary concepts seem to be working well. Even in these models, there are problems that have been identified and skills needed that team members are only beginning to acquire. If the approach is to be successful, team communication techniques, team building activities, and conflict resolution skills must be integral parts of inservice and preservice education. Personnel preparation programs must include content and practice related to developing team effectiveness. Early intervention advocates must continue to address policy and procedural issues that affect team functioning. Finally, ongoing evaluation of transdisciplinary team models should be conducted to determine which specific approaches are most useful in assessment and intervention with young children and their families.

QUESTIONS FOR DISCUSSION

1. What are two of the aspects of transdisciplinary assessment and intervention that are most likely to improve services to young children and families?
2. What are two of the aspects of transdisciplinary assessment and intervention that are most problematic in attempts to develop team approaches that work effectively?

PROBLEMS OF PRACTICE

Visit an early intervention program and observe a team meeting. Then, interview individually the program director, a teacher, and a support specialist. Ask each of them the same questions regarding their views of the model they use, its effectiveness level, and its problems. Relate what they say to your observation of the team and to the content of this chapter.

SUGGESTED READINGS

Hanson, M., & Lovett, D. (1992). Personnel preparation for early interventionists: A cross-disciplinary survey. *Journal of Early Intervention, 16,* (2), 123–135.

Woodruff, G., & McGonigel, M. (1988). Early intervention team approaches: The transdisciplinary model. In J. Jordan, J. Gallagher, P. Hutinger, & M. Karnes (Eds.), *Early Childhood Special Education: Birth to Three.* Reston, VA: Council for Exceptional Children.

Doris Bergen

THE FUTURE OF TRANSDISCIPLINARY ASSESSMENT AND INTERVENTION

In the introduction to this book, I discussed the theoretical and practical rationale for advocating a transdisciplinary team approach to assessment and intervention. In the chapters, the perspectives presented have made clear the complex nature of this teamwork; it involves young children, their diverse families, numerous professionals from specialized and disparate disciplines, the social service and educational systems, and policy makers who represent a range of constituencies. Although there are many practical problems yet to be resolved and some difficult policy issues that must still be clarified, it is clear that the benefits in a collaborative and responsive early intervention team approach are only beginning to be appreciated.

Dialogue among all of the stakeholders must be continued and expanded, but it is evident that they already have a common base of interests and understandings that can be used as a foundation. This common base includes the following understandings:

1. Early assessment and intervention must be grounded in knowledge of human development, including not only that of infants and toddlers, but also that of their parents and other family members.
2. Families are integral members of the early intervention team and their participation as observers, caregivers, and educators of their young children can positively influence the family system as a whole and their child's educational experiences.
3. Team approaches enable professionals to provide better assessment and intervention services and, in addition, professionals are pro-

vided with collaborative skills that can be useful to them in many other facets of their work.

4. The planned intervention experiences that result from well-designed, developmentally appropriate, multifactored assessments are of primary benefit to young children, who also profit from the environment of caring that results when many persons are working together to reach common goals related to their development and education.

5. The empowerment of families and professionals that occurs through networks facilitating access to the systems of the society can influence social policy initiatives to promote the overall welfare of children and families.

The future of transdisciplinary assessment is unclear. As with most new approaches, it has encountered resistance from those who have found value in other assessment models or who see it as a threat to their present work style or discipline. It has already undergone a number of transformations, elaborations, or truncations, depending on the agendas of the people who have embraced the model and those who have resisted it. I hope its fate will not be that of many other reforms of the past, which is to be half-heartedly tried and then whole-heartedly rejected, without any real evidence being collected about the effectiveness of the reform.

I think it is very important for those of us who value this approach and see it as ultimately more humane, informative, and valid to think about systematic ways to gather data that can help us evaluate its development and overall effectiveness. Thus, if you participate in a model of transdisciplinary assessment, I urge you to document what you are doing and engage in assessment of your approach, even as you are using it. Try to determine the needs it addresses well and the strengths it draws on, the interpersonal conflicts and collaboration it elicits, the support systems it must have to work well, and the policies that promote its development. Further, as you become empowered along with the other members of your team, working with young children who have disabilities or who are at risk for developmental delay, perhaps you can raise (and help us answer) the "American" question—

Why is American society not concerned about the developmental potential of every child and every family and why are we so slow to realize that our future is in the hands of all of these young children?

EXAMPLES OF CLINICAL, INTERVIEW, AND OBSERVATION INSTRUMENTS

PEDIATRIC NEUROLOGY HISTORY

Name _____   Date _____

Date of birth _____   Hospital # _____

Chief complaint:

Present illness:

Current medication:

Past history:

    Pregnancy, birth, neonatal:

       (birth wt. _____)

    Development: (<5-years-old, do Denver)

       (age walked alone _____)

    School:

    Behavior:

    Major illnesses, injuries, hospitalizations:

    Misc. (include immunizations):

    Previous medications (for seizures, headaches):

Review of Systems:

    Seizures:

    Headaches:

    Other:

Social History:

Family History:

Source Note: Used with permission of Francis S. Wright, Department of Pediatrics, Ohio State University.

PEDIATRIC NEUROLOGY EXAMINATION

General Appearance:
    (describe dysmorphic features)
    *(draw abnormalities on picture)
H.C. _____ cm (%); Wt. _____ kg (%); Ht. _____ cm (%)
Medical Examination: (include only pertinent features)
    *(draw abnormalities on picture)
    Head: (shape, size of fontanels, suture abnormality)
    ENT:
    Skin:
    Heart, lungs:
    Abdomen (organomegaly):
    Skeletal, extremities:
    Vascular (cranial, neck bruits):
    Other:
Mental Status:
    Level of consciousness:
    Estimate of intelligence:
    Language, speech:
    Handedness, foot preference:
Neuro-Opthalmological Examination:
    Visual acuity: R: L:
    Visual fields (confrontation):
    Pupil size, reaction: R: L:
    Funduscopic examination:
    EOMs:
    C.N.s III, IV, VI:
    Gaze pareses, nystagmus, misc.:
Cranial Nerves, other:
    C.N.'s I, V, VII, IX-X:
      VIII (include hearing):
      * circle abnormalities; check if normal
Motor Examination:
    Weakness:
    *(Fill out Muscle Testing Chart for localized, lower motor neuron, or
    muscle disease.)

Neck, trunk:

Upper extremities: R: L:
    proximal
    distal

Lower extremities: R: L:
    proximal
    distal

Tone (describe distribution):

   Spacticity, rigidity:

   Hypotonia:

Deep tendon reflexes:

   Biceps: R: L:

   Triceps: R: L:

   Quadruceps: R: L:

   Gastrocnemius: R: L:

   Other:

Primitive Reflexes:

   Plantar reflexes (Babinski sign):

   Other: (Infants—check appropriate reflexes)

      Moro:

      Tonic neck reflexes:

      Palmar, plantar grasp reflexes:

      Parachute, Landau:

      Other:

Involuntary Movements (describe):

   chorea, athetosis, dystonia, tics, other

Coordination (Cerebellar) Examination:

   head tilt, titubation, truncal ataxia:

   upper extremities: R: L:
      (finger–nose)

   lower extremities: R: L:
      (heel–knee–shin)

Alternate Motion Rate: (finger wiggle, knee pat, foot pat)
                 R: L:

Other: (fasciculations, atrophy, hypoplasia)

Sensory Examination:

   Primary Sensations: (pin, touch, deep pain, vibration, position sense)
   (draw spinal levels, root, plexus, peripheral nerve lesions)*
     upper extremities: R: L:
     lower extremities: R: L:

Cortical Sensations: (stereognosis, graphaesthesia, 2-pt., DSS):
     upper extremities: R: L:
     lower extremities: R: L:

Miscellaneous Observations: (nuchal rigidity, Kernig's sign,
straight leg raising, etc.)

*ALL OBSERVATIONS TO BE NOTED ON FIGURES

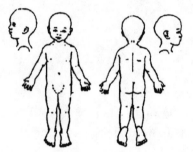

Summary of History and Examination:

Impression (Conclusions):

Recommendations:
Tests Recommended:
Treatment Recommended:

Other:

Signed: _____   _____, M.D.
         (medical student, resident,   (attending physician)
           nurse associate)

Source Note: Used by permission of Francis S. Wright, Department of Pediatrics, Ohio State University.)

PARENTAL INTERVIEW SUGGESTIONS

These questions are designed to supplement the medical history, developmental milestone, social interaction, and adaptive behavior information gathered from questionnaires used by medical or psychological personnel during an intake interview. They are not all inclusive, but examples of the kind of open-ended questions that often foster communication between professionals and parents. Interviews may use all sections or only those for which additional information is needed. They are typically used in an informal manner, with encouragement of the parent to talk in some detail about relevant items.

I.   Communication:
     How does _____ let you know what s/he wants?
        Expressive prompts:
           Telling needs?
           Making choices?
           Labeling objects?
           Showing different crying?
           Who in the family understands _____'s communication?
        Receptive prompts:
           Responding to directions?
           Appropriate response to yes and no?
           Identifying body parts?
           Listening to story?

II. Play/Social Relating:
     How does _____ get along with other kids? adults? sibs? pets?
        Prompts:
           Sharing?
           Using toys?
           Interest in play/interaction with other kids?
           Imitates adults and other kids?
           Play social mode—parallel, solitary, interactive?
           Play symbolic mode—using pretend?

III. Sensory Responses:
     Does _____ have any unusual responses to sensory stimuli?

Prompts:
    Taste?
    Touch?
    Smell?
    Vision?
    Hearing?

IV. Behavior:

What kinds of behaviors are typical of _____?
  Prompts:
    Does s/he have tantrums?
    What is usual mood?
    How does s/he act in public? (e.g., at store)
    What is sleeping schedule?
    What are eating habits?
    What kinds of fears?
    How do you manage _____?
    What are most useful techniques?

V. Self-Help:

What ways does _____ try to help take care of his/her own needs?
  Prompts:
    What food can _____ feed him/herself?
    Does _____ help with dressing?
    How does _____ react when bathing?

VI. Family Support:

What are the concerns of your family regarding _____?
  Prompts:
    What have you been told is wrong with _____?
    What advice have you been given?
    How can we best help you?
    Do family/spouse/parent agree with your concerns?

Source Note: Adapted from guidelines developed at The University of North Carolina, by Drs. Eric Shopler and Gary Meisibov.

TWO-DIMENSIONAL PLAY OBSERVATION FORM

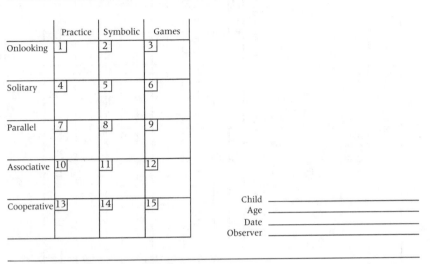

	Practice	Symbolic	Games
Onlooking	1	2	3
Solitary	4	5	6
Parallel	7	8	9
Associative	10	11	12
Cooperative	13	14	15

Child _____
Age _____
Date _____
Observer _____

- **Examples of play coded by cell**

Cell

1. **Onlooking–Practice:** Slowly walking through gross motor area, observing children going up and down slide and rocking in boat.
2. **Onlooking–Symbolic:** Observing another child "feeding" popcorn to a puppet.
3. **Onlooking–Games:** Standing, intently watching teacher and two children play Ring-Around-the-Rosy.
4. **Solitary–Practice:** Walking alone on tiptoe over pillows, carpet, tile, up and down stairs.
5. **Solitary–Symbolic:** Making animal puzzle pieces "walk" around and "talk" to each other.
6. **Solitary–Games:** Arranging cars in special order in line, selecting them according to self-designed rule, moving them in certain sequence so that one will "win."
7. **Parallel–Practice:** Painting with fingers on table beside other children, all of whom are focused on their own play.
8. **Parallel–Symbolic:** Setting table and "feeding" doll in house area, while other children are engaged in similar but separate play.

9. **Parallel–Games:** Running along with other children but not racing against them, only with self.
10. **Associative–Practice:** Rolling on pillows with another child, laughing and escalating activity in response to other child's action.
11. **Associative–Symbolic:** Building a "barn" with another child, helping by handing blocks, suggesting how to make the roof, adding to the wall, but also doing some independent building.
12. **Associative–Games:** Playing a "turn-taking" game with another child, such as pulling child in wagon, then sitting in wagon as other child pulls, then pulling child, then being pulled.
13. **Cooperative–Practice:** Throwing ball back and forth to another child for an extended time period.
14. **Cooperative–Symbolic:** Engaging in sociodramatic play as "mother" or "daddy" and demonstrating appropriate role actions for extended time period.
15. **Cooperative–Games:** Participating in a game of tag or hiding and finding, following rules for an extended time period.

Source Note: Reprinted from Bergen, 1988.

AUDIOGRAM FORMAT

MIAMI UNIVERSITY
Speech and Hearing Clinic
Oxford , Ohio 45056
(513)523-2500

AUDIOLOGICAL EVALUATION
Date _____
Supervisor _____
Clinician _____

Name _____ D.O.B. _____ Age _____ Phone _____
Address _____ City/State _____ Zip _____

Frequency (Hz)

	125	250	500	1000	2000	4000	8000

Hearing Level in dB (re: ANSI 1969)

-10
0
10
20
30
40
50
60
70
80
90
200
110
120

LEGEND		Right	Left
Air	Unmasked	O	X
	Masked	△	□
Bone	Unmasked	∨	∧
	Masked	⌐	⌐
Abbreviations or other symbols			

Pure Tone Average
(2 Freq./3 Freq.)
Right _____ Left _____

264

Comments
_____
_____
_____
_____

Into	R/L	R/L	R/L	R/L	R/L	R/L
AC						
BC						

Masking Levels

Discrimination in % Correct

	SRT/SAT	MCL	UCL/LDL	%	db HL	S/N	%	dB HL	S/N	%	dB HL	S/N
Right												
Left												
Aided												
Unaided												

Sound Field

Word Lists _____

Competing Signal(s) _____   Masking Levels _____

Impedance Test Summary (Tympanogram Type, Compliance, Middle Ear Pressure, Acoustic Reflex Pass/Fail)

Right ear _____

Left ear _____

Source Note: Used by permission of Miami University, Department of Communication.

265

INTERVIEW STYLE FAMILY NEEDS SURVEY, PILOT FORM

Name _____ Date _____

Introductory Statement to Be Read to Parents by Interviewer

The process for developing the IFSP consists of collecting, sharing, and exchanging information between families and team members to enable families to make informed choices about the early intervention services they want for their children and themselves. This questionnaire is designed to help families collect and organize information needed to identify their own strengths and needs.

Your participation and input when answering these questions is completely voluntary. The information obtained here is considered confidential, and will only be shared with your invited members of the IFSP team.

Questions to Be Used by the Interviewer (Prompts Are in Parentheses.)

Tell me about your child.

Describe a typical day with your child.
    (What else can you tell me?)

What times of day do you enjoy most with your child?
    (Why do you think this is?)

What times of day are most difficult with your child?
    (Why do you think this is?)

Tell me about meal time.

Tell me about your child's medical and dental care.
    (Including therapy)

What have you been told by doctors, therapists, or others about your child?

Do you need more information about your child's disability?
(What kind would you like?)

Does your family understand your child's disability?
    (How do they show this?)
    (Who does/doesn't understand?)

What are some of the ways your family and friends support you?
  (Are there any other ways?)

Do you have reliable baby sitting so you can get out occasionally?
  (Why or why not?)
  (Who?)

Would you like to find additional financial support to help provide for your family?
  (If answer is yes, ask "In what ways have you tried to find additional support?")

Would you like to know more about services provided in our community?
  (What types of services?)

What do you want for your child during this next year?
  (What else?)
  (Help parents prioritize desires.)

What do you want for your family during this next year?
  (What else?)
  (Help family prioritize desires.)

What would you like to know more about?
  (Is there anything you would like me to know that I haven't asked?)

Ending Statement

Thank you for your cooperation in answering these questions today. The information collected here will help identify and prioritize family strengths and needs for the upcoming IFSP meeting.

Source Note: Used by permission of Marjorie Pitzer, Hamilton County, OH, Early Intervention Collaborative.

SAMPLE INDIVIDUAL FAMILY SERVICES PLAN

Section 1: General Information

Child information: Name, gender, birth date, age(s) at testing

Parent/Guardian information: Name, address, phone, guardianship/relationship (if other than parent)

Present date and dates of earlier reviews:

Plan initiated by:

Service coordinator/IFSP meeting participants (signature page):

Section 2: Family Information Summary

Persons living in household:

Relevant family circumstances, strengths, needs:

Family activities/objectives (if in IFSP):

Section 3: Child Service Inventory

Early Intervention Services currently in use: Services from other agencies currently in use:

Section 4: Child Medical Information Summary

Ongoing health concerns:

Physicians involved with child: Frequency of visits, purposes

Physician activities/objectives (if in IFSP):

Section 5: Parent's Summary of Child's Present Levels

For each area of development, the following questions are answered:

Already can:

Is beginning to:

We'd like to work on:

Family questions about the assessment:

Activities/objectives (if in IFSP):

Section 6: Summary Assessment Information

For each area of development and for all assessment measures the following are described:

Area of development:

Assessment measure/method used:

Assessment personnel and date of assessment:

Results:

Family questions about the assessment:

Activities/objectives (if in IFSP):

Section 7: Outcome and Service Action Plan

For each outcome the following is described:

Outcome (What we want):

Family strengths and needs (Family resources/capacity to achieve outcome):

Service/action plan (What is going to happen):

Criteria (How we will know if plan is working):

Review of outcome/service action plan: (Completed for last review before new plan is developed)

Section 8: Transition Plans

For transition periods the following is described:

Transition information: What is happening, when, where; transition activities to ensure support of plan

Unanswered questions concerning transition:

Section 9: Review To-Do List

Activities/objectives (To-do lists) from other sections are combined for IFSP

Section 10: Authorization for Release of Information

Family selects persons/organizations with whom information can be shared.

Source Note: Adapted from IFSP format of Hamilton County, OH, Early Intervention Collaborative. Used by permission.

SAMPLE ECOLOGICAL INVENTORY

Child name _____   Date of birth _____

Background information (Summary from records):

Observation Plan

Domains to be observed: Domestic, community, leisure

Environments to be observed:
    Domestic: Family home, grandparent's home
    Community: Neighborhood walk, grocery store, church
    Leisure: Fast food restaurant, backyard

Sub-environments to be observed:
    Domestic, homes: Kitchen, family room, bedroom, bathroom
    Community, neighborhood: Sidewalk, street, yards
    Community, store: Supermarket
    Community, church: Sunday school classroom
    Leisure, restaurant: Ordering area, seating area, parking lot area
    Leisure, backyard: wading pool, surrounding yard area, garage

Observation Results

Skills observed and rated: Possesses skill (+), is learning skill (+ –), is skill
that is ready to be learned (*)

Kitchen: Feeding self with spoon
    Skills: Grasping spoon with palmar grasp (+)
             Scooping food (mashed potatoes) (+ –)
             Bringing food to mouth (+ –)
             Taking food off spoon with mouth (+ –)
             Chewing and swallowing food (+ –)
             Indicating needs with "more" (+ –) (instead of crying)
             Scooping unmashed food (*)

Restaurant: Eating a meal
    Skills: Picking up sandwich (+)
             Taking bites from sandwich (+)
             Chewing and swallowing food (+ –)
             Eating at appropriate pace (*)
             Indicating needs with "more" (*) (instead of crying)
             Waiting till meal is over (*)

(*Note:* Many more examples would be listed before the summary information would be described.)

Summary of Skills Across Domains:

Recommendations/Objectives:

Source Note: Adapted from student work, Department of Educational Psychology, Miami University, Used by permission of Sue Skinner-Kidd.

OVERVIEW OF SELECTED ASSESSMENT INSTRUMENTS

TITLE: The Ainsworth Strange Situation Assessment Procedure

AUTHORS: M.D. Ainsworth, M.C. Blehar, E. Waters, and S. Wall

PUBLISHER AND ADDRESS: Lawrence Erlbaum Associates, 365 Broadway, Hillsdale, NJ 07642

COPYRIGHT DATE: 1979

LEVEL: Infants 10 to 24 months

PURPOSE: To determine how infants organize behavior with caregivers and unfamiliar persons in an environment having varying conditions that elicit distress.

DISTINGUISHING CHARACTERISTICS: Requires an 8-episode, 22- to 24-minute structured laboratory observation, with infant and attachment figure. Separations from that person are assumed to elicit mild to moderate levels of fear and distress, which lessen child's tendency to explore the unfamiliar environment.

ADMINISTRATION: Two observers administer, one with whom the child becomes familiar and one who acts as stranger. Child is observed interacting with observers and attachment figure in the planned situations. Need observer inter-rater reliability.

SCORING AND INTERPRETATION: Behavior rated along six dimensions: Proximity/contact seeking, contact maintenance, resistant, avoidant, distance interaction, and search during separations. Infants are categorized in three major patterns of attachment: Secure, avoidant, and resistant.

OVERALL EVALUATION: Useful in assessing quality and security of infant-caregiver relationship. A research tool with variety of populations. Classification system representative of infants in middle-income, low-risk families. Patterns in some high-risk populations differ; use with caution with these children.

TITLE: Battelle Developmental Inventory (BDI)

AUTHORS: J. Newborg, J. Stock, L. Wnek, J. Guidubaldi, and J. Svinicki.

PUBLISHER AND ADDRESS: DLM Teaching Resources, One DLM Park, Allen, TX 75002

COPYRIGHT DATE: 1988

LEVEL: Birth to 8 years

PURPOSE: (Screening form) To identify children at risk for developmental handicaps who need more comprehensive evaluation. (Full scale form) To identify young children's developmental strengths and weaknesses; to assist in designing, monitoring, and evaluating educational plans.

DISTINGUISHING CHARACTERISTICS: A standardized assessment battery of key developmental skills. Full BDI comprises 341 test items in five domains: Personal–social, adaptive, motor, communication and cognitive. Screening test has 96 items. Norm group of 800 children stratified by geographic location, race, sex, and socioeconomic level. High test–retest reliability and adequate validity data.

ADMINISTRATION: By early intervention personnel; data collected through a structured test, interviews with parents and teachers, and observations of child in natural setting. Modifications for children with disabilities are suggested. Screening takes 10 to 30 minutes; full BDI, 1 to 1 1/2 hours (less for younger children).

SCORING AND INTERPRETATION: Score in each domain and total performance score. Total raw score can be converted to percentile ranks, standard scores, and age equivalents. Case studies facilitate interpretation.

OVERALL EVALUATION: Provides both norm-referenced and criterion-referenced data and is appropriate for children who have disabilities. Because of limited number of items at each age level, a single subdomain score should not be used to determine early intervention eligibility. Very few items for the under 6-month age level; thus, not useful for that age.

TITLE: The Bayley Scales of Infant Development–Second Edition (BSID-II)

AUTHOR: N. Bayley

PUBLISHER AND ADDRESS: The Psychological Corporation, PO Box 839954, San Antonio, TX 78283-3954

COPYRIGHT DATE: 1993

LEVEL: 1 to 42 months

PURPOSE: To diagnose developmental delay in infants and young children; to provide information for planning and monitoring interventions.

DISTINGUISHING CHARACTERISTICS: A revision of a widely used scale for young children. Three scales: Motor, Mental, and Behavior Rating. Second edition includes more items assessing social behavior, visual and auditory habituation, object permanence, problem solving, language, fine motor skills, and number concepts. Normative data from sample of 1,700 children, stratified by age, gender, race, geographic location, and parent education level, and validity information for clinical groups (premature, HIV+, drug exposed, asphyxia, Down's syndrome, otitis media, developmental delay) provided. Reliability and validity are acceptable. A Spanish language version is also available.

ADMINISTRATION: By a psychometrically trained professional. Items are administered based on the child's chronological age. Has basal and ceiling rules.

SCORING AND INTERPRETATION: Raw scores converted to Mental Development Index (MDI) and Psychomotor Development Index (PDI); developmental age level comparisons also available.

OVERALL EVALUATION: Scales have empirical and theoretical support, are psychometrically and technically sound, and are sensitive to performance differences between children in the normative sample and children with various conditions of risk. Designed to capture the attention and interest of very young children. Can also be used as a parental teaching tool and for research on developmental issues. Complicated to administer.

TITLE: Brigance Diagnostic Inventory of Early Development, Revised

AUTHOR: A. H. Brigance

PUBLISHER AND ADDRESS: Curriculum Associates, Inc., 5 Esquire Rd., North Billerica, MA 01862

COPYRIGHT DATE: 1991

LEVEL: Birth to 6 years

PURPOSE: To assess development of young children; to support diagnosis or referral for developmental delay; to assist in educational planning and monitor progress.

DISTINGUISHING CHARACTERISTICS: Criterion-referenced inventory that assesses, diagnoses, assists record keeping, fosters educational planning. Various tests are contained in a notebook; materials used are familiar to child. Field tested in programs for young children in 19 states and Canada. Normative data from field testing used to validate skill sequences and developmental ages; no reliability information provided.

ADMINISTRATION: By early intervention personnel without specialized training. Examiner decides on skill areas to assess and selects appropriate skill levels. Tests are not timed.

SCORING AND INTERPRETATION: The Developmental Record Book lists developmental milestones for primary skills; the Comprehensive Skill Sequences identifies secondary skills leading to primary skills and can be used for children with severe disabilities or delays. Record-keeping systems color-coded. Child performance levels used to plan skill objectives.

OVERALL EVALUATION: Easy to use; provides information for educational planning. Technical data are not provided, and comparability of results with other assessment measures not yet demonstrated. Use in a multi-test team assessment, not as only assessment instrument.

TITLE: The Carolina Curriculum for Handicapped Infants and Infants At Risk (CCHI)

AUTHORS: N. Johnson-Martin, K. Jens, and S. Attermeier

PUBLISHER AND ADDRESS: Paul H. Brookes Publishing Co., PO Box 10624, Baltimore, Maryland 21285-0624

COPYRIGHT DATE: 1990

LEVEL: Handicapped children functioning in the birth- to 24-month developmental range

PURPOSE: To provide assessment information for planning curricular intervention strategies appropriate for children with disabilities.

DISTINGUISHING CHARACTERISTICS: Criterion-referenced checklist; measures 24 areas of development, with sequences of skills within each area. Provides curricular intervention strategies related to items not achieved. The birth- to 12-month section was field-tested with 150 children from 22 different early intervention programs in the US. Lists materials needed, specific teaching procedures, and learning and evaluation criterion standards. Inter-rater reliability high, but no validity data are given.

ADMINISTRATION: By early intervention staff; does not require specific training. Rapport built with infant and parents in first stage. Then child is observed demonstrating skills, or items may be credited based on parent report. No time limit.

SCORING AND INTERPRETATION: A+ is marked if the item is passed. If many attempts are required before correct response, the item is marked E (emerging skill). An item should not be scored as passed if accomplished in an atypical fashion. An assessment log and developmental progress chart included for monitoring progress over time.

OVERALL EVALUATION: Easily administered criterion measure for direct service providers, with teaching suggestions for items missed. Although simply worded and free of jargon, it takes a long time to administer and has been criticized for its organization. Most useful for children with mild and moderate disabilities.

TITLE: Child Behavior Checklist for Ages 2–3 (CBCL/2–3)

AUTHOR: T. Achenbach

PUBLISHER AND ADDRESS: Thomas Achenbach, Dept. of Psychiatry, University of Vermont, Burlington, VT 05401

COPYRIGHT DATE: 1992

LEVEL: 2 to 3 years old

PURPOSE: To obtain ratings of behavioral and emotional problems in young children in a variety of contexts.

DISTINGUISHING CHARACTERISTICS: A rating scale for parents or primary caretakers, modeled on the Child Behavior Checklist for Ages 4 to 18. Can be filled out independently by parents with at least 5th-grade reading skills. Has moderate-to-high reliability and validity with other measures. Normed on a sample of 368 toddlers across ethnic groups, geographic locations, and SES conditions.

ADMINISTRATION: By a trained professional (for interpretation). Caregiver answers questions about perceptions of child's behaviors. Takes approximately 10 minutes to complete. Can be filled out by an interviewer if parents lack adequate reading skills; can also be translated into different languages for non-English speakers.

SCORING AND INTERPRETATION: Scored by hand or computer. Scaled scores, percentiles, and normalized t scores are obtained. Profile of child is interpreted based on six syndromes: Anxious/depressed, withdrawn, sleep problems, somatic problems, aggressive, and destructive. Combined scores interpreted as Internalizing or Externalizing profiles; a total problem score can also be obtained.

OVERALL EVALUATION: A well normed checklist with adequate technical data. Has modifications for administration to caretakers having varied reading skill levels. Potential for widespread research and practical applications. Should be used as part of a multifactored assessment that includes direct observation and assessments by professional personnel to avoid labeling of child on basis of parent's perception.

TITLE: Child Development Inventory (CDI)

AUTHOR: H. Ireton

PUBLISHER AND ADDRESS: Behavior Science Systems, Inc., Box 580274, Minneapolis, Minnesota 55458

COPYRIGHT DATE: 1992

LEVEL: 6 months to 6 years; older children functioning in this age range

PURPOSE: To measure young children's development and learning in areas meaningful to clinicians, teachers and parents; to identify developmental problems for further assessment

DISTINGUISHING CHARACTERISTICS: Replaces the Minnesota CDI (1972). A parent report measure, with 270 items in eight developmental areas: Social, self-help, gross motor, fine motor, expressive language, language comprehension, letters, and numbers. Includes a General Development Scale and a section describing symptoms and behavior problems of young children. Normed on a sample of 568 children 1 year to 6 years, 3 months. Screening versions for 6 to 15 months (Infant DI); 15 to 36 months (Early Child DI); and an interview version (Child Development Review) also available. Moderate to high reliability and validity data.

ADMINISTRATION: Parent is asked to indicate statements that describe child's behavior by marking yes or no on the answer sheet. Should be completed before other assessment measures are administered.

SCORING AND INTERPRETATION: Total number of yes responses scored using a template. These are then recorded on the child profile sheet and compared to the normative sample.

OVERALL EVALUATION: Derived from a strong developmental research base. It is a useful resource for development of educational plans, especially when supplemented with teacher observations. Involves parents in thinking about their child's developmental achievements and needs.

TITLE: Denver Developmental Screening Test II (DDST-II)

AUTHORS: W. Frankenburg, J. Dodds, P. Archer, B. Bresnick, P. Maschka, N. Edelman, and H. Shapiro

PUBLISHER AND ADDRESS: Denver Developmental Materials, Inc., PO Box 6919, Denver, Colorado 80206-0919

COPYRIGHT DATE: 1990

LEVEL: Birth to 6 years

PURPOSE: To identify possible problems and screen for referral to further evaluation; to confirm clinical suspicions with an objective measure; to monitor children at risk for developmental problems.

DISTINGUISHING CHARACTERISTICS: Revision of original Denver. Consists of 125 items distributed across four domains: Social–emotional, fine motor, gross motor, and language. Revision includes more items in the language category. Norms developed using a quota sample from the Denver area, controlled for maternal education, residence, and ethnicity. Has adequate reliability and validity data. Spanish language version available.

ADMINISTRATION: By medical or early intervention personnel who have received training. (Video training tape available.) Most items scored by observation; others can be scored by parental report. Item level for initiating the test begins below child's age and continues until three failures are recorded. Takes 15 to 20 minutes.

SCORING AND INTERPRETATION: Each item is marked pass, fail, no opportunity to perform, and refusal to perform. Scores are interpreted as normal (no delays); abnormal (2 or more delays); questionable (1 delay or 2 or more cautions); untestable (depending on the number of potential delays or cautions, if scored as failures). Children with abnormal scores are referred to other assessment sources; those with questionable or untestable scores are to be retested at a later date.

OVERALL EVALUATION: Easily administered, standardized screening measure; useful as an initial screening tool for determining at-risk children who need further assessment. Not intended as a predictor of later development.

TITLE: Developmental Activities Screening Inventory (DASI-II)

AUTHORS: R. Fewell and M. Langley

PUBLISHER AND ADDRESS: ProEd, 8700 Shoal Creek Blvd, Austin, TX 78758-9965

COPYRIGHT DATE: 1984

LEVEL: Birth to 60 months

PURPOSE: To provide early detection of developmental difficulties in infants.

DISTINGUISHING CHARACTERISTICS: Non-verbal screening instrument with 67 items. Provides list of developmental activities that precede the attainment of each item on the test; can be incorporated into the IFSP or IEP of child. Initially field tested with over 200 multiply handicapped children. Concurrent validity demonstrated with other tests measuring similar abilities, but lacks adequate information on reliability or other types of validity. No norm group information or other technical data are reported.

ADMINISTRATION: By early intervention personnel after minimal level of training. Starts one level below the child's estimated developmental age and attains a basal when all items within one developmental level have been failed. The test is not timed; sequence of item administration can be varied. Specific adaptations for administering to visually impaired children are provided.

SCORING AND INTERPRETATION: Specific criteria for passing are provided for each item. All items below basal are considered passed and the child receives 1 point for each item passed beyond that point. Raw scores can be converted to developmental quotient.

OVERALL EVALUATION: Especially useful for assessing young children with severe disabilities or visual impairments. Easily translated into practical applications and instructional programming. Has only a few items at each developmental level, but can be a useful prescriptive tool for teachers.

TITLE: Developmental Profile II (DPII)

AUTHORS: G. Alpern, T. Boll, and M. Shearer

PUBLISHER AND ADDRESS: Western Psychological Services, 12031 Wilshire Blvd., Los Angeles., CA 90025

COPYRIGHT DATE: 1980

LEVEL: Birth to 9 years

PURPOSE: To provide a multidimensional description of a child's development.

DISTINGUISHING CHARACTERISTICS: Parent report instrument that gives profile of the child in five areas of development: Physical, self-help, social, academic, and communication. Revised in 1980 and normed on predominantly urban, black and white children in the midwest. Good inter-rater and test–retest reliability but insufficient validity studies.

ADMINISTRATION: By teachers or other trained school personnel; conducted as interview, observation. Questions may be rephrased to facilitate parent's understanding, as long as content remains unchanged. Two methods of administration: Regular and short-cut.

SCORING AND INTERPRETATION: Items scored pass or fail; noted if examiner has directly observed or gained information from interviewee. Child's chronological age compared to five developmental ages to interpret functioning. Shows whether child is "advanced" or "delayed" in the five developmental areas.

OVERALL EVALUATION: An easily administered and scored test, providing a quick and inexpensive description of the child's development. Should not be used as the only instrument for placement purposes, because validity is not strongly demonstrated.

TITLE: Differential Ability Scales (DAS), Preschool Level

AUTHOR: C. Elliot

PUBLISHER AND ADDRESS: The Psychological Corporation, PO Box 839954, San Antonio, TX 78283-3954

COPYRIGHT DATE: 1990

LEVEL: 2 years, 6 months to 5 years, 11 months (to age 7 for children with delays)

PURPOSE: To assess verbal, reasoning, perceptual, and memory abilities in young children.

DISTINGUISHING CHARACTERISTICS: Revision and extension of British Ability Scales. Cognitive battery divided into two levels: lower preschool (ages 2–6 to 3–5) and upper preschool (ages 3–6 to 5–11). Lower preschool comprises four subtests and two diagnostic subtests. Well standardized across all age levels, with representativeness of norms and fair reliability and validity data.

ADMINISTRATION: By a psychometrically trained professional. Specific instructions provided for determining the basal and ceiling items at each age level.

SCORING AND INTERPRETATION: Two cluster scores derived, for verbal and nonverbal abilities. Score interpretation based on normative sample and on individual child's profile of strengths and weaknesses. A GCA (general conceptual ability) score gives picture of child's conceptual and reasoning abilities.

OVERALL EVALUATION: The DAS is a well standardized, useful tool for determining cognitive functioning of toddlers, with items that are of intrinsic interest to them. Its ease of administration makes it especially noteworthy.

TITLE: Fagan Test of Infant Intelligence

AUTHORS: J. Fagan and P. Shepherd

PUBLISHER AND ADDRESS: Infantest Corporation, 11000 Cedar Ave., Cleveland, Ohio 44106.

COPYRIGHT DATE: 1987

LEVEL: 6 to 12 months

PURPOSE: To assess cognitive potential of young children; to identify children with cognitive deficits.

DISTINGUISHING CHARACTERISTICS: A novel test of infant intelligence, using infant attention to visual stimuli to identify infants who are at risk for cognitive delay. Predictive validity is good in comparison to other early cognitive assessment instruments.

ADMINISTRATION: Requires training in use of equipment and measurement techniques. With special apparatus, "novelty problems" (e.g., pictures of diverse faces) are presented visually to infant sitting on parent's lap. Tester sits behind apparatus, observes infant's visual fixations through peephole, and records length of fixations.

SCORING AND INTERPRETATION: Computerized scoring system prints out description of infant's current status relative to other infants of that age. Used to designate infants at high risk, suspect for risk, or at low risk for later cognitive deficit.

OVERALL EVALUATION: Has potential for providing a very early measurement of potential cognitive delay. Use has been primarily by hospital clinics, in combination with traditional assessment measures; cost relatively high in comparison to other assessment instruments. Predictive validity is promising. Potential for assessing cognitive development in toddlers with severe physical disabilities not yet explored.

TITLE: Family Needs Scale

AUTHORS: C. J. Dunst, C. S. Cooper, J. C. Weeldreyer, K. D. Snyder, and J. H. Chase

PUBLISHER AND ADDRESS: In C. J. Dunst, C. Trivette., and A. Deal (1988). Enabling and empowering families: Principles and guidelines for practice. Cambridge, MA: Brookline Books. (May be reproduced.)

COPYRIGHT DATE: 1988

LEVEL: Adult family members

PURPOSE: To determine whether a family of a child with disabilities has needs for help or assistance.

DISTINGUISHING CHARACTERISTICS: A family report form, with 41 areas of potential need, which are rated on a Likert-type scale. Includes need related to finances, living conditions, special care for child, and social support. High split-half reliability and item correlation. Criterion validity for total scale score, factor scores, and number of dimensions of parental beliefs show adequate levels.

ADMINISTRATION: Family member circles responses with assistance of early intervention staff member.

SCORING AND INTERPRETATION: Likert scale ranges from "almost never" or "almost always" in relation to each need area. The level and type of need of the family is determined from the need strength of the responses (i.e., many "often" or "almost always" answers). Also permits interpretation of the types of needs (e.g., mainly child care, medical, educational, financial).

OVERALL EVALUATION: Useful as one method that provides a picture of the range of needs the family may have, as well as the strength of each need. Delivery of services can be guided by the information.

TITLE: Family Needs Survey

AUTHORS: D. Bailey and R. Simeonsson

PUBLISHER AND ADDRESS: Frank Porter Graham Child Development Center, CB#8180, University of North Carolina, Chapel Hill, NC 27599 (Contact authors for information.)

COPYRIGHT DATE: 1990

LEVEL: Adult family members

PURPOSE: To assess the expressed needs of families of young children with disabilities or delays; to assist in developing the IFSP.

DISTINGUISHING CHARACTERISTICS: A parent self-report, which measures family needs for information, social support, help in explaining child's condition, community services, financial resources, and family functioning assistance. Authors recommend combining it with open-ended interview. Test–retest reliability higher for fathers than mothers; additional data on validity still needed.

ADMINISTRATION: Parent is asked to check the items, indicating how great the need is for each. Authors recommend each parent answer separately. Can be administered by early intervention staff at intake.

SCORING AND INTERPRETATION: A 3-point scale (no, not sure, yes) used to indicate type and strength of the family's need on each item. If needs are identified, the information may be discussed further in open-ended interview or used in identifying family goals for the IFSP.

OVERALL EVALUATION: Useful method for making parents aware of areas in which the family may have needs and providing information to professionals on the needs families choose to identify. May be considered intrusive by some parents. Parents have option of not answering the questions; those who prefer not to answer may keep the survey for reference.

TITLE: Family Support Scale

AUTHORS: C. Dunst, V. Jenkins, and C. Trivette

PUBLISHER AND ADDRESS: In C. J. Dunst, C. M. Trivette, and A. G. Deal (1988). Enabling and empowering families: Principles and guidelines for practice. Cambridge, MA: Brookline Books. (May be reproduced.)

COPYRIGHT DATE: 1988

LEVEL: Adult family members

PURPOSE: To determine sources of people helpful to a family raising a young child, in particular a child at risk for developmental delay.

DISTINGUISHING CHARACTERISTICS: Questionnaire lists 18 different people and groups who help families raising young children; parents rate how helpful these sources have been on a 6-point scale. It has adequate reliability and validity, although test–retest reliability declines as family needs change.

ADMINISTRATION: Typically administered to the parent or primary caretaker by early intervention staff.

SCORING AND INTERPRETATION: Descriptive information used to guide case management and delivery of services.

OVERALL EVALUATION: Appears to be a helpful source of information on whether the family is making optimal use of available family and community resources, and the extent to which they find these resources helpful. May be considered intrusive by some parents, who have option of not answering such questions.

TITLE: Greenspan-Leiberman Observation System for Assessment of Caregiver-Infant Interaction during Semi-Structured Play (GLOS-Revised)

AUTHORS: S. Greenspan, A. Lieberman, and S. Poisson

PUBLISHER AND ADDRESS: Contact Sue Poisson, Regional Center for Infants and Young Children, 11710 Hunters Lane, Rockville, MD 20852

COPYRIGHT DATE: 1990

LEVEL: Ages 2–30 months

PURPOSE: To define observable and measurable indicator behaviors and characterize clinical aspects of the mother/caregiver-infant interaction process.

DISTINGUISHING CHARACTERISTICS: Covers 45 maternal/caregiver behaviors and 43 infant behaviors related to interaction processes. Behaviors are rated according to percentage of occurrences observed in the session. Interobserver reliability and stability of behavioral results have been reported.

ADMINISTRATION: Administered by professional trained in the procedure. The videotaped observation totals 10 minutes of mother/caregiver– infant interaction in a free play situation. Directions to caregiver are to do "whatever you wish to do." Although a box of toys are in the room, no specific instructions to use them are given.

SCORING AND INTERPRETATION: Behaviors of child and mother/caregiver are coded every 15 seconds; several behaviors can be simultaneously coded. Behaviors are rated on a continuum from never occurring (0%) to occurred at every observation (100%).

OVERALL EVALUATION: Useful to assess social–emotional behaviors and to determine characteristics of mother/caregiver–infant interactions that might affect child's development. Because of the complexity of the coding system, a skilled clinician must supervise the assessment.

TITLE: Hawaii Early Learning Profile (HELP)

AUTHORS: S. Furuno, K. O'Reilly, C. Hosaka, T. Inatsuka, T. Allman, and B. Zeisloft

PUBLISHER AND ADDRESS: Vort Corporation, PO Box 60132, Palo Alto, CA 94306

COPYRIGHT DATES: 1984, 1988

LEVEL: Birth to 36 months

PURPOSE: To assist in planning individualized programs for children with a wide range of disabilities.

DISTINGUISHING CHARACTERISTICS: Criterion-referenced; divided into HELP Charts and HELP Activity Guide, both normed using disabled infants in Hawaii. Provides a month-to-month sequenced list of typical developmental skills in six areas: Cognitive, expressive–language, gross motor, fine motor, self help, and social–emotional; based on information from developmental scales and standardized tests. No data on reliability and validity. Focuses on skills that are teachable and amenable to intervention.

ADMINISTRATION: Recommended to be administered by a multidisciplinary team, making adaptations for the child's disabilities. Several sessions, each less than an hour, are necessary for completing this untimed assessment.

SCORING AND INTERPRETATION: Results entered on the scoring chart with a colored pencil; age range is identified. Charts are updated using a different color at each new assessment date. Current skill levels are used to plan interventions.

OVERALL EVALUATION: Easily administered and understood by parents; intended use by multidisciplinary and transdisciplinary teams is a plus. Lack of technical data is major caution in using it; should be supplemented by other measures.

TITLE: Home Observation for Measurement of the Environment for Infants and Toddlers (HOME)

AUTHORS: B. M. Caldwell and R. Bradley

PUBLISHER AND ADDRESS: Child Development Research Unit, University of Arkansas at Little Rock, 33rd and University Avenue, Little Rock, AR 72204

COPYRIGHT DATES: 1978, 1984

LEVEL: Birth to 36 months; adult interactions

PURPOSE: To assess quality of child care and environmental support available to the child in the home; to identify risks for developmental delay due to these factors; to assist in the planning of appropriate interventions.

DISTINGUISHING CHARACTERISTICS: Observational and interview instrument, developed from a list of positive environmental characteristics likely to foster early development. Standardization data was gathered using 176 families. Has high reliability and validity ratings. Good predictor of developmental normality or potential delay.

ADMINISTRATION: Administered in the home by early intervention staff. Observations of parent–child interactions and parental interview are included. Interview takes approximately 1 hour. A checklist notes absence or presence of interactional behaviors and specified environmental factors.

SCORING AND INTERPRETATION: Each of the 45 items on the checklist are marked as yes (present) or no (absent). Scores are computed for the total inventory and 6 subscales: Caregiver emotional and verbal responsivity, avoidance of restriction and punishment, organization of environment, provision of appropriate play materials, caregiver involvement with the child, and variety of daily stimulation.

OVERALL EVALUATION: An innovative method for assessing environmental factors in the home that may predict later delay. Validated in research and clinical settings. Standardization sample cannot be considered to be nationally representative. Use in combination with other measures recommended.

TITLE: Movement Assessment of Infants (MAI)

AUTHORS: L. Chandler, M. Andrews, and M. Swanson

PUBLISHER AND ADDRESS: Infant Movement Research, PO Box 4631, Rolling Bay, WA 9806

COPYRIGHT DATE: 1981

LEVEL: Birth to 12 months

PURPOSE: To give a comprehensive appraisal of motor development in the 1st year of life; evaluates risk, but is not intended to provide a diagnosis of movement disabilities.

DISTINGUISHING CHARACTERISTICS: Neurodevelopmental, criterion-referenced, measuring four components of movement: Tone, primitive reflexes, automatic reactions, and volitional movement. Assesses precursor movement behaviors that lead to later movement behaviors. Establishes baseline for treatment; can be used to assess children over 12 months functioning below that age level. Recently standardized with normative samples for ages 4, 6, 8 months. Screening instrument with norms from 2–12 months also available.

ADMINISTRATION: Requires training prior to administration; takes 20 to 30 minutes.

SCORING AND INTERPRETATION: Items scored on a scale of 1 to 4, except the tone items, which are scored on a scale of 1 to 5. A risk score for each of the four sections is used to make assumptions about the neurological nature of the deficit. The profile of scores is used in interpretations. A total risk score for children at 4, 6, and 8 months can also be derived.

OVERALL EVALUATION: Provides method of evaluating precursors of severe motor delays. Especially useful in clinical and research settings.

TITLE: Neonatal Behavioral Assessment Scale (NBAS) (2nd Edition)

AUTHOR: T.B. Brazelton

PUBLISHER AND ADDRESS: J.B. Lippincott, East Washington Square, Philadelphia, PA 19105 (Distributer: Cambridge University Press)

COPYRIGHT DATE: 1984

LEVEL: Neonates (37–44 weeks gestational age)

PURPOSE: To provide profile of overall behavioral organization of the normal full-term newborn; to describe coping capacities and adaptive strategies elicited by stresses in extrauterine environment; to describe changes over time in these behaviors; to identify individual differences in responsivity; to predict infants who might be at risk and in need of early intervention.

DISTINGUISHING CHARACTERISTICS: Assesses newborn behavioral repertoire on 28 behavioral and 20 neurological responses, observed within 6 states of consciousness (from deep sleep to crying). Originally developed in 1973, revised version includes 9 supplementary items to be used with high-risk infants.

ADMINISTRATION: Requires examiner trained to reliability, who must be competent in handling infants and learn to be responsive to reading their behavioral cues. Good reliabilty and validity, with training. Standardization and normative data not available. Repeated administration recommended at 1–3 days, 2 weeks, and 4 weeks. With high-risk samples, may be used up to 2–3 months.

SCORING AND INTERPRETATION: Behavioral items scored on a 9 point scale; reflexes on a 4 point scale. Items are clustered into 7 dimensions: habituation, orientation, motor processes, range of state, regulation of state, autonomic stability, and reflexes. Best performance profile tells how the infant performs under optimal conditions. Examiner plays a critical role in gaining infant's best performance. A total score is not obtained.

OVERALL EVALUATION: Currently the most widely used assessment method for newborn populations. Extensive use as a research instrument in study of high-risk infant behaviors, obstetric medication effects, maternal substance abuse effects, cross-cultural comparisons, prediction of later development, and as a form of intervention. NOTE: Training available from J. K. Nugent, Child Development Unit, Children's Hospital, Boston, MA.

TITLE: Nursing Child Assessment Satellite Training Instrument (NCAST) (Originally called Barnard Teaching and Feeding Scales)

AUTHOR: K. Barnard

PUBLISHER AND ADDRESS: Available from G. Summer, NCAST, WJ10, University of Washington, Seattle, WA 98195; distributed as part of NCAST training sequence

COPYRIGHT DATE: 1978

LEVEL: Children 6 to 36 months and their caregivers

PURPOSE: To identify early factors that predict later child development outcomes, to assist in determining interactive patterns that influence development, and to evaluate high-risk characteristics.

DISTINGUISHING CHARACTERISTICS: Parental and child behaviors are coded in two structured situations: Feeding (NCAFS) and Teaching (NCATS). Four categories of responses are coded for parents: Sensitivity to cues, response to child's distress, social–emotional growth-fostering, and cognitive growth-fostering. Two categories of responses are coded for child: clarity of cues and responsiveness to parent. Standardized on a population of predominantly white, healthy, middle-income women and their infants, half of whom were born with complications. Although NCAST has moderately high reliability and validity ratings, two administrations with high-risk families before judgment of interaction quality is reached are recommended.

ADMINISTRATION: Administered by a professional (nurse or early interventionist) who has been trained in observing parent–child interactions in teaching and feeding situations. Training must be taken in order to obtain instruments.

SCORING AND INTERPRETATION: Items are scored as occurring or non-occurring for each of the sections. Overall score is derived for each section.

OVERALL EVALUATION: The utility of feeding situations as ideal for observation has been debated; useful for situations where reciprocity of interaction is in question. NCAST has good technical standards and is being used increasingly as an outcome measure in early intervention projects. It should be used with caution in high-risk populations.

TITLE: Peabody Developmental Motor Scales (PDMS)

AUTHORS: M. R. Folio and R. R. Fewell

PUBLISHER AND ADDRESS: DLM Teaching Resources, One DLM Park, Allen, TX 75002

COPYRIGHT DATE: 1983

LEVEL: Birth to 6 years, 9 months

PURPOSE: To gather developmental information on gross and fine motor functioning that can be used for program planning.

DISTINGUISHING CHARACTERISTICS: Evaluates gross and fine motor development in young children, in five gross motor skill areas: reflexes, balance, nonlocomotor, locomotor, and receipt and propulsion; and in four fine motor areas: grasping, hand-use, eye–hand coordination, and manual dexterity. Small, but representative normative sample. Good reliability; moderate validity data reported.

ADMINISTRATION: Administered by trained professional with knowledge of motor functioning. Each section takes about 30 minutes to administer, and it is suggested that the two sections be administered within 5 days of each other.

SCORING AND INTERPRETATION: Each item is scored 0 when the child fails the response, 1 when the criteria are not fully met, and 2 when criteria have been met easily. The raw scores are converted to age equivalents, developmental quotients, percentiles and z-scores for each of the nine skill areas.

OVERALL EVALUATION: A good instrument for systematic assessment of motor skills that does not require a trained psychometrician; often used by physical and occupational therapists. Correlates well with the Bayley Motor Scale.

TITLE: Preschool Language Scale-3 (PLS-3)

AUTHORS: I. L. Zimmerman, V. G. Steiner, and R. E. Pond

PUBLISHER AND ADDRESS: The Psychological Corporation, PO Box 839954, San Antonio, TX 78283-3954

COPYRIGHT DATE: 1992

LEVEL: Birth to 6 years, 11 months

PURPOSE: To measure receptive and expressive language of young children; to identify and describe maturational lags; to assist in planning language interventions.

DISTINGUISHING CHARACTERISTICS: Developmentally sequenced test of receptive (auditory comprehension) and expressive language, originally developed in 1969; revised in 1979. Third edition features pictures and manipulatives of interest to young children, optional supplementary articulation and spontaneous language measures, and a parent report measure. Below 12 months, test focuses on language precursors, such as attention, vocalization, and pragmatics. For over 12 months, syntax and semantics (e.g., vocabulary, concept words) are stressed. Test is now norm-referenced, with normative data based on performance of a representative national sample of 1,900 children across the age span. Moderate to high reliability and validity data. A Spanish language version is available.

ADMINISTRATION: Administered by speech pathologists and by early intervention personnel with knowledge of language development principles. Although time may vary, it is usually completed in 30 minutes.

SCORING AND INTERPRETATION: Test items begin 1 year below child's chronological age. Recorded as correct, incorrect, and no response, score of 1 for correct items. Basal is 3 consecutive items passed; ceiling is 5 consecutive items failed. A receptive, expressive, and total score can be generated. Standard scores, percentile ranks, and age equivalents may be determined.

OVERALL EVALUATION: Easy to administer; jargon-free and the materials are of interest to children. In wide use in early intervention programs and language clinics because it provides a relatively quick index of child language performance. Lack of technical information continues; the addition of normative data is a strength.

TITLE: Receptive–Expressive Emergent Language Scale (REEL-2)

AUTHORS: K. Bzoch and R. League

PUBLISHER AND ADDRESS: ProEd Inc., 8700 Shoal Creek Boulevard, Austin, TX 78758

COPYRIGHT DATE: 1991

LEVEL: Birth to 3 years

PURPOSE: To identify young children who may have specific language handicaps requiring early habilitative and educational intervention.

DISTINGUISHING CHARACTERISTICS: A diagnostic interview that measures the child's level of emergent language. Direct observation is recommended prior to the interview. Comprises 66 expressive and 66 receptive items, broken down into 22 different age levels. Standardization information is not given, although reliability and validity studies are provided and indicate moderately high technical adequacy.

ADMINISTRATION: Administered by speech pathologists or other early intervention staff with understanding of language; takes approximately 20 minutes.

SCORING AND INTERPRETATION: Individual items are scored "plus," "minus," or "emergent." Three scores are available: Receptive Language Age, Expressive Language Age, and Combined Age. Language quotients are derived using an equation that weighs the receptive and expressive items equally.

OVERALL EVALUATION: A well-crafted instrument based on linguistic theory. One advantage is that it measures receptive and emergent language, as well as expressive language. Another is that it engages the caregiver in the assessment process.

TITLE: Revised Infant Temperament Questionaire (RITQ)

AUTHORS: W.B. Carey and S. McDevitt

PUBLISHER AND ADDRESS: Contact W. B. Carey, M.D., Division of General Pediatrics, Children's Hospital of Philadelphia, Philadelphia, PA 19104 (requested prepaid contribution of $10)

COPYRIGHT DATE: 1978

LEVEL: 4 to 8 months

PURPOSE: Identifies infant behavior styles that may be of concern to parents or be clinically significant; is used to describe infant temperaments that may affect their initiation and response modes and their parents' interactions.

DISTINGUISHING CHARACTERISTICS: A 95-item parent response questionnaire that measures infant temperament in 10 categories: Activity, rhythmicity, approach, intensity, adaptability, mood, attention span, persistence, distractibility, and threshold to stimulation. Has internal consistency reliability and validity; scores correlate with later cognitive and developmental milestones and presence of clinical problems such as colic. Standardized using 203 infants aged 4 to 8 months, from different SES levels, primarily white middle- and upper-middle-class backgrounds.

ADMINISTRATION: Parent rates the child's functioning using a six-point Likert scale ranging from "almost never" to "almost always."

SCORING AND INTERPRETATION: Summary score for each category obtained from the questionnaire used to classify infant into one of the diagnostic clusters: Difficult (arrhythmic, withdrawing, low adaptibility, intense, negative); Easy (the opposite of those characteristics), Slow-to-warm-up (inactive, slow in approach and adaptibility, mild, negative) or Intermediate (all others).

OVERALL EVALUATION: Not a screening device for abnormal behavior and development, but used when there are parental concerns about infant behavioral styles or clinical problems like a sleep disturbance that may require different parenting styles. Measures parental ratings of infant temperament using objective descriptions on each item and also asks for parental overall perceptions. Easily administered but scoring is complex; useful for initiating parenting discussions. NOTE: Similar questionnaires for other age levels are available from B. Medoff-Cooper, University School of Nursing, Philadelphia, PA 19104-6096 (early infancy) and W. Fullard, Department of Educational Psychology, Temple University, Philadelphia, PA 19122 (toddler).

TITLE: The Rossetti Infant–Toddler Language Scale

AUTHOR: L. Rossetti

PUBLISHER AND ADDRESS: Lingua Systems, 3100 4th Ave., PO Box 747, East Moline, IL 61244

COPYRIGHT DATE: 1990

LEVEL: Birth to 36 months

PURPOSE: To provide a comprehensive assessment of preverbal and verbal aspects of young children's communication and interaction.

DISTINGUISHING CHARACTERISTICS: Includes a parent questionnaire, a child language sample (at least 50 child utterances), and a child–examiner interaction period. The items are based on developmental knowledge and author observation, with six developmental areas observed. No normative group, reliability, or validity data reported.

ADMINISTRATION: By early intervention staff with expertise in child development and language. Clear directions, criteria, and information on methods that get best responses are provided. Parent questionnaire is completed first and used to guide level at which to begin testing. Entire procedure may take up to 1 hour.

SCORING AND INTERPRETATION: Basal and ceiling levels must be obtained. Items are scored as passed when the examiner observes them, when they are elicited, or when caregiver reports they occur. Basal and ceiling levels in each area are obtained; a profile of scores can also be charted. Mean length of utterance is obtained from spontaneous language sample. Results are interpreted in relation to educational plans for the child.

OVERALL EVALUATION: Provides a comprehensive picture of spontaneous and elicited language expression and reception and uses an informal, play-based approach. Parent questionnaire is thorough, and test instructions are clear. Lack of technical information suggests caution in interpretation. A useful addition to a transdisciplinary, multifactored, team assessment.

TITLE: The Symbolic Play Scale

AUTHOR: C. Westby

PUBLISHER AND ADDRESS: Discussed in Westby, C. E. (1980). Assessment of cognitive and language abilities through play. Language, Speech and Hearing Services in Schools, 11, 154–168.

COPYRIGHT DATE: 1980

LEVEL: 9 to 36 months

PURPOSE: To determine if a child should be given priority for receiving language remediation, and, if language remediation is indicated, to determine what communicative functions, semantic concepts, and syntactic structures should be taught; to assess play development and language within a naturalistic setting.

DISTINGUISHING CHARACTERISTICS: A procedure that evolved from a Piagetian-based language program for severely retarded and trainable retarded children. Explores language development through the medium of play. The play is classified into 1 of 10 symbolic play stages and the language sample is analyzed for syntactic, semantic, and pragmatic quality.

ADMINISTRATION: By professional knowledgable about linguistic and play development from Piagetian theoretical perspective. An estimate of child's developmental age is obtained from a norm-referenced psychometric instrument (e.g., the Bayley). Children are then given developmentally appropriate choices of play materials and observed during play. The session is tape recorded.

SCORING AND INTERPRETATION: The child's symbolic play level is compared with the language level to determine whether language and cognition are developing congruently. Need for remedial services by the speech pathologist can then be determined.

OVERALL EVALUATION: A naturalistic and developmentally appropriate method for assessing cognitive, play, and language developmental problems, and planning the language skills that should be taught.

TITLE: System to Plan Early Childhood Services (SPECS)

AUTHORS: S. J. Bagnato and J. Neisworth

PUBLISHER AND ADDRESS: American Guidance Service, 4201 Woodland Rd., PO Box 99, Circle Pines, MN 55014-1796

COPYRIGHT DATE: 1990

LEVEL: Ages 2 to 6

PURPOSE: To assist teams to organize informed judgments in order to make decisions for children with disabilities or at risk for disability; to plan and evaluate interventions for these children.

DISTINGUISHING CHARACTERISTICS: An innovative team system using clinical judgments rather than test scores. Three rating forms: Developmental Specs (DS), Team Specs (TS), and Program Specs (PS), used in sequence. Field tested with 1,300 children. Moderate to high inter-rater and test–retest reliability and concurrent validity.

ADMINISTRATION: By transdisciplinary team that includes parent; after using observation, interviews, or testing, team members rate child's development in six domains: Communication, sensorimotor, physical, self-regulation, cognition, and self–social (on DS). DS requires 15 to 20 minutes for rating plus time taken by team member to gather information needed to rate.

SCORING AND INTERPRETATION: Using clinical judgment, team members summarize ratings (TS); discuss and arrive at consensus for programming among 10 options (PS). Develop summary sheets for monitoring progress. Together, TS and PS require 25 to 30 minutes.

OVERALL EVALUATION: Designed to be an efficient method of assessment and consensus decision making among team members. Organizes structure of team meetings and promotes team interaction; assessment process still requires time for team members to gather child developmental data.

TITLE: Transdisciplinary Play-Based Assessment–Revised

AUTHOR: T. W. Linder

PUBLISHER AND ADDRESS: Paul H. Brookes, PO Box 10624, Baltimore, MD 21285-0624

COPYRIGHT DATE: 1993

LEVEL: Toddlers and preschool-age

PURPOSE: To provide a flexible, holistic, developmentally appropriate method of assessing young children's development; to enable transdisciplinary teams to identify young children with developmental delays within a naturalistic setting.

DISTINGUISHING CHARACTERISTICS: A book that explains rationale, assessment procedures, scoring and report writing method, with examples. Specifically designed for team-based arena-type assessment.

ADMINISTRATION: By early intervention team that includes parent facilitator, play facilitator, observing team members, and video camera operator. Occurs in playroom in following phases: Unstructured play facilitation, structured play facilitation, child–child interaction, parent–child interaction, motor play, and snack time. Observing team members record observations during all phases.

SCORING AND INTERPRETATION: After session, team discusses observations recorded on worksheets for each developmental area. Summary sheets for each domain are prepared. Video tape used for review of observations and for documentation.

OVERALL EVALUATION: An innovative and child-sensitive method of assessment that structures the transdisciplinary team members' roles to gain integrative report. Includes parent in all portions. No information on normative or technical data.

TITLE: Uzgiris and Hunt Scales of Infant Psychological Development

AUTHORS: I. Uzgiris and J. M. V. Hunt; protocol revised by C. J. Dunst

PUBLISHER AND ADDRESS: University Park Press, 233 East Redwood Street, Baltimore, Maryland, 21202. (Revised scale)

COPYRIGHT DATES: 1975 (Uzgiris & Hunt); 1980 (Dunst)

LEVEL: Birth to 24 months

PURPOSE: To assess the sensorimotor development of infants and older children who are at risk for delays.

DISTINGUISHING CHARACTERISTICS: An ordinal measure based on Piagetian-defined stages of sensorimotor development. Revised by Dunst, with manual to guide administration. Term "ordinal" indicates that abilities demonstrated at one level of a domain is evidence that all lower levels in that domain can also be performed. Seven sensorimotor domains are assessed: object permanence, means–ends, vocal imitation, gestural imitation, operational causality, spatial relationships, and scheme actions. High concurrent validity with psychometric instruments; high reliability coefficients.

ADMINISTRATION: By professional with knowledge of Piagetian developmental theory. After establishing rapport with child and parents, assessment begins with items developmentally two or three steps below level at which child is currently functioning. There is no specified order of presentation; assessment may be extended over 2 to 3 days to ensure optimal performance.

SCORING AND INTERPRETATION: Items are administered until the ceiling is obtained; scored as "correct," "correct after demonstration," "emerging skills," or "not observed." Estimated developmental ages (EDA) are provided for each scale step. Age placements have no normative value; considered to be estimates of the "modal" age at which children ordinarily attain the scale landmarks. Interpretation based on evidence of delayed or non-delayed sensorimotor performance, typical or atypical patterns of sensorimotor performance, and extent and nature of discrepancies. Child profile is also charted.

OVERALL EVALUATION: A theoretically sound, relatively informal means of assessing cognitive developmental age. Especially useful to assess children of chronological ages over 2½ years, who are performing in the sensorimotor developmental stage.

TITLE: Vineland Adaptive Behavior Scales

AUTHORS: S. Sparrow, D. Balla, and D. Cicchetti

PUBLISHER AND ADDRESS: American Guidance Service, Circle Pines, MN 55014-1796

COPYRIGHT DATES: 1984, 1985

LEVEL: Birth to 18 years, 11 months; also low functioning adults

PURPOSE: To provide a general assessment of adaptive behavior; to assist in diagnostic evaluations, program planning, and research.

DISTINGUISHING CHARACTERISTICS: Interview instrument measures child adaptive behavior in four domains: communication, daily living skills, socialization, and motor skills. A maladaptive behavior domain may also be measured at examiner's discretion. Available in survey form (297 items) and expanded form (577 items). Classroom report edition for age 3 and up also available (244 items). Provides norm-referenced information (sex, race or ethnic origin, community size, region of country, parent level of education) based on the performance of a representative national standardization sample of 4,800 handicapped and non-handicapped individuals. Compares parent's description of child behavior with descriptions other parents have given. Moderate to high reliability and validity data reported.

ADMINISTRATION: Parent interview instrument administered by trained professional. The entry point of interview is determined by examiner, who may select child's chronological, mental, or social age. Criteria should remain consistent for each domain tested. Basals and ceilings need to be determined. The test is untimed.

SCORING AND INTERPRETATION: Score is based on respondent's indication of child performance of the activities. A score of 2 indicates the behavior is a usual one; 1 indicates it is a partial or occasional activity; and 0 indicates no engagement in the behavior. Some items may be scored N (no opportunity to perform) or DK (not aware of behavior). Raw scores convert to percentiles, stanines, age equivalents, and standard scores.

OVERALL EVALUATION: A widely used, well-standardized, measure of strengths and weaknesses in adaptive behavior domains. Often used by psychologists in combination with a norm-referenced cognitive measure.

References

Abidin, R. R. (1986). *Parenting Stress Index* (2nd ed.). Charlottesville, VA: Pediatric Psychology Press.

Able-Boone, H. (1992, December). *Family participation in the IFSP process.* Paper presented at the annual meeting of the Division of Early Childhood, Washington, DC.

Able-Boone, H., Sandall, S. R., Stevens, E., & Frederick, L. L. (1992). Family support resources and needs: How early intervention can make a difference. *Infant-Toddler Intervention, 2*(2), 93–102.

Achenbach, T. (1988). *Child Behavior Checklist for Ages 2–3.* Burlington: University of Vermont.

Achor, S. (1978). *Mexican Americans in a Dallas Barrio.* Tucson: University of Arizona Press.

Acredolo, L. P., & Hake, J. L. (1982). Infant perception. In B. B. Wolman (Ed.), *Handbook of developmental psychology* (pp. 244–283). Englewood, NJ: Prentice Hall.

Ainsworth, M. D. S. (1979). Infant–mother attachment. *American Psychologist, 34,* 932–937.

Alexander, R. (1990). Oral–motor and respiratory–phonatory assessment. In E. D. Gibbs & D. M. Teti (Eds.), *Interdisciplinary assessment of infants* (pp. 63–76). Baltimore: Paul H. Brookes.

Alpern, G., Boll, T., & Shearer, M. (1984). *Developmental Profile II.* Los Angeles: Western Psychological Services.

American Academy of Otolaryngology: Guide for the evaluation of hearing handicap. (1979). *Journal of the American Medical Association, 241,* 2055–2059.

American Association of Mental Retardation (AAMR). (1983, May). *Position statement on witholding medical and other treatment from defective newborn children.* Washington, DC.: Author.

American National Standards Institute. (1969). *American National Standard Specifications for Audiometers* (ANSI S3.6, revision 1989). New York: Acoustical Society of America.

American National Standards Institute. (1982). *American National Standard Specifications for Hearing Aids* (ANSI S3.22). New York: Author.

American Nurses Association. (1988). *Nursing case management.* Kansas City, MO: Author.

American Physical Therapy Association (APTA). (1991). *Competencies for physical therapists in early intervention.* Washington, DC: Author.

American Psychological Association. (1993). *Ethical principles of psychologists.* Washington, DC.: Author.

Anastasi, A. (1988). *Psychological testing* (6th ed.). New York: Macmillan.

Anastasiow, N. J., & Harel, S. (1993). *At-risk infants: Interventions, families and research.* Baltimore: Paul H. Brookes.

Anderson, C. J. (1981). Enhancing reciprocity between mother and neonate. *Nursing Research, 30,* 89–93.

Anderson, E. R., Bell, N. J., Fischer, J. L., Munsch, J., Peek, C. W., & Sorell, G. T. (1993). Applying a risk-taking perspective. In N. J. Bell & R. W. Bell (Eds.), *Adolescent risk taking* (pp. 165–185). Newbury Park, CA: Sage.

Angell, R., & McWilliam, R. A. (1992, December). *What North Carolina families think of early intervention services: A survey.* Paper presented at the meeting of the Division of Early Childhood, Washington, DC.

Apgar, V. A. (1953). A proposal for a new method of evaluation of a newborn infant. *Anaesthesia and Analgesia, 32,* 260–267.

Arikian, V. L. (1991). Total quality management: Applications to nursing service. *Journal of Nursing Administration, 21*(6), 46–50.

Association for Childhood Education International. (1993). Infants and toddlers with special needs and their families. Position paper. *Childhood Education, 69*(5), 278–286.

Association of Teacher Educators/National Association for the Education of Young Children. (1991). Position paper. *Young Children, 47*(1), 16–21.

Association of Teacher Educators, Division of Early Childhood, National Association for the Education of Young Children. (1994, Spring). *Personnel standards for early education and early intervention. Position paper.* Washington, DC: Author.

Ausubel, D. P., Sullivan, E. V., & Ives, S. W. (1980). *Theory and problems of child development* (3rd ed.). New York: Grune & Stratton.

Baer, D. M. (1981). A hung jury and a Scottish verdict: "Not proven." *Analysis and Intervention in Developmental Disabilities, 1,* 91–98.

Bagnato, S. J., & Neisworth, J. T. (1987). The developmental school psychologist: Professional profile of an emerging early childhood specialist. *Topics in Early Childhood Special Education, 7*(3), 75–89.

Bagnato, S. J., & Neisworth, J. T. (1990). *System to Plan Early Childhood Services (SPECS).* Circle Pines, MN: American Guidance.

Bagnato, S. J., & Neisworth, J. T. (1991). *Assessment for early intervention: Best practices for professionals.* New York: Guildford Press.

Bailey, D. (1988). Rationale and model for family assessment in early intervention. In D. Bailey & R. Simeonsson (Eds.), *Family assessment in early intervention* (pp.1–26). Columbus, OH: Merrill.

Bailey, D. B., Buysse, V., Edmondson, R., & Smith, T. M. (1992). Creating family-centered services in early intervention: Perceptions of professionals in four states. *Exceptional Children, 58*(4), 298–309.

Bailey, D., DeWert, M., Thiele, J., & Ware, W. (1983). Measuring individual participation on the inter-disciplinary team. *American Journal of Mental Deficiency, 88,* 247–254.

Bailey, D., Palsha, S., & Simeonsson, R. (1991). Professional skills, concerns, and perceived importance of work with families in early intervention. *Exceptional Children, 58*(2), 156–165.

Bailey, D., & Simeonsson, R. (1984). Critical issues underlying research and intervention with families of young handicapped children. *Journal of the Division for Early Childhood, 9,* 38–48.

Bailey, D., & Simeonsson, R. (1988). *Family assessment in early intervention.* Columbus, OH: Merrill.

Bailey, D., Simeonsson, R., Yoder, D., & Huntington, G. (1990). Preparing professionals to serve infants and toddlers with handicaps and their families: An integrative analysis across eight disciplines. *Exceptional Children, 57*(1), 26–35.

Bailey, D., & Wolery, M. (1989). *Assessing infants and preschoolers with handicaps.* New York: Macmillan.

Bailey, L., & Slee, P. T. (1984). A comparison of play interactions between non-disabled and disabled children and their mothers: A question of style. *Australia and New Zealand Journal of Developmental Disabilities, 10*(1), 5–10.

Baldwin, D. A., Markman, E. M., & Melartin, R. L. (1993). Infants' ability to draw inferences about nonobvious object properties: Evidence from exploratory play. *Child Development,64*(3), 711–728.

Ball, W., & Tronick, E. (1971). Infant responses to impending collision: Optical and real. *Science, 171,* 818–820.

Baltes, P. B. (1989). The dynamics between growth and decline. *Contemporary Psychology, 34,* 983–984.

Barnard, C. P., & Corrales, R. G. (1979). *The theory and technique of family therapy.* Springfield, IL: Charles C. Thomas.

Barnett, D. W., & Carey, K. T. (1992). *Designing interventions for preschool learning and behavior problems.* San Francisco: Jossey-Bass.

Barona, A. (1991). Assessment of multicultural preschool children. In B. A. Bracken (Ed.), *Psychoeducational assessment of preschool children* (2nd ed.) (pp. 379–391). Orlando, FL: Grune & Stratton.

Bates, E., Bretherton, I, & Snyder, L. (1988). *From first words to grammar.* Cambridge, England: Cambridge University Press.

Bayley, N. (1993). *Bayley Scales of Infant Development* (2nd ed.). San Antonio, TX: The Psychological Corporation.

Beckwith, L. (1985). Parent–child interaction and social–emotional development. In C. C. Brown & A. W. Gottfried (Eds.), *Play interactions: The role of toys and parental involvement in children's development* (pp.152–159). Skillman, NJ: Johnson & Johnson.

Beninghof, A., & Singer, A. (l992). Transdisciplinary teaming: An inservice training activity. *Teaching Exceptional Children, 58*(3), 58–61.

Bennett, F. C. (l982). The pediatrician and the interdisciplinary process. *Exceptional Children, 48,* 306–314.

Bergan, J. R., & Feld, J. K. (1993). Developmental assessment: New directions. *Young Children, 48*(5), 41–47.

Bergen, D. (1988). Methods of studying play. In D. Bergen (Ed.), *Play as a medium for learning and development* (pp. 27–44). Portsmouth, NH: Heinemann.

Bergen, D. (1988). Stages of play development. In D. Bergen (Ed.), *Play as a medium for learning and development* (pp. 49–66). Portsmouth, NH: Heinemann.

Bergen, D. (1989). Characteristics of young children's expression of humour in home settings as observed by parents. *International Journal of Educology, 3*(2), 124–135.

Bergen, D. (1991). *Play as the vehicle for early intervention with at-risk infants and toddlers.* Chicago: American Educational Research Association. (ERIC Document Reproduction Service No. ED 305 182).

Bergen, D., & Raver, S. A. (1991). Techniques for infants and toddlers at-risk. In S. A. Raver, *Strategies for teaching at-risk and handicapped infants and toddlers* (pp. 200–233). New York: Merrill.

Berko-Gleason, J. (1985). *The development of language.* Columbus, OH: Merrill.

Bess, F. H., & McConnell, F. (1981). *Audiology, education and the hearing impaired child.* St. Louis: C.V. Mosby.

Bingol, N., Fuchs, M., Diaz, V., Stone, R. K., & Gromisch, D. S. (1987). Teratogenicity of cocaine in humans. *Journal of Pediatrics, 110,* 93–96.

Blacher, J. (1987, April). *Attachment between severely impaired children and their mothers: Conceptual and methodological concerns.* Paper presented at the biennial meeting of the Society for Research in Child Development, Baltimore, MD.

Bobath, K. (1980). *The neurophysiological basis for treatment of cerebral palsy* (2nd ed.). Philadelphia: J. B. Lippincott.

Bornstein, M. H. (1988). Perceptual development across the life cycle. In M. H. Bornstein & M. E. Lamb (Eds.), *Developmental psychology: An advanced textbook* (pp. 151–204). Hillsdale, NJ: Erlbaum.

Bowlby, J. (1989). The role of attachment in personality development and psychopathology. In S. I. Greenspan & G. H. Pollock (Eds.), *The course of life, Volume I: Infancy.* Madison, CN: International Universities Press.

Boyce, W. T. (1992). The vulnerable child: New evidence, new approaches. *Advances in Pediatrics, 39,* 1–33.

Boyce, W. T., Sobolewski, S., & Schaefer, C. (1989). Recurrent injuries in school-aged children. *American Journal of Diseases in Children, 143,* 338–342.

Boykin, A., (1985). The academic performance of Afro American children. In J. Spence (Ed.), *Achievement and achievement motives* (pp. 324–371). San Francisco: W. Freeman Press.

Bracken, B. A. (1985). A critical review of the Kaufman Assessment Battery for Children (KABC). *School Psychology Review, 14,* 21–36.

Bracken, B. A. (1987). Limitations of preschool instruments and standards for minimal levels of technical adequacy. *Journal of Psychoeducational Assessment, 4,* 313–326.

Bracken, B. A. (1991). The clinical observation of preschool assessment behavior. In B. A. Bracken (Ed.), *The psychoeducational assessment of preschool children* (pp. 40–52). Boston: Allyn & Bacon.

Bradley, R. H., & Caldwell, B. (1976). The relation of infants' home environments to mental test performance at 54 months: A follow-up study. *Child Development, 47,* 1172–1174

Brazelton, T. B. (1984). *Neonatal Behavioral Assessment Scale* (2nd ed.) Spastics International Medical Publications. London: Blackwell; Philadelphia: Lippincott.

Brazelton, T. B., Koslowski, B., & Main, M. (1974). The origins of reciprocity: The early mother–infant interaction. In M. Lewis & L. A. Rosenblum (Eds.), *The effect of the infant on its caregiver* (pp. 49–77). New York: Wiley.

Brazelton, T. B., Nugent, J. K., & Lester, B. M. (1987). Neonatal behavioral assessment scale. In J. D. Osofsky (Ed.), *Handbook of infant development (2nd. ed.,* pp. 780–817). New York: Wiley.

Bredekamp, S. (Ed.). (1987). *Developmentally appropriate practice in early childhood programs serving children from birth through age 8.* Washington, DC: National Association for the Education of Young Children.

Bretherton, I., O'Connell, B., Shore, C. & Bates, E. (1984). The effect of contextual variation on symbolic play development from 20 to 28 months. In I. Bretherton (Ed.), *Symbolic play: The development of social understanding* (pp. 271–298). New York: Academic Press.

Brigance, A. H. (1991). *Brigance Diagnostic Inventory of Early Development, Revised.* Woburn, MA: Curriculum Associates.

Briggs, J. (1970). *Never in anger: Portrait of an Eskimo family.* Cambridge, MA: Harvard University Press.

Bronfenbrenner, U. (1993). The ecology of cognitive development: Research models and fugitive findings. In R. H. Wozniak & K. W. Fischer (Eds.), *Development in context* (pp. 3–44). Hillsdale, NJ: Erlbaum.

Bronfenbrenner, U. (1979) *The ecology of human development.* Cambridge, MA: Harvard University Press.

Brooks-Gunn, J., Klebanov, P. K., Liaw, F., & Spiker, D. (1993). Enhancing the development of low-birthweight, premature infants: Changes in cognition and behavior over the first three years. *Child Development, 64(3),* 736–753.

Brophy, K., & Stone-Zukowski, D. (1984). Social and play behaviour of special needs and non-special needs toddlers. *Early Child Development and Care, 13(2),* 137–154.

Brown, L., Nietupski, J., & Hamre-Nietupski, S. (1976). Criterion of ultimate functioning. In M. A. Thomas (Ed.), *Hey, don't forget about me! Education's investment in the severely, profoundly, & multiply handicapped,* (pp. 2–15). Reston, VA: Council for Exceptional Children.

Brown, P. (1980). Fitness and play. In P. F. Wilkinson (Ed.), *In celebration of play* (pp. 282–295). New York: St. Martin's Press.

Brown, R. (1973). *A first language: The early stages.* Cambridge, MA: Harvard University Press.

Bruder, M. B., & Nikitas, T. (1992). Changing the professional practice of early interventionists: An inservice model to meet the service needs of Public Law 99-457. *Journal of Early Intervention, 16,(2),* 173–180.

Bruner, J. (1983). *In search of mind.* New York: Harper & Row.

Bruner, J. S., & Sherwood, V. (1976). Peek-a-boo and the learning of rule structures. In J. S. Bruner, A. Jolly, & K. Sylva (Eds.), *Play: Its role in development and evolution* (pp.277–285). New York: Basic Books.

Burkhardt, L. J. (1981). *Homemade battery powered toys and educational devices for severely disabled children.* Millville, PA: Burkhardt.

Bzoch, K., & League, R. (1991). *Assessing language skills in infancy (Receptive-Expressive Emergent Language Scale-2).* Baltimore, MD: University Park Press.

Caldwell, B., & Bradley, R. (1979/1984). *Home Observation for Measurement of the Environment.* Little Rock: University of Arkansas.

Campbell, P., McInerney, W., & Cooper, M. (1984). Therapeutic programming for students with severe handicaps. *American Journal of Occupational Therapy, 38,* 594–602.

Carey, W. B., & McDevitt, S. C. (1978). Revision of the Infant Temperament Questionnaire. *Pediatrics, 61(5),* 735–738.

Carpignano, J., & Bigge, J. (1991). Assessment. In J. Bigge, *Teaching individuals with physical and multiple disabilities* (pp. 280–326). New York: Merrill.

Casby, M. W., & Ruder, K. F. (1983). Symbolic play and early language development in normal and mentally retarded children. *Journal of Speech and Hearing Research, 26(3),* 404–411.

Case, R. (1986). The new stage theories in intellectual development: Why we need them; what they assert. In M. Perlmutter (Ed.), *Perspectives for intellectual development* (pp. 57–96). Hillsdale, NJ: Erlbaum.

Cazden, C. B. (1976). Play with language and metalinguistic awareness. In J. S. Bruner, A. Jolly, & K. Sylva (Eds.), *Play: Its role in development and evolution* (pp.603–608). New York: Basic Books.

Chan, S. (1986). Parents of exceptional Asian children. In M. Kitano & P. Chinn (Eds.), *Exceptional Asian children and youth* (pp. 36–53). Binghamton, NY: Haworth Press.

Chandler, L. S. (1990). Neuromotor assessment. In E. D. Gibbs & D. M. Teti (Eds.), *Interdisciplinary assessment of infants* (pp. 45–62). Baltimore, MD: Paul H. Brookes.

Chandler, L. S., Andrews, M., & Swanson, M. (1980). *Movement Assessment of Infants.* PO Box 4631, Rolling Bay, WA.

Chasnoff, I. J., Griffith, D. R., Freier, C., & Murray, J. (1992). Cocaine/polydrug use in pregnancy: Two-year follow-up. *Pediatrics, 89,* 284–289.

Chess, S., & Thomas, A. (1989). Temperament and its functional significance. In S. I. Greenspan & G. H. Pollock (Eds.), *The course of life* (Vol. II) (pp. 163–228). Madison, CN: International Universities Press.

Chukovsky, K. (1963). *From two to five.* Berkeley: University of California Press.

Cicchetti, D. (1985). Caregiver–infant interaction: The study of maltreated infants. In C. C. Brown & A. W. Gottfried (Eds.), *Play interactions: The role of toys and parental involvement in children's development* (pp. 107–113). Skillman, NJ: Johnson & Johnson.

Cicchetti, D., & Sroufe, L. A. (1976). The relationship between affective and cognitive development in Down's syndrome infants. *Child Development, 47,* 920–929.

Cicchetti, D., & Toth, S. L. (1987). The application of a transactional risk model to intervention with multi-risk maltreating families. *Zero to Three, 7*(5), 1–8.

Cipani, E. (1990). "Excuse me: I'll have...": Teaching appropriate attention-getting behavior to young children with severe handicaps. *Mental Retardation, 28,* 29–33.

Claflin, C. J., & Meisels, S. J. (1993). Assessment of the impact of very low birth weight infants on families. In N. J. Anastasiow & S. Harel (Eds.), *At-risk infants: Interventions, families, and research* (pp. 57–79). Baltimore, MD: Paul H. Brookes.

Clune, C., Paolella, J. M., & Foley, J. M. (1979). Freeplay behavior of atypical children: An approach to assessment. *Journal of Autism and Developmental Disorders, 9,* 61–72.

Columbo, J. (1993). *Infant cognition.* Newbury Park, CA: Sage.

Constantino, J. N. (1993). Parents, mental illness, and the primary health care of infants and young children. *Zero to Three, 13*(5), 1–10.

Cooper, J. M., & Griffith, P. (1978). Treatment and prognosis. In M. Wyke (Ed.), *Developmental Dysphasia* (pp. 159–176). London: Academic Press.

Correa, V. I. (1989). Involving culturally diverse families in the education process. In S. H. Fradd & M. J. Weismantal (Eds.), *Meeting the needs of culturally and linguistically different students: A handbook for educators* (pp. 130–144). Boston, MA: College Hill Press.

Council for Exceptional Children (CEC). (1993). CEC policy on inclusive schools & community settings. Supplement to *Teaching Teaching Exceptional Children, 25.*

Craig, H. K., Evans, J. L., Meisels, S. J., & Plunkett, J. W. (1991). Linguistic production abilities of 3-year-old children born premature with low birth weight. *Journal of Early Intervention, 15*(4), 326–337.

Crisler, J. R. (1979). Utilization of a team approach in implementing Public Law 94-142. *Journal of Research and Development in Education, 12,* 101–108.

Cummins, J. (1980). The cross lingual dimensions of language proficiency: Implications for bilingual education and the optimal age issue. *TESOL Quarterly, 14*(2), 175–187.

D'Amato, E., & Yoshida, R. K. (1991). Parental needs: An educational life cycle perspective. *Journal of early Intervention, 15,*(3), 246–254.

Damon, W. (1988). *The moral child.* New York: Macmillan.

Daniel, J. H., Hampton, R. L., & Newberger, E. H. (1983). Child abuse and accidents in black families: A controlled comparative study. *American Journal of Orthopsychiatry, 53*(4), 645–653.

Darwin, C. (1877). Biographical sketch of an infant. *Mind, 2,* 285–294.

Delpit, L. D. (1988). *When the talking stops: Paradoxes of power in educating other people's children* (31 pp.). Paper presented at the 9th annual Ethnography in Education Research Forum, Philadelphia, PA.

Diamond, K. E., & Squires, J. (1993). The role of parental report in the screening and assessment of young children. *Journal of Early Intervention,17*(2), 107–115.

Diaz, R. M., Padilla, K. A., & Weathersby, E. K. (1991). The effect of bilingualism on preschoolers' private speech. *Early Childhood Research Quarterly, 6,* 377–393.

Division for Early Childhood (DEC)/Council for Exceptional Children (CEC). (1993). *DEC recommended practices: Indicators of quality in programs for infants and young children with special needs and their families.* Reston, VA: Author.

Donnellan, A. M., Mirenda, P. L., Mesaros, R. A., & Fassbender, L. L. (1984). Analyzing the communicative functions of aberrant behavior. *TASH, 9,* 201–212.

Drew, C. J., & Turnbull, H. R. (1987). Whose ethics, whose code: An analysis of problems in interdisciplinary intervention. *Mental Retardation, 25,* 113–117.

Dunn, J. (1993). *Young children's close relationships.* Newbury Park, CA: Sage.

Dunn, J., & Kendrick, C. (1981). Social behavior of young siblings in the family context: Differences between same-sex and different-sex dyads. *Child Development, 52,* 1265–1273.

Dunst, C. J. (1980). *A clinical and educational manual for use with the Uzgiris and Hunt Scales of Infant Psychological Development.* Baltimore, MD: University Park Press.

Dunst, C. J. (1985). Rethinking early intervention. *Analysis and Intervention in Developmental Disabilities, 5,* 165–201.

Dunst, C. J., Johanson, C., Trivette, C. M., Hamby, D. (1991). Family-oriented early intervention policies and practices: Family-centered or not? *Exceptional Children, 58,* 115–126.

Dunst, C. J., & Trivette, C. M. (1987). Enabling and empowering families: Conceptual and intervention issues. *School Psychology Review, 16,* 443–456.

Dunst, C. J., Trivette, C. M., and Deal, A. (1988). *Enabling and empowering families.* Cambridge, MA: Brookline Books.

Edmondson, R., & Smith, T. (1992). *Temperament and behavior of cocaine-exposed*

infants. Paper presented at the annual meeting of the Division of Early Childhood, Washington, DC.

Education of Handicapped Act Amendments of 1986 (P. L. 99-457). (1986). 20 U.S.C.
Secs. 1400–1485.

Egan, J., Schaefer, S., & Chatoor, I. (1988). Clinical evaluation of nonorganic failure to thrive. In C. J. Kesstenbaum & D. T. Williams (Eds.). *Handbook of clinical assessment of children and adolescents* (Vol. 1, pp. 831–841). New York: New
York University Press.

Eimas, P. D., & Miller, J. L. (1992). Organization in the perception of speech by
young infants. *Psychological Science, 3*(6), 340–345.

Elkind, D. (1976). *Child development and education: A Piagetian perspective.* New York:
Oxford University Press.

Elkind, D. (1981). *Children and adolescents: Interpretive essays on Jean Piaget* (3rd Ed.).
New York: Oxford University Press.

Elliot, C. (1990). *Differential Ability Scales (DAS), Preschool level.* San Antonio, TX:
The Psychological Corp.

Emde, R. N. (1980). Toward a psychoanalytic theory of affect. In S. Greenspan &
G. Pollock (Eds.), *The course of life: Psychoanalytic contributions toward under-
standing personality development and early childhood* (pp. 63–112). Washington,
DC: Mental Health Study Center, National Institute of Mental Health.

English, R. (1983, November). *The challenge for mental health minorities and their world
views.* Paper presented at the 2nd annual Robert L. Sutherland lecture, University of Texas at Austin, Austin, TX.

Epstein, H. T. (1978). Growth spurts during brain development: Implications for
educational policy and practice. In J. S. Chall & A. F. Mirsky (Eds.), *77th
National Society for the Study of Education Yearbook: Education and the brain* (pp.
343–370). Chicago: University of Chicago Press.

Erikson, E. H. (1963). *Childhood and society* (2nd ed.). New York: W. W. Norton.

Erikson, E. H. (1968). *Identity: Youth and crisis.* New York: Norton.

Evans, E. D. (1985). Longitudinal follow-up assessment of differential preschool
experience for low-income minority children. *Journal of Educational Research,
78,* 4, 197–202.

Fagan, J. F. & Shepherd, P. (1987). *Fagan Test of Infant Intelligence.* Cleveland, OH:
Infantest Corp.

Fagan, J. F., & Singer, L. T. (1983). Infant recognition memory as a measure of
intelligence. In L. P. Lipsett (Ed.), *Advances in infancy research* (Vol. 2, pp. 31–78).
Norwood, NJ: Ablex.

Fagan, J. F., Singer, L. T., Monte, J. E., & Shepherd, P. A. (1986). Selective screening device for the early detection of normal or delayed cognitive development
in infants at risk for later mental retardation. *Pediatrics, 78,* 1021–1026.

Fagan, T. F., & Sachs Wise, P. (1993). *School psychology: Past, present, and future.* New
York: Longman.

Fagot, B. I. (1988). Toddlers' play and sex stereotyping. In D. Bergen (Ed.), *Play
as a medium for learning and development: A handbook of theory and practice* (pp.
133–135). Portsmouth, NH: Heinemann.

Fagot, B. I., Hagen, R., Leinbach, M. D., & Kronsberg, S. (1985). Differential reactions to assertive and communicative acts of toddler boys and girls. *Child Development, 56,* 1499–1505.

Falvey, M. A. (1989). *Community-based curriculum: Instructional strategies for students with severe handicaps* (2nd ed.). Baltimore: Paul H. Brookes.

Fantz, R. L. (1963). Pattern vision in newborn infants. *Science, 140,* 296–297.

Featherstone, H. (1980). *A difference in the family: Life with a disabled child.* New York: Basic Books.

Feinman, S. (1991). Bringing babies back into the social world. In M. Lewis & S. Feinman (Eds.), *Social influences and socialization in infancy* (pp. 281–326). Genesis of Behavior, Vol. 6, Series Editors, M. Lewis & L. A. Rosenblum. New York: Plenum Press.

Fenson, L. (1984). Developmental trends for action and speech in pretend play. In I. Bretherton (Ed.), *Symbolic play: The development of social understanding* (pp.249–270). New York: Academic Press.

Fernald, A., & Morikawa, H. (1993). Common themes and cultural variations in Japanese and American mothers' speech to infants. *Child Development, 64*(3), 637–656.

Feuerstein, R. (1979). *The dynamic assessment of retarded performers.* Baltimore, MD: University Park Press.

Fewell, R. R. (1986). *Play Assessment Scale.* Unpublished manuscript. New Orleans: Tulane University.

Fewell, R. R. (1991). Trends in the assessment of infants and toddlers with disabilities. *Exceptional Children, 58*(2), 166–173.

Field, T. M. (1979). Games parents play with normal and high-risk infants. *Child Psychiatry and Human Development, 10,* 41–48.

Field, T. (1980). Interactions of preterm and term infants with their lower- and middle-class teen-age and adult mothers. In T. Field, S. Goldberg, D. Stern, & A. Sostek, (Eds.), *High risk infants and children* (pp. 113–132). New York: Academic Press.

Field, T. M. (1982). Affective displays of high-risk infants during early interactions. In T. M. Field & A. Fogel (Eds.), *Emotion and early interaction* (pp. 101–125). Hillsdale, NJ: Erlbaum.

Field, T. (1993). Enhancing parent sensitivity. In N. J. Anastasiow & S. Harel (Eds.), *At-risk infants: Interventions, families, and research* (pp. 81–89). Baltimore, MD: Paul H. Brookes.

Fike, R. D. (1993). Personal relationship-building between fathers and infants. *Focus on Infancy, 5*(4), 1–2.

File, N., & Kontos, S. (l992). Indirect service delivery through consultation: Review and implications for early intervention. *Journal of Early Intervention, 16*(3), 221–233.

Finnie, N. (1975). *Handling the young cerebral palsied child at home.* New York: E.P. Dutton.

Fischer, K. W. (1980). A theory of cognitive development: The control and construction of hierarchies of skills. *Psychological Review, 6*(87), 477–531.

Fischer, K. W., Bullock, D. H., Rotenberg, E. J., & Raya, P. (1993). The dynamics of competence: How context contributes directly to skill. In R. H. Wozniak & K. W. Fischer (Eds.), *Development in context* (pp. 93–120). Hillsdale, NJ: Erlbaum.

Fischer, K. W., & Lazerson, A. (1984). *Human development: From conception through adolescence.* New York: Freeman.

Flavell, J. H. (1993). Young children's understanding of thinking and consciousness. *Current Directions in Psychological Science, 2*(2), 40–46.

Flower, J. (1991). Come the revolution. *Health Care Forum Journal,* Sept/Oct, 34–37, 70.

Foley, G. M. (1990). Portrait of the arena evaluation: Assessment in the transdisciplinary approach. In E. D. Gibbs & D. M. Teti (Eds.). (1990). *Interdisciplinary assessment of infants: A guide for early intervention professionals* (271–286). Baltimore, MD: Paul H. Brookes.

Folio, M. R. & Fewell, R. R. (1983). *Peabody developmental motor scales and activity cards.* Allen, TX: Developmental Learning Materials.

Folven, R. J., & Bonnevillian, J. D. (1991). The transition for nonreferential to referential language in children acquiring American Sign Language. *Developmental Psychology, 27,* 806–816.

Fordyce, W. (1982). Interdisciplinary process: Implications for rehabilitation psychology. *Rehabilitation Psychology, 27,* 5–11.

Fox, N. A., Kagan, J., & Weiskopf, F. (1979). The growth of memory during infancy. *Genetic Psychology Monographs, 99,* 91–130.

Fradd, S. H. (1987). The changing focus of bilingual education. In S. H. Fradd & W.J. Tikunoff (Eds.), *Bilingual education and bilingual special education: A guide for administrators* (pp. 1–44). Boston: College Hill Press.

Fraiberg, S. (1974). Blind infants and their mothers: An examination of the sign system. In M. Lewis & L. A. Rosenblum (Eds.), *The effect of the infant on its caregiver* (pp. 215–232). New York: Wiley.

Fraiberg, S. (1980). Clinical assessment of the infant and his family. In S. Fraiberg (Ed.), *Clinical studies in infant mental health: The first year of life* (pp. 23–48). New York: Basic Books.

Frankenburg, W. K., & Dodds, J. B. (1990). *Denver II.* Denver, CO: Denver Developmental Materials, Inc.

Fredericks, H. D., Anderson, R., & Baldwin, V. (1979). The identification of competency indicators of teaching of the severely handicapped. *American Association for the Education of the Severely and Profoundly Handicapped Review, 4,* 81–95.

Freud, S. (1923–1924). The ego and the id. In *The standard edition of the complete psychological works of Sigmund Freud* (Vol.19, pp. 3–66). London: Hogarth Press.

Frisby, C. L. (1992). Issues and problems in the influence of culture on the psychoeducational needs of African-American children. *School Psychology Review, 21*(4), 532–551.

Frodi, A., & Lamb, M. (1980). Child abuser's responses to infant smiles and cries. *Child Development, 51,* 238–241.

Furuno, S., O'Reilly, K. A., Hosaka, C. M., Inatsuka, T. T., Allman, T. L., & Zeisloft, B. (1979/1985). *Hawaii Early Learning Profile (HELP)* Palo Alto, CA: VORT.

Gallagher, R. J., & Cech, D. (1988). Motor assessment. In T. D. Wachs & R. Sheehan (Eds.), *Assessment of young developmentally disabled children* (pp. 241–254). New York: Plenum Press.

Gardner, H. (1983). *Frames of mind: The theory of multiple intelligences.* New York: Basic Books.

Gardner, H. (1993). *Multiple intelligences: The theory in practice.* New York: Basic Books.

Gargiulo, R. M. (1985). *Working with parents of exceptional children.* Boston: Houghton Mifflin.

Garland, C. W., & Linder, T. W. (l988). Administrative challenges in early intervention. In J. B. Jordan, J. J. Gallagher, P. L. Hutinger, & M. Karnes (Eds.), *Early childhood special education: Birth to three* (pp. 5–28). Reston, VA: Council for Exceptional Children.

Garland, C., Woodruff, G., & Buck, D. (l988, June). *Case management.* Division for Early Childhood Special Education White Paper.

Garshelis, J. A., & McConnell, S. R. (1993). Comparison of family needs assessed by mothers, individual professionals, and interdisciplinary teams. *Journal of Early Intervention, 17*(1), 36–49.

Geertz, C. (1973). *Interpretation of cultures.* New York: Basic Books.

Gesell, A. (1925). *The mental growth of the preschool child: A psychological outline of normal development from birth to the sixth year.* New York: Macmillan.

Gesell, A., (1928). *Infancy and human growth.* New York: Macmillan.

Gesell, A. (1949). *Gesell Developmental Schedules.* New York: The Psychological Corporation.

Gibson, E. J. (1969). *Principles of perceptual learning and development.* New York: Appleton-Century-Crofts.

Gibson, E. J., & Walk, R. D. (1960). The "visual cliff." *Scientific American, 202,* 64–71.

Gibson, J. J. (1979). *The ecological approach to visual perception.* Boston: Houghton Mifflin.

Gilliam, J. E., & Coleman, M. (l98l). Who influences IEP committee decisions? *Exceptional Children, 47,* 642–644.

Goldberg, S., & Lewis, M. (1969). Play behavior in the year-old infant: Early sex difference. *Child Development, 40,* 21–32

Goldman, R., & Fristoe, M. (1986). *Goldman-Fristoe Test of Articulation.* Circle Pines, MN: American Guidance Service.

Gonzalez-Mena, J., & Eyer, D. W. (1993). *Infants, toddlers, and caregivers* (2nd ed.). Mountain View, CA: Mayfield.

Goodman, S. H., Radke-Yarrow, M. & Teti, D. (1993). Maternal depression as a context for child rearing. *Zero to Three, 13*(5), 10–16.

Goodwyn, S. W., & Acredolo, L. P. (1993). Symbolic gesture versus word: Is there a modality advantage for onset of symbol use? *Child Development, 64*(3), 688–701.

Gould, R. I. (1980). Transformations during early and middle adult years. In N. J. Smelser & E. H. Erikson (Eds.), *Themes of work and love in adulthood* (pp. 213–237). Cambridge, MA: Harvard University Press.

Govle, R. M. (1982). *Maternal social networks and cognitive development of preschool children: An hypothesis and exploratory study of rural Appalachian families.* Unpublished doctoral dissertation: University of Tennesee. (Dissertation Abstracts No. AAC8303718).

Green, G. (1993, May/June). Q. & A.: What is the balance of proof for or against facilitated communication? *AAMR News and Notes, 6*(3), 5.

Green, M. (1986). Vulnerable child syndrome and its variants. *Pediatric Review, 8,* 75–80.

Green, M. (1991). On making a difference. *Pediatrics, 87*(5), 712–718.

Greenfield, P., & Smith, J. (1976). *The structure of communication in early language development*. New York: Academic Press.

Greenspan, S., & Greenspan, N. T. (1985). *First feelings: Milestones in the emotional development of the child*. New York: Viking.

Greenspan, S., Leiberman, A., & Poisson, S. (1990). *Greenspan-Lieberman Observation System for Assessment of Caregiver-Infant Interaction During Semi-structured Play (GLOS-Revised)*. Division of Maternal and Child Health, HRSA, DHHS, Rockville, MD.

Grossman, H. J. (1984). *Educating Hispanic students*. Springfield, IL: Charles Thomas.

Gunnar, M. R., Malone, S., & Fisch, R. O. (1987). The psychobiology of stress and coping in the human neonate: Studies of the adrenocortical activity in response to stress in the first week of life. In T. Field, P. McCabe, & N. Scheiderman (Eds.), *Stress and coping* (pp. 179–196). Hillsdale, NJ: Erlbaum.

Haggerty, R. J., Roghmann, K. J., & Pless, I. B. (Eds.). (1975). *Child health and the community*. New York: Wiley.

Hale-Benson, J. (1986). *Black children: Their roots, culture and learning styles*. Baltimore, MD: Johns Hopkins University Press.

Hamilton, S. E., Oscar, N., & Atkins, J. (1993, August). *The identification and education of African-American culturally diverse optimal performers between preschool and 12th grade*. Paper presented at the National Association of Black Psychologists Conference, Toronto, Canada.

Hamric, A. B., & Spross, J. A. (1989). *The clinical nurse specialist in theory and practice* (2nd ed.) Philadelphia: W. B. Saunders.

Haney, M. & Falvey, M. (1989). Instructional strategies. In M. A. Falvey, *Community-based curriculum instructional strategies for students with severe handicaps* (2nd ed.) (pp. 63–90). Baltimore: Paul H. Brookes.

Hanson, M., & Lovett, D. (1992). Personnel preparation for early interventionists: A cross-disciplinary survey. *Journal of Early Intervention, 16*(2), 123–135.

Haring, K., Sterling, J. & Myse, J. (1992, December). *Family systems project: First year report*. Paper presented at the annual meeting of the Division of Early Childhood, Washington, DC.

Harley, B., Hart, D., & Lapkin, S. (1986). The effects of early bilingual schooling on first language skills. *Applied Psycholinguistics, 7*(4), 295–322.

Harrington, R. G. (1984). Preschool screening: The school psychologist's perspective. *School Psychology Review, 13*(3), 363–374.

Hawley, T. L., & Disney, E. R. (1992). Crack's children: The consequences of maternal cocaine abuse. *SRCD Social Policy Report, 6*(4), 123 pp.

Hay, D. F., Nash, A., & Pedersen, J. (1983). Interaction between six-month-old peers. *Child Development, 54*, 557–562.

Hay, D. F., Ross, H. S., & Goldman, B. D. (1979). Social games in infancy. In B. Sutton-Smith (Ed.), *Play and learning* (pp. 83–107). New York: Gardner Press.

Haynes-Seman, C., & Hart, J. S. (1987). Doll play of failure to thrive toddlers: Clues to infant experience. *Zero to Three, 7*(4), 10–13.

Heath, S. B. (1989). Oral and literate traditions among Black Americans living in poverty. *American Psychologist, 44*, 367–373).

Heffernan, L. & Black, F. W. (1984). Use of the Uzgiris and Hunt scales with handicapped infants: Concurrent validity of the Dunst age norms. *Journal of Psychoeducational Assessment, 2*, 159–168.

Hill, P.M., & McCune-Nicolich, L. (1981). Pretend play and patterns of cognition in Down's syndrome children. *Child Development, 52,* 611–617

Hilliard, A. G. (1976). *Alternative to IQ testing an approach to the identification of "gifted" minority children.* Final Report, Sacramento Division of Special Education, California State Department of Education (ERIC Document: Reproduction Services No. ED147009).

Hilliard, A. G. (1987). Testing African American students [Special Issue]. *Negro Education Review, 38,* 2–3.

Hills, T. W. (1993). Assessment in context: Teachers and children at work. *Young Children, 48*(5), 20–28.

Holm, V. A. and Kunze, L. H. (1969). Effects of chronic otitis media on language and speech development. *Pediatrics, 43,* 833–839.

Horn, E., & Jones, H. (1992). *Experimental analysis of early motor skills intervention for infants with neuromotor disabilities.* Paper presented at the meeting of the Division of Early Childhood, Washington, DC.

Horwitz, S., McLeaf, P. J., Leventhal, J. M., Forsyth, B., & Speechley, K. N. (1992). Identification and management of psychosocial and developmental problems in community-based, primary care pediatric practices. *Pediatrics, 89*(3), 480–485.

Hughes, H. M., & Barad, S. J. (1983). Psychological functioning of children in a battered women's shelter: A preliminary investigation. *American Journal of Orthopsychiatry, 52*(3), 525–531.

Hymovich, D. B. (1988). *Parent Perception Inventory.* King of Prussia, PA: D. Hymovich.

Ilg, F. L., & Ames, L. B. (1955). *The Gesell Institute's Child Behavior.* New York: Dell.

Individuals with Disabilities Education Act (P.L. 100-476) (1990). 20 U.S.C. Secs. 1400–1485.

Ireton, H. (1988). *Early Child Development Inventory.* Minneapolis, MN: Behavior Science Systems.

Iwacha, A. C. (1983). Coyote in the classroom. In O. N. Saracho & B. Spodek (Eds.), *Understanding the multicultural experience in early childhood education* (pp. 3–15). Washington, DC: National Association for the Education of Young Children.

Iwata, B. A., Dorsey, M. F., Slifer, K. J., Bauman, K. E., & Richman, G. S. (1982). Toward a functional analysis of self-injury. *Analysis and Intervenion in Developmental Disabilities, 2,* 3–20.

Izard, C. (1980). The emergence of emotions and the development of consciousness in infancy. In J. M. Davidson, & R. J. Davidson (Eds.), *The Psychobiology of consciousness* (pp.193–216). New York: Plenum Press.

Johnson, L., Kilgo, J., Cook, M., Hammitte, D., Beauchamp, K., & Finn, D. (l992). The skills needed by early intervention administrators/supervisors: A study across six states. *Journal of Early Intervention, 16*(2), 136–145.

Johnson-Martin, N. M., Jens, K. G., & Attermeier, S. A. (1990). *Carolina Curriculum for Handicapped and At-risk Infants.* Baltimore, MD: Paul H. Brookes.

Johnston, E. B. (1992). *Early communication intervention with toddlers—through dyad building and repair.* Paper presented to Ohio Speech & Hearing Association Convention, Cincinnati, OH.

Johnston, E. B., & Johnston, A. V. (1984). *The Piagetian language nursery: An intensive group language intervention program for preschoolers.* Rockville, MD.: Aspen Systems Corp.

Kagan, J. (1984). *The nature of the child.* New York: Basic Books.

Kagan, J. (1987). Perspectives on infancy. In J. D. Osofsky (Ed.), *Handbook on infant development* (2nd ed.) (pp. 1150–1198). New York: Wiley.

Kagan, S. L. (1992). Readiness past, present, and future: Shaping the agenda. *Young Children, 48*(1), 48–53.

Kalmanson, B. (1989). Assessment considerations: Developmental vulnerabilities. *Early Childhood Update, 5*(4), 6–7.

Kaplan-Sanoff, M., Brewster, A., Stillwell, J., & Bergen, D. (1988). The relationship of play to physical/motor development and to children with special needs. In D. Bergen (Ed.), *Play as a medium for learning and development* (pp. 137–162). Portsmouth, NH: Heinemann.

Kaufman, A. S., & Kaufman, N. L. (1983). *Kaufman Assessment Battery for Children.* Circle Pines, NM: American Guidance Services.

Kaufmann, R. K, Hurth, J. L., & Johnson, B. H. (1991). Future directions for the IFSP. In M. J. McGonigel, R. K. Kaufmann, & B. H. Johnson (Eds.), *Guidelines and recommended practices for the Individualized Family Service Plan* (2nd ed.) (pp. 79–83).

Kelley, M. F., & Surbeck, E. (1991). History of preschool assessment. In B. A. Bracken (Ed.), *The psychoeducational assessment of preschool children* (2nd ed.) (pp. 1–17). Boston: Allyn & Bacon.

Keogh, J. F. (1978). Movement outcomes as conceptual guidelines in the perceptual–motor maze. *Journal of Special Education, 12*(3), 321–329.

Kirby, R. S., Swanson, M. E., Kelleher, K. J., Bradley, R. H., & Casey, P. H. (1993). Identifying at-risk children for early intervention services: Lessons from the Infant Health and Development Program, *Journal of Pediatrics, 122,* 680–686.

Kopp, C. B. & Kaler, S. R. (1989). Risk in infancy: Origins and implications. *American Psychologist, 44*(2), 224–230.

Kramer, M. & Schalenberg, C. (1988). Magnet hospitals: Part I, institutions of excellence. *Journal of Nursing Administration, 18*(1), 13–24.

Krauss, M. W., Upshur, C. C., Shonkoff, J. P., & Hauser-Cram, P. (1993). The impact of parent groups on mothers of infants with disabilities. *Journal of Early Intervention, 17*(1), 8–20.

Kravitz, R. I., & Driscoll, J. M. (1983). Expectations for childhood development among child-abusing and nonabusing parents. *American Journal of Orthopsychiatry, 53*(2), 336–344.

Lahey, M. (1988). *Language disorders and language development.* New York: Macmillan.

Lamb, M. E. (1977). The development of mother-infant and father-infant attachments in the second year of life. *Developmental Psychology, 13,* 637–648.

Laosa, L. M. (1982). Families as facilitators of children's intellectual development: A causal analysis. In L. M. Laosa & I. E. Sigel (Eds.), *Families as learning environments for children* (pp. 1–45). New York: Plenum Press.

Lazar, I., Darlington, R., Murray, H., Royce, J., & Snipper, A. (1982). Lasting effects of early education. *Monographs of the Society for Research in Child Development, 47,* (2–3, Serial No. 195).

Leighty-Troester, E., Doubledee, S. L., Deakin, C., & Ruder, K. (1981). An intensive preschool summer language program. *Infant Toddler Intervention, 1*(2), 125–135.

Lenneberg, E. H. (1967). *Biological foundations of language*. New York: Wiley.

Levinson, D. J. (1978). *The seasons of a man's life*. New York: Knopf.

Lewis, M., & Feinman, S. (Eds.) (1991). *Social influences and socialization in infancy*. Genesis of Behavior, Vol. 6, Series Editors, M. Lewis & L. A. Rosenblum. New York: Plenum.

Linder, T. W. (1993). *Transdisciplinary play-based assessment–Revised*. Baltimore, MD: Paul H. Brookes.

Ling, D. (1976). *Speech and the Hearing Impaired Child: Theory and Practice*. Washington, DC: Alexander Graham Bell Association.

Lozoff, B. (1989). Nutrition and behavior. *American Psychologist, 44*(2), 231–236.

Lusthaus, E. (1985). "Euthanasia" of persons with severe handicaps: Refuting the rationalizations. *Journal of the Association for Persons with Severe Handicaps, 10,* 87–94.

McAdoo, H. P. & McAdoo, J. L. (Eds.). (1985, 1988). *Black children: Social, educational and parental environments*. Beverly Hills: Sage.

McCall, R. (1979). Stages in play development between zero and two years of age. In B. Sutton-Smith (Ed.), *Play and learning* (pp. 35–44). New York: Gardner Press.

McCarthy, D. (1972). *McCarthy scales of children's abilities*. Chicago: The Psychological Corporation.

McClennen, S. E. (1991). *Cognitive skills for community living: Teaching students with moderate & severe disabilities*. Austin, TX: Pro-ed.

McCune-Nicolich, L. (1981). Toward symbolic functioning: Structure of early pretend games and potential parallels with language. *Child Development, 52,* 785–797.

McGee, G. G., Feldman, R. S., & Chernin, L. (1991). A comparison of emotional facial display by children with autism and typical preschoolers. *Journal of Early Intervention,15*(3), 237–245.

McGonigel, M. J., Kaufmann, R. K., & Johnson, B. H. (Eds.). (1991). *Guidelines and recommended practices for the individualized family service plan* (2nd ed.). Bethesda, MD: Association for the Care of Children's Health.

McLaughlin, C. P., & Kaluzny, A. D. (1990). Total quality management in health: Making it work. *Health Care Management Review, 15*(3), 7–14.

McLean, J. E. & Snyder-McLean, L. K. (1978). *A transactional approach to early language training*, Columbus, OH: Merrill.

Mahler, M. S., Pine, F., & Bergman, A. (1975). *The psychological birth of the human infant: Symbiosis and individuation*. New York: Basic Books.

Martin, F. (1986). *Introduction to audiology* (3rd ed.). Englewood Cliffs, NJ: Prentice–Hall.

Martin, S. S., Davis, C. A., & Brady, M. P. (1992, December). *Increasing motor behaviors and social responses of young children with severe disabilities in integrated daycare*. Paper presented at the annual meeting of the Division of Early Childhood, Washington, DC.

Meisels, S. J. (1993). Remaking classroom assessment with the work sampling system. *Young Children, 48*(5), 34–40.

Meisels, S. J. (1987). Uses and abuses of developmental screening and school readiness testing. *Young Children, 42*(1), 4–6, 68–73.

Meltzoff, A. N. (1988). Infant imitation and memory: Nine-month-old infants in immediate and deferred tests. *Child Development, 59,* 217–225.

Meltzoff, A. N. (1990, June). *Infant imitation.* Invited address at the University of Texas at Dallas, School of Human Development and Communication Sciences, Richardson, TX.

Mercer, J. R. (1989). Alternative paradigms for assessment in a pluralistic society. In J. A. Banks & C. A. McGee Banks (Eds.), *Multicultural education: Issues and perspectives* (pp. 289–304). Boston: Allyn & Bacon.

Meyer v. Nebraska, 262 U.S. 390 (1923).

Miller, P., & Garvey, C. (1984). Mother–baby role play: Its origins in social support. In I. Bretherton (Ed.), *Symbolic play: The development of social understanding* (pp. 101–130). New York: Academic Press.

Morrow, R. D. (1989). What's in a name? In particular, a Southeast Asian name? *Young Children, 44*(6), 20–23.

Morrongiello, B. A., & Clifton, R. K. (1984). Effects of sound frequency on behavioral and cardiac orienting in new born and five-month-old infants. *Journal of Experimental Child Psychology, 38,* 429–446.

Morsink, C. V., Thomas, C. C., & Correa, V. I. (1991). *Interactive teaming.* New York: Macmillan.

Mueller, E. C., Brenner, J., (1977). The origins of social skills and interaction among playgroup toddlers. *Child Development, 48*(3), 854–861.

Mueller, E. C., & Lucas, T. (1975). A developmental analysis of peer interaction among toddlers. In M. Lewis & L. Rosenblum (Eds.), *Peer relations* (pp. 223–257). New York: Wiley.

Myers, L. J. (1988). *Understanding an afrocentric world view: Introduction to an optimal psychology.* Dubuque, IA: Kendall-Hunt.

National Association of Early Childhood Teacher Educators. (1991). *Endorsement of ATE/NAEYC Position Statement.* Unpublished document.

National Association for the Education of Young Children (NAEYC). (1988). Position statement on standardized testing of young children 3 through 8 years of age. *Young Children, 45*(3), 21–38.

National Association of School Psychologists. (1987, Sept.). *Position statement on early intervention services.* Silver Springs, MD: Author.

National Association of School Psychologists. (1993, April). *Position statement on inclusive programs for students with disabilities.* Silver Springs, MD: Author.

Neighbors, H. W., Jackson, J. S., Bowman, P. H., & Gurin, G. (1982). Stress, coping and black mental health: Preliminary findings from a national study. *Prevention in Human Services, 2,* 5–29.

Neisworth, J. T., & Bagnato, S. J. (1986). Curriculum-based developmental assessment: Congruence of testing and teaching. *School Psychology Review, 15,* 180–199.

Nelson, K. (1973). Structure and strategy in learning to talk. *Monographs of the Soci-*

ety for Research in Child Development, 38(1–2), 1–135.

Nelson, K. (1985). *Making sense: The acquisition of shared meaning.* New York: Academic Press.

Nelson, N. W. (1993). *Childhood language disorders in context.* New York: Merrill/ Macmillan.

Neugarten, B. L. (1964). *Personality in middle and late life.* New York: Atherton Press.

Neugarten, B. L. (1988, August). *Policy issues for an aging society.* Paper presented at the meeting of the American Psychological Association, Atlanta, GA.

Newborg, J., Stock, J., Wnek, L., Guidubaldi, J., & Svinicki, J. (1988). *Battelle Developmental Inventory.* Allen, TX: DLM Teaching Resources.

Nine, S., Bayes, K., Christian, S., & Dillon, B. (1992). Organizing quality assurance in a maternal-child health division. *JOGNN, 21*(1), 28–32.

Nobles, W. (1980). African philosophy: Foundations for black psychology. In R. Jones (Ed.), *Black psychology* (pp.23–35). New York: Harper & Row.

Nobles, W. (1986). *African psychology: Toward its reclamation, reascension, and revitalization.* Oakland, CA: Black Family Institute.

Noonan, M. J., Brown, F., Mulligan, M., & Rettig, M. A. (1982). Educability of severely handicapped persons: Both sides of the issue. *Journal of the Association for the Severely Handicapped, 7,* 3–12.

Norris, M. K. G., & Hill, C. (1991). The clinical nurse specialist: Developing the case manager role. *Dimensions of Critical Care Nursing, 10*(6), 346–353.

Northern, J. L. and Downs, M. P. (1984). *Hearing in Children* (3rd ed.). Baltimore, MD: Williams & Wilkins.

Nugent, J. K. (1985). *Using the NBAS with infants and families.* White Plains, NY: March of Dimes.

Nursing Child Assessment Satellite Training (NCAST). (1978a) *Nursing Child Assessment Feeding Scale.* (Manual from NCAST training.) Seattle, WA: University of Washington.

Nursing Child Assessment Satellite Training (NCAST). (1978b). *Nursing Child Assessment Teaching Scale.* (Manual from NCAST training.) Seattle, WA: University of Washington.

Oden, S. (1988). Alternate perspectives on children's peer relationships. In T. D. Yawkey & J. E. Johnson (Eds.), *Integrative processes and socialization: Early to middle childhood* (pp 139–166). Hillsdale, NJ: Erlbaum.

O'Dougherty, M., & Brown, R. T. (1990). The stress of childhood illness. In L. E. Arnold (Ed.), *Childhood Stress* (pp. 325–349). New York: Wiley.

Ogbu, J. (1981). Origins of human competence: A cultural-ecological perspective. *Child Development, 52,* 413–429.

Ogbu, J. (1988). Black education: A cultural-ecological perspective. In H. P. McAdoo (Ed.), *Black Families* (pp.169–184). Newbury Park, CA: Sage.

Ohio Dept. of Education. (1991). *Rules for the education of preschool children with disabilities served by public schools and county boards of mental retardation and developmental disabilities.* (Ch. 3301–31). Columbus, OH: Author.

Ohio Revised Code. *Occupational therapy.* Sec. 4755.01.

Ohio Revised Code. *Physical therapy.* Sec. 4755.40.

Olson, D. H. , Portner, J., & Lavee, Y. (1985). Faces III. In D. H. Olson, H. I. McCubbin, H. Barnes, A. Larsen, M. Muxen, & M. Wilson. (Eds.), *Family inventories: Inventories in a national survey of families across the family life cycle* (pp. 1–42). St. Paul: University of Minnesota.

Orelove, F. P. & Sobsey, R. J. (1991). *Educating children with multiple disabilities: A transdisciplinary approach* (2nd ed.). Baltimore, MD: Paul H. Brookes.

Ostfeld, B. M. & Gibbs, E. D. (1990). Use of family assessment in early intervention. In E. D. Gibbs & D. M. Teti (Eds.), *Interdisciplinary assessment of infants* (pp. 249–260). Baltimore, MD: Paul H. Brookes.

Outtz, J. H. (1993). A changing population's call to action. *National Voter, 42*(4), 5–6.

Owens, R. E., (1988). *Language development: An introduction* (2nd ed.). Columbus, OH: Merrill/Macmillan.

Paget, K. D. (1991). The individual assessment situation: Basic consideration for preschool-age children. In B. A. Bracken (Ed.), *The psychoeducational assessment of preschool children* (32–39). Boston: Allyn & Bacon.

Pastor, D. L. (1981). The quality of mother-infant attachment and its relationship to toddlers' initial sociability with peers. *Developmental Psychology, 17,* 326–335.

Patton, J. M. (1992). Assessment and identification of African American learners with gifts and talents. *Exceptional Children, 59*(2), 150–159.

Piaget, J. (1954). *The construction of reality in the child.* New York: Basic Books.

Piaget, J. (1962). *Play, dreams and imitation in childhood.* New York: Norton.

Pierce v. Society of Sisters, 268 U.S. 510 (1925).

Pitzer, M. W. (1992). *Family needs survey: An interview to help identify family strengths and needs in the IFSP process.* Unpublished master's thesis, Miami University, Oxford, OH.

Pizzo, P. D. (1990). Family-centered Head Start for infants and toddlers: A renewed direction for Project Head Start. *Young Children, 45*(6), 30–35.

Pollitt, E., Gorman, K. S., Engle, P. L., Martorell, R., & Rivera, J. (1993)*Early supplementary feeding and cognition. Monographs of the Society for Research in Child Development, 58*(7) (Serial No. 235), 1–122.

Porter, P. L. (1993). *Enhancing motor development in early intervention through adapted physical education.* Unpublished master's thesis, Miami University, Oxford, OH.

Powell, D. R. (1986). Parent education and support programs. *Young Children, 41*(3), 47–52.

Power, T. G., & Parke, R. D. (1983). Patterns of mother and father play with their 8-month-old infant: A multiple analysis approach. *Infant Behavior, 6,* 453–459.

Rainforth, B., & York, J. (1991). Handling and positioning. In F. P. Orelove & D. Sobsey, *Educating children with multiple disabilities: A transdisciplinary approach* (2nd ed.) (pp. 79–117). Baltimore, MD: Paul H. Brookes.

Ramirez, M. (1991). *Psychotherapy and counseling with minorities: A cognitive approach to individual and cultural differences.* New York: Pergamon.

Raver, S. A. (1991). *Strategies for teaching at-risk and handicapped infants and toddlers: A transdisciplinary approach.* New York: Merrill.

Raver, C. C., & Zigler, E. F (1991). Three steps forward, two steps back: Head Start and the measurement of social competence. *Young Children, 46*(4), 3–8.

Redding, R. E., Harmon, R. J., & Morgan, G. A. (1990). Relationships between maternal depression and infants' mastery behaviors. *Infant behavior and development, 13,* 391–395.

Reiser, D. J. (1992, Summer). The parent-child unit in the NICU. *Perinatal Hotline, 6*(1).

Rheingold, H. L. (1979, March). *Helping by two-year-old children.* Paper presented at the biennial meeting of the Society for Research in Child Development, San Francisco.

Riguet, C. B., Taylor, N. D., Benaroya, S., & Klein, L. S. (1981). Symbolic play in autistic, Down's and normal children of equivalent mental age. *Journal of Autism and Developmental Disorders, 11*(4), 439–448.

Rogers, S. J. (1988). Cognitive characteristics of handicapped children's play: A review. *Journal of the Division for Early Childhood, 12*(2), 161–168.

Rogers, S. J., & Puchalski, C. G. (1984). Development of symbolic play in visually impaired young children. *Topics in Early Childhood Special Education, 3*(4), 57–63.

Rogoff, B. (1991). The joint socialization of development by young children and adults. In M. Lewis & S. Feinman (Eds.), *Social influence and socialization in infancy: Vol. 6. Genesis of Behavior* (pp. 253–280). New York: Plenum Press.

Rogoff, B. (1993). Children's guided participation and participatory appropriation in sociocultural activity. In R. H. Wozniak & K. W. Fischer (Eds.), *Development in context* (pp. 121–153). Hillsdale, NJ: Erlbaum.

Rosenblith, J. F. (1992). *In the beginning: Development from conception to age two.* Newbury Park, CA: Sage.

Rosenfeld, A., & Stark, E. (1987, May). The prime of our lives. *Psychology Today,* pp. 62–72.

Rossetti, L. (1990). *The Rossetti Infant-Toddler Language Scale.* East Moline, IL: Lingua Systems.

Rossetti, L. (1991) Infant-toddler assessment: A clinical perspective. *Infant Toddler Intervention, 1*(1), 11–24.

Roth, F. P. (1990). Early language assessment. In E. D. Gibbs & D. M. Teti (Eds.), *Interdisciplinary assessment of infants* (pp. 145–160). Baltimore, MD: Paul H. Brookes.

Rovee-Collier, C. (1993). The capacity for long-term memory in infancy. *Current Directions in Psychological Science, 2*(4), 130–135.

Ruff, H. A. (1982). Effect of object movement on infants' detection of object structure. *Developmental Psychology, 18,* 462–472.

Ruiz, R. (1981). Cultural and historical perspectives in counseling Hispanics. In D. Sue (Ed.), *Counseling the culturally different: Theory and practice* (pp. 186–215). New York: Wiley.

Ruiz, R., & Padilla, A. (1979). Counseling Latinos. In D. Atkinson, G. Morten, & D. Sue (Eds.), *Counseling American minorities: a cross-cultural perspective* (pp. 169–190). Dubuque, IA: William Brown.

Sandall, S., Able-Boone, H., & Speirer, J. (1992, December). *Home visiting: Parents' and professionals' impressions.* Paper presented at the annual meeting of the Division of Early Childhood, Washington, DC.

Santos de Barona, M. S., & Barona, A. (1991). The assessment of culturally and linguistically different preschoolers. *Early Childhood Research Quarterly, 6,* 363–376.

Santrock, J. W. (1992). *Life-span development.* Dubuque, IA: William Brown.

Saracho, O. N., & Spodek, B. (Eds.). (1983). *Understanding the multicultural experience in early childhood education.* Washington, DC: National Association for the Education of Young Children.

Sattler, J. (1992). *Assessment of children* (3rd ed., revised). San Diego, CA: Jerome M. Sattler.

Savage, J. E., & Adair, A. (1980). Testing minorities: Developing more culturally relevant assessment systems. In R. Jones (Ed.), *Black Psychology* (pp. 196–200). New York: Harper & Row.

Savage-Rumbaugh, E. S., Murphy, J., Sevcik, R. A., Brakke, K. E., Williams, S. L., Rumbaugh, D. M. (1993). Language comprehension in ape and child. *Monographs of the Society for Research in Child Development, 58*(3–4), 1–256.

Scarr, S. (1991). *Developmental theories for the 1990's.* Presidential address, biennial meeting of the Society for Research in Child Development, Seattle, WA.

Scharenaker, S. K., Snelling, T. M., and Ferrer-Vincent, S. T. (1987, Fall). The otitis media clinic: a multipdisciplinary approach to the treatment of otitis media in children. *Rocky Mountain Journal of Communication Disorders, 5,* 3–7.

Schiele, J. L. (1991). An epistemological perspective on intelligence assessment among African American children. *Journal of Black Psychology, 17*(2), 23–26.

Scholdroth, A. (1988). Recent changes in the educational placement of deaf students. *American Annals of the Deaf, 133*(2), 61–67.

Schweinhart, L. J. (1993). Observing young children in action: The key to early assessment. *Young Children, 48*(5), 29–33.

Shea, V. (1984). Explaining mental retardation and autism to parents. In E. Shopler & G. B. Mesibov (Eds.). *The effects of autism on the family* (pp. 265–288). New York: Plenum Press.

Shirley, M. M. (1931). *The first two years.* Minneapolis: University of Minnesota Press.

Shonkoff, J. P., Hauser-Cram, P., Krauss, M. W., & Upshur, C. C. (1992). Development of infants with disabilities and their families: Implications for theory and service delivery. *Monographs of the Society for Research in Child Development, 57*(6) (Serial No. 230), 1–165.

Simeonsson, R. J. (1988). Unique characteristics of families with young handicapped children. In D. B. Bailey & R. J. Simeonsson (Eds.), *Family Assessment in Early Intervention* (pp. 27–44). Columbus, OH: Merrill.

Singer, L., Farkas, K., & Kliegman, R. (1992). Childhood medical and behavioral consequences of maternal cocaine use. *Journal of Pediatric Psychology, 17*(4), 389–406.

Skinner, B. F. (1945, 1972). Baby in a box. In B. F. Skinner (Ed.), *Cumulative record: A selection of papers* (3rd ed.) (pp. 419–426). New York: Appleton–Century–Crofts.

Slade, A., & Bergman, A. (1988). The clinical assessment of toddlers. In C. J. Kestenbaum & D. T. Williams (Eds.), *Handbook of clinical assessment of children and adolescents* (Vol. 1, pp. 1809–1896). New York: New York University Press.

Slentz, K. L., & Bricker, D. (1992). Family-guided assessment for IFSP development: Jumping off the family assessment bandwagon. *Journal of Early Intervention, 16*(1), 11–19.

Slobin, D. (1972, July). Children and language: They learn the same way all around the world. *Psychology Today,* 71–76.

Smith, D. B., & Luckasson, R. (1992). *Introduction to special education.* Boston: Allyn & Bacon.

Smith, P. D. (1989). Assessing motor skills. In D. B. Bailey & M. Wolery (Eds.), *Assess-*

ing infants and preschoolers with handicaps (pp. 301–338). New York: Merrill.

Snarey, J. (1993). *How fathers care for the next generation.* Cambridge, MA: Harvard University Press.

Snow, C. E. (1983). Literacy and language: Relationships during the preschool years. *Harvard Educational Review, 55,* 165–189.

Sparrow, S. S., Balla, D. A., & Cicchetti, D. V. (1984, 1985). *Vineland Adaptive Behavior Scales.* Circle Pines, MN: American Guidance Services.

Spencer, M. B., & Dornbusch, S. M. (1990). Challenges in studying minority youth. In S. S. Feldman & G. R. Elliott (Eds.), *At the threshold: The developing adolescent.* Cambridge, MA: Cambridge University Press.

Squires, J., & Bricker, D. (1991). Impact of completing infant developmental questionnaires on at-risk mothers. *Journal of Early Intervention, 15*(2), 162–172.

Stanley v. Illinois, 405 U.S. 645 (1971).

Starfield, B., Hankin, J., Steinwachs, D. M., Horn, S., Benson, P., Katz, H., & Gabriel, A. (1985). Utilization and morbidity: Random or tandem? *Pediatrics, 75,* 241–247.

Starfield, B., Katz, H. Gabriel, A., Livingston, G., Benson, P., Hankin, J., Horn, S., & Steinwachs, D. (1984). Morbidity in childhood: A longitudinal view. *New England Journal of Medicine, 310,* 824–829.

Starfield, B., Van Den Berg, B. J., Steinwachs, D. M., Katz, H. P., & Horn, S. D. (1979). Variations in utilization of health services by children. *Pediatrics, 63,* 633–641.

Stayton, V., & Johnson, L. (l990). Personnel preparation in early childhood special education: Assessment as a content area. *Journal of Early Intervention, 14,*(4), 352–359.

Stein, R. K., & Jessop, D. J. (1982). A noncategorical approach to chronic childhood illness. *Public Health Report, 9,* 354–362.

Steiner, J. E. (1979). Human facial expressions in response to taste and smell stimulation. In H. Reese & L. Lipsitt (Eds.), *Advances in child development and behavior* (Vol. 13, pp. 257–295). New York: Academic Press.

Stern, D. N. (1974). Mother and infant at play: The dyadic interaction involving facial, vocal, and gaze behaviors. In M. M. Lewis & L. Rosenblum (Eds.), *The effect of the infant on its caregiver* (pp. 187–213). New York: Wiley.

Stern, D. N. (1977). *The first relationship.* Cambridge, MA: Harvard University Press.

Sternberg, L. (1988). Future educational concerns: Crucial questions. In L. Sternberg (Ed.), *Educating students with severe or profound handicaps* (3rd ed.) (pp. 475–483). Rockville, MD: Aspen.

Sternberg, L., & Taylor, R. L. (1988). Systems and procedures for managing behavior. In L. Sternberg (Ed.), *Educating students with severe or profound handicaps* (3rd ed.) (pp. 157–182). Rockville, MD: Aspen.

Steward, M., & Steward, D. (1973). The observation of Anglo-, Mexican-, and Chinese-American mothers teaching their young sons. *Child Development, 44,* 329–337.

Stokes, T. R. & Baer, D. M. (1977). An implicit technology of generalization. *Journal of Applied Behavior Analysis, 10,* 341–367.

Super, C. M. (1976). Environmental effects on motor development. *Developmental Medicine and Child Neurology, 18,* 561–567.

Super, C. M. Herrera, M. G., & Mora, J. O. (1990). Long-term effects of food supplementation and psychosocial intervention on the physical growth of Columbian infants at risk of malnutrition. *Child Development, 61,* 29–49.

Super, C. M., Herrera, M. G., & Mora, J. O. (1991, April). *Cognitive outcomes of early nutritional intervention in the Bogota study.* Paper presented at the biennial meeting of the Society for Research in Child Development, Seattle, WA.

Susman, E. J., Trickett, P. K., Iannotti, R. J., Hollenbeck, B. E., & Zahn-Waxler, C. (1985). Child-rearing patterns in depressed, abusive, and normal mothers. *American Journal of Orthopsychiatry, 55*(2), 237–259.

Sutton-Smith, B. (1979). Epilogue: Play as performance. In B. Sutton-Smith (Ed.), *Play and learning* (pp. 295–322). New York: Gardner Press.

Switzky, H. N., Ludwig, L., & Haywood, H. C. (1979). Exploration and play in retarded and nonretarded preschool children: Effects of object complexity and age. *American Journal of Mental Deficiency, 83,* 637–644.

Tanner, J. M. (1978). *Foetus into man.* Cambridge, MA: Harvard University Press.

Task Force on Education. (1990). *Educating America: State strategies for achieving the national education goals.* Washington, DC: National Governors' Association.

Teti, D. M., & Nakagawa, M. (1990). Assessing attachment in infancy: The strange situation and alternate systems. In E. D. Gibbs & D. M. Teti (Eds.), *Interdisciplinary assessment of infants* (pp. 191–214). Baltimore, MD: Paul H. Brookes.

The Association for Severely Handicapped (TASH). (1983) *Resolution on Infant Care* Seattle, WA: Author.

The Association for Severely Handicapped (TASH). (1988) *Supported Education Resolution.* Seattle, WA: Author.

The Association for Severely Handicapped (TASH). (1993) *Resolution on Life in the Community.* Seattle, WA: Author.

Thelen, E., Corbetta, D., Kamm, K., Spencer, J.P., Schneider, K., & Zernicke, R., F. (1993)The transition to reaching: Mapping intention and intrinsic dynamics. *Child Development, 64*(4), 1058–1098.

Thomas, A., & Chess, S. (1977). *Temperament and development.* New York: Brunner/Mazel.

Thorndike, R. L., Hagen, E. P., & Sattler, J. M. (1986). Stanford-Binet Intelligence Scale: Fourth Edition. Chicago: Riverside.

Thorton, A., & Cambrun, D. (1989). Religious participation and sexual behavior and attitudes. *Journal of Marriage and the Family, 51,* 641–653.

Thousand, J. S., & Villa, R. A. (1993). Strategies for educating learners with severe disabilities within their local home school and communities. In E. L. Meyan, G. A. Vergason, & R. J. Whelan (Eds.), *Challenges facing special education* (pp. 285–322). Denver, CO: Love Publishing.

Torrance, E. P. (1990). Torrance Tests of Creative Thinking: Norm-Technical Manual. Bensenville, IL: Scholastic Testing Service.

Tjossem, T. (Ed.). (1976). *Intervention strategies for high risk infants and young children.* Baltimore, MD: University Park Press.

Trevarthen, C. (1977). Descriptive analyses of infant communicative behavior. In H. R. Schaffer (Eds.), *Studies in mother-infant interaction* (pp. 227–270). London: Academic Press.

Turnbull, A. P. (1991). Identifying children's strengths and needs. In M. J. McGonigel, R. K. Kaufmann, & B. H. Johnson (Eds.), *Guidelines and recommended practices for the individualized family service plan* (2nd. ed.) (pp. 39–55). Bethesda, MD: Association for the Care of Children's Health.

Turnbull, A. P., Summers, J. A., & Brotherson, M. J. (1984). *Working with families with disabled members: A family systems approach.* Lawrence: Kansas University Affilitated Facility.

Turnbull, A. P., Summers, J. A., & Brotherson, M. J. (1987). From parent involvement to family support. In S. M. Pueschel, C. Tingey, J. E. Pynders, A. C. Crocker, & D. M. Crutcher (Eds.), *New perspectives on Down Syndrome* (pp. 289–306). Baltimore, MD: Paul H. Brookes.

Tyler, A. H., & Gregory, V. R. (1992). Assessment of physical and sexual abuse in the preschool child. In E. Vazquez Nuttall, I. Romero, & J. Kalesnik (Eds.), *Assessing and screening preschoolers.* (pp. 369–382). Needham Heights, MA: Allyn & Bacon.

Ungerer, J. A., & Sigman, M. (1981). Symbolic play and language comprehension in autistic children. *Journal of the American Academy of Child Psychiatry, 20*(2), 318–337.

Upshur, C. C. (1991). Mothers' and fathers' ratings of the benefits of early intervention services. *Journal of Early Intervention, 15*(4), 345–357.

U. S. Dept of Education, Office of Special Education and Rehabilative Services (1981). Third annual report to Congress on the implementation of Public Law 94-142: The Education for All Handicapped Act. Washington, DC: Author.

Uzgiris, I. C. (1976). Organization of sensorimotor intelligence. In M. Lewis (Ed.), *Origins of intelligence* (pp. 123–164). New York: Plenum Press.

Uzgiris, I. C., & Hunt, J. (1975). *Assessment in infancy: Ordinal scales of psychological development.* Urbana: University of Illinois Press.

Vaillant, G. E. (1977). *Adaptation to life.* Boston: Little, Brown.

Vandell, D. L., & Mueller, E. C. (1978). Peer play and friendships during the first two years. In H. C. Foot, A. J., Chapman, & J. R. Smith (Eds.), *Friendships and social relations in children* (pp. 181–208). London: Wiley.

Van Dijk, J. (1986). An educational curriculum for deaf-blind multi-handicapped persons. In. D. Ellis (Ed.), *Sensory impairments in mentally handicapped people* (pp. 374–382). San Diego, CA: College Hill Press.

Vazquez Nuttall, E., Romero, I., & Kalesnik, J. (Eds.). (1992). *Assessing and screening preschoolers.* Needham Heights, MA: Allyn & Bacon.

Vygotsky, L. (1962). *Thought and language.* Cambridge, MA: MIT Press.

Vygotsky, L. (1967). Play and the role of mental development in the child. *Soviet Psychology, 5,* 6–18.

Wachs, T. D., & Chan, A. (1985). *Physical and social environment correlates of three aspects of 12 month language functioning.* Paper presented at the meeting of the Society for Research in Child Development, Toronto, Canada.

Walton, G. E., & Bower, T. G. R. (1993). Newborns form prototypes in less than 1 minute. *Psychological Science, 4*(3), 203–205.

Weeks, Z. R., & Ewer-Jones, B. (1991). Assessment of perceptual-motor and fine motor functioning. In B. Bracken (Ed.), *Psychoeducational assessment of preschool children* (pp. 259–283). Needham Heights, MA: Allyn & Bacon.

Werner, E. E., & Smith, R. S. (1982). *Vulnerable but invincible: A study of resilient children.* New York: McGraw-Hill.

Werner, E. E., & Smith, R. S. (1992). *Overcoming the odds: High risk children from birth to adulthood.* Ithaca, NY: Cornell University Press.

Weschler, D. (1989). Weschler Preschool and Primary Scale of Intelligence–Revised. San Antonio, TX: Psychological Corporation.

Westby, C. E. (1980). Assessment of cognitive and language abilities through play. *Language, Speech & Hearing in the Schools, 10*(3), 154–168.

Wheeler, D. L., Jacobson, J. W., Paglieri, R. A., & Schwartz, A. A. (1993). An experimental assessment of facilitated communication. *Mental Retardation, 31,* 49–60.

White, S. J., & White, R. E. (1987). The effects of hearing status of the family and age of intervention on receptive and expressive oral language skills in hearing-impaired infants. In H. Levitt, N. McGarr, & D. Geffner (Eds.), *Development of language and communication skills in hearing impaired children.* (ASHA Monograph No. 26, 2–24). Washington, DC: American Speech-Language and Hearing Association.

Widmayer, S. M., & Field, T. M. (1980). Effects of Brazelton demonstrations on early interactions of preterm infants and their teenage mothers. *Infant Behavior and Development, 3,* 79–89.

Widmayer, S. M., & Field, T. M. (1981). Effects of Brazelton demonstrations for mothers on the development of preterm infants. *Pediatrics, 67,* 711–714.

Williams, H. G. (1990). Assessment of gross motor functioning. In B. Bracken (Ed.), *Psychoeducational assessment of preschool children* (pp. 284–316). Needham Heights, MA: Allyn & Bacon.

Wolery, G., & Dyk, L. (1984). Arena assessment: Description and preliminary social validity data. *The Journal of the Association for the Severely Handicapped, 9,* 231–235.

Wolery, M. (1989a). Assessing play skills. In D. B. Bailey & M. Wolery, (Eds.), *Assessing infants and preschoolers with handicaps* (pp. 428–446). Columbus, OH: Merrill.

Wolery, M. (1989b). Using direct observation in assessment. In D. B. Bailey & M. Wolery (Eds.), *Assessing infants and preschoolers with handicaps* (pp. 64–96). Columbus, OH: Merrill.

Wolery, M., Bailey, D. B., & Sugai, G. (1988). *Effective teaching: Principles and procedures of applied behavior analysis for exceptional students.* Boston: Allyn & Bacon.

Wolff, P. (1989). The concept of development: How does it constrain assessment and therapy? In P. R. Zelazo & R. G. Barr (Eds.), *Challenges to developmental paradigms: Implications for theory, assessment, and treatment* (pp. 13–28). Hillsdale, NJ: Erlbaum.

Woodruff, G. (1980). Transdisciplinary approach for preschool children and parents. *The Exceptional Parent, 10*(1), 13–16.

Woodruff, G. (1993). Women and children and HIV. *Readings: A Journal of Reviews and Commentary in Mental Health, 8*(2), 18–22.

Woodruff, G., & McGonigel, M. (1988). Early intervention team approaches: The transdisciplinary model. In J. Jordan, J. Gallagher, P. Hutinger, & M. Karnes (Eds), *Early Childhood Special Education: Birth to Three* (pp. [AU: supply page nos.]). Reston, VA: Council for Exceptional Children.

Worobey, J., & Belsky, J. (1982). Employing the Brazelton Scale to influence mothering: An experimental comparison of three strategies. *Developmental Psychology, 18*, 736–743.

Wright, M. O., & Masten, A. S. (in press). Vulnerability and resilience in young children. In S. I. Greenspan, J. D. Osofsky, & K. Pruett (Eds.), *Handbook of Child and Adolescent Psychiatry. Section on Infancy and Early Childhood.* New York: Basic Books.

Xiaohe, X., & Whyte, M. K. (1990). Love matches and arranged marriages. *Journal of Marriage and the Family, 52*, 709–722.

Young, V. H. (1970). Family and childhood in a southern Georgia community. *American Anthropologist, 72*, 269–288.

Zigler, E. (1993, August). *Reshaping early childhood intervention to be a more effective weapon against poverty.* Keynote address presented at the annual meeting of the American Psychological Association, Toronto.

Zigler, E., Abelson, W., & Seitz, V. (1973). Motivational factors in the performance of economically disadvantaged children on the Peabody Picture Vocabulary Test. *Child Development, 44*(2), 294–303.

Zigler, E., & Black, K. B. (1989). America's family support movement: Strengths and limitations. *American Journal of Orthopsychiatry, 59*, 6–19.

Zimmerman, I. L., Steiner, V., & Pond, R. E. (1992). *Preschool Language Scale—3.* San Antonio, TX: The Psychological Corp.

Index

About the Authors and Contributors

Doris Bergen, Ph.D., is Professor and Chair, Department of Educational Psychology at Miami University, Oxford, OH. She teaches infant–toddler and preschool assessment and intervention, play development, lifespan human development, psychology of the learner, and educational research. She has also taught numerous other courses in early childhood, early childhood special education, and developmental psychology. Her research has focused on the play development of typically developing and at-risk young children, cross-cultural views of early childhood education, and humor development from early to middle childhood. She is the author of two books on play and of numerous articles and chapters on the development and education of young children. She has established early childhood special education degree/certification programs at three universities, and she now serves as director of the Miami University Center for Human Development, Learning, and Teaching, which focuses on furthering knowledge of at-risk populations. She is also past president of the National Association of Early Childhood Teacher Educators, a member of the NAEYC Professional Development Institute Panel, and a member of the DEC Personnel Standards Committee.

Caroline Everington, Ph.D., is an Associate Professor, Department of Educational Psychology, Miami University. She is coordinator of the special education programs, including early intervention. Her teaching specialization is ecological assessment and curriculum intervention for infants and older individuals who have severe and multiple disabilities and she provides consultation to schools implementing inclusion practices. She is also a nationally recognized expert in the assessment of the competency of mentally retarded offenders to stand trial, and the author of an assessment instrument for this purpose used by agencies throughout the country.

Kathleen Hutchinson, Ph.D., is a Professor, Department of Communication, Miami University. She is coordinator of the Audiology Clinic, a specialist in audiologic assessment of infants and young children, and teaches courses in audiology and assessment of hearing impairments. Her publications focus on topics such as the effects of acoustic amplification on young children's language development, the use of signing and speaking to facilitate language learning, factors influencing auditory brainstem response (ABR) results, and context effects on speech reception.

ELIZABETH JOHNSTON, ED.D., is an Assistant Professor, Department of Communication, Miami University. She designed and implemented the university Preschool Language Nursery and serves as its director. She is a specialist in Piagetian-based early language intervention and teaches courses in language acquisition and diagnostics. She has also designed and conducted parent–child programs that focused on facilitating development of young children with language-related problems. Her publications are related to Piagetian-based methods of facilitating language learning and source books in language and pragmatic therapy. She is also author of a communication abilities diagnostic test.

SUSAN MOSLEY-HOWARD, PH.D., is an Associate Professor, Department of Educational Psychology, Miami University. She is chair of the educational psychology program committee and teaches counseling techniques, assessment, learning theories, research design, and African-American psychology. She is a member of the interdisciplinary Black World Studies faculty and co-director of a nationally recognized interactive video project promoting racial understanding among college-age students. Her publications focus on issues related to multicultural education, counseling, and African-American psychology.

SHARON RAVER-LAMPMAN, PH.D, is a Professor, Department of Child Study/Special Education, at Old Dominion University in Virginia. Her specialization is early education of children with disabilities and she teaches a range of early intervention and special education courses. She is particularly interested in family-centered approaches to early assessment and is the author of a book on transdisciplinary team approaches to working with infants and toddlers who are at-risk for developmental problems. In 1993–1994, as a Fulbright Scholar, she shared her early intervention expertise with students and faculty at Palacky University in Czechoslovakia.

JULIE RUBIN, PH.D., is a Visiting Assistant Professor, Department of Psychology, Miami University. She is a psychologist in private practice and also has a degree in special education. Presently, she is director of the Psychology Clinic and she teaches courses in assessment and psychopathology. She has had experience as a member of an interdisciplinary medical assessment team, as coordinator of an infant research project, and as director of an augmentative communications program. Her publications are related to these program topics.

ALEX THOMAS, PH.D., is an Associate Professor, Department of Educational Psychology, Miami University. He is coordinator of the school psychology graduate program and has had extensive experience as a practicing school psychologist. His teaching expertise is in assessment, intervention, and consultation techniques, including curriculum-based measurement and intervention assistance team functioning. His books and other publications focus on innovations in school psychology practice, including the school psychologist's role on transdisciplinary teams. He is a past president of the National Association of School Psychologists.

MARGARET WRIGHT, PH.D., is an Associate Professor, Department of Psychology, at Miami University. She is a clinical psychologist with special expertise in developmental neuropsychology and pediatric neuropsychologic assessment. Her experience includes designing a behavioral neurology program and working as a psychologist on interdisciplinary infant and preschool assessment teams in hospital and pediatric settings. She has had a number of grants focusing on young children with multiple disabilities, heart defects, hyperactivity, and seizure disorders, and on medically fragile infants and toddlers. Her publications address these topics. She has also written a book on counseling the chronically ill child.